AFRICAN ETHNOGRAPHIC STUDIES
OF THE 20TH CENTURY

Volume 40

AN AFRICAN ARISTOCRACY

AN AFRICAN ARISTOCRACY

Rank Among the Swazi

HILDA KUPER

R Routledge
Taylor & Francis Group

LONDON AND NEW YORK

First published in 1947 and reprinted in 1961 with a new preface by Oxford University Press for the International African Institute.

This edition first published in 2018
by Routledge
2 Park Square, Milton Park, Abingdon, Oxon OX14 4RN

and by Routledge
711 Third Avenue, New York, NY 10017

Routledge is an imprint of the Taylor & Francis Group, an informa business

British Library Cataloguing in Publication Data
A catalogue record for this book is available from the British Library

ISBN: 978-0-8153-8713-8 (Set)
ISBN: 978-0-429-48813-9 (Set) (ebk)
ISBN: 978-1-138-58550-8 (Volume 40) (hbk)
ISBN: 978-1-138-58612-3 (Volume 40) (pbk)
ISBN: 978-0-429-50479-2 (Volume 40) (ebk)

Publisher's Note
The publisher has gone to great lengths to ensure the quality of this reprint but points out that some imperfections in the original copies may be apparent.

Disclaimer
The publisher has made every effort to trace copyright holders and would welcome correspondence from those they have been unable to trace.

Due to modern production methods, it has not been possible to reproduce the fold-out maps within the book. Please visit www.routledge.com to view them.

AN AFRICAN ARISTOCRACY

RANK AMONG THE SWAZI

HILDA KUPER

Published for the
INTERNATIONAL AFRICAN INSTITUTE

by the
OXFORD UNIVERSITY PRESS
LONDON   NEW YORK   TORONTO

Oxford University Press, Amen House, London E.C.4
GLASGOW NEW YORK TORONTO MELBOURNE WELLINGTON
BOMBAY CALCUTTA MADRAS KARACHI KUALA LUMPUR
CAPE TOWN IBADAN NAIROBI ACCRA

First published 1947
Reprinted (with New Preface) 1961

PRINTED IN GREAT BRITAIN
3344 · SB 459

ACKNOWLEDGEMENTS AND PREFACE

I N this new foreword to *An African Aristocracy* I would like once again
to acknowledge the help I received in the collection and presentation
of my original material. It is impossible to mention by name all the people
who contributed to my writings since every anthropological work is a joint
effort in which the anthropologist depends for data on the co-operation
of the people studied and draws on the works of colleagues past and present
for analysis and interpretation.

Looking back on my period of fieldwork, I realise how fortunate I was
to have met with such courtesy and friendliness from all sections of the
population. I occasionally revisit Swaziland, and each time the welcome
I receive evokes a promise to return. It is difficult to express my indebtedness to the Swazi for accepting me as they did, but I wish in particular to
put on record my lasting gratitude to Sobhuza II, his mother Lomawa,
his Queens who 'adopted' me, his sisters Sencabaphi and Nengwase, his
ritual blood-brother Ngolotsheni Motsa, and my faithful assistant
Mnyakaza Gwebu. My work also brought me into contact with White
officials, missionaries, traders, miners and farmers, many of whom
extended to me a warm hospitality and discussed with me their points of
view. Members of the technical and administrative staff of the Territory
constantly provided me with information and assistance, and I take this
opportunity to offer special thanks to Mr. A. G. Marwick, one time
Resident Commissioner, Mr. G. Elder, Principal Veterinary Officer, and
the medical officers Drs. Jamieson, Keen and Mossbaum.

In the previous edition, I paid tribute to my teachers Dr. Winifred
Hoernlé and Professor Bronislaw Malinowski. Since then they have both
died, but their ideas are alive in their students and the memory of my
association with each remains for me a stimulus and inspiration. My
colleagues, particularly Dr. Audrey I. Richards, Professor Max Gluckman,
Professor Isaac Schapera and Professor Meyer Fortes, know how greatly
I benefited from their criticism and encouragement. My fieldwork was
financed by a Research Fellowship from the International African Institute, which also undertook publication of my work.

How much has happened since 1940, when I completed my intensive
fieldwork in Swaziland! In a historic speech made in the Union of South
Africa, in April 1960, the British Prime Minister, Harold Macmillan,
spoke of the 'wind of change' that was sweeping across the African
continent. This wind has been gathering momentum over the past fifteen
years. In Swaziland it has blown more gently than in many other parts of
the Commonwealth, and though it would be interesting to speculate why,
this obviously is not the place in which to do so. We can merely point out
that the Swazi, who were never strongly militaristic and who were conquered by concessions rather than direct force of arms, were encouraged
to retain much of their traditional culture under their own hereditary
leaders who received recognition from the time of annexation by the
British. Again, though there are a fairly large number of Whites who own
land and property in Swaziland they are not directly represented in the
government, and for the Swazi in Swaziland there is comparative freedom

from the oppressive racial laws that have evoked violent opposition in the adjoining Union of South Africa.

At the same time, change has not altogether passed the Swazi by. The years after the Second World War were marked by a more positive approach than previously to the political rights, the economic development, and the educational and social needs of the people. The position of the traditional ruler and Councils was formally proclaimed, new personnel were appointed, and 'Native authorities' were invested with more specific powers. New administrative machinery for liaison with the White admini-stration was inaugurated and experiments made in local government. Recognition was given to selected Native Courts and a somewhat different legal hierarchy was established. A Swazi National Treasury was officially proclaimed replacing other sources of financial control, and affording new avenues for economic responsibility to men with western education. But compared with changes introduced in other parts of Africa, for example in Ghana, or even Basutoland, these changes are not fundamental.

On the other hand, more conspicuous than deliberate political changes, are the economic. Large amounts have been invested by privately owned companies and grants have been made available from the Colonial Development and Welfare Fund and the Colonial Development Corpora-tion. As a result the pattern of land utilisation has changed considerably. Vast areas in the highveld have been planted with forests; in the lowveld three big irrigation schemes have been started and several new industries and townships have been opened. Everywhere there is evidence of im-proved agricultural techniques, new cash crops, and more careful siting of villages in relation to garden and pasturage. Additional land was acquired for the Swazi and, according to the most recent figures (1958), a little more than half the territory has become available for Swazi occupation. Oppor-tunities for local employment have increased, while the numbers recruited for mine labour in the Union remain fairly constant.

Reading the preceding paragraph, the reader may wonder to what extent *An African Aristocracy* describes present-day Swazi society. During my period of intensive fieldwork, I became aware both of the distinctiveness of traditional Swazi relationships and also of the resilience of traditional Swazi loyalties. Thus it came about that I was able to publish my material in two separate books—*An African Aristocracy* (published by the Interna-tional African Institute) and *The Uniform of Colour* (published by the Witwatersrand University). Together they described the Swazi way of life at a particular period of history, but they also reflected a duality within the Swazi world. *An African Aristocracy* analysed traditional Swazi social relationships which were still actively maintained, and *The Uniform of Colour* indicated the interaction of Swazi and Whites in a rapidly changing milieu.

Two world views—the traditional or conservative and the western— existed simultaneously, influencing each other. Thus, in *An African Aristocracy* we analysed the balance of power within a nation ruled by the Ingwenyame and his mother, the Indlovukati, and in *The Uniform of Colour* we discussed their status and role as the 'Paramount Chief' and the 'Queen Mother' *vis-à-vis* White administration as well as their own westernised and conservative subjects. Again, in *An African Aristocracy* we dealt with the great dramatic and symbolic ritual of kingship, in the *Uniform of Colour* we showed the affects of Christian Missions and western education on traditional ritual and beliefs. While situations of conflict and modes of resolving or diverting conflicts are inherent in society, the situations and resolutions reflect changes in relationships.

The post-war changes that I have mentioned have been directly introduced into the White-Black milieu but, because of the complexity of social interaction, they have further, indirectly, influenced alignments between Swazi themselves. These changes and their repercussions, which would be considered in any new edition of *The Uniform of Colour* rather than in *An African Aristocracy*, are being studied by Mr. John Hughes, for the Swaziland Administration.

Like other African tribes, the Sawzi did not develop in isolation and many characteristics of their society spread far beyond their borders. They borrowed from some tribes and influenced the development of others. Recent studies by John Barnes and Margaret Read show the persistence of social and cultural affinities between the Swazi of Swaziland and the Ngoni of Northern Rhodesia and Nyasaland despite distance and time. And even in the face of technical and social change, traditional beliefs and methods of organisation may continue to exercise a powerful influence.

Many excellent monographs on African tribes have appeared in recent years, and important contributions have been made to our understanding of tribal government, law, economics, political structure, kinship, ritual and symbolism. Advances have also been made in comparative work and abstract analysis and techniques are being devised to quantify quality.

In itself *An African Aristocracy* is a work of limited pretensions; it is a study of the orientation of a particular society in a particular environment at a particular time. The essential starting point in an analysis of human society is that it is human, that its basic components are men, women, and children—and all that implies in emotional interaction—able to perpetuate and if necessary deliberately to change their social heritage.

In *An African Aristocracy* the emphasis is on the specific not the general, the personal not the abstract, and the theory guiding my description is nowhere explicitly stated. But I tried to handle my material in such a way as to indicate both the complexity of structural principles and the richness of cultural content, and I appreciate the extent to which this book has been used by others in efforts to further anthropology as a science. In this I particularly acknowledge the contribution of Max Gluckman, who, in his stimulating Frazer lecture 'Rituals of Rebellion' added to an understanding of my description of the Swazi Incwala and illuminated an important field of social behaviour.

Durban   HILDA KUPER
April 1960

CONTENTS

PAGE

ACKNOWLEDGEMENTS AND PREFACE . . . v
PRAISE SONG OF SOBHUZA II xi

PART I

INTRODUCTION AND HISTORICAL BACKGROUND

CHAPTER I. INTRODUCTION 1
Conditions of work and the status of the anthropologist—the scope of the book—the approach to time.

CHAPTER II. CONQUERING ARISTOCRACIES:
1. THE DLAMINI 11
The period of clans—amalgamation of the clans—a military king.

CHAPTER III. CONQUERING ARISTOCRACIES:
2. THE EUROPEANS 19
Europeans enter into Swazi political organization—the Swazi king and European pioneers—concessions—a period of unrest—the period of acceptance—conclusion.

PART II

THE BASIS OF CONSERVATISM

CHAPTER IV. THE TEMPO OF PEASANT LIFE . . 34
The country—the seasonal rhythm—the homestead—royal villages—the plan of royal villages—rights to land—moving of homesteads.

CHAPTER V. THE CONSERVATIVE POLITICAL HIERARCHY 54
The *Ingwenyama* and *Indlovukati*—the princes—limits of nepotism—leading commoners—the voice of the people—central and local administration—vassallage and slavery—the character of Swazi authorities.

CHAPTER VI. RITUALIZATION OF THE KING . . 72
Royal villages reflect the development of kingship—childhood of the king—transference of the king's blood—polygyny as part of ritualization—the health of the king.

CHAPTER VII. CHOICE OF THE HEIR 88
The danger of friction—the council responsible for choosing the heir—the first wife—the main wife—women of little importance—*Lobolo*—death of a main wife—failure of main issue—guardianship and regency—character.

CHAPTER VIII. BLOOD, KINSHIP AND LOCALITY   .   105
Blood and kinship—blood and social situations—heredity
—the clan hierarchy—kinship and locality.

CHAPTER IX.   THE AGE-CLASS SYSTEM   .   .   . 117
The attitude to age—organization of men's age classes—
orientation to warfare—labour—education—organization of
women's age classes—activities.

CHAPTER X.   WEALTH IN THE PEASANT SOCIETY   . 137
Technical limitations—division of labour—specialization—
work parties and communal enterprises—distribution of
wealth—prestige and generosity.

CHAPTER XI.   INDIVIDUAL VARIABILITY AND
RITUAL   158
Recognition of individual variability—why and how Swazi
become specialists in ritual—specialists at work—rulers and
specialists—sorcery, witchcraft and the *status quo*.

CHAPTER XII.   DEATH AS AN INDEX OF RANK .   . 177
Explanations of death—gradations of mortuary rights—
social meaning of death—power of the dead—approaching the
ancestors.

CHAPTER XIII.   THE DRAMA OF KINGSHIP   .   . 197
The actors—sun and moon—the little *Incwala*—the interim
period—fetching the sacred tree—the bull—the great day—
seclusion—the fire—the ceremony during the king's minority
—interpretation.

CHAPTER XIV.   CONCLUSION   226

APPENDICES

   I. GENEALOGY OF KINGS 232
  II. SWAZI CLANS 233
 III. PLAN OF CAPITAL 235
  IV. PLAN OF EMBRYO CAPITAL 236
   V. A MYTH OF KINGSHIP .   .   .   .   :   . 237
  VI. FAILURE OF MALE ISSUE   238
 VII. REBUILDING THE SHRINE HUT OF THE CAPITAL 240

BIBLIOGRAPHY   243
INDEX   245
MAP .   .   .   . *at end*

LIST OF ILLUSTRATIONS

Since it has not been possible to reproduce all the illustrations used in the first edition of this book, references in the text to plate numbers of the original edition should be ignored. For those illustrations in this edition which also appeared in the first edition the original plate numbers are indicated in brackets.

Facing page

Plate I 74

    (*a*) Building the Shrine Hut at the Capital: old women laying the first mat (*Umcengo*)

    (*b*) The Hut, decorated with branches of *Lugagane*, in which a wife of the King gives birth to her child.
                                        (*Original Plate V*)

Plate II 75

    (*a*) Fixing the Head-ring: Luhogo Mandzeɓele was very deft with his fingers and also held a high position as Councillor
                                  (*Original Plate VI (a)*)

    (*b*) Queens binding mealies: part of the work at harvest time

Plate III 164

    (*a*) Warriors dancing

    (*b*) An *Inyanga* stirring frothy medicines used to treat patients suffering from *mfufunyane*, a type of spirit possession

Plate IV 165

    (*a*) Princesses in their *Incwala* Dress (*Original Plate XVI (a)*)

    (*b*) Sobhuza II on the first day of the Little *Incwala*

PRAISES OF SOBHUZA II[1]

Chanted by Lohoko Mndzebele

Dawn, you of the Inner House!
Dawn, Strong Lion with mighty claws
That grabbed protection overseas!
Thou art cold. Cold as the waters
of Mangwaneni.
Thou art the ice of Mangwaneni.[2]
I call Sobhuza, Sobhuza of the High Mountains.
Cast your shadow on the hills.
Cast your shadow on the huts.
You play with the waters
And they speak.
Sobhuza, Somkiti, born amidst black shields.[3]
He himself is fearful
He has outwitted me.
Miraculous body that grows feathers in winter
while others are without plumage.
Master in weapons.
Your voice brings joy to people,
Even unto your mother's people
of the far Magudu mountains.[4]
I appeal to you,
You enter into all matters
You, son of Mkatshwa's daughter,
Son of a Zulu woman.
You condescended to white authority,
You from the fountain of a Zulu clan.
The Zulu shall drink of your waters.
They drink of the waters of friendship.
Waters cleanse Sobhuza, lave his feet,
Cleanse him of pollution.
He is polluted. He trod the grave of wizards,
The grave of Mkiza of the Mapoko clan.[5]
Sobhuza is a mighty force
Concentrated in mystic waters.[6]
He destroys people when he handles them,
He tracked Shaka like an antelope.

[1] This is a free translation of part of Sobhuza's praise song.

[2] A waterfall in Central Swaziland.

[3] Black shields are associated with the national ritual of kingship.

[4] Sobhuza's mother, an MKatshwa, came from Zulu stock living near the Magudu in Zululand.

[5] No member of the royal clan may come into contact with anything associated with death without being polluted. Sobhuza when a child accidentally trod on the grave of the man mentioned.

[6] At the great national ceremony Sobhuza is treated with special water collected from the sea and big rivers.

He danced in two worlds.
Sobhuza danced in the compounds of Robinson Deep and Havelock.[7]
Danced he with tools and hammers
While Ndungunye and his men attacked but with spears.[8]
You pointed a spear at the Sotho,[9]
Black hero of the Swazi.
They hate Sobhuza and are right to hate.
Jaw that cracks all bones,
Spotted Beast! Great Conqueror!
Hail! You of the Inner House!

[7] These are two of the many gold-mine compounds in the Transvaal where Swazi go to work.

[8] Ndungunye was one of the former Swazi kings.

[9] A number of wars were fought between the Swazi and the Sotho.

PART I

CHAPTER I

INTRODUCTION

1. *Conditions of Work and the Status of the Investigator*

I MET Sobhuza II, Chief of the 'primitive people' I was to study, attending the New Education Conference at the Witwatersrand University in July 1934. Sobhuza II, *Ingwenyama* (Lion) of the Swazi nation, had travelled nearly 300 miles from his home in the Protectorate to hear a series of lectures in English by world-famous educationalists and anthropologists.

Most educated Africans, more particularly detribalized Africans and men with little standing in tribal life, distrust anthropology. They see in it a weapon to keep natives in their 'traditional milieu' (arbitrarily stripped of actions judged 'barbarous' by Europeans) and to prevent them on pseudo-scientific grounds—retaining the 'soul of the people', their 'primitive mentality'—from assimilating European culture. Sobhuza, on the other hand, is interested in anthropology; he has read a number of books on the subject, subscribes to anthropological journals, enjoys descriptions of the customs of other people, and is proud of his own. He one day explained, 'Anthropology makes possible comparison and selection of lines of further development. European culture is not all good; ours is often better. We must be able to choose how to live, and for that we must see how others live. I do not want my people to be imitation Europeans, but to be respected for their own laws and customs.'

In the hierarchical Swazi society, the support of the *Ingwenyama* is an essential prerequisite for the acceptance of any stranger, and without his sympathetic assistance anthropological research would have been difficult.

I spent over two years in the Swaziland Protectorate. My first visit, beginning October 1934, lasted sixteen months. I returned in September 1936 for another eight months' intensive research. Since then I have been back for short periods to check up data, to witness ceremonies, and to pay friendly visits. In Johannesburg, where I have lived since I left Swaziland, I worked with a number of Swazi, some newcomers from the country, others old city-dwellers.

In the Protectorate I stayed in native homesteads. My headquarters was Lobamba, the capital. At my disposal was the most Westernized house in the village—a square brick room with a wooden door about six feet high, glass windows, and a partition dividing the room into two sections. In it were a few leather chairs—the only chairs in the capital and used mainly for European guests. Till I arrived, this special hut was occupied by the most important relatives of the *Ingwenyama* on their state calls to the capital.

From Loɓamba I travelled to various principalities, and in Swazi society it was taken for granted that, except when I went to a ceremony in a commoner's family, I should stay in the homestead of the chief. 'At the homes of the great appear the laws of our people', Umnyakaza Gweɓu, my retainer, often explained. 'The chief alone can arrange for you to see all you wish and call anyone to speak to you.' The co-operation I received from the subjects depended largely on the character of the chiefs.

Umnyakaza was 'given me' by Sobhuza as my *umfana*. The basic meaning of *umfana* is 'boy'; in the context of political relations it is a subject bound by personal loyalty. His position is very different from that of a servant to a European. The *umfana* becomes a member of the over-lord's intimate circle of dependents, regards him as a father and is treated much like a son. Umnyakaza, a warrior from Sobhuza's own bodyguard, acted as my teacher, interpreter, cook, and travelling companion. In addition to an unusually extensive Swazi and Zulu vocabulary, he had a grasp of Sesotho, spoke a graphic, ungrammatical English, a smattering of Afrikaans, and a few words of Portuguese. Intelligent and neurotic, with moods veering from sullen depression to unrestrained gaiety, he believed he was possessed of spirits, and when last I heard of him, he was roving the hills, undergoing the painful training of a diviner. In addition to Umnyakaza, who went everywhere with me and worked for me in Johannesburg for six months, Sobhuza selected other assistants and companions for special occasions.

Despite the open friendship of Sobhuza, the dominant attitude towards me, especially the attitude of the semi-educated Swazi, was fear and suspicion; they were afraid that I was a spy—a European who had ingratiated her way into the confidence of the rulers in order to betray them later. I was *maɓalana*, a scribe; in my right hand I held the most dangerous of all spears, the pen, and in my left an impenetrable shield, my notebook. I was introduced by the governor of the capital to the council of the nation as 'a European brought by the Lion (Sobhuza). Fear her, respect her. Forget not she is a European. The King says her work is to show we are not wild animals, we do not live in the mountains, we have our laws. Do not trouble her.' Sobhuza's patronage made the people superficially friendly, but it was a hard task to win their confidence. As a woman once said, pityingly, 'We deceive you like anything because you are white.'

I established intimate contact with a limited circle of people, and these I used as my main informants. The rest of the community were actors in the situations that are the laboratory experiments of the anthropologist: I wrote down words and watched their behaviour, but the individuals themselves were of little assistance for detailed discussions, since I had not broken down their reserve, antagonism, and suspicion. In selecting cases for intensive interviewing, I bore in mind factors of birth, education, age, and religious belief.

To obtain information, I used the techniques of observation, genealogies, texts, essays set to schoolchildren, interviews, letters from Swazi to each other and to me, and questionnaires. I have used the orthography decided upon by a conference held in 1933, except for the spelling of occasional proper names which are more familiar in other forms, e.g. Sobhuza instead of Sobuza.

It was essential to learn the language as quickly and thoroughly as possible. Most Swazi know little or no English; the few who speak it fluently still use Swazi in their homes. Educated Swazi preferred to write their texts for me in Zulu (the dialect related to Swazi and used in the schools) rather than in English. English is a foreign tongue dealing with foreign concepts, and when a man speaks English his behaviour and mode of thought seem to change. A Swazi teacher once commented 'I only enjoy selling cattle when I speak English.' The significance of this remark is appreciated when one knows the reluctance of the average Swazi to part with his cattle. The process of learning Swazi was of great assistance to me, for seeing a European struggle to acquire their language seemed to give people a certain satisfaction and pleasure, while I think that teaching it to me gave them a sense of importance. They were tolerant of blunders, proud of progress, and they expressed their joy when they did not constantly have to repeat and explain their statements. Then only did they themselves speak freely and not in a peculiar garbled language (a parallel of the European's pidgin English), which they thought was easier for me to understand.

It was also necessary for me to grasp other tools of their culture in order to break down the barrier between black and white. I learned to grind grain and make beer; I participated in dancing, singing, the judging of cases, and so on. Often I identified myself with a particular section of actors: at wedding ceremonies I went as a member sometimes of the bride's and sometimes of the groom's group; sometimes with the mother-in-law, sometimes with the sisters; at work parties I sometimes sat and distributed food with the host, and sometimes toiled with the workers. When I started field work, I was only allowed to join in the activities of the girls; after my marriage a new status was mine, and wives considered me their equal and treated me as a confidante. As a woman the sphere of my participation was restricted and my data on certain topics reflects this. Just as each individual has only a circumscribed knowledge of his culture, so each status group has its bias and limitations.

Complete identification with the Swazi was neither possible nor, from the point of view of obtaining a comprehensive picture of Swazi life, desirable or necessary. In the Protectorate black and white are closely interdependent. To understand modern Swazi culture, it is necessary to study situations of black and white co-operation, antagonism, and segregation, and the direction of European control. The two colour groups are interdependent, but distinct in culture and interests. To have 'gone native' would have ruined any chance of obtaining data from most of the Europeans.

The anthropologist is inevitably an influence in the lives of the natives, and vice versa. Through me a number of Swazi saw for the first time a typewriter, camera, petrol lamp, collapsible bath, and other material elements of Western civilization. The headmaster of the national school and I, on Sobhuza's request, took about forty children to the Empire Exhibition in Johannesburg (1936), where they gazed with wonder on a new world. Apart from goods introduced or increased by me, I, as an anthropologist, was used as a source of knowledge on European modes of thought and action. Questions put to informants were returned—with interest. Moreover, I was in a position different frcm that usually held by the European. I did not blame, try to convert, or seek labourers. I represented a type with whom the Swazi are rarely in contact—the liberal intellectual. The greatest honour shown me by the Swazi was when Sobhuza and his Councillors asked me to become 'headmaster' of the Swazi National School during the absence, on active service, of Mr. T. Keen.

On entering any community a new arrival is automatically assigned a 'place'. No man or woman can remain in complete isolation; he (or she) is forced to participate to some degree in the life around. Nor can a community admit within its bounds any member who acts without reference to his (or her) fellow men.

A stranger is catalogued on arrival. In Swaziland the first and most important quality noted is skin colour. Everyone falls automatically into the 'white', 'black', or 'coloured' group, and is expected to conform to the attitudes of that group. Throughout the book, therefore, I use the term 'white' as synonymous with Europeans; 'black' with African, native, and Bantu; 'coloured' with Eur-African (the result of miscegenation between Africans and Europeans, and also between coloureds, Africans, or Europeans, as well as of unions within the coloured group itsel.f) Secondly, obvious economic factors such as type of equipment, make of car, and spending power, affect the classification. Thirdly, different Churches in this small 'Christian country' create their own categories of believer and heathen. Fourthly, in the backward Protectorate, occupations are limited and there is both a jealous monopoly of existing trades and a suspicion of 'the specialist', more especially one whose calling is unfamiliar. The anthropologist, in the same way as government official, chief, trader, or anyone else, is accorded a definite position in the society he investigates. Anthropologists were no novelty to Europeans in Swaziland, but each anthropologist evoked specific reactions. Finally, characteristics such as nationality, sex, education, age, evoke fairly stereotyped patterns of behaviour.

The reactions are not uniform; they vary with different classes of the population. By class I mean, in this book, a group distinguished from others by economic and social standards. The Europeans in Swaziland fall roughly into three classes: the upper—leading government officials, professional men, big traders, prosperous landowners, and mine managers; the middle—small traders, farm managers, and lower Civil Servants; and the lower—labelled the 'poor whites'. The Swazi are not yet stratified into economic classes, though there is a growing tendency towards this division. In their own society they differentiate primarily the noble-born from the commoner.

Associational interests, interests of a group or groups organized for particular purposes, also affect the attitudes towards the anthropologist. Government officials considered research might assist administration. Farmers and miners were suspicious lest I disorganize labour, and certain missionaries read into my work an attempt to revive traditional religious practices.

The anthropologist reacts according to his own training and interests to the people among whom he works. This inevitably affects both the facts he selects from the welter of data he records and the interpretation he gives to them. I am handicapped by not being able to publish certain data: my friendship with Sobhuza gave me important information that I bound myself not to disclose. Secondly, I am prevented from using certain documents for fear of being involved in cases of defamation. Thirdly, some official correspondence was shown to me, provided that I did not make it public. Fourthly, and this is most important, my own outlook has undoubtedly affected my interpretation of the facts. This does not mean that I came to Swaziland to prove a preconceived thesis. The process of scientific rationalization is not so conscious.

Originally I intended to write a general monograph. I collected innumerable facts and fitted them into stereotyped headings—Economics, Politics, Religion, Magic, and so on. After a few months in the field, the 'pattern' of the culture slowly emerged for me. Unfortunately, I persevered in collecting all the usual material of an ethnographic account. Even after I left Swaziland I devoted some months to forcing these facts into the artificial chapters of a standard monograph. Finally, I decided to write on what appeared to me the essential orientation of Swazi life—rank. The question arose: Did my evaluation of the facts agree with that of the Swazi? I discussed the matter with informants in Johannesburg; the problem when formulated was an intellectual abstraction that they had not considered. I discussed specific situations and posed definite questions. The final interpretation was mine as a sociologist. My facts, I hope, will not be challenged; my assessment may. No human being can be objective in his interpretation and evaluation of social facts; the colour, the class, the creed directs thought and classification. Anthropological doctrines have time and again been proved to reflect social currents, for anthropology deals with crucial issues in society and anthropologists themselves are involved in these issues. All the investigator can do is to attempt to guard against arbitrarily selecting facts which he is aware can be refuted by the facts he has consciously omitted.

This book will meet with criticism, not only by Europeans, but also by educated Swazi. Anthropologists in most parts of the world are no longer describing the lives of illiterates, unable to speak for themselves or to judge the books to which they contribute the living substance.

2. The Scope of the Book

This book is not an all-embracing monograph on Swazi culture. The material is co-ordinated and presented from the approach of rank and status—the social evaluation of individuals and groups. Much of the data that I collected has therefore been omitted as irrelevant, and will be published separately. For further information on the Swazi, the reader is referred to books and articles cited in the bibliography.

Nor does this volume cover the whole rank situation in modern Swaziland. It deals exclusively with the traditional orientation, and thereby involves an arbitrary limitation. To complete the picture, we require a description of European domination, accomplished by European culture agents—administrators, farmers, missionary recruiters, and

B

traders—and the changing alinements which they caused in the traditional structure. This section has been omitted for reasons of space, and
will be published independently.

Rank is measurement of social status. A graded scale of individuals
and of social groups exists in every society. Almost any conceivable
factors—wealth, birth, colour, age, sex, occupation, creed, ability—may be
culturally selected as bases for discrimination. The factors vary in force
and recognized importance; they are integrated in such a way as to form
a coherent system characterized by dominant emphasis. The stress may
be on one or more factors, associated with similar or diverse groups.
Within the social framework every action is intelligible and is evaluated
by the people concerned.

A study of the Swazi in the twentieth century is largely an analysis of
the privileges of pigmentation and pedigree and of the way in which they
affect and are affected by other cultural principles. Rank controls the
behaviour of individuals and groups; it determines their rights, obligations, and attitudes. In any social situation the modes of action and of
thought depend primarily on whether the actors are black or white,
nobles or commoners, men or women, adults or children, specialists or
laymen, married or unmarried, or fall into any other category of relationships evaluated by the people in the society. Every human being combines a number of such categories or statuses and co-ordinates them
psychologically as best he can. Within the course of a few hours, one
and the same man may act as father, son, headman, specialist in ritual,
and judge. For each occasion the pattern is more or less culturally
determined and the response fairly automatic, though sometimes there
are conflicting status obligations which each individual resolves, only
partly, for himself or herself.

The average individual is never conscious either of the sum total of the
status norms in his society or of his own limitations. He has a distorted
vision and a partial knowledge dictated by his participation in, rather
than his observation of, his cultural surroundings. A European and a
native, a king and a slave, a man and a woman, often hold different points
of view because each is a stranger in the world of the other. The transitory
existence of individuals is usually soon forgotten and the ritual that is
enacted on their deaths marks them primarily as status types in a continuous culture scheme.

Within the scheme there must be some consistency. It would be an
impossible situation if wealth gave power, yet natives, recognized as the
inferior group, owned the best property in the country; or if pedigree
bestowed honour in politics while religion denied any benefits to the
aristocracy of birth. Consistency is, however, rarely the result of conscious effort: a planned society is unknown to most peoples, and even
leaders who have deliberately introduced radical changes have not perceived the full effects of their innovations. The consistency is the result
of interacting social forces—economic, legal, ethical—which are never so
perfectly adjusted as to eliminate all conflict. Individuals do not need
absolute consistency, since the life of the average man is limited to
episodes not co-ordinated by clear-cut principles, and man himself is
often actuated by a variety of warring motives. From morning till night

each man passes through a series of situations which need have no connection apart from their reaction on his own complex physical and mental build. The generous father is not a stranger in the body of the grasping trader, and as long as they do not confront each other in the same situations, they may cause no obvious strain.

Individual differences are insignificant compared with status types. The average human being appears sufficiently malleable to fit more competently rather than less so into any position to which he is trained from childhood; and the ideal status personality of any group is known, no matter to what extent the individual falls below standard. Limited maladjustment is frequent, but of little social effect. Severe maladjustment is rare and becomes widespread in periods of rapid social change such as native tribes are experiencing at the present time through the impact of Western civilization. This is potentially more than the maladjustment of isolated individuals; it is the nucleus of new status types which may oust the old.

The change an individual can effect on the pattern of his culture usually depends more on the status structure than on his personal qualities. In a society where noble birth is accepted as synonymous with leadership, there is little possibility of innovations being introduced by commoners. Few societies give much scope to individual ability; in most, people are trained to the duties and privileges of a rank ordained by birth, age, or sex. The more stable a society, the less desire and usually the less opportunity there seems to be to break loose from these restrictions. Free competition for the highest positions is often a sign of disintegration of an established order.

It is this conception of rank that I intend to apply in my analysis of Swazi society.[1] It involves a selection and correlation of facts from a particular viewpoint, and a viewpoint which I consider brings out the major interests of the society at the present time.

3. The Approach to Time

Any study of a people is a study of a particular period of time, since culture is forever changing, more or less gradually, according to the structure of the society and the type of stimulus. Every change reacts throughout the society, with uneven effects on different activities. Items of culture have varying mobility, even though they form part of an interlocking whole: the imposition of tax reacted more directly on the relation of chief and subject than on the religion of the ancestral cult, and more strongly on the economic than on the linguistic apparatus of the culture.

In this book I discuss certain aspects of Swazi society as I observed it during my years in the Protectorate; I am primarily concerned with the present. In Part I, I describe the main historical processes that resulted in the existing structure; in Part II, I discuss the traditional orientation as a basis of conservatism. In Part III (which will appear separately), I indicate the forces of change. The situation that confronted me in

[1] This conception of status types has much in common with Ralph Linton's analysis of 'orientations' in *The Study of Man*, Appleton Century, 1936, Chap. 25, and with Ruth Benedict's *Patterns of Cultures*, Routledge, 1935.

Swaziland was fundamentally similar to that confronting other anthropologists dealing with simple, homegeneous societies undergoing revolutionary change through contact with complex, highly specialized societies. Anthropologists have advanced different methods of dealing with such material: some have argued for historical reconstruction (I. Schapera), the finding of a zero point (L. P. Mair), or the finding of a base line (M. J. Herskovits); and others (B. Malinowski, M. Fortes) have vehemently attacked the scientific validity or the utility of describing a past for which no accurate records exist.[1]

Apart from Part I, I have not attempted a historical reconstruction, but I have tried in Part II to show what organizations and interests of the traditional culture survive, and are active and resistant. Reconstruction of an unwritten past, more especially one that is no longer evident in the present, would have been inaccurate and incomplete. There *was* a past to which my informants constantly referred, and which influenced their reactions to the present. But that past was not, as they believed, the period of Mbandzeni, the last of the independent Swazi kings, the man in whose reign Europeans first settled in the country and whose death marked the end of an epoch in Swazi history. The details of that actual past are blurred, forgotten and distorted, and it is the blurred, distorted, rationalized past that operates at the present time.

There is always the difference between evidence and proof, between memory of participation in an activity and an actual activity, between a statement and a situation, between the ideal and the practice. When I started my work I was intent on obtaining observable facts, but I soon realised that the attitudes to, and ideas about, the facts were equally important to record, since these motivated action. The distortions and idealizations of the past give to a people their standards of value for the present. One finds expressed two entirely different social attitudes to one event: thus many Swazi, when describing a period 'before the white man', lament a golden age, whereas others rejoice in the passing of barbarism.

The historical method is particularly difficult because of the approach of the Swazi to time, and the absence of written records. Swazi do not co-ordinate events and the social settings in which they occur in any clear time sequence. Events of outstanding importance are remembered, but are torn from their social context. Like other primitive people, the Swazi are without the concept of historical evolution and contrasting stages of development. Famines, wars, epidemics are remembered in isolation. For the Swazi there is but the present and the immediate past that merges imperceptibly with the long, long ago on a single time plane. Myth and legend become part of history, and outstanding men and women become mythological beings. Time is marked by important social episodes; it is not measured in equal time units. The major unit of Swazi reckoning is an *umbuso* (reign), and the genealogy of rulers links the units together. The ruling lineage can be traced back accurately for eight generations, more remote royal names are remembered with little certainty in their order of succession. The time depth of the Swazi is determined by a limited interest in the past.

[1] For a discussion of this, see *Methods of Study of Culture Contact*. International African Institute, Memorandum XV.

A reign is obviously not an even unit of measurement, comparable to a decade or a century: it is the identification of time with a dominant social personality. A reign ends abruptly with death. Between the reigns of two Swazi kings there is a period of gradual transition, a lengthy mourning of the dead and a training of the successor. The personal growth of the king is punctuated by national ceremonies that serve as points of time reference for the nation. Carried over into each reign are customs that have their origin in a distant as well as in an immediate past. The deaths of leading men do not break the continuity of the social structure in which they paraded. The tenacity of certain customs and the ease with which others are abandoned and forgotten depends on factors that cannot be controlled by any individual in the society. Social factors are more powerful and lasting than any dictator.

In actual time, less than a century elapsed between the reign of Mbandzeni and that of his grandson, the present Paramount Chief, but the changes that took place in the structure of the society within twenty years of Mbandzeni's accession are more radical than those that occurred in the much longer period between Mbandzeni and his ancestor, Ngwane I. In the earlier period contact was between groups roughly similar in culture, and, above all, at the same technological level, whereas the later contact was between carriers of an advanced industrial civilization and a primitive peasant people. No individual within the earlier system could have invented so many alien objects or conceived such revolutionary ideas, for every man has his vision and his material setting limited by the culture that has produced him. Not only is a prophet rarely recognized in his own country, but his prophecy is limited by his dependence on the people with whom he has spent his days. Contact of European and Swazi was different from any internal development: it was an impact from an outside group with its own activities and beliefs that were parallel to, and often in conflict with, those of the Swazi in-group. The impetus to change was largely beyond Swazi control. The culture that I studied in Swaziland is a new culture, and one of uneven and conflicting parts. To split up each part and apportion the constituent elements to the 'traditional' culture and to 'Western' culture gives as little idea of the real emergent culture as the dissection of a corpse would give of the personality of the individual when alive. The existing culture must not be considered as a harmonious and well-integrated whole; on the contrary, it is composed of groups and individuals that are often actively hostile to each other. Modern Swazi culture cannot be measured by the degree of assimilation of 'Western culture'; the 'culture' brought in by Europeans is not complete, but consists of elements drawn from various countries and classes, transported across the seas to a strange environment.

How can one describe the conflicts observable in the present culture? To divide each chapter into two parts—(1) the traditional activities and (2) the innovations that challenge them—would introduce a false dichotomy, since both sets of activities operate simultaneously. Moreover, each has different affiliations and involves different social attitudes. Let me illustrate this point: Witch doctors in Swazi conservative society are the leading specialists; witch doctors in the black-white milieu are regarded as criminals (witches) on the one hand, and are linked with doctors and missionaries on the other. Thus Swazi witch doctors at the present time fit into two distinct but overlapping and contemporary social milieus. In order to bring out the dominant interests of each, I divided the material according to the milieu. This volume provides a relevant historical and sociological background, and a description of the orientations in the traditional milieu.

CHAPTER II

CONQUERING ARISTOCRACIES: 1. THE DLAMINI

ONQUEST of a territory implies invasion and direct or indirect use of force. Invaders defeat a settled population either by open warfare, through the use of superior weapons and more effective organization, or by diplomacy and economic coercion backed, in cases of non-submission, by the threat of annihilation. Both techniques are well known in all stages of history. The methods of administering the conquered then depend on the degree of cultural similarity between conquered and conquerors and the social attitudes to such factors as religion, race, and tradition.

In this chapter I outline the techniques of conquest and control observable in two main phases of Swazi history. The first dates roughly from the beginning of the sixteenth to the early nineteenth century, and the second extends from then to the present time. The first period is characterized by the relationship of Bantu people with relatively homogeneous cultures, and the second by contact between three distinct cultures, Bantu, Boer, and British. The first period can be subdivided into (1) the period of migration of Bantu kinsmen organized into small patrilineal clans; (2) the contact of different clans and the growth of rival clan heads into petty chiefs with non-clansmen among their subjects; and (3) the dominance of one clan and the organization of subjects on a military non-kinship basis under the leadership of the head of the ruling clan. In the second phase there is (1) initial recognition of a native king as the leader of his people; (2) an interim period of economic and political rivalry between Boer and Briton expressed in their reaction towards the Bantu; and (3) the curtailment by the European Government of the powers that made Bantu leadership effective. My aim is to show the main trends in these historical stages and to illustrate thereby the techniques used by conquering aristocracies.

1. *The Period of Clans*

Groups of Bantu-speaking people migrated into South-eastern Africa in the late fifteenth century. Leading one of the groups was Dlamini, a man of Embo Nguni stock, and founder of the royal clan of the Swazi. He led his followers eastwards along the Komati river towards the coast.[1] The size of his tribe is unknown;[2] the nucleus of the people were his

---

[1] For my account of this period, I rely on clan histories and traditions; on pointers in the present social structure (persistence of certain groups, and principles of territorial distribution); on historical documents. I have selected one of the better-known versions of early Swazi history. There are many and often contradictory chronicles, but the main principles are the same.

[2] I use the word *nation* for a number of tribes owing allegiance to a central authority; *tribe* for a group composed predominantly of kin and under the leadership of the dominant kinship group; *clan* for the furthest extension of kinsmen traced either through the father or the mother; *lineage* for a subdivision of a clan, the lineage members being able to trace genealogical relationship with each other. Theoretically the functions of each of these units can be the same, but at any period in a given society they are different.

patrilineal kinsmen, the rest were married women and a few men of other clans. Marriage within the Dlamini circle was, apparently, prohibited to all but the leader, so that most females joined other groups on maturity and alien women took their places. Occasionally a husband moved to the home of his wife, or a man, discontented with his own people, or exiled from them, proffered attachment elsewhere.

For over two hundred years the descendants of Dlamini dwelt in the area of Lourenço Marques. They built scattered patriarchal homesteads, pastured their cattle, and tilled the soil. Sometimes segments hived off through the ambition of brothers or sons, or to facilitate marriages which were otherwise prohibited. The new group thus formed adopted a new name and became politically independent. The Mkize, Hluɓi, Ɓele, Natal Dlamini are among those who seceded from the main line of the first Dlamini. The 'true Dlamini' established peaceful and intimate contact with at least one other Bantu group, the Tembe, a people highly skilled in agriculture and in industry. Modern Swazi state: 'We are one with the Tembe; their king, like ours, marries his sisters.' Inter-marriage between the ruling Tembe and Dlamini was, moreover, prohibited till, in the reign of the Dlamini king Mbandzeni, the Swazi sent Princess Dzambile, classificatory sister of Mbandzeni, as wife of the Tembe ruler. A bond of marriage was substituted for the unity of blood.

The order of Dlamini's direct descendants is confused until the appearance of Ngwane II, who inaugurates a new stage of Swazi history (Appendix I). From the names of ancient kings it seems that approximately seventeen generations elapsed between Dlamini and Ngwane II.

2. Amalgamation of the Clans

Ngwane II is the first king commemorated in present-day Swazi ritual. For some unknown reason he left his ancestral home and with his tribe of kinsmen and retainers crossed the high and wild Lubombo range, an achievement recorded in the praise song famed to this day throughout the nation, the praise song of the royal clan. 'Nkosi! Dlamini! You scourged the Lubombo in your flight. . . .' He led his people along the northern bank of the Pongolo, and finally built his village, Loɓamba,[1] in what is now South-eastern Swaziland. Here he died, and annual pilgrimages have ever since been made to the cave in the tree-covered hill where he and later kings lie buried in state. The people whom we speak of as Swazi usually refer to themselves as *Bantu Baka Ngwane*, 'People of Ngwane'.

The area which the Swazi consider the birthplace of their nation is known as Eshiselweni (the Place of Burning),[2] a name descriptive of ruthless methods of conquest. Stories are still told of the tyranny of Ngwane's son, Ndungunye, and grandson, Sobhuza I. They laid waste the homes of those who dared to flout their commands. Ndungunye, or it may have been Sobhuza I, would summon warriors to pluck between their teeth meat impaled on the point of a spear; if blood spurted on the sharp metal he would shout: 'Who is it that soils the spear of the Lion. Let him be

---

[1] This is not the present capital.
[2] Sobhuza I named his first village Eshiselweni. Some informants say the name refers to the fact that huge quantities of ash were seen at the site.

killed.' Sobhuza's mother, Somtjalose of the Simelane clan, is said to have restrained her son and won for the mother of the Dlamini ruler a special place in ritual and in government.

Throughout Southern Africa in the late eighteenth century nations were rising rapidly to power under ambitious rulers. The land needs of an increasing peasant population made it more difficult for independent groups to roam about without coming into conflict over garden lands or pasture. Moreover, Europeans had established mastery in parts of the south and the east of South Africa; fugitives and spies brought back reports of military domination; and the area available for Bantu habitation was diminishing. Contemporary with Ndungunye and Sobhuza I were Dingiswayo, chief of the Mtsetfwa, Zidze of the Ndwandwe, and later, in the nineteenth century, came Shaka, whose Zulu hordes ravaged Southern Africa at the same time that Mzilikazi and Soshangane spread to the north and north-east the pattern of disciplined warrior nations. The Dlamini avoided battle with the Mtsetfwa, and occasionally sent tribute to Dingiswayo.[1] The people of Zidze were many and mobile; a friendship of long standing with the followers of Sobhuza eventually foundered on a politico-economic issue, a dispute over the possession of fertile garden lands along the Pongola banks. Sobhuza's tribe had either to fight or flee.

Unwilling to accept the territorial claims of Zidze, yet conscious of numerical weakness, Sobhuza I fled northwards with all his followers, across the healthy western mountains, avoiding the fever-stricken, tsetse-ridden lowlands. Sobhuza's people were immigrants with women and children in their midst, not an army on the march, and with them they drove their most valuable possession, their cattle. Most of the migrants were Dlamini relatives with their wives, but there were also forerunners of many clans important at the present time: Matse6ula, Hlophe, Thwala, and others, with genealogies extending beyond their amalgamation at Eshiselweni. They were not all of Embo Nguni stock; but their differences were merged in loyalty to the Dlamini leader: they are acknowledged as the true, original Swazi, the *Bomdzaßu* (*ko*) ('Those who originated at Eshiselweni'). They performed special duties to enhance the power of the ruling clan, and with some of their members the Dlamini king created a ritual bond of blood brotherhood.

The 'true Swazi' entered a country already occupied by alien groups of Nguni and Sotho stock from whom Sobhuza demanded allegiance. They lived in scattered patriarchal homesteads and most of them were loosely organized under a few clan leaders who had non-relatives among their followers. Some clans had already divided into independent sub-clans through quarrels over leadership. Thus the Maseko, Kubonye, and Lala were related through an ancestor, Mancamana, and did not intermarry, but there was no political unity between them.

Groups that submitted humbly, implicity acknowledged their inferior strength. They gave occasional tribute in food and service, and were permitted, as long as they remained loyal, to retain their hereditary chiefs,

---

[1] Some informants deny this; others say that it was definitely the case. Possibly only those people who were nearest to the Mtsetfwa, and not the main group of the Dlamini subjects, placated Dingiswayo.

their land and a limited autonomy. Those who resisted were defeated and plundered; the men were usually slain and the women and children were assimilated by marriage and adoption into the nation. Unimportant families were sometimes left to 'sweep the ashes' in the denuded area and to attend on the Dlamini representative sent to rule there. One small group, the Mapoko,[1] simply moved out of the immediate range of conquest: an insult remembered and, later, revenged. The prior inhabitants who formed the second time group in the growing nation were labelled *Emakhandzambili* ('Those found ahead'). After some time those who became loyal subjects active in the Dlamini interests tended to be classed as 'true Swazi'.

Sobhuza I eventually established himself in the region of the Mdzimba hills, Central Swaziland, to this day the district in which most royal villages are situated. He built his homestead, Elangeni ('In the sun'), and stabilized his position. He as *Inkosi*, king, had among his prerogatives the waging of wars, the power of life and death, possession of the most potent magic, distribution of land. To his kinsmen he gave districts and he incorporated his subjects into the army to support him against attacks from rival relatives as well as from outside enemies.

It was Sobhuza's policy to avoid conflict with superior forces; by marriage alliances he sought the goodwill of powerful kings and demonstrated his own peaceful intentions. He took the daughter of Zidze as his main wife and gave two of his own daughters to Shaka. The great Zulu paid Sobhuza I a personal visit and was received with extravagant hospitality. Later Shaka, fearful of a successor, murdered the Swazi princesses because they became pregnant by him, but apparently Sobhuza did not consider this a *casus belli*. When, in 1828, Dingane assassinated Shaka his half-brother, and sent marauding impis into Swaziland, Sobhuza ordered his people not to engage in pitched battles, but, if necessary, to take refuge in the mountain caves. Only after Dingane's power was destroyed by the Boers in 1836 did the Swazi fight a Zulu regiment on the open plains.[2]

When Sobhuza died, he left to his successor a strong kingdom respected and feared by the neighbouring Bantu. The defeat of rival populations was followed by their incorporation in a common polity. His followers numbered several thousand people of different culture and origin, and the boundaries of his domain extended roughly as far as Barberton in the north, Carolina in the west, the Pongola in the south, and the Ubombo in the east.

3. A Military King

The daughter of Zidze bore to her royal husband two sons and a daughter; the older son, Umzimandzi, died in infancy and the younger,

---

[1] Better known as the Mapôrs or Ndzundza, and classified by Van Warmelo as Southern Transvaal Ndeɓele. *A Preliminary Survey of Bantu Tribes of South Africa*, Pretoria, 1935, p. 38.

[2] Then the Swazi regiments fought in the battle spoken of as *impi yobuya*. According to the Swazi, Dingane wanted to settle in Swaziland, and sent his army to clear the way. Dingane was killed by a Swazi chief in the south, who reported his independent action to the Swazi king.

Mswati, the recognized heir, was an immature youth on his father's death. While his grandmother and a close Dlamini uncle were acting as regents, one of his adult half-brothers tried to seize the kingship. In a battle waged to settle the issue the warriors of the capital were loyal to Mswati and killed the would-be usurper and many of his men. To prevent further trouble, Mswati was fully installed as king as soon as the proper period of national mourning had elapsed though, some say, neither he nor laZide[1] were fully trained in the secrets and duties of their future position. The people saw that 'without a king the country would rot', since 'the country needs a king'.

Mswati was the greatest of the Swazi fighting kings. Until his reign the army was organized on a local basis, each chief having authority to call up the men in his district. The local group was in many cases predominantly a kinship group. Mswati, encouraged by his mother, organized all subjects into age groups that cut across local boundaries and kinship loyalties. Each man was automatically conscripted, and his life was controlled by rigid discipline dictated from the capital.[2] Mswati established special royal villages as mobilizing centres for men in the adjacent districts, and he also created military outposts for attack on neighbouring independent tribes. From Hoho (Northern Swaziland), Emtshindini, and Embuleni (in the present Transvaal), he deployed his impis. They pillaged the Sotho for cattle and captives; they supported Mawewe against his brother Mzila in a dispute for the kingdom of their father Soshangane, founder of the Ngoni kingdom in Gasaland; they reached Southern Rhodesia in their raids, and they made the name of Mswati the terror of the north. They did not fight to gain new territories, but rather for wealth and excitement. The warriors brought their plunder to the king, who redistributed most of it, giving due preference to the *emaqawe*, the heroes. Important captives were sometimes ransomed (infinitive—*kuhlenga*) for cattle or exchanged for Swazi prisoners of war.

Destruction of the fighting forces of an army did not necessarily involve the permanent extinction of the group or a lasting hostility to the victors. The Dlamini emphasized the sanctity and power of hereditary chieftainship, and as long as a chief or his heir survived, the Dlamini ruler acknowledged him as the foundation on which the conquered group could be rebuilt. Mswati reinstated heirs of certain clan chiefs in the districts of their fathers, once their allegiance was assured. In this way he made staunch allies of once powerful enemies. This transition in attitude and behaviour resulted from the treatment the future chief received from the Dlamini king, the building up of economic and political interdependence and the creation of bonds of kinship and friendship. The technique can be documented by many clan histories, and I give in some detail that

[1] Daughters of important men are known by their father's name plus the prefix 'la'.

[2] The Swazi were in close contact with the rising Zulu nation and appear to have 'borrowed' much of its military organization. Shaka broke down the clan structure and brought men from all clans into a centralized military zone. (See article by H. M. Gluckman, 'The Kingdom of the Zulu', *African Political System*, edited by M. Fortes and E. E. Pritchard, Oxford, 1940.)

of the Mngometfulu[1] as an illustration of certain of the principles involved:

'We were kings indeed in our day before the *impi* of Mswati destroyed
us. Our first ancestor, Mngometfulu, came from a stone between the
Ngwetse and Ngwavuma rivers holding in his hand rain magic, later
stolen by his young brother Magagule. In the days of Mswati we were
at the Lubombo mountains under our King Lubelo, son of Udlakadla.
Lubelo was great; he defeated many tribes,[2] he had numerous regiments; one was called Ticelecele, a name already belonging to the men
of Mswati, who, when he heard of the imitation exclaimed: "Does he
think he is equal to me? Destroy the people of Mngometfulu." When
the big birds (heralds of an army) were seen, spies reported to Lubelo
the approach of Mswati's warriors. Lubelo said: "Let us attack them
at the neck of Ngwempisi river, near the waterfall, for they cannot cross
in great numbers." He spoke to Mbete his brother, but Mbete was
wooden-headed and led the army to a plain. The people of Mswati
arrived shouting of their great victories and flourishing their spears as
they jumped high in the air, and the Mngometfule seemed few and
their praises were not heard. The Swazi encircled us as in pincers.
Lubelo spat *tse tse* in anger and his eyes were fearful. He rejoiced only
that the killing of his brother fell to his enemies and not to himself.
Then Lubelo in his fury decided to attack the neighbouring Gumbi
under their chief, but huts hear, and they quickly allied with the strong
Sambane, head of the Nyawo. Councillors of Lubelo advised him
against the battle, pointing to the wounds (the gaps) in his ranks. But
he heeded not, and spoke contemptuously of those tribes. When the
attack was made the Mngometfulu were caught in a cleft stick. The
Nyawo struck first, the Gumbi came from behind. They destroyed.
Then Lubelo said in despair: "Better be killed by the king of Ngwane,
because we are really one, than by those foreigners."[3] At that time the
White people were entering the country, and Lubelo with his young
son Mbikiza and a few women went in a wagon, while warriors followed
on foot. Mswati's men saw them and gave fight. Lubelo was killed
in the wagon, but before he died he handed his son Mbikiza to a
warrior of the enemy saying, "Take him. Care for him. He is the chief
for the Mngometfulu." Most of his people died that day and those
who survived were mocked for not dying with their king.[4] They paid
allegiance to Mswati, not knowing that the child still lived, till one day
the king asked a brother of Lubelo if he knew the order of the royal
huts of the Mngometfulu. The brother told of the supposed death of

[1] I took down this story from Sukani Mngometfulu, an old man, 'father' of
the present Mngometfulu chief, and I checked it with informants. It is sub-
stantially the same as that recorded in Bryant, pp. 343–5, but it is in many
respects different from that in the Blue Book Cmd. 6,200, 1890, p. 206.

[2] The Myeni and Matenjwa.

[3] This refers to the fact that some years earlier the Mngometfulu had been
assisted by the Swazi to re-establish themselves after defeat by a third party.

[4] The Mngometfulu who remained behind at the Lubombo obtained the help
of Ziβeβu, the Zulu, to take revenge on Sambane.

the heir in the wagon, with his father. Then Mswati produced the child who had been looked after by the warrior, Ngolotsheni, at his home at Esikoteni (South Swaziland), Ngolotsheni, whose daughter bore our king Sobhuza. He had been like his own child and wept at parting. Mswati gave Mbikiza many cattle, saying: "I have already eaten the Mngometfulu. Return to your home." So our kingship woke again.'

Disruption of rival Bantu kingdoms magnified Mswati's power and many survivors fled 'to his armpit'. His fame also attracted distant relatives of established tribesmen anxious for a protector in this period of unrest. Some were humble and insignificant, and others were once powerful and honoured. He established large groups in sparsely populated districts under their own chiefs, and he settled people who were without leaders under his nominees. The immigrants, known as *tikhondzi* (lieges), form a third time group in the Swazi nation.

Loyal subjects could anticipate protection from external foes and a limited security of person and property within a system of law. Only occasionally the king directed his army against a quiescent group to 'wash the spear' of a favoured son anxious for the taste of battle, or for no more obvious reasons than pleasure and to demonstrate his authority. Victories were propaganda of royalty. But as a rule force was reserved to deal with open antagonists, and the peaceful tribesmen participated in the deliberations of the national councils, rallied for labour, danced in an annual ceremony to strengthen the Dlamini king, were eligible for promotion in the army and for posts of ritual and administrative importance. Local and kinship loyalties were subordinated in national activities.

The nation revolved round the king. He controlled the army, was the supreme judge, disbursed wealth, and possessed unique ritual. All officials were dependent on him for their positions: princes, chiefs, and councillors emphasized his power. At the same time they were in a position to stop him from abusing his privileges. His mother in particular acted as a check, and, on occasions, as a leader of the opposition.

Diplomatic marriages continued to be made for national purposes. Wives were selected for Mswati from many subject groups, and marriage ties were created, not only with powerful chiefs, but with insignificant commoners. His harem was the largest in the land and, by the custom of *ukuqoma*, he enjoyed the privilege of seizing by force any unmarried girls he desired. His kinsmen also, because of their high status and the wealth that went with it, possessed many women. The Dlamini clan multiplied more than all others and the bond of Dlamini blood ramified throughout the nation.

Members of the different stocks also intermarried, since the laws of exogamy forced them to seek wives outside the clan. Between conquered and conquerors, and between the conquered themselves, there was established a complex network of economic and social obligations, gifts and services, based on 'in-law' relationship.

The contact between the diverse elements enriched the nation with new ideas, words, rituals, and tools. The Dlamini benefited most because they, through the king, acquired and monopolized certain ritual and material possessions. While they did not seek to impose their customs and tolerated the cultural peculiarities of others, the prestige that attached to the Dlamini made their customs appear desirable. Some were imitated by the aliens and became national characteristics. These included slits in the lobes of the ears, a special mode of costume, the dialect known as *siswati* (verb—*kuswata*), certain rituals, and laws of property and person.

In the final heterogeneous nation there were over seventy clan names, approximately one-fifth were 'true Swazi', one-seventh were 'prior' inhabitants, and the remainder were migrants. About 70 per cent were Nguni, and 30 per cent were Sotho—the Nguni-Sotho classification cutting across the time stratification. The Dlamini clan far outnumbered any of the other clans, some of which had only one member—a refugee to the Swazi kingdom. Every clan had its history, and the combined history of all the clans gave the mandate of superiority to the Dlamini conquerors.[1]

When the Europeans first entered the country in the reign of Mswati they found a nation organized for defence and attack and the maintenance of internal order through the leadership of a Dlamini monarch.

[1] See Appendix II for some of the main Swazi clans.

CHAPTER III
CONQUERING ARISTOCRACIES: 2. THE EUROPEANS

1. *Europeans enter into Swazi Political Organization*

UNTIL the reign of Mswati contact with the Europeans was indirect, and its effect was more psychological than economic or political. The first Europeans entered Southern Africa before the different tribes were united into the Swazi nation. As early as the fifteenth century, the Portuguese established contact with East Coast natives. In 1502, a Portuguese captain seized as slaves a few unsuspecting Tembe, the clan with whom the Dlamini claim kinship; when the next galleon arrived it was greeted with a shower of assegais. Furthermore, the coastal natives witnessed the power of Western arms in a long battle between European groups for the harbour of Delagoa Bay, desired as a base for inland traffic and as a port of call on the voyage to the riches of the East. While the Dlamini kings were welding together the nation, Europeans settled to the north and south-east of Swaziland, and there filtered through to the native people a few beads, cloths, and other wonders of the white man. When the Great Trek began (1836), news of the migration and of battles between whites and blacks spread among the Bantu. The land of Mswati's father, Sobhuza I, was steadily encircled by white influences.

Sobhuza I, informants report, dreamed that people of a strange species entered his country. They were the colour of the red mealies; their hair resembled the tails of cattle; their houses were built on platforms and dragged by oxen; they spoke an unknown tongue and they knew not the courtesies of humanity. The men carried weapons of terrible destruction. This dream was interpreted as a warning from the ancestors never to fight the white people, 'and see', the story-teller added, 'we have obeyed'. Before the Europeans penetrated Swaziland, before there was any direct contact, the Swazi acknowledged their difference and the white man's military strength.

During the reign of Mswati the European advance guard arrived in the country and was received in peace. Farmers drifted through on their way to the coast, traders bartered their wares for ivory and skins, hunters shot the wild game teeming in the low and middle veld, and a missionary settled for a while in the south. The Europeans came as individuals, but were not isolated—they were members of different white communities. Boer and British had established themselves as two powerful and antagonistic groups in Southern Africa.

The Swazi considered that the Europeans would be useful as allies. Mswati, soon after his accession in 1838, requested the protection of the Queen of England through her Agent-General in Natal, Sir Theophilus Shepstone, in the hope that this might check the raids of the powerful Zulu, under Mpande, into Swaziland. Protection was refused, but Shepstone, through his strong influence in Zululand, curbed Mpande. Swazi remembered this service when at a later date they wanted a European to assist them in their internal affairs.

19

Sporadic, peaceful contacts prepared the way for permanent relationships. Boer farmers required land. In 1845, Mswati ceded to the 'Dutch South Africa Nation' (Boers in the Transvaal) for one hundred breeding cattle, a large district inhabited by subordinated Sotho. Ten years later, seventy head of cattle and services (unspecified) bought for the Lydenburg Republic an area which, though vaguely defined, seems to have covered the whole of Mswati's land. Soon after, he regranted a portion of this in a land concession to an individual Boer farmer. The concession period, the period of 'paper conquest' had begun.

The relationship between the Swazi and the European groups was friendly and co-operative. In 1864, the Swazi helped the Boers to defeat tribes in the Lydenburg district, aware that among them were the Mapoko, the proud folk who had refused to accept Dlamini domination. Of this battle Theal writes: 'A Swazi army fell upon Mapok and routed him. It next attacked Malewu and nearly annihilated his clan, leaving in one place alone the corpses of 854 men and 2,840 women and children.'[1]

The Boers were, however, anxious for some control over the powerful warrior nation living in fertile country, and when Mswati died, tribal dissension gave them an opportunity to intervene in internal government. Mswati's mother and one of his half-brothers, Ndwandwe, were acting regents for the young heir, Ludönga. Suddenly Ludönga died. The council held that the Prince Regent had murdered him in order to obtain power for himself, and so the Prince Regent was clubbed to death. Thereupon, older sons of Mswati wrangled and intrigued, coveting the kingship, and the army was divided behind rival claimants. Finally, influenced mainly by the Queen Regent, the nation through its representative councils and chiefs agreed to accept the quiet, motherless Mbandzeni as king. The Transvaal Republic sent a commando of four hundred men to 'crown him',[2] and the State President claimed that his people put an end to the internal disputes by which the Swazi would otherwise have exterminated themselves. After the ceremony the leaders of the troops had Mbandzeni make his mark on a document confirming all concessions granted by his father.

2. The Swazi King and European Pioneers

Swazi government remained apparently unchanged by the presence of Europeans in the early years of Mbandzeni's reign. He continued in the traditions that glorified Dlamini pedigree and military strength. His regiments raided tribes in the Zoutpansberg and Lydenburg districts,[3] and he punished with death any attack on his privileges. At his command, sanctioned by his supporters in the council, the queen mother, mother of Ludönga, was executed for plotting against him. Another wife of Mswati was appointed in her stead. The British, soon after they had defeated and exiled the Zulu chief, Cetshwayo (1880), requested the assistance of the Swazi against Sekukuni, Chief of the Pedi, and as a result some 6,000 Swazi went into battle under their great general, Mbovana Fakudze.

[1] Theal, *History of South Africa*, 4th Edition, Volume IV, p. 456.
[2] C. M. Rudolph, Cmd. 6.200, 1890, p. 134.
[3] They raided districts already ceded by Mswati in 1846 to the 'Lydenburg Republic'.

Throughout South Africa in the latter half of the nineteenth century Boer and Briton were delimiting their boundaries and defining their spheres of interest.[1] The Boers needed land. They saw that the soil in Swaziland was fertile and well-watered, the grass was good for pasturage, and the country conveniently situated as a route for a proposed harbour at Kosi Bay. Most Boers identified themselves with the expansionist and republican policy of the Transvaal government. England, on the other hand, towards the middle of the nineteenth century, after the loss of her American colonies and the rise of free trade, wanted to consolidate her Empire rather than expand it, but the danger of losing the prized products of colonies to other Western Powers forced her to resume her imperialist drive. She had no desire to annex Swaziland, envisaging the control of that tiny area, isolated from her other territories, as both costly and troublesome. At the same time, she was not prepared to let the Boers gain control in a country of unknown promise, or divert trade from her own southern ports. In two conventions (1881 and 1884) entered into between the British and Boer governments, the independence of the Swazi was guaranteed.[2]

The discovery of gold in the north-west in 1882 lured European fortune-hunters to Swaziland. Adventurers with their worldly wealth slung in knapsacks over their shoulders trudged along the native footpaths; the more fortunate travelled in wagons that laboriously carved tracks over hills and valleys till they reached Embekelweni, Mbandzeni's home, east of the Mdzimba. Companies were floated, largely with capital from overseas, and the possibilities of a harbour and a railway were investigated. The men bribed their way past the councillors to obtain personal interviews with the king. They brought him cash, blankets, dogs, horses, liquor, and other products of the 'civilized world'; in return, he was merely requested to make crosses on the documents that they placed before him.

It seems from all accounts that several hundreds of Europeans passed through the country and visited Mbandzeni. While some concessionaires stayed for months and years, others drifted away after their interviews. It is doubtful if there were more than a hundred permanent inhabitants, and these were mainly traders and Boer farmers who annually brought in their sheep for winter pasturing.

Swazi principles for incorporating alien Bantu were applied to the Europeans. They received from the king the right to live in the country, permission to use the land, and a limited protection of person and property. In return, Mbandzeni required them to recognize him as sovereign in Swaziland, to acknowledge his authority, and to obey his judgements in all matters affecting the Swazi people.

At the same time the Europeans held a unique position, since they were not assimilated into Swazi life; they did not serve the Swazi king, and they employed his subjects as their servants; they came as individuals

[1] References in this section are to the Blue Books on Swaziland: Cmd. 5,089, 1887; Cmd. 6,200, 1890; Cmd. 6,217, 1890; Cmd. 7,212, 1893; Cmd. 7,611, 1895.

[2] See Convention for the Settlement of the Transvaal Territory, 1881, and the London Convention, 1884.

C

without the quality of royal birth, and yet commanded the privileges of chiefs; they took no active part in national ceremonies and followed their own religious practices; they were in language and all cultural traits distinct, and frequently showed in their treatment of the natives that they were proud of the distinction. Finally, they maintained loyalties beyond the borders with their own national groups.

Among the immigrants were a few lawless men who, respecting neither the life nor the property of others, flouted all authority. Mbandzeni's subjects complained that Boers along the western border demanded tax, stole cattle, seized children, moved beacons, and treated Swazi, even of the highest rank, with injustice and brutality. Raids for stock and tabourers were a constant menace. An eyewitness reported on one occasion that Boers 'carried off about forty head of cattle, shot one Kafir through the leg, cut one Kafir's ear off and took a boy about nine years of age along with them'.[1] There were rumours of an intended invasion by a strong 'filibustering expedition' of Boer adventurers, said to be sponsored by their Government, which, however, denied all knowledge and disclaimed responsibility.

The presence of the Europeans gradually disturbed the alliances between Swazi authorities and their subjects. Service was deflected from the king and chiefs to European employers; criminals fled from judgements in Swazi courts to white homes for protection; Mbandzeni's failure to restrain European lawbreakers undermined his authority; and the conspicuous wealth of the Europeans overshadowed his prestige. He complained that his people 'seemed to favour the white man more than himself'; that each white man behaved 'like a king'. European governments outside Swaziland abstained from taking action against miscreant Europeans who lived in Mbandzeni's country. Mbandzeni's security was also threatened externally. Learning of a threatened Boer invasion, he appealed to Sir Hercules Robinson, Governor and High Commissioner, and received the advice 'that if his country is entered and occupied without his permission by a gang of marauders, he should not remain inactive, but should collect a force and expel them'.[2] Mbandzeni, however, knew from the fate of other native chiefs that it was disastrous to fight Europeans. Unable to control them either as groups or as individuals, and appreciating the danger of conflict between the two sections of the Europeans and between Europeans and his own people, Mbandzeni was forced to introduce new administrative machinery. The treatment of all inhabitants on the same terms was impossible. Persuaded by some of the more responsible concessionaires, he appealed to the British High Commissioner for a British resident, but was refused. He thereupon made use of a principle of government already developed among his own people— hereditary privileges in a trusted family. He turned to Sir Theophilus Shepstone, who had assisted the Swazi against the attacks of Mpande and who was deeply respected by the natives, and asked him to send one

[1] Extract from *Mercantile Advertiser* posted to the Acting High Commissioner for South Africa, 21 December, 1886. Cmd. 5,089, p. 2, also p. 13. For a similar episode see *Cape Times*, 29 September, 1886.

[2] Telegram from Sir Hercules Robinson, Governor and High Commissioner, to Sir H. T. Holland, 29 March 1887. Cmd. 5,089, 1887, p. 40.

of his sons to help the Swazi in their dealings with other Europeans.[1] Thus it came about that on 18 February 1887, 'Offy', Theophilus Shepstone, Junior, a young adventurer,[2] was formally installed by the Swazi king as Resident Adviser and Agent of the Swazi nation with powers to act in all matters concerning white people in Swaziland.[3]

Shepstone's position was difficult and unique. It was not analogous to that of Europeans in other native kingdoms who were made 'white chiefs'; he was without a district, and without a recognized following, and the terms of his appointment specifically excluded him from dealing with matters affecting natives only. He received a high salary for his services and could be dismissed if the Swazi government lost confidence in him.[4] Mbandzeni and his men, afraid that the appointment might be misunderstood, constantly reiterated to the Europeans that he, Mbandzeni, was king in his own country. 'Offy' was his subordinate: he was to guard Swazi interests threatened by his own people. The Europeans did not regard Shepstone as their representative. As a white man, he was affiliated to the white groups, and because he was an Englishman the Boers identified him with the English. But no European government sanctioned his powers and one section of English concessionaires disliked him as much as did the Boers. The Europeans did not accept the principle of selection by virtue of birth, and the fact that 'Offy' was the son of 'Somtseu' was to them no reason why he should receive sufficient support to make his decisions effective. It was the counterpart of the situation in which a European government chooses its own nominees from among the subject people, and ignores traditional leaders and accepted laws of succession to leadership.

Mbandzeni attempted to control the Europeans through their own institutions, and at the same time to retain his sovereignty. With his sanction, Shepstone called a meeting of concessionaires, and a white committee of fifteen property-owners representing land, mining, and other interests was elected, with five additional members as king's nominees. To this committee Mbandzeni gave somewhat reluctantly[5] a charter of self-government, but he expressly reserved to himself the right to veto any decisions. He was still the king; he told the Europeans that nobody should force natives to work on concessions or beat them if they refused. He stated publicly that he had not sold the ground, but simply leased it to white men; that he would be displeased if they interfered with the girls, or burnt grass, or made roads where his cattle grazed, or demanded payment from his subjects for thefts without first proving

---

[1] Memo by Sir T. Shepstone, 20 April 1889. Cmd. 6,200, 1890, p. 148.

[2] Harry Shepstone, an older son, was first approached, but, appreciating the difficulties, he refused.

[3] He was in no way accredited by the British government as its representative. Cmd. 5,089, 1887, p. 9.

[4] Shepstone fell out of favour and was actually dismissed for some months in 1889, and Mr. A. M. Miller was appointed in his stead. Cmd. 6,200, 1890, p. 195.

[5] He was finally swayed by the advice of Prince Jokova, a leading councillor and a man extremely opposed to the Europeans; he wanted them to live their lives without impinging on his people.

guilt; and he still considered that he had the right to maintain his position over his own people by force, administered in accordance with Swazi law.[1] Thus in December 1888 he explained in a letter to the Governor of Natal:[2] 'I discovered a dangerously treasonable conspiracy in this my country, which, had it not been brought to light, would have plunged the nation into civil war and caused endless bloodshed among my people. For the protection of my people, my country, my children, and my throne, I was compelled to take severe and decisive action. From the time of my forefathers to the present, the law of my country has allowed and allows but one punishment for convicted rebels and traitors, and that punishment is death. . . . And so, unprejudiced by any strictly personal motives, and acting as I sincerely believed for the safety and welfare of my people, the security of the many interests vested in my country by white people, and for the prevention of eternal war, sentence of death was passed upon the ring-leaders, the majority of whom were executed.'

Soon after Mbandzeni died. Europeans who knew him well stated that he was a man of singularly kind and gentle disposition, a man of remarkable shrewdness and tact.[3] His own people venerate him as a good king, duped by unscrupulous white men posing as his friends. Mbandzeni saw his heritage dwindling, his domain restricted by European boundary commissions, his power questioned by European governments. When he was near to death he mourned, 'Swazi kingship ends with me.'

3. *Concessions*

Swazi were subjugated through concessions, a type of economic warfare eventually sanctioned by powerful European governments.[4] Neither Boer nor British pioneers were organized primarily for open battle, and in Swaziland the flag followed trade. The history of the concessions in Swaziland is probably without parallel; the king and his council signed away the entire country and all rights over future development. Swazi talk of the 'documents that killed us'.

Early concessions dealt primarily with land and minerals. Later, more especially in the years when a paid and trusted European adviser was in control (1887–9), a prodigious number of industrial monopolies were granted. Some of the land grants were for grazing, others for leases, and a few were outright transfers; the period of use varied from fifty years to 'as long as grass grows and water runs'; the country was not surveyed, and the boundaries were vaguely defined. Among the documents are two known as the 'Unallotted Lands', and 'Unallotted Minerals Concessions'. They respectively assigned for one hundred years rights of farming over

---

[1] Cmd. 5,089, 1887, pp. 69–74.

[2] The writer of the letter is not specified; Mbandzeni's cross and seal and the cross of three councillors were witnessed by three members of the white committee. Cmd. 6,200, 1890, pp. 104–5. Mbandzeni usually had his Secretary and Agent, Shepstone, and later Miller, to write all letters. Shepstone was fluent in Zulu; Miller used John Gama, a Swazi educated in Natal, as his interpreter. Gama was also employed directly by Mbandzeni. Cmd. 9,200, 1890, p. 235.

[3] See report by Sir F. de Winton, 1890. Cmd. 6,201, 1890, p. 8.

[4] It must be remembered that the 'concession phase' was spread throughout African and other areas conquered by Europeans.

unallotted territory in Swaziland south of the Komati, and of mining over the entire unallotted country. Land and mineral rights that lapsed under other concessions were to revert, not to the Swazi nation, but to the holders of the two concessions. Monopoly grants covered every conceivable activity of an agricultural and industrial country; tanning and tanneries; printing, publishing, and advertising; the collection and receiving of customs; the importation of machinery; the power of attorney to collect the king's private revenue; the manufacture and import of tobacco; the extraction of oil; the building of townships; the sole rights of auctioneering and photography, pawn-broking and Orphan Chambers, insurance and assurances; the right 'to bill batteries, to trent bailings and concentrates' (*sic*); the use of steam; 'the treatment of tailings', the right to apply for concessions.[1]

The majority of the documents were obviously incomprehensible to an illiterate chief and council of a peasant people, despite the grantee's attestation in each case that it was 'truly and duly' interpreted. Land grants dealt with principles of tenure shaped in a foreign culture; leasehold, freehold, sale, and private ownership were concepts that did not exist among the Swazi. Swazi naïvely trusted in a clause whereby Mbandzeni specifically reserved his 'sovereign rights' over the land and protected his subjects from 'detrimental interference' by concessionaires. Minerals and chemicals had no place in Swazi economy, while the processes of extraction detailed in the concessions were patently untranslatable. The monopoly rights dealt with material assets that were the product and not the starting point of an industrial system. To take but one example, how could the Swazi understand the right 'to carry on the business of banking in all its branches, and in particular to advance money upon property and securities of all kinds, to discount bills, notes, and other securities, to deal in exchange and specie, and to receive money on deposit at interest or otherwise, to borrow or raise money by the issue of, or upon, bonds, debentures, bills of exchange, notes or other obligations or securities, and generally to carry on the banking business (1 May 1888)'? The Swazi explained: 'We hold the feather and sign. We take money, but we do not know what it is for' (Meeting, 9 December 1889). For each concession Mbandzeni, and as a rule his courtiers, received money or gifts. Never had there been such wealth in the country, so many new articles, so much excitement. It was estimated that the Swazi king's annual income, derived from rents, obligations and transfer dues under concessions, ranged from £15,000 to £20,000. The Swazi considered that this money was tribute to their king; the Europeans were satisfied that it secured them the rights they desired.

In the meantime, Boer-British antagonism crystallized round their respective economic interests, and concessions were used to further national ambitions. Boers predominated in farming, British in mining and trade. Land and mineral rights frequently overlapped, and though many of the former were only for winter grazing and many of the latter were not operated, the territorial coincidence of dual interests was made a bitter political issue. Moreover, the Boers, anxious to annex the

---

[1] For list of concessions, see Cmd. 6,201, 1890, pp. 59–74.

country, had obtained rights which were essentially powers of government. The South African Republic had acquired for itself the vital concession of railways, posts and telegraphs, navigation and surveying. It was not the British Government, but individual investors and companies, that desired Britain to assume responsibility. The Chambers of Commerce of London, Leeds, Bradford, Liverpool, Birmingham, and Sheffield, the Forbes Reef Co., the Napootaland Syndicate, the Umbandine Swaziland Concession, Birds' Swaziland Concession, Acton's Swaziland Concession, and others 'humbly protested' against any cession of Swaziland to the South African Republic.[1]

4. A Period of Unrest

The death of Mbandzeni was followed by a period of national unrest, intensified, yet superficially restrained, by the presence of Europeans. Representatives of the British and Boer Governments, despite repeated verbal recognition of Swazi sovereignty, had frequently protested against the royal prerogative of 'killing off' and had threatened the Swazi that 'action would be taken'. At one meeting Jokova (the leading councillor) pointed out the inconsistency of Europeans: 'We thank you for the words that have been said, but you talk about the independence of the Swazi nation. We do not see that unless you allow us to rule in our own way there is any independence at all. Our way of ruling is to kill each other, and what shall the rule be if we are not allowed to kill?'[2] The Queen Regent pleaded for permission to destroy 'for just one day' the wizards who had murdered the king. Permission was refused, and the national leaders resentfully submitted to the British Queen's 'detestation of the practice'.[3] After heated discussion they selected as main wife and future queen mother, Gwamile Mdluli, a woman of unusual intelligence and ability, whose eldest son, Bunu, was a headstrong youth of sixteen years. A rival candidate was sent far from the capital. Sporadic violence continued; stories of Swazi atrocities were splashed by the Press; there was a recognized increase in crime and armed feuds between native groups in the country.

The affairs of the European pioneers were equally chaotic. The White committee failed to exercise control; from the beginning Boer extremists refused to support any Englishman; decisions were frustrated by personal intrigues; members were untrained and inefficient; their executive powers were challenged. After Mbandzeni died, the committee was dissolved by order of the Swazi nation, who had lost all confidence in it.

A Joint Commission from the two European governments, and originally sanctional by Mbandzeni, came to investigate racial and economic conditions. It reiterated the guarantee of independence of the Swazi nation and appointed a Provisional Government representing the three

[1] Cmd. 6,200, 1890, pp. 243–50. Over £2,000,000 was invested by companies in the United Kingdom. See also Cmd. 6,201, 1890, pp. 51–8. The Aborigines Protection Society, London, also sent in a plea. Cmd. 6,200, 1890, p. 207.

[2] Meeting, 18 December 1889, Cmd. 6,201, 1890, p. 47.

[3] See Telegrams, Despatches, etc. Cmd. 6,200, 1890, pp. 268–74.

groups, with Shepstone as the Swazi nominee.[1] A legal tribunal, with Shepstone again speaking for the Swazi, confirmed 352 out of 364 concessions.

The Provisional Government, torn by national and personal rivalry, muddled along for over three years. It was 'probably the most expensive (administration) in the world'. The revenue, derived from licences, taxes, and customs dues, was roughly one-fifth of the cost of government and 'accrued under laws so imperfectly drawn that the salaried Attorney-General whose special function is to maintain the law, thought it becoming to refuse, in his private capacity, to pay any import dues'.[2] The cost was shared by the Boers and British; the Swazi, who derived most money from concessions, paid nothing towards the maintenance of the Provisional Government.

To responsible Europeans, settled in the country or having interests there, the necessity for a single administration became increasingly obvious. European residents at this stage numbered some 750, of whom about 450 claimed British nationality.[3] There was the danger that at any moment war might break out between Boer and Briton, European and native, as a result of the actions of irresponsible sections of the white population. In the meantime, black and white were becoming increasingly interdependent and the black man's institutions thwarted the white man's ambitions and autonomy. At the same time a basis was required for dispossessing the Swazi of their sovereignty without violating too blatantly the pledges of the 1881 and 1884 Conventions! The Joint Commission had reaffirmed the integrity of the nation and declared that 'no inroad on their independence shall be allowed, even with the consent of the Swazi Government, without the consent of both her Majesty's Government and the Government of the South African Republic'. Sir Arthur Havelock declared that the only justification for the abrogation of the independence of the Swazi would be the complete failure of existing institutions, and, he had added, this was imminent.[4]

The Boers persistently advanced reasons why Swaziland should be annexed to the Republic. President Kruger, moreover, offered, in return for this and other territories required by his people, that the Republic would (according to British phraseology) 'withdraw her pretensions to extend her influence north of the Limpopo'. After lengthy correspondence, the Republic, in 1893, received sanction from the British Government to negotiate with the Swazi for control over the affairs of Europeans, subject to special stipulations to protect Swazi interests and customs, and not to incorporate their country.[5] The document was placed before the Queen Regent and her council. They read it with amazement, refused to

[1] The Swazi issued an 'Organic Proclamation' in which they set forth the constitution and powers of the Provisional Government. Cmd. 7,212, 1893, pp. 12–15. This document was later repudiated by the Swazi.

[2] Cmd. 7,212, 1893, p. 101.

[3] Cmd. 7,212, 1893, p. 142.

[4] Cmd. 7,212, 1893, pp. 123 ff. Also *Hansard*, Vol. 347, 3rd Series, pp. 1,138 and 1,715, for correspondence and discussion between the British Colonial Office and the South African Republic.

[5] Convention of 1893. Cmd. 7,212, 1893, pp. 149–51.

sign, denied all knowledge of various documents that they feared might be used against them,[1] and finally sent a deputation to England to plead British protection. The men returned with assurances of the benevolent intentions of Her Majesty's Government, which was, however, precluded by its treaty engagements from accepting their allegiance (16 November 1894). The two European governments were not diverted from their plan by the opposition of the natives. In December 1894, Great Britain and the South African Republic concluded a convention whereby the need to obtain the prior consent of the Swazi was waived and the country became a 'protected dependency' of the South African Republic. Unwilling to suffer the doom of openly rebellious Bantu nations, the Swazi temporarily submitted.

They found European rule oppressive; they were required as labourers and were treated as *Emakafula* (Kafirs). The 1894 Convention provided for the introduction of a native hut tax after the expiration of three years. Whereas concessions were negotiated with the king and councillors and did not obviously and immediately affect each individual, tax was a direct attack against which the Swazi had previously successfully protected themselves. They resented it as 'money to keep the white man in the country'. Furthermore, their cattle were depleted by a scourge of rinderpest attributed by many to the white invaders. Swazi had not yet accepted the principle of working for Europeans in order to pay tax. There were rumours that they would resist the collectors and that the specialists in war ritual had been summoned to prepare the army for attack against the Europeans.

Hostility culminated in an internal political episode that was not directly related to white contact.[2] In 1898, the first year of tax collection, Mbaba Sibandze, a leading councillor, was executed at the capital. The young King Bunu was implicated, and the Republican authorities summoned him for trial before the landdrost's Court. They claimed this power by virtue of a clause in the 1894 Convention that retained to Bunu 'the usual powers of Paramount Chief in so far as the same are not inconsistent with civilized laws and customs'. Irresponsible concessionaires told the king he would be killed; the nation mobilized; rumours of the preparation of war ritual again startled the country. The Republican Government rushed in extra armed police from the Transvaal with artillery. Bunu refused to appear before the Court, and with a few trusted followers rode by night to the British resident magistrate at Ingwavuma, Zululand. 'I have fled my country', he said simply, 'because Boers are invading it, and bringing in arms to kill me. I have seen their troops with my own eyes. I have stolen no sheep and shed no white man's blood.' The British intervened on behalf of the Swazi, holding that there was no court then in existence competent to try the king. The State President of the Republic, in one of the innumerable letters between the two governments, admitted that he was anxious to be rid of a Paramount Chief after Bunu, and considered that by his flight he had already abandoned his throne. The Swazi insisted that 'If the king is dead, the queen

[1] Cmd. 7,611, 1895, p. 17.

[2] A detailed account is published in Cmd. 9,206, 1899, pp. 1–157.

is the king.' The British contended that it was premature to treat the king as non-existent. Eventually the Republican authorities agreed that the murder of the councillor would not be 'judged too harshly since it was the act of a young uncivilized paramount chief of a barbaric people'. After a most interesting and unusual trial, they reinstated Bunu, imposed a fine of £500, and, in a Protocol drawn by both White governments, radically curtailed his criminal jurisdiction.

When in the next year the Anglo-Boer War broke out, Boer and British both advised the Swazi not to join the 'enemy'. Individual volunteers assisted both sides as spies and runners, but no regiment left the capital. The Swazi watched the white men fight among themselves; Bremersdorp, Boer headquarters, was razed to the ground and the Republican administration withdrew.

Bunu died during the war. He had been an unhappy as well as a dissolute young man, and, aware of his unpopularity, he was constantly afraid that he was bewitched. His loyal subjects, temporarily freed from white control, took vengeance on those whom they believed had caused his early death. No damage was done to families, homes, and possessions left by the white soldiers. The council selected as Bunu's main wife laNgolotsheni (Lomawa) Ndwandwe, daughter of the chief who tended the Mngometfulu heir and a member of the great Zidze's stock. Her child, Sobhuza, was a baby, and Bunu's mother, Gwamile, and his brother, Malunge, acted as regents. Both were people of intelligence and courage; they strove for the rights of their people within the framework of a domination they realized they could not overthrow.

5. *The Period of Acceptance*

The years of friction merge with a period of interdependence and voluntary acceptance of British control. In 1902, Britain, as part of the sour fruits of military victory, assumed the role of protector of Swaziland. The Swazi anticipated a restoration of their sovereign rights and the expulsion of troublesome concessionaires. These hopes were gradually shattered, but in the course of time, through economic and political forces, the natives recognized the Europeans as a vital part of their society, and under their leader Sobhuza II showed, despite sporadic conflicts, positive co-operation with, and loyalty to, the *Uhulumeni* (White government).

After the Boer War, a Special Commissioner took charge, and the Administration consisted of little more than a police force whose primary concern was to restrain the hostility of natives and to collect tax. In 1903, the Council was placed directly under the Governor of the Transvaal, laws of the Transvaal were applied to Swaziland, a few local administrators were appointed, and technical development was directed from the Transvaal. The personnel and duties were formally extended. When, in 1906, the Transvaal received self-government, control of Swaziland was transferred to the British High Commissioner for South Africa and the present system was inaugurated. A Proclamation (1907) provided for a full administrative staff with a Resident Commissioner at the head, and experts for different activities; Swazi chiefs became essential cogs in the machine; duties and powers were defined.

Before there could be either security or development it was essential to settle the question of the concessions. Britain considered it impossible to annul them, since they had been recognized by the legal tribunal she herself had supported. Therefore a Commission was appointed to define the boundaries between land and mineral grants, to decide on the exact nature and priority of claims, and to expropriate at pre-war value the monopoly and industrial concessions. There still remained a major issue. What was to be done with the natives, who, living in the country, regarded it as their own? They were no longer consulted on vital issues. Lord Selborne, the High Commissioner, investigated the land position, and with the sanction of the Secretary of State introduced a Partition Proclamation (1907). The Resident Commissioner announced its provisions to a meeting of concessionaires and natives: one-third of every land and grazing concession—that is, one-third of the country—was alienable for the sole and exclusive rights of the natives; the remaining two-thirds belonged to the holders of Mbandzeni's documents. The selection of areas for natives was to be left to a Special Commissioner with power to choose any portion, whether it be more or less than one-third of a particular concession. If more, the holder received compensation either in other land or in money; if less, the difference became a reserve of Crown land for government purposes. Where Mbandzeni had made the concession leasehold for fifty or ninety-nine years with a right of renewal for fifty years, the title could, at the choice of the holder, be converted on expiry of the period into 'freehold', or else revert to the Crown; it did not revert to the Swazi nation. Natives living outside native areas were protected from interference for a period of five years and they could thereafter remain on his property only with the permission of the European owner and on his terms.

Europeans were satisfied with the partition; the natives were aghast. They were still almost entirely a peasantry, though the need for tax money drove the younger men to work periodically for Europeans.[1] They won their subsistence from the soil, their major rituals were directed to increase its yield; the land was ritually identified with the king, with prosperity, health, and power; it was a focal point of national sentiment. To lose their land struck at the roots of their economic and political system. They sent a deputation to protest to the King of England, but the proclamation was irrevocable.

Before the new system was inaugurated, all rifles and ammunition had been taken from the Swazi. George Grey, a man of remarkable ability and sincerity, was selected for the difficult task of apportioning the land. He was guided by two main principles: firstly, the less migration, the less trouble there was likely to be; and, secondly, the natives were entitled to a fair share of well-watered and fertile land. He therefore chose areas where the people were already densely settled, and at the same time he strove to include land along river banks and flat, cultivable stretches inland. He accomplished his task in eighteen months. Local officials were left to execute it. Bitter though the natives were, the partition was

---

[1] By 1908, 1,087 natives were employed on local mines and 7,906 obtained passes to seek work outside the Protectorate. Cmd. 4,448, 1908, pp. 25, 36–40, 44–8, for figures of the different districts.

carried out with little friction. The reasons are clear: Grey had mapped the area with great skill and the most important chiefs were not immediately affected; concessionaires were restrained from summarily ejecting the native people and many remained as squatters; finally, the Swazi authorities were aware that they no longer had the power to order Europeans to leave the country.

The natives submitted, but they were not reconciled. They attempted to fight the Europeans with their own weapons. 'In what does the white man's power lie?' the Queen Regent Gwamile once asked Robert Grendon, a coloured man she brought from Natal as tutor to her grandson. Before he could answer, she continued: 'It lies in money and in books. We too will learn; we too will be rich.'[1] She encouraged her people to go out to work, and in 1914 she sent out men to collect money from her people to buy back farms from European holders. Unfortunately, the Swazi had not acquired, in their contact with Europeans, honest methods of business, and large sums were misappropriated. On Gwamile's request, the Administration had finally to take charge, and 36,404 morgen were purchased by the nation. Gwamile also started a school for princes and sons of leading commoners. She aimed especially at educating the young king so that he could regain for his people the land lost by documents. In the year following his accession (1922), she thought her dream would be realized.

Supported by the council, the young king, in 1922, petitioned before the Special Court of Swaziland against the ejectment of his subjects from an area covered by the Unallotted Land Concession. The Court dismissed the petition and the nation appealed to the Privy Council in London. Gwamile and the newly trained queen mother Lomawa issued a levy of £5 on each adult male to defray the expenses of the case; in that year there was no shortage of labour on farms or mines, while those who were reluctant to pay did well to spend the nights in the mountains to avoid the warriors of the Queen Regent. A great deal of money stuck to the palms of unscrupulous collectors. Sobhuza II, his highest councillors, a noted Swazi doctor, a legal representative (Dr. Seme, a Zulu who had qualified at the English Bar), and a representative of the European Administration travelled overseas. Douglas, the Swazi's counsel, put forward their arguments; the case ostensibly against the holders of the concession was in reality against the Crown and contested the validity of its Orders in Council. The Swazi nation lost the case. In his judgement, Viscount Haldane stated: 'This method of peacefully extending British Dominion may well be as little generally understood, as it is (where it can operate) in law, unquestionable.' The moneys collected by the Swazi were insufficient to meet the expenses, so the White administration, at Gwamile's request, levied a special tax of £5 on each adult male, and supervised the sale of one of the farms, 3,979 morgen, purchased by the nation.

Thus it came about that in the Protectorate, until 1943, slightly under two-thirds of the land (1,145,000 morgen) including Crown lands, were owned by some 500 Europeans, of whom roughly 40 per cent were

[1] Told me by Mr. Grendon.

absentee landlords, and a little over one-third (806,290 morgen), scattered in thirty-one blocks, was Native Area. In 1936, the white population numbered 2,740, the black 153,270. Increasing more rapidly than either was a coloured group of 705 people. Roughly 15,000 of the natives were tenants on European farms and Crown land.

Swazi bitterness over the land situation did not diminish with the passing years, accompanied as they were by an increase in population, and in 1941 Sobhuza, in a petition to His Majesty the King, complained, *inter alia*, that deterioration of his people was inevitable unless they could be assured of wider areas. His claims were supported by a few influential and liberal Europeans both in South Africa and in England. An investigation, moreover, satisfied the High Commissioner that the provision of additional areas of land for landless Swazi, who, it was estimated in 1943, numbered over 25,000 people, representing more than 5,000 families, was a matter of urgent and vital importance. In consequence, steps were taken to add to native areas partly by the utilization of Crown land and partly by purchase of suitable properties with funds provided by the British Government under the Colonial Development and Welfare Act of 1940. This scheme is now under way, and a new phase of Swazi development may be inaugurated.

6. Conclusion

I have briefly surveyed two methods of conquest and control in a single area. In the Bantu system, conquest was by open force followed by reintegration and fusion of the cultures of conquered and conquerors. An aristocracy of birth was established, but it was prevented from ruthlessly exploiting the people by the diffusion of power among various officials and councils. There was a nobility of the élite and a recognition of loyal service.

The European conquerors used economic pressure of a type incomprehensible to their opponents, although this economic pressure was in fact backed by the power of force. Bitter political conflict between white groups affected the particular method of government of the subjugated Swazi, and gave the Swazi an opportunity to play one European group against the other. When domination was finally established, the Europeans asserted themselves as a white ruling aristocracy.

A few facts of more general interest have been indicated in this chapter thereby relating data on the Swazi to some current sociological problems:[1] the relationship between kinship and territorial aspects of political structure; the process whereby a centralized government came into being; the circumstances under which a ruling aristocracy arose. I have shown the continuity that underlay the development from a mode of government based on kinship (clanship) to an integrated political system operating within fixed territorial boundaries.

In the 'clan period' locality and kinship overlapped, and the local unit was invested with its political structure by the clan system. Sub-clans that hived off from the main clan and settled in other districts became

[1] See, for example, Lowie, *The Origin of the State*, New York, 1927; Fortes and Evans Pritchard, *African Political Systems*. Oxford, 1940.

separate political (local) units, and conversely individuals who joined another clan unit were incorporated on the basis of a kinship fiction.

In the period of centralized government under a king, the emphasis on territorial loyalties did not exclude the appreciation and use of kinship in administration.

The main features of the process of the growth of the Swazi nation can be restated: friendly co-operation between the clans was not sufficient to induce a political federation with a central authority. The clans remained politically distinct even though they intermarried and borrowed from each other culturally. Nor did war between clans inevitably result in a centralized State. A clear distinction must be drawn between different types of warfare. In the clan period fighting was largely ceremonial; in the reign of the early kings incorporation was a result rather than the aim of war; in the middle period wars were waged to wrest territory from neighbours and also to win booty from distant peoples over whom there was apparently no intention of establishing control.

To transform a temporary victory into a permanent conquest required administrative foresight such as that displayed by Sobhuza I and Mswati, and I suggest that the development of this essential quality was stimulated by contemporary events in Southern Africa, notably the arrival of Europeans and their treatment of the indigenes. It is possible, but unlikely, that a tradition of State organization remained active among the Swazi; if it is true that the original elements constituting the 'Bantu' broke off from large, organized kingdoms, that mode of government had remained in abeyance for over 200 years and the cause for its revival must be sought in the context of the time of its revival.

The 'nation' developed by the Dlamini had no clearly defined caste structure such as characterizes the present 'British Empire' period. This notable difference can, probably, be accounted for by a number of factors. (1) The 'true Swazi', the early conquerors, were themselves a recent amalgam, and many of the people over whom they established control were of the same stock as themselves. The Europeans were from the beginning conscious of their racial difference. (2) The cultures of the different components of the Swazi nation, though distinguished by local peculiarities, were at the same stage of technological development. The Europeans established themselves on the unknown technique of concessions and the civilization these implied.

PART II

CHAPTER IV

THE TEMPO OF PEASANT LIFE

1. *The Country*[1]

THE Protectorate lies wedged between the Union of South Africa on three sides and Portuguese territory on the fourth. It is a small country, with a rich variety of scenery, climate and soil.

Moving from west to east, Swaziland falls roughly into three topographical regions. In the west is the high veld, 3,000 to 6,000 feet above sea-level, wild and broken, frequently veiled in mist and drizzle. On clear days serried mountain peaks are visible, rising to the supreme Makonjwa spur, a beacon between Swaziland and the Transvaal. Short grass covers the mountain sides, and clumps of trees and ferns grow near the streams that sparkle down narrow gorges into steep, sheltered valleys. The country slopes towards the plateaus of the middle veld, 1,500 to 3,000 feet, its gentle undulations interrupted by odd-shaped kopjes—outcrops of dolerite, basalt, and granite. The river beds are wider, cultivable stretches larger, the grass longer and the weather warmer and drier than in the high lands. The midlands merge with the lowlands (700 to 1,500 feet), where the eye roves over thick bush, low thorn trees, short, sparse grass. Here in the heat of summer days there gleams the mirage of water in the unattainable distance. On the extreme east, forming a boundary with Portuguese territory, the Ubombo range rises abruptly. The bush country has a fascination and richness of its own: it is the haunt of wild game; there is fine timber in the scattered forests; when rain is sufficient, corn sprouts luxuriantly in the rich turf soil, the best in the country; cattle thrive on the bush foliage and, except in years of drought, remain sleek and heavy-uddered when those in the middle and high veld are lean and withered.

Four main rivers—the Komati, Mbuluzi, Usutu and Ingwavuma—and their tributaries, water the country. Generally speaking, they flow from west to east into the warm Indian Ocean. Here and there are lovely waterfalls and deep, still pools, and many strange tales are told of creatures that live in the water and affect the lives of men.

There is no system of irrigation, and Swazi rely almost entirely on rain for their water supply. Rain is expected from September, the beginning of spring, until February, the end of summer. Steady showers fall in the high lands, torrential storms break in the low veld. Over a period of ten years, 1922 to 1931, the annual rainfall averaged 57·572 inches at Mbabane in the high veld, 32·32 inches at Bremersdorp in the middle veld, and 18·322 inches at Balegane in the low veld. Throughout the country, but more particularly in the eastern flats, there is constant danger of drought.

The climate, for the most part, is delightful and exhilarating. In the winter the air is cold and still, and the sun shines from a cloudless

[1] For a full description of the country, the reader is referred to D. M. Doveton, *The Human Geography of Swaziland*, London, 1937.

34

sky. But sometimes in summer the heat in the bush veld is over 120 degrees in the shade, and Swazi say they are too 'burnt' to work. On the whole, the country is healthy, though there is the danger of bilharzia in some of the rivers and of malaria in the lower altitudes. Men from the mountains are well aware of the danger of 'the fever of the bush'; many refuse to believe that it is carried by a mosquito.

Throughout the Protectorate Swazi plant grain, tend cattle, and hunt game. They distinguish different types of soil and judge their fertility by the vegetation they carry. The land is the basis of Swazi livelihood.

2. *The Seasonal Rhythm*

The tempo of peasant life is set by the rhythm of seasonal changes, the periods of heat and cold, the time of rain and dryness, for on those depend the growing and ripening of crops, the condition of the herds, and the work of the people.

Swazi divide the year into four seasons, each with its specific activities (see chart pp. 50–53). In spring (August to October), when the first rains fall, the garden work begins. The women hoe and sow maize or millet in small plots along the river banks, where the soil is always slightly damp and the seed germinates quickly. By the time the first gardens are planted, the rains have moistened the inland fields, and the women, aided to some extent by the men, turn to the larger gardens and plant maize, millet, and various subsidiary foods (species of ground nuts, gourds, sugar-cane, and pumpkins).

With full summer (November to January) come the heavy rains, the weeds grow rank, and agricultural work is intensified. The last gardens are planted, and communal work parties, specially for weeding, are frequent. The homesteads are emptied of all able-bodied women, and even the young children and the men spend most of their day toiling in the fields. In the height of summer the early crops ripen, and the regiments of the nation assemble at the capital to celebrate the *Incwala*, whereby the nation receives strength for the new year.

In autumn (February to March), women spend long days cutting the full maize cobs, which they tie into bundles and then carry home with the help of the men. Millet slowly ripens in the fields, where a few watchers remain on guard to drive away thieving birds.

During winter (April to July), the last maize is harvested and the millet gleaned. The scene of activity changes from the fields to the homesteads. Men and women rub and beat mealies from the cob, and thresh and winnow the corn. The best quality grain is reserved for storage in the underground pits; the inferior grain is used for immediate consumption and to reward workers.

Winter is also the hunting season and the time when new huts are built and old ones repaired. Freed from their rigorous gardening tasks, women take the opportunity to visit their parents; headmen, aware of the full grain bins, entertain on a lavish and often wasteful scale. It is in winter, too, that widows, in the third year after the death of their husbands, shed their mourning weeds, and, with the spring, resume their normal life.

Like many primitive peasants, Swazi live on a precarious subsistence

level,[1] and their food supply fluctuates annually between plenty and a
scarcity bordering on famine. Winter is the time of satisfaction, of
physical well-being, while in summer, before the new crops ripen, comes
the moon named 'to swallow the pickings of the teeth'. In summer, when
the highest output of energy is required, the food supply is at its lowest;
in autumn and winter, when there is relatively little work, food is plentiful.
The uneven balance of work and a grain diet is to some extent offset by
the fact that in midsummer, when grain is scarce, the cattle yield a
greater supply of milk than they do in winter when the grass is dry. But
milk is largely the food of children; beer made from grain takes its place
in adult life. In addition to cultivated crops and domesticated animals,
Swazi eat as relishes and delicacies certain wild greens, roots, fruits, wild
game, and various types of insects. These, too, are seasonal, and never a
reliable source of food. Apart from the actual seasonal fluctuation,
Swazi are threatened with famine in years when drought whitens the
crops and cattle die of thirst; when torrential rains fall, flooding the
rivers, washing away the gardens on the banks and rotting the plants in
the inland areas; or when locusts and other pests, only too frequent in
southern Africa, strip the fields or kill the herds.

The agricultural routine is the principal standard for reckoning periods
of time. Other activities are said to take place at 'the time of ploughing',
'the time of reaping', and so on. Even the care of the cattle, the most
precious economic possession, is largely dependent on the agricultural
activities. In spring and summer great attention is given to herding the
animals, so that they will not stray into the cultivated fields; in winter
they are turned into the harvested gardens to feed off the stalks, and
herders relax their vigilance.

The year is measured by observation of the sun; Swazi say that the
earth is stationary and the 'Great Sun', the 'Male of the Heavens', moves
regularly back and forth in a set and limited course. Space is bounded
by distances that have actually been experienced and remembered; until
the Europeans came either 'from across the sea', or 'out of the sea', the
world was still small. Conservative Swazi believe that there is nothing
beyond the points where the sun rises and sets; that the land in which
they live was 'from the beginning' old, unchanged and unchanging; that
in stones in the south are marks of the footprints of the gigantic 'First
Being'; that between a people and its land is a mutual dependence—a
bond of life.

3. *The Homestead*

Within the peasant society the major social unit is the *umuti* (homestead), under the control of an *umnumzana* (headman). He sometimes
subdivides his homestead into local subsections, each of which may be
described as an *umuti*, but all are under his control and are recognized
as parts of a single and effective unit.

Swazi homesteads lie scattered at irregular intervals over the countryside. In the middle and high veld people build on the hills and mountain
slopes; their beehive huts of dried grass can scarcely be distinguished

[1] For a full description, see my article, 'Notes on the diet of Swazi in the
Protectorate', *Bantu Studies*, Vol. 18, pp. 199–236.

from the rounded granite boulders. Unfenced and irregularly-shaped gardens straggle over the lower slopes, in the sheltered valleys, and on the open plains. In the bush veld, homes and gardens are made in clearings in thickly-wooded country.

The ideal homestead is polygynous; polygyny, however, is attained for the most part only by aristocrats and wealthy, elderly commoners. The following figures were obtained for me from the tax books of the Bremersdorp area by Joshua Lukele, a clerk in the administrative office:

	Polygynous	Monogamous	Single
1931	651	1,523	761
1932	656	2,430	815
1933	642	2,761	821
1934	657	2,716	858
1935	669	1,836	932
	3,275	11,266	4,187

Total, 18,728

That is, over a period of five years, 22·35 per cent of the taxpayers (males over eighteen years) were unmarried, 60·3 per cent were monogamous and 17·3 per cent were polygynous. Of the polygynists in 1933, there were 254 with two wives, 36 with three wives and 45 with four wives or more.[1] In a census that I took in sixty-six homesteads in the fairly progressive Matsapha district, the total number of inhabitants was 980, of whom 237 were adult (taxpaying) men, 224 were married or betrothed women, and 519 were children. 113 men of taxpaying age were bachelors, 85 were monogamists, and 39 were polygynists. Of the polygynists, 21 had two wives; 12 three wives; 2 four wives; 1 six wives; 2 eight wives, and 1 twelve wives. Thus monogamy is the rule, and even most polygynists rarely marry more than two women. Very few ordinary Swazi can attain double figures in wives.

A homestead is seldom occupied solely by a single biological family. For economic and/or ritual benefits, additional kinsmen or even unrelated dependents attach themselves to the immediate family. Single men stay with older brothers on the parents' death; widows sometimes return to their fathers or brothers; children of relatives or of friends are often 'borrowed' to assist in the herding of cattle and nursing of infants; married sons often remain on the patriarchal estate.

The number of occupants in the homestead varies with factors of wealth and status. The smallest homestead that I know belongs to a Christian widow, who lives with her two unmarried sons several miles from their nearest kin; the largest is that of the ruling family. The average number of occupants of the Matsapha sample was 7·2 for

[1] Marwick gives the following figures for the Mbabane subdistrict. He does not, however, state the year. 1,019 taxpaying bachelors; 485 monogamists; 146 with two wives, 26 with three wives, 20 men with four wives and over. Thus 60·1 per cent of the taxpayers were unmarried or monogamous and 39·9 per cent polygynous. *Swazi*, Oxford Press, 1940, p. 40.

D

commoners' families and 22·5 in the homesteads of princes and chiefs.

On the whole, homesteads appear to be smaller than they were in the early days. Several reasons are given for the decrease: (1) there is less need for united defence against attack from man or beast; (2) harmony is maintained more easily in small homesteads; (3) young people, more especially converts, are becoming increasingly independent of their kinsmen; (4) it is difficult nowadays to obtain tracts of land sufficiently extensive to support large families. Since Swazi return to their homesteads every evening, gardens cannot lie very far away.

The headman of the homestead is rarely completely isolated from relatives by blood or marriage. Of the sixty-six homesteads in Matsapha, only fifteen headmen were more than one day's journey on foot from paternal kin, and in a less advanced part of Hlatikulu, five out of fifty-two headmen were unrelated to anyone in the vicinity. Three of the five were recent immigrants from Zululand.

Homesteads are built according to a fairly standardized plan. In each homestead or local division there are three key structures: the *siβaya* (cattle byre), *indlunkulu* (great hut), and *lilawu* (bachelors' quarters). The cattle byre is usually constructed first. If the lie of the land permits, it is built facing the rising sun—a symbol in family and national ritual. The *siβaya* is a circular enclosure palisaded with strong logs, the interstices filled with tough, pliable branches. In it are dug flask-shaped grain pits (about 8 feet deep and 2 feet across the mouth), their openings sealed with dung and marked with stones. Swazi say this type of granary was devised in the days of tribal warfare to hide the harvest from the enemy. Placing the pits in the cattle byre serves another purpose as well, for it gives the headman an opportunity to control the food stores. Women, especially young and inexperienced housekeepers, may only enter the cattle byre on rare occasions. If they want grain from the pits, they must send a child, who is usually assisted in taking out the grain by an older woman or by the headman himself. Men have complete freedom of access to the *siβaya*. Homesteads without the *siβaya* are few and usually belong to insignificant people—men without cattle or without sons to herd them.

Facing the cattle byre is the *indlunkulu* (great hut), associated with the elders of the headman's lineage, and decorated with the skulls of cattle sacrificed to the ancestors. The erection of the *indlunkulu* marks a complete homestead; until it is ready there are restrictions on normal behaviour in the partly-built home: no fire should be lit, and sexual relations are prohibited. When a homestead is moved, the great hut is carefully lifted after all the other huts have been transferred, and is carried with special songs and ceremonies to the central position at the new site. Alongside it, within a single reed enclosure, are other huts used for sleeping, cooking, and storing food. They are arranged so as to leave ample space for the *siβuya* (yard), where people often sit, cook, or work. In charge of the *indlunkulu* is the *inkosikati vomuti* (chief woman of the homestead). She is the mother of the headman, the link between him and his 'fathers'. If she is dead, a classificatory mother, or the first wife of the headman, or a wife of the same clan as the dead mother, is substituted. She, too, is called 'mother' and assumes the duties of the real mother. Ordinarily the great hut is taboo to wives, since it is the sanctuary of the husband's male ancestors whom they must *hlonipa* (avoid and respect). The importance of the mother, and her control in all matters affecting the homestead, is an outstanding feature of Swazi family and national life.

The *lilawu* (barracks) for unmarried men and male visitors guards the entrace to a homestead. In large homesteads there are often two barracks, one on either side of the cattle byre, each with a few huts surrounded by a strong wall of branches. Between the barracks and the great hut, forming with them a rough arc round the cattle byre, are the quarters of wives and married dependents.

Each married woman, after a year's apprenticeship to the 'mother' of the headman, usually receives her own huts and yard. These are enclosed for privacy and protection by high reed fences strengthened with heavy poles and thick bands of grass. The whole enclosure is described as *indlu yaBaniBani* (huts of So-and-So). Here a woman and any very young children in her care live and eat. To them it is *ketfu*—our place. Since wives may not enter the enclosure of the great hut without observing special restraints on behaviour, clothing, and language, the husband usually visits them in their own quarters. A 'modern husband' may build a room for himself to which he will summon a wife.

Senior wives are usually placed close to the main hut. Sometimes a senior wife has an *inhlanti* (subordinate co-wife), who contributes to her larder and shares her kitchen, and who builds her living huts close by. A growing daughter has her *intsanga* (girl's hut) near her mother's, and there receives a recognized lover. A married son also often builds his huts near to his mother, who is in charge of his young wives.

Rigid allocation of wives on the left- and right-hand sides of the main hut, an indication of status amongst most South-eastern Bantu, is only found in southern Swaziland, where Zulu influence is strong. Elsewhere the arrangement depends largely on the whim of the headman and his mother, and a great deal of latitude obtains.

The plan of the polygynous homestead, with its clear demarcation of each married woman and her own children, facilitates subdivision into separate local groups. Subdivision is said to prevent quarrels between co-wives and between half-brothers; to give more space from which to select good land for cultivation; and to extend a headman's prestige over a wide area. The section of the homestead where the 'mother' lives is known as the *umpakatsi* (capital); it alone has the real *indlunkulu*, and in relation to it any other homestead of the headman is merely the *lilawu* (barrack).

When a headman dies, it is the duty of his main heir to perpetuate his father's homestead. The son is bound by his inheritance to maintain the family line. He is expected to place a wife or wives at the local subdivisions 'to wake the huts of his father so that they will not perish'. If he does not put one of his own wives there, it is good for the homestead to be maintained by a friendly brother and his family. The emphasis on family land and tradition is particularly marked in the case of chiefs.

Two examples will indicate the way in which ancestral homes are continued from one generation to another:

At Esikoteni in the south, Ngolotsheni was the first Ndwandwe to be appointed chief, and he established three homesteads—Entlangana, Emlanjwaneni, and Enkalakutaɓa. On his death, his son Mlokotwa was appointed and ruled from Entlangana. Mlokotwa died before he branched out into new homesteads. Some of his half-brothers lived with their mothers at the two remaining villages. Mlokotwa's heir, Silwane, governs from Entlangana and is thinking of putting up other homesteads, but if no Ndwandwe remains at Emlanjwaneni or Enkala-kutaɓa, Silwane will send some of his wives with their children to 'wake father's home'.

Among the Simelane, the emphasis on the ancestral home is clearly formulated. The Simelane have a well-developed chieftainship, and the village where the last chief is buried becomes the capital of his heir who is also bound to maintain other homesteads of the paternal line. In addition to perpetuating the old homesteads, each heir starts a new one (his *lilawu*). Thus Maɓonya, grandfather of Ntshingile, had Ntshaɓa as his capital and Ekuhlaleni as his new homestead. He died at Ntshaɓa, but the law of the Simelane dictated that he be buried at Ekuhlaleni. This became the capital of his son Mbozongo, who also maintained Ntshaɓa by sending there one of his wives with the clan name of Maɓonya's mother. Mbozongo died at Ekuhlaleni and was buried at Gwegwe, the homestead he had started. Gwegwe became the capital of his heir Ntshingile. Ntshingile died there and was buried at Godloza, the homestead he started. Ntshingile's heir is still a child, and his mother, the main wife of Ntshingile, will remain at the old capital, Gwegwe, till he is full grown. They will then go to Godloza, the new capital. After a time, the heir will build his own *lilawu*, which will be the next capital. The result is that at the present time there are six villages of the Simelane chiefs going back three generations. At each there lives a close kinsman of the ruling chief, and the capital in each generation is under the control of the mother of the chief.

The characteristics of the average Swazi homestead can now be briefly reiterated: it is essentially a kinship group under the care of the senior male, the patriarch. The polygynous homestead is the ideal, and allows for subdivision. The unit of major importance is under the 'mother' of the headman, who is the link between a man and the paternal lineage which gives him standing.

4. *Royal Villages*

The homestead of the king is organized on principles similar in many respects to those that govern the homesteads of other important polygynists. The family is the nucleus of the royal homestead; queens are established in many local subdivisions; the homestead of the mother of the king is the most important in ritual; and the homesteads of royal predecessors are kept alive under their old names.

But there are also noteworthy differences between the royal homestead and any other. Mother and son have separate homesteads associated with them; ancient royal centres may be in the charge of non-relatives; and the main sections of the royal homesteads are so large and include so

THE TEMPO OF PEASANT LIFE

many non-kinsmen that they are more aptly termed 'villages'. Each royal homestead is called an *umuti wenkosi* (king's homestead) and is an *umpakatsi* (capital) of the nation, but the real *umpakatsi* is the homestead controlled by the queen mother.

These characteristics can be shown clearly by a description of the present situation, taking as starting point the precedent set Sobhuza II by his father, Bunu.

Bunu's capital was Zombodze, controlled by his mother, Gwamile Mdluli. When Bunu had acquired a few wives, he built his first independent establishment, Eza6eni. This was known as his *lilawu* (bachelor's quarters); it was 'merely' the administrative, and not the sacred, centre of national life. Later he started the royal villages of Emampondweni and Nsuka, and he also sent queens to a few homes of royal predecessors. But Bunu died . young, his harem included merely eight wives and fourteen betrothed girls, and many royal villages had no direct representative of the immediate ruling family.

Each king starts his own capital, and when Sobhuza reached manhood he and his mother, Lomawa Ndwandwe, established Lo6amba. When he had already taken a number of queens he branched out into his *lilawu*— Lozitehlezi. Later he placed wives at three other royal centres—Zombodze, Nsuka, and Entonjeni. Main homesteads of past kings since the time of Sobhuza's great great grandfather, Ngwane II, are perpetuated by successors of the first governor or, more rarely, by distant relatives of the first founder. Thus at Enkanini, capital of Mbandzeni, Malangatonke is successor to the governor, Makambane. Again at Embekelweni, another of Mbandzeni's villages, the post of governor is held by Sha6angwane Gininza, a member of a family that has provided many trustworthy national officials. At Eza6eni, village of Bunu, the Sukati family who had charge is dying out, and will probably have to be replaced. Logo6a, village of Sobhuza I, is carried on by Prince Mgwazenjani.

Of all the royal villages Lo6amba is the largest, Lozitehlezi ranks second, and Zombodze, the former capital, third in size and importance. In October 1934 the population of Lo6amba numbered 265, Lozitehlezi 137 and Zombodze 70. At Lo6amba there were 19 wives and 30 children of Sobhuza. 17 of the 49 citizens' huts belonged to men of the royal family, 2 to local chiefs, and the remainder to commoners. The population varies with seasonal activities, but, Swazi insist, at no time in former reigns was it as low as at certain periods of the present régime.

Any one may obtain permission to live at a royal village on the understanding that he or she becomes an attendant of the person in charge. This happens particularly at the three main villages. Descendants of founders of other royal villages consider such villages their 'shelter', and sometimes live there themselves or send wives, knowing that they will be well cared for.

A new village started by a king, or an old royal village woken by him through establishing a few queens there, becomes the main village of the oldest son of the most important queen in residence. Thus Nsuka, under the governor, Mahutfulo Magutfulela, will later have as its leading prince, Sikova, son of the senior queen in the Nsuka harem.

Royal villages vary in size and importance with (*a*) the genealogical nearness of the original founders to the ruling king, (b) the character of the governor, and (c) the active interest shown in them by the rulers.

5. *Plan of Royal Villages*

Royal villages conform to a stereotyped plan indicative of groups of status. This is most evident in the capital. Glancing at the diagram of Loɓamba (Appendix III), one has the impression of a horseshoe, or, in Swazi analogy, of horns meeting at the base. The pivotal structures are again the *siɓaya*, the *indlunkulu*, and the *emalawu* (plural of *lilawu*).

Loɓamba's cattle byre is the largest in the country—roughly 180 feet in diameter. In addition to the usual purposes of a *siɓaya*, the national cattle byre serves as the amphitheatre for the great annual ceremony, the *Incwala*. At the upper end is the *inhlambelo* (sanctuary) (A), where the king is doctored with special medicines. On ordinary days calves of the royal herd are kept overnight in the sanctuary, while the calves of other people are tied elsewhere.

Facing the sanctuary is the *indlunkulu*. Whereas in commoners' homes, *indlunkulu* is applied only to the main hut itself, at the capital the term is extended to all huts in the enclosure. The *indlunkulu* (here translated as Great Abode), is in the charge of the queen mother, and in 1935 contained eleven huts. On the right-hand side is the national shrine hut (D), popularly known as *kaɓayethe*, the hut one enters with the royal salute, *Ɓayethe*. Ritual mats and ropes, handed down from generation to generation, are woven into the framework of the hut. At the back of the hut is the *luphandze* (a reed fence) about 3 feet high, behind which sacred objects are hidden. They include calabashes, a type of grain no longer grown, and occasional offerings of beer. The supports of the hut are strongly doctored, and above the door are two tiny holes in the inner layers of thatching through which the king spits on certain occasions, thereby radiating his power over the nation. Over the doorway, on the outside, are skulls of sacrificial cattle. The *kaɓayethe* is not a place for ordinary activities or for merry-making. Here the king and the queen mother speak to the ancestral spirits on behalf of their subjects, and perform rites to bring rain; here princes and princesses gather for important family occasions; and here matters of national concern may be discussed. No one impure, no one who has recently had sexual relations, no menstruating women, no one with the ropes of mourning may enter. Swazi say that such a person would bring madness on himself or herself, and disaster on the land. Swazi in European dress take off their shoes and hats before going inside, and accept the rules of behaviour dictated by tradition. The king's wives may not enter, nor even pass in front of the low doorway: it is the hut of the powerful males of their husband's clan, and queens must avoid them more rigorously than ordinary wives avoid their in-laws. Royal children, on the other hand, perpetuators of the paternal lineage, sleep in the *kaɓayethe*, except when it is required for special ceremonies. Behind it lies a sacred store hut, containing in pots and 'shop-bought' boxes ancient ceremonial objects. The remaining huts are for sleeping, storing grain, and cooking. They are more numerous than in ordinary homesteads, because of the number of grandchildren in the care of the queen mother and the reserves of food kept ready for use.

To the left of the queen mother's enclosure is the *sigodlo* (harem for the queens), surrounded by a high reed fence with a single narrow gateway. The harem is divided into two sections, the 'white' and the 'black'. The 'white' (H) is at the entrance, and is associated with the king's marriage to his first recognized, his ritual wife. In the 'white' *sigodlo* is a large hut in which the king sleeps with this woman, or a second ritual wife, on the nights when he is most strongly doctored (see Chapter XIII). The hut itself is known as the *sigodlo* (H), which can be translated as 'core of the harem'. Most of the other queens have never been inside, and are afraid to enter. Like the *kaɓayethe*, it has ritual apertures, supporting poles, and many sacred associations. The king's ceremonial shields are hung on the grass wall. When Sobhuza comes to Loɓamba, he often sits in this hut with important counsellors, and when he is away it is occupied by two warriors who guard the entrance to the queen's quarters during the night. Behind the 'white' *sigodlo* hut is a storeroom which is only entered by certain of the queens, two old men, and specialists in national rituals.

The 'white' *sigodlo* is in front of the 'black' *sigodlo*, the queens' living quarters. Unlike commoners' wives, queens share a common yard. Queens are carefully ranked on a basis of seniority and each 'big queen' has a few 'little queens' attached to her; these form a close co-operative unit, share the same huts, and help in each others' fields. Deep in the harem is the king's private sleeping hut.

Surrounding the *indlunkulu* and the *sigodlo* is a double semicircle of citizens' quarters. The inner (C) is inhabited by men of very high rank, some of whom officiate in national ritual. Because of their status, they are protected by a bulwark of civilians. The outer semicircle is known as *tinhlentlwini*, and there live other subjects who have paid allegiance direct to the queen mother. Sometimes a man brings one of his wives to the capital, keeping others at his own homestead where he is the master. In olden times, practically every important Swazi had a wife living at the capital or at the king's village, and he stayed with her when he paid his long state visits.

On the extreme right of the outer semicircle, facing east, is the hut normally occupied by the *indvuna yenkulu* (big governor), the chief civil authority, and on the extreme left lies the hut of the *indvuna yemaɓutfo* (governor of the age classes), the chief military authority. Their main homesteads are some distance from the capital. At Loɓamba the enclosure of the main civil authority is not in the usual position. This happened because when Maniginigi Nkambule, Governor of Loɓamba, died, his assistant, Mshudulwane Zwane, was promoted to the position, but remained in his enclosure within the arc of citizens' quarters. A new assistant, Xlaya, of the same clan as the late governor, was appointed, and installed because of the clan bond in the hut of the deceased at the point of the semicircle. My hut was immediately behind his (P).

The barracks, placed on either side of the cattle byre, guard access to the heart of the capital and protect the inhabitants. The oldest regiments are quartered on the outside, covering the younger. When an enemy approaches, or in the event of danger such as fire, the alarm is given and the warriors are able to run, without hindrance from the people or obstruction from buildings, to assist the most important members of the nation. The queen mother and her daughters-in-law are the first people to be safeguarded, and the valued national property must also be protected.

Other royal villages are built on a simpler plan than the capital. Ritual is the core of Swazi kingship and is enacted at the village of the woman who links the king with the line of kings. When he establishes his *lilawu*, he moves to it with some of the regiments and a few queens and citizens, but the queens who are important in ritual and most of the objects required for national ceremonies remain in the village of the queen mother. Thus Lozitehlezi, *lilawu* of Sobhuza II, has no *kaɓayethe*, no ritual huts in the harem, no sacred store huts, and no inner semicircle of ritual functionaries. But since it is the military and administrative headquarters, it has at least as many warriors as Loɓamba, and because the king is also important in ritual, there is a small sanctuary in his cattle byre. The plan of the remaining royal villages ranges from the *lilawu* to that of a typical homestead. Wherever the king places a queen there should be a band of men to protect her, and she becomes the most important person in the village.

The main royal villages are centres of the greatest national activity. Important foreigners and subjects from all parts of the country come there; courtiers compete for royal favours; intrigues occur; leading cases are discussed; the most important festivals are celebrated, and major labour enterprises are organized. Among non-literate peoples personal contacts are the principal means of disseminating news and knowledge, and Swazi emphasize how much greater are the wisdom and etiquette of those who grow up in the homes of the great, than of those people who live in small and more homogeneous units, 'away from people'.

6. Rights to Land

The organization of the homestead of commoner and king depends to a great extent on the rights to land. People cannot build and cultivate where they like; nor has every Swazi an equal claim to the soil. Swazi land tenure is determined by the hierarchical political structure, the main principles of which will be outlined here and more fully developed in later chapters.

National territory is described as *live lakaNgwane* or *live lenkosi. Live* means both 'country' and 'nation'; *lakaNgwane* means 'of the place of Ngwane' (the name of the first founder). The king (*inkosi*) is regarded as the head of the land. Sometimes instead of *live* the word *umhlaɓa* is used, which has as its primary meaning 'arable lands', and in its extended form is applied to the people who use the land. In Swazi ideology the land and the people are interlocked, and the political bond between rulers and subjects is based largely on the power that the rulers wield over the soil on which the people live.

The country is divided into a number of *tiganga* (areas) defined by natural features—rivers, dongas, and hills. Each area is named, and the names do not change though the political divisions may be altered. The place-name serves as one mode of identification. When a stranger is asked from where he comes, he may reply with a place-name that covers a wide area; within it are names of small areas not as well known. Thus in Johannesburg, a Swazi will reply to the question, 'From where do you come?' that he comes from *live lakaNgwane*. The question, 'What part of Swaziland?' will elicit the name of a major *siganga*—perhaps Matsapha, and this will again be narrowed down to one of the smaller *tiganga*, such as Hambakußo or Lancabani; and if all this is familiar territory to the interrogator, the main homestead of the chief and finally of the man himself is named. The process of identifying a man may also work along the political units. 'Who is your *inkosi*?' asked in Johannesburg, meets with the reply, 'Sobhuza', and from there one works down to the immediate local superior.

The king and his mother have special privileges over the whole land: they can take any gardens that they wish and can move subjects from one part of the country to another. They realize, however, that arbitrary use of their power invokes opposition; therefore they usually adjust their demands to the needs of their subjects and only move chiefs and their followers for specific reasons. A king on his accession finds his country already divided into political units, and the land allotted to his subjects by his predecessors, and does not interfere unless there is trouble or the royal family needs land. It is understood that if rulers take land from a loyal, established chief for national purposes (e.g. for extension of a royal homestead, for royal grazing land, etc.), they will give him adequate land elsewhere as compensation. King Mswati, for example, gave Madzanga Motsa an area named Incangamatshe. Later, King Mbandzeni wanted to extend his village, Embekelweni, to Langaße, and he had to find land for the Langaße folk. He· transferred them to Incangamatshe, and removed some of the Motsa to Ubulinga, where he wanted trustworthy scouts. Early kings also moved groups that were quite reliable from near the royal villages to buffer positions on the border. This was done, for example, to a section of the Gweßu in the reign of Mbandzeni.

One of the duties of a king's advisers is to keep him informed of the distribution of his people and the adequacy of land in various areas. In 1937, Sobhuza sent two emissaries to travel the country and report in which areas there was the greatest congestion, and where there was room for a denser population. He must know this before he can give political power to any of his brothers, sons, or other subjects.

As representative of the nation, the king allots land to his people. This is never spoken of as *tsengisa* (to sell); instead Swazi use the word *kuphakela*, a word applicable to the serving of food; food which is the recognized right of every individual and which is never sold in the traditional milieu. If a stranger drops in on a family he must be invited to share the meal; if a neighbour is hungry he should be given food. One of the main duties of a woman is to *pakhelatitsha*—serve bowls of food—for every member of her household and also one for the unexpected guest. The land from which food is produced is also considered a universal right, hence the aptness of the phrase *Inkosi iyaphakela live*. Sometimes Swazi use the word *ukwaßa*, the allocation of the meat of a slaughtered beast according to strict principles of status. The division is in the hands of the headman, who apportions the sections with care, forethought, and discrimination, so that each person obtains some, but the more important receive the choicest parts. Swazi talk figuratively of the country as *inkomo* (a beast) of the nation.

It must be emphasized that each king on his accession finds his domain already divided into local units, and he does not interfere with the local overlords nor alter their boundaries unless there is good reason. Stability is necessary from one reign to another, and it would create dissatisfaction and chaos if a new king reorganized on any large scale the units which were loyal to his father. Only if a chief is insubordinate, or if there are violent quarrels between adjoining areas, or if there is urgent need to bestow political honours on new and deserving individuals, does a king dispose of the land of an accepted chief.

National territory is subdivided into principalities ruled by *ßantfwa-ßenkosi* (princes), *tikulu* (hereditary chiefs), and *tindvuna* (governors). These authorities are either appointed by the king or have their hereditary positions ratified by him. For simplicity, I speak of all these men as 'chiefs' of the principality. Each principality is described as *indzawo yaßani ßani* (place of So-and-So), or as his *sive* (country), or *sigodsi* (hollow).[1] The principalities overlap the geographical areas (*tiganga*). Some chiefs have followers in two *tiganga* and more than one chief may live in the same *siganga*. The boundaries of a principality often remain vague until a clash occurs, when the matter is settled by representatives sent from the central government.

The size of principalities and the number of inhabitants vary. The areas range from about four square miles to over twenty square miles, and the density from less than three per square mile to more than 100 per square mile. While some chiefs (e.g. Vilikazi Dlamini) have under 100 taxpayers in their principality, others (e.g. Mtunzi Mdluli, Ndaßazezwe Dlamini, and ßokweni Mamba) have over 2,000. The density of the population is lowest in the fever-ridden bush country and highest in the healthy midlands.

The head of a principality exercises definite privileges over the land, but his power does not depend directly on the size of his own gardens. His prestige derives from the number of people who owe him allegiance and bring him tribute. One informant expressed this clearly: 'Land only matters when it is cultivated and occupied; just as a man prefers cattle to a byre so people make known the name of a chief, for the soil itself does not speak.'

The head of a principality has the power to accept subjects and grant them land, and also to evict subjects from land. He may not, however, accept subjects from another tribe without first reporting to the king, and he must accommodate any man sent him by the king. If a subject leaves a principality the land reverts to the chief and he may re-allot it; but if the man or one of his kinsmen returns he can ask for it back.

The average Swazi commoner, headman of an ordinary homestead, has his claim to land sanctioned by his citizenship. This entitles him to appeal to the king or queen mother if he feels himself unjustly evicted from an area or is unable to obtain sufficient gardens for his requirements. Apart from this general title, most Swazi claim a stake in specific areas

---

[1] *Sigodsi* is used among the neighbouring Zulu, whose land is characterized by undulating hills and valleys, and is not common among Swazi.

through kinship ties. When a man dies his main heir inherits his land and is expected to provide also for younger brothers. This claim is voiced even after many years. The main heir will point to family graves —beacons that establish his right to ancestral soil.

Sons are not encouraged to remove men to whom their fathers had given land unless the sons can definitely prove that they themselves need the fields. Ndzaɓankulu once rebuked a youth who, on his father's death, drove off a family that had used a plot for three years. 'Remember', said the chief, 'that this land is not yours, nor is it his. It returns to me and it is not mine either. It belongs to the king and all Ngwane. A man to whom I give beer does not keep the bowl.' A chief, under exceptional circumstances, may even refuse to recognize a son's claim to his ancestral land. This happens if the sons are found guilty of the death of their father or have abandoned him.[1]

Relatives outside the immediate homestead may give a person land as a sign of affection. Thus in one instance a maternal uncle assisted his sister's child; in another a maternal grandparent gave a grandson land. Nowadays, parents sometimes allot married daughters gardens. If the husbands' homesteads are nearby, the wives cultivate these gardens themselves, but if they are far away the relatives work them for the women and send them the harvest. A man may help his very close friend with the loan of gardens that he himself is not using.

People who live in the homestead retain a strong sentimental attachment to the soil and the surroundings. A Swazi who returned from a long absence in Johannesburg explained to a number of less sophisticated fellow men: 'Europeans do not love their homes as we do. They always sell their houses and move far away, never returning to see who is living there. They like their chairs, tables, and pictures more than their homesteads.'

The familiar hill and river are often incorporated into family praise songs; men point out the old sites of their homes; women after marriage often express a longing to 'see the place of their childhood'. Frequently in Johannesburg I have heard the words *ngyagodvuka*—'I have nostalgia for my home', and it is not only for people ('people change'), but for the locality marked by the family graves, and for the peasant life.

7. *Moving of Homesteads*

Yet Swazi homesteads are not permanent. They are moved from one site to another and in some instances abandoned altogether. Movement of subjects takes place both within a principality and from one principality to another. When the headman or another important inmate dies, the cattle byre and all the huts (except that of the deceased) are literally carried a short distance from the old site and re-established on the old pattern under the old name. Sometimes sons move away and form independent homesteads.

[1] Thus Mnisi told me that he once drove away a man who had moved without reason from his father's homestead when the father had adequate land and was anxious to have his son nearby. The son did not visit his father nor give him any help. But on the father's death the boy returned 'to gobble the inheritance'. Mnisi declared that he did not want such men in his principality.

The homestead is also transferred if there is an epidemic; if the pasture and garden lands become exhausted; if quarrels break out with neighbours, or, most important, if the headman has a dispute with his political overlord. Only if the family moves a great distance are the huts abandoned, since to build up an entirely new homestead is an expensive and arduous task. The homesteads of chiefs are the only permanent ones within the boundaries of the principality.

When a headman moves his homestead, two sets of factors, the one utilitarian and the other social, guide his choice. On the one hand, he looks for adequate garden land for himself and his dependents, good pasture land for his cattle, wood and water conveniently close for domestic needs, a building site which is not too damp and not too exposed. On the other hand—and here he is in a weaker position than a political leader— he must seek a congenial social environment. There are many men who abandoned their old homes solely because the land became 'tired' and no more was available nearby, but there are others who move because of personal difficulties. Out of the 126 homesteads in the Matsapha area, 38 came to their present sites in search of better land, 32 to find safer neighbours, and the remainder were on ancestral land. A man wants to be under a chief renowned for his *umpatfo* (handling) and close to friends, for well he knows how much his happiness and prosperity depend on neighbourliness. Should he find that he has made a mistake, and he has his proof in the unaccountable failure of his crops, the sudden illness of his children, unnecessarily frequent demands on his services, gossip whispered him by his cronies, he moves with his family, his huts, and other property.

Progressive Swazi who have planted trees and built solid houses that cannot be transported, but who consider themselves victims of witchcraft, are torn between their economic interests and their sense of personal insecurity. Sometimes the one and sometimes the other wins. If the headman considers that the chief is a 'good man who treats me well' he r ay remain within the principality, but move to a different neighbourhood. He tries to find out which people are 'all right'—generous, and eager to assist. At the same time, however, it is risky to rely entirely on the opinion of others, and wise to have one neighbour who is not a stranger.

A man who seeks a new home thinks of his relatives and friends. Most men consider a kinship tie adds to local security. Pagans in particular try to see that among the neighbours is a relative. They know that in most mundane activities strangers can assist, but that on the more important legal and ritual occasions a kinship personnel is essential. Frequently, until everything is settled, he does not mention to the people he is leaving why he is paying these preliminary visits. He fears lest any hostile neighbour in his old environment send witchcraft against him at his new home.

Having found a suitable area, both physically and socially, the commoner opens his negotiations. He cannot assume that, because land is unoccupied and uncultivated, he will receive permission to live and work there. In the more crowded areas, such as Mankaiana and Hlatikulu, men already in occupation are afraid to welcome new arrivals, and try to keep a reserve of fallow land for their own future needs. A man always speaks to the people near whom he wishes to build before he approaches their chief. He tells the size of his family and may mention the reason for leaving his old home. There is always someone who already has the right to the land he desires, since, in the original allocation of land, boundaries were defined by those of the nearest neighbours. The newcomer thus often receives land from an earlier arrival who introduces him to the chief.

Sometimes the seeker for new land is rebuffed because the people have heard that he is a thief or a wizard, and when he comes to talk to them they try to keep him away by telling him that there is really no room, they themselves are cramped, but they suppose that he can build there if he must. Swazi are very sensitive; they 'feel shame' quickly and few would stay after such an invitation. A man who is thick-skinned—or desperate— tells the chief through his councillor that he has found a place he likes, but So-and-So (the firstcomer) says there is no room. The chief calls the objector, and if he thinks he is 'trying to make himself big, as though the land were his', he interferes and welcomes the stranger.

Usually the earlier arrival finds it hard to turn away the man who has sought him out, and if he himself has no land to give away, might even plead the other's cause elsewhere. The first stereotyped response is 'Here there is no land', but the supplicant continues unperturbed. He 'begs to make a fire here', or asks to be allowed to 'crawl under your armpit'. A man who finds himself among strangers tries assiduously to cultivate their friendship, knowing that he will need it sooner or later. Swazi do not make judgements quickly and a common remark even after two years of trial is: 'I do not know him; I am still scrutinizing him, for he is new and trying to impress.'

Before a man finally moves from one principality he must *valelisa* (bid farewell) to his chief or he will not be accepted elsewhere. The subject sometimes pays the overlord £1 'to wipe the name from the tax book'. If a chief evicts a subject the price of farewell is not demanded, 'lest it be given with a bad heart and bring danger'. Fifty years ago the farewell custom did not exist: men had greater freedom of movement, and chiefs benefited to such an extent by followers that they did not bother to find out why men had left their old homes. Now that chiefs have little land, they are not prepared to risk harbouring bad characters. Should a chief suspect the man as a sorcerer, he may send a messenger to find out the real reason for the departure before he accepts him as his subject.

Thus there is a definite correlation between the movement of home-steads, the laws of land tenure, and the political structure. The most permanent homesteads are those of the political overlords who have the privileges of choosing their land and of controlling their subjects; the most mobile members of the population are commoners who have not inherited sufficient land for their needs or who are hounded from place to place by personal misfortunes.

SEASONAL CHART IN THE MIDDLEVELD [1]

Calendar month	Swazi moon	Season	Garden work	Animal husbandry	Other activities	Ceremonial	Food cycle
JANUARY.	*Bimbidwane* (everyone satisfied—kuɓimbi szela).	SUMMER (*Lihloɓo*) (End of summer). Last rain	Last maize fields planted. Early gardens harvested. Weeding of later fields. Very active.	Cattle pastured away from gardens. Milked twice a day. Herders busy.	Little time for distant visits. Daily work. Law-suits (all year).	No national ceremony unless *Incwala* is late. Individual rites.	Plentiful food. Fresh mealies, pumpkins, aloe bulbs, cow peas, monkeynuts, pumpkin leaves. Fruits.
FEBRUARY.	*Indlovana* (little elephant).	AUTUMN	Harvesting green maize. Weeding last fields of maize. Guarding corn from birds.	Cattle taken to pasture in harvested gardens. Milked twice a day.	Preparing granaries. Shelling dried mealies. *Palula* (virgin soil) turned.	Individual and local, e.g. chiefs call magicians to drive away birds.	As above. Marula beer in bushveld.
MARCH.	*Indlovuyenkulu* (big elephant).	(*Likwindla*)	Harvesting. Very busy in fields. Millet needs watching.	As above.	As above. Storing maize. Beer feasts, mainly for work parties.	As above.	As above.

[1] Planting can continue longer in lowveld where there is later frost.

Calendar month	Swazi moon	Season	Garden work	Animal husbandry	Other activities	Ceremonial	Food cycle
APRIL.	*Mabasa* (*kubasa*—to make a fire).	WINTER (*Ubusika*)	Maize harvest reaching end. First millet gleaned.	Milk decreasing. Cattle graze on dried maize stalks (*emahlanga*). Herdboys relax.	As above. Burning of grass begins.	Ceremonies prohibited during rainy seasons begin, e.g. doctoring homes against storms.	Green foods old and bitter. Dry maize. Fresh millet. Pumpkins, etc.
MAY.	*Inkwekweti* (*kwekweta*—pick up everything you have).		Harvest of millet.	As above.	Burning of grass. Hunting season. Building. Cutting grass for homes, mats, ropes, etc. Pottery begins.	Time for many ceremonies, e.g. weddings, end of widows' mourning period, safety of homes.	As above. Game killed. *Umfuso* (dried greens).
		Little rain.					
	Inhlangala (*kuhlangula*—brush off leaves). (Month omitted in order to correlate moons with month).	Wind.	As above. (Restful period.) Work only in millet fields.	As above. (Little work.)	As above. (Very busy social activities.)	As above. (Active ceremonial period.)	As above. Beer of dry maize and millet.
JUNE	*Inhlaba* (aloe blossoms).	No rain. Cold.	As above.	As above.	As above.	As above.	As above.

Calendar month	Swazi moon	Season	Garden work	Animal husbandry	Other activities	Ceremonial	Food cycle
JULY.	*Kolwane* (hawk that nests in this moon).	—	As above.	As above.	As above.	As above. Height of hunting season.	As above. Many people down to one meal a day.
AUGUST.	*Inci* (small wolf breeds in this month).	SPRING (*Emaḥloɓo Tudlana*— LITTLE SUMMER).	Preparing soil for first planting. Millet ripe for storage.	Cattle still feeding from stalks. Burnt pastures.	Burning grass. Building. Hunting. Visiting. (End of social period; work in fields again.)	National and individual doctoring of fields. Cattle sent to royal graves.	Still adequate in storage.
SEPTEMBER.	*Inyoni* (special bird mates).	First rains.	Maize planting begins in early gardens. Subsidiary crops— pumpkins, monkey-nuts, sweet cane, peas, etc.— planted.	Cattle to summer pasturage.	Hunting ends. Grass - cutting ends. Building continues. Pottery ends.	Cattle return from royal graves. Doctoring of homestead ends. Burning of grass round royal graves.	Stores get low. If rain falls, green vegetables, e.g. *msoɓo*, mushrooms, etc. Price of maize 12s. 6d. per bag at central shop in 1935. Price of maize `17s. per bag in outlying districts in 1935.

Calendar month	Swazi moon	Season	Garden work	Animal husbandry	Other activities	Ceremonial	Food cycle
OCTOBER.	*Impala* (antelope bears its young).		Great activity. Planting, weeding, hoeing, ploughing.	As above.	Threshing of millet. Building.	National rain ceremony if necessary.	Stored food and new greens (Sweet potatoes round Stegi.)
NOVEMBER.	*Lweti* (star visible when women begin work in early morning). Also *Inkosi Yencane* (LITTLE CHIEF).	SUMMER (*Lihloɓo*).	Great activity of women, men and children.	Careful herding begins. Milk increases.	As above. End of building.	National rain ceremony may continue. Little *Incwala*. (May begin in December — new moon.)	Green vegetables, e.g. *Ligusha*. Stores very low. Hunger moon.
DECEMBER.	*Mavulangamithi* (to swallow pickings of teeth). Also *Inkosi Yenkulu* (BIG CHIEF).	Heavy rains.	Very busy.	As above.	Preparations for big *Incwala*.	Big *Incwala* — festival of the nation. First fruits of limited number of crops.	Peak of hunger before first crops ripen and may be eaten.

E

CHAPTER V

THE CONSERVATIVE POLITICAL HIERARCHY

A<small>T</small> the peak of the political hierarchy are the king and his mother, each with a hereditary title and special insignia of office, each with political power sanctioned on the familiar African pattern by ritual and belief. Administratively, the monarchs combine the functions divided in Western countries into legislative, executive, and judicial, and they are aided in the discharge of their duties by a hierarchy of officials whose activities have not the rigid departmentalism characteristic of modern European constitutions.

The local divisions within the tribe are administered by officials appointed or recognized by the national rulers, assisted by subordinates of their own choosing. A local authority may be responsible to the king and his mother either directly or through a series of intermediate local superiors.

1. *The Ingwenyama and Indlovukati*

The king inherits his position in the male line. He is chosen from among the other sons of his father by virtue of his mother's rank in the harem. The complex principles of succession are described in Chapter VI; here it is sufficient to state that the king is regarded as having in his body the 'blood of kingship' (*ingatiyebukhosi*) from both the paternal and maternal side. Marriage cattle contributed by the nation for his mother make her the 'mother of the people of the country' and her son the 'child of the people'. When they are fully installed, she is given the title of *Indlovukati* (Lady Elephant) and he of *Ingwenyama* (Lion).

The king and his mother hold positions of unique privilege and authority. They are the central figures of all national activities: they preside over the highest courts; they summon national gatherings, control the age classes, allocate land, disburse national wealth, take precedence in ritual, and help to organize important social events.

Any offence against the person or property of the king or his mother is considered more heinous than one committed against any other individual. It is a crime for the average Swazi to wear the rulers' clothes, use their medicines, approach too close to their persons. Adultery with a queen was formerly punished as treason. Until Bunu's reign the rulers exercised the power of life and death over their subjects, and even to-day they may banish subjects whom they consider dangerous to the nation, or to themselves, its representatives.

Royal prerogatives are balanced against royal obligations. The manifold duties of the rulers, if conscientiously performed, take up a great deal of time and energy. The monarchs receive complaints, discuss matters of national importance, interview local authorities, listen to major cases, represent the people in negotiations with foreign diplomats, and supervise ceremonies. Their ritual duties sometimes keep them intensively occupied for weeks on end. Their functions in the various spheres will be further elaborated in subsequent chapters.

Between the *Ingwenyama* and the *Indlovukati* there is a delicate balance of powers, legal, economic, and ritual. He presides over the highest court, and formerly he alone could pronounce the death sentence. But she is in charge of the second highest court, her counsellors may take part in discussions at her son's court, and her hut is a sanctuary even for men sentenced to death. He controls the entire army, but the commander-in-chief may reside at the queen mother's village. He has his own chosen regiments stationed at his home; she has regiments at the capital under the leadership of princes. He has power to distribute land; together they work the rain that fructifies the soil. He may take cattle from the royal herds; she may rebuke him if he wastes national wealth. She is the custodian of the sacred objects of the nation, but they are not effective without his co-operation in manipulating them. He represents the line of past kings; she speaks to the dead in the shrine hut of the capital and provides beer for the libations. He is made great and rejuvenated in the annual ceremony held at her home; she receives special treatment on that occasion and takes precedence over other participants. In all activities they should assist and advise each other, for he is *Inkosi* and she is also *Inkosi*. Together they are spoken of as twins, and when one dies the other must be more strongly fortified than for any other national or personal loss.

Conflict between the two rulers is a menace to the entire nation. In the reign of Mbandzeni it led to civil war. Drought and flood have sometimes been attributed to 'bad feelings', 'bitterness' between the king and his mother. Above all, the administration of the entire country requires their harmonious co-operation: it is considered difficult to maintain law and order if the rulers ignore their obligations towards each other.

In order to obviate friction, Swazi formulate certain rules of behaviour. 'A king is ruled by his *tindvuna* (counsellors)'; and 'A king is king by his people'. Pressure is put on the rulers, as will be shown later, by various officials and councils, who share the responsibility of control.

Antagonism because of personality difference is appreciated in a society built essentially on a close personal, kinship basis. Swazi have therefore ruled that '*Inkosi kayilanywa*' (a king is not followed, i.e. has no full brothers born after him). This prevents a woman from encouraging a favoured younger son to usurp the birthright of the older brother. The value of this precaution was proved in cases where the queen mother was not chosen at the time of her marriage, and bore more than one son. Gwamile's preference for her younger son Malunge is the notorious example.

The separation of the villages of the king and his mother also minimizes potential conflict. The distance varies in different reigns, and increases as the king develops in status. Mswati's village, Hoho, was one day's journey on foot from the capital, Elangeni; Sobhuza's village, Lozitehlezi, is only a few hours by foot from Loɓamba and under an hour by car. There is no necessity for the rulers to see each other daily, and sometimes a couple of weeks pass without the king visiting his mother. She very rarely moves from the capital. Diplomatic intermediaries are sent to and fro, however, and are useful in situations where friction might be engendered or aggravated by face-to-face talk. The indirect approach, tact and evasion, is evident in many Swazi negotiations, but nowhere did I find it more marked than in internal politics.

Most Swazi refer the dual control by mother and son to *umdzabuko* (creation, the origin), but, when encouraged to discuss the matter further, a number of informants accounted for it in terms of patterns of behaviour inculcated by the domestic situation. 'A mother always loves her child, and he loves her. They respect each other greatly and so work together peacefully. With wives it is different; to-day they love you and to-morrow they hate you, and when you think that a wife loves you then there is jealousy in her heart. In your love you may confide in her, but she is treacherous, and will deceive you so that her child and no other will rule. Perhaps the people do not want her son, then two sons will strive for kingship, and this will breed family friction.'[1]

The extent to which co-operation between the *Ingwenyama* and the *Indlovukati* is harmonious, depends on conditions of the times and on personal qualities. In the past, when both rulers were illiterate, and the nation was more homogeneous, the duties were more evenly shared between the queen mother and her son; at present the educated Sobhuza shoulders most of the administrative responsibilities and the balance of power has changed (see Chapter XV).

2. *The Princes*

Swazi political power radiates primarily from the king. Aristocrats are graded by proximity to the ruling line. The first generation of a king's descendants are titled the *Bantfwaßenkosi* (children of a king), *emacandza welive* (eggs of the country), *BoMalangene* (early scions of the royal family). The second and third generations are addressed as *Bantfwaßenkosi* but are more accurately described as *Bantfwaßantfwaßenkosi* (children of children of a king). Heirs of important collateral lines who rule over principalities are also respectfully called *Bantfwaßenkosi* and their privileges are referred back ultimately to the link with the ruling lineage. Thus Ndzabankulu does not state that he holds his principality from Mbaimbai, but from Mbaimbai, son of Mswati. The more distant and unimportant relatives of a king merely retain the clan name, Nkosi Dlamini.

The king relies a great deal on the support of members of his lineage. His close relatives, particularly his uncles and half-brothers, wield great influence. The senior princes are consulted on all important issues; they, together with other counsellors, are the king's advisers and teachers, as well as his most fearless critics. Formerly they spent many months at the royal villages, and had wives living there to look after them when they paid state visits and also to serve the rulers. Nowadays, princes have less contact with the rulers, but they are still summoned for major events (selection of an heir to a noble line, allocation of widows of princes, the annual ceremony of kingship, property disputes that involve their kinsmen, the death of an important prince). The duties of *Bantfwaßenkosi* are

---

[1] The dual monarchy is more fully developed among the Swazi than in neighbouring tribes, where the emphasis is on the male. It would be useful to plot the distribution of the 'dual monarchy' type of monarchy throughout Africa, for it may well be that the Swazi system has been influenced by contact with other tribes.

similar to those of senior members of a commoner's lineage, but the issues at stake affect the nation and not only the small circle of relatives.

Between male agnates—fathers and sons, full and half-brothers, the patrilineal Swazi recognize an ambivalent reaction. On the one hand there is affection, co-operation and mutual interest; on the other there is jealousy, ambition, and aggression. Because of the positive and constructive aspects of the bond of blood, princes are sent to act as *titfundzi telive* (literally, shadows, i.e. personalities, of the realm), to report important events, investigate rumours of treason, and see that subjects respond to the summons for national service. They are expected to keep alive the prestige of royalty by generosity to commoners and tribute to the central rulers. But the bond of blood also makes the princes rivals of the king. Examples of conflict between the heir and male relatives, both before and after his installation, were mentioned in Chapter II. The axiom is '*Inkosi inye kupela*' (there is only one king). Uncles and brothers must be subordinate. They are princes, they are powerful, but they must not be his equals in ritual, wealth or prestige.

Kingship has been desired by ambitious princes and Swazi cannot imagine a peaceful and voluntary abdication. When they learnt that the English king (Edward VIII) had abdicated, they were amazed and expressed their opinions in the idiom of their own culture. 'How can a king run away from kingship?' 'There will be trouble.' 'He is mad, poor man, and the people should wait till he recovers, not encourage his brother to steal from him.' 'What does the queen mother say? Is the younger son her favourite?' 'My! but the Europeans have no law.' The queen mother considered: 'The people were right. They cannot accept a woman of no rank as queen. They must send the king far away, and give him enough work so that he will not bother his brother.'

Important princes should never be settled too near the king lest they usurp his powers and interfere with his 'personality' by ritual. No close brother may live permanently at the capital, eat from the king's dish, be at all familiar with his queens, or treat the queen mother's enclosure as though it were his own mother's. Sobhuza is severely criticized by conservatives for not taking the same precautions as did his forefathers, and for having 'brothers' among his intimate personal attendants.

Swazi consider that the best way to avoid trouble between princes and the king is to grant them limited power over local units. The eldest sons of most senior queens receive principalities as their birthrights. We saw in Chapter III how queens were distributed at royal centres throughout the country, and mentioned that the main heir of each leading queen of the village became prince over the surrounding people. Other sons and their mothers may also be sent to take charge of areas. The position is inherited by their heirs, and the royal links are perpetuated. Principalities given to sons of kings from the reign of Mswati are still under their descendants. From among 169 chiefs listed by the government, 75 are Dlamini; the number would be even greater if some of the leading princes of the past had not been killed or banished.

Formerly the king could find principalities for his relatives by expanding his terrain; now that all land is allocated and the boundaries of the country are fixed, he can only satisfy the claims of immediate kin at the

expense of existing chiefs of royal or common descent. If the king sends
a prince to take over a principality, the former ruler remains in the area
and becomes the great *indvuna* (counsellor) of the prince. A king does
not necessarily remove non-relatives to give princes their opportunity.
Hereditary chiefs of other clans are as secure as Dlamini. The men
whom the king demotes are those who displease him, and are troublesome; they may or may not be kinsmen. Sometimes the king com-
promises and allocates to the prince only a portion of the land, or appoints
him ruler over a frontier, and claimants on either side recognize his
superiority. Thus Umshengu, important half-brother of Sobhuza,
received land contested by two neighbouring chiefs, both of whom are
willing to recognize his overlordship. The reception accorded a prince
depends largely on the character of the men affected; while subjects of a
harsh and mean ruler are prepared to welcome a change, those who have
been under a good and generous man resent the newcomer as an intruder
and flout his commands. He, however, has it in his power to dismiss
disloyal occupants, and the king will, if satisfied, endorse his action.
The question of adapting the claims of princes to the limitations of the
land is coming to the fore as Sobhuza's sons are reaching maturity.

More closely identified with the king than the princes are two officials
known as *tinsila*. These are men chosen from special clans; they are
never Dlamini, but a ritual transference of blood between them and the
king places them in an intimate physical and mental relationship. Their
loyalty determines very directly the health of the king. It is in
their interests as well as part of their duty to watch and guide the
princes and report any hint of treason. *Tinsila*[1] have administrative
authority equal to that of the most important princes; they mediate in
disputes and above all endeavour to keep the peace between the various
sections of the people. This role of peacemaker was brought home
clearly when Sobhuza banished a young prince from the capital, and he
fled to the *insila*, Ngolotsheni Motsa, to fend off the king's displeasure,
which even the queen mother could not curb. The *tinsila* are primarily
associated with the ritual of kingship, and will be more fully discussed
in Chapter VI.

3. *The Limits of Nepotism*

Female relatives of the king are politico-economic assets to be judici-
ously invested. The more important princesses are given as wives to
foreign rulers and non-Dlamini chiefs. In this way they link the king
with important local units, and serve as useful informants on local politics
and interests. Out of twenty-five chiefs who were not of the Dlamini
clan and whose genealogies I examined, twenty were related to Sobhuza
through marriage. Eight were married to his paternal aunts (in Swazi
terminology they are his 'female fathers'); three were married to daughters
of his mother's co-wives (i.e. to his 'sisters') and nine were married to
daughters of his father's 'brothers' (i.e. to women also known as his
'sisters'). Because of their noble birth, these women hold special

---

[1] There are more than two *tinsila*, but here I refer to the two senior *tinsila*
only.

privileges in the harems of their husbands, and are potentially mothers of the successors to the chieftainships (see Chapter VII).

The king's full sister is considered next in rank to the *Indlovukati* and the king's leading wives.[1] She is titled the *inkosatan yelive* (princess of the country), and has an important voice on the council which chooses the heir to the kingship on her father's death. Her brother's children regard her, the 'female father', with marked respect and her own children are their equals.

Since, however, princesses on marriage live away from the capital, they take little active part in the central government. On their occasional visits 'home' (*kuɓo*) they are treated with honour[2] and are lavishly entertained, but, unlike princes, they do not attend the court, nor are they often summoned for national discussions.

Swazi stress the political rights of paternal kinsmen more than those of maternal, but the queen mother's close relatives also influence national affairs. The man who receives marriage cattle for his daughter or sister has high standing in the home of her husband; he is her legal representative in charges laid against her, and he acts as intermediary in ritual involving her own ancestors. The close maternal relatives of the king, more especially his *ɓomalume* (maternal uncles), usually receive, if they do not already hold, posts in the central government, and even the less important are shown special deference.

Relatives of queen mothers living outside Swazi territory were formerly granted land and power, in addition to protection from enemies, 'because through their women Swazi kings were born'. In this way the Simelane, to give but one example, were established in South Swaziland. When Somnjalose Simelane was queen mother, a group of her kinsmen living in Zululand were attacked by the Zulu. Suka Masuku, an attendant of the Simelane chief, put the heir, Mɓozongo, on his back and fled with him to Somnjalose, the child's paternal aunt. She cared for the child and later, when a chief in Hlatikulu waxed pretentious and demonstrated magical powers beyond his status (it is said that he held corn in his closed fist and when he opened his fingers the corn had sprouted), Mɓozongo was sent to take his place.

While the political privileges granted to the Dlamini are their prerogative, those bestowed on maternal relatives depend largely on character and affection. On the appointment of a new king, the maternal relatives of his predecessor may lose their influence, even though they retain their social prestige.

The queen mother's co-wives—that is, the mothers of princes—exercise a strong influence in the homes of their own sons, and are also called to the capital for special occasions. The senior wives in particular, the *ɓomage* (classificatory mothers) of the king are required for such national rituals as the moving of royal villages, the annual ceremony of kingship and the annual dedication of cattle to the dead.

[1] As usual, if there is no full sister, a half-sister is selected for the position of honour.

[2] Thus, to give a minor illustration, when Sobhuza entertained his paternal great-aunt, Sencaɓaphi, daughter of Mbandzeni, he sat on the floor of his office since she would not take a chair.

The wives of the ruling king are recognized as 'mothers of the people', but they lead fairly secluded lives during the lifetime of their husband. Sobhuza is particularly strict towards his queens; they may not go about singly, and are always also accompanied by small boys, who drive men from their pathways and keep a watch on the women's conduct. The queens take part in national celebrations and must periodically provide food for the people. They achieve their fullest power through the positions accorded their sons after the king's death.

Relatives of these queens—the king's own in-laws—have no prescribed role in Swazi government, but may receive help from the nation because of the status of their daughters. The parents of the king's main wife become the maternal relatives of his heir.

A wise king recognizes the value of *ɓunini* (kinship). It extends throughout the nation, linking him by blood and marriage with chief and commoner, wealthy and poor. The success of a chief's reign depends to a great extent on his treatment of his kinsmen and their friendship towards him.

4. *Leading Commoners*

The king is careful not to give too much power to male kinsmen, and certain highly-coveted administrative posts are monopolized by commoners. In this fashion a balance is maintained between the rights of the Dlamini aristocrats and members of other clans.

The monarchs rely to a great extent on *tindvuna* (councillors) of the royal villages. They are usually selected after consultation with trusted advisers, including senior princes, and come from a few well known lineages of commoner clans—more particularly from the Fakudze, Nkambule, Zwane, and Hlophe. The post is not necessarily given to the main heir of a former *indvuna*; an insignificant son or even a brother's child may be appointed. The quality desired above all others is 'respect for people'; the *tindvuna* are the people's representatives. While their ultimate appointment rests with the king, they may only be dismissed by the king in council.

In every reign a new *indvuna* is chosen for the new capital (see Chapter IV) and publicly introduced to the nation gathered in the cattle byre. He becomes the *indvuna lenkulu* (great councillor or governor) in the land, but he is expected to consult with the *tindvuna* of other royal villages, more especially with the great counsellor of the previous reign, who continues to reside at the former capital. Thus Mshudulwane Zwane, the great counsellor of Loɓamba, co-operates with Mandanda Mtsetfwa, counsellor of the former capital Zombodze. When necessary, they call on Malangatonke Fakudze of Enkanini, Ndala Fakudze of old Loɓamba, Mahutfulo Magutfulela of Nsuka, and a few others. Each of these men is respectfully addressed by the populace as *Mngane* (Noble One or Sir) or *Baɓe* (Father).

While Mshudulwane is nominally the *indvuna lenkulu*, Mandanda Mtsetfwa exercises more influence, by reason of his greater ability. Both are completely illiterate. Mandanda is shrewd, superficially genial, and is intensely suspicious of Europeans. To the conservative Swazi, he is the ideal official. Since the position of *indvuna* is not strictly hereditary, greater attention is paid to their character than in the case of aristocrats.

Tindvuna help the rulers in all spheres of work. It is a platitude among the Swazi that the *Inkosi* (male or female) is ruled by *tindvuna*. They hear cases; give judgements; advise on the temper of the people; look after the distribution of royal cattle; organize labour for the fields; arrange that national ritual is performed on time; interview strangers and bring them to the rulers; report illnesses, accidents, and any untoward event. Should the king or his mother be too autocratic, wasteful or negligent, the *tindvuna* join with the senior princes in reminding them of their duties.

The post of *indvuna lenkulu* gives so deep an insight into national secrets and so great a hold over national resources that Swazi recognize the danger of his intriguing against the established rulers. Two well-known *tindvuna* (Sandlana Zwane and Mbaɓa Siɓandze) were executed for treason. Sandlana supported a prince against Mbandzeni and was also rumoured to be too intimate with the queen mother. Mbaɓa was proved to have stolen a leg of an animal sacrificed to the ancestors, and to have sent it to some Sotho who were hiding in the Mdzimba mountains. This sacrilege was considered tantamount to witchcraft directed against the ruling king, Bunu.

Tindvuna have intrigued with princes and queen mothers against kings; *tindvuna* themselves are never eligible for kingship, because they are without the royal blood. Leading *tindvuna* are, however, drawn into the web of fictional kinship with the ruling clan through their national responsibilities. Consequently, they may not marry a close relative of the king; they may eat from the same dish as princes; and when they die they are buried with the ritual of the royal clan.

The great *indvuna* appoints an assistant, and if he shows himself very efficient, he may succeed to the post when the senior dies or becomes completely useless. The assistant is always a younger man; he goes on messages, represents the rulers in distant villages, and generally executes the more arduous duties. In addition he takes orders from the senior and helps him with his work in the court. *Tindvuna* of other royal villages may also have assistants.

Apart from the *tindvuna* and their assistants are a number of essential minor civil officials. They include personal servants and courtiers (*tinceku*), messengers (*emancusa*), cooks (*ɓapheki*), and herders (*ɓelusi*). Because they are employed by the rulers, their status is high. In Swazi society there is little specialization of labour, and it is the rank of the people for whom one works rather than the type of work that may give prestige.

Civil officials cannot be rigidly distinguished from the military staff which was so important in former days and still controls labour. Every man belongs to the age-class regiments (*emaɓutfo*, singular *liɓutfo*), and the distinction between regimental and administrative authorities is often one not of persons but of situations. Linking together the military-cum-age class and the civil administration are aristocrats who hold privileges in both groups by virtue of pedigree, and leading commoners whose civil duties overlap with regimental activities. Thus Mshengu is the prince of a regimental division and also a member of the Inner Council (see p. 62); again, Mandanda Mtsetfwa presides over the court at Zombodze and leads the regiments in the annual national ceremony.

But there are distinct titles and duties associated with the *emaButfo* whether or not the same people also hold office in civil life. The age-class system is fully discussed in Chapter IX; here I am interested in indicating its position in the political organization. The division on the basis of age is different from the hierarchy built on rank by birth, but hereditary officials exercise authority through the age classes. A young prince may be appointed as leader of a senior age group; his power depends on its support. The king stands for the principle of hereditary power, and is at the head of all age groups. Since intertribal warfare has ceased, the *emaButfo* has become subordinate to the civil administration, and labour for national, hereditary authorities is the main function of the age classes.

Among the officials considered essential for national security are the *tinyanga* (specialists in ritual). National ritual is usually monopolized by special clans which co-operate with, and support, the Dlamini. Medicines required for national ritual are transmitted from father to son, subject always to the ultimate approval of the Dlamini king.

All Swazi officials, civil, military, and ritual, normally hold office for life and are only dismissed for treason or witchcraft. Incompetence, habitual drunkenness, stupidity, or weakness of character are qualities that are criticized, but as long as an official is loyal he retains his position. The only way to counteract his defects is to appoint capable men as his assistants.

To sum up the position of commoners in the central government, it is clear that the majority of officials are drawn from plebeian clans, but owe their position to the king and the queen mother. Swazi officials are never elected; they hold their positions either by hereditary right or by individual qualifications, among which trustworthiness and a generous nature are the most essential. The system is best adapted to a society where there is little need for rapid decisions and quick change of policy.

5. *The Voice of the People*

In administering the affairs of the nation, the rulers are also assisted by the organized advice of their subjects. The people are represented on the central government by two councils, the *Liqoqo* (Inner Council) and the *Libandla* (General Council). Swazi say of the king: 'He has no children; the people are his children.' His own sons and daughters are taught to reply to the question, 'Who is your father?' with the name of one of his brothers. The king-father, however, is not permitted to be a despot.

In a useful memorandum, Sobhuza discusses the relationship between the king, *Liqoqo* and *Libandla*. 'In all the national bodies the people hold the highest position, hence the king, as the people's representative, holds a higher position than any other body in the government. The power of the people can be appreciated when something shows signs of going wrong on the part of the king, when the councillors (of the *Liqoqo*) may be heard to say: "The people of Ngwane (i.e. the *Libandla*) will kill us—for our part in the wrong doing"; and similarly when councillors (of the *Liqoqo*) suspect that the *Libandla* is acting wrongly or unwisely they may be heard to say: "The king will kill or punish us." '

The *Liqoqo* is a development of the family council, and hence is predominantly aristocratic. It is under a prince who is specially 'pointed out' to the people. Not every royal kinsman is a member: members are chosen by the king-in-council mainly from senior princes and from able commoners. In addition to princes, a few chiefs not of the royal family and a few intelligent, devoted, and influential attendants are on the present *Liqoqo*. The principal qualifications are, therefore, ability, interest, and general standing. The king, his mother (the only woman on the council), and the great counsellor are *ex officio* members.

The rulers continue to consult the *Liqoqo* of their predecessors. They may also make suggestions for additional suitable members. For convenience, the council is limited in numbers, and Sobhuza has kept it down to less than thirty. No public announcement is made of any new candidate, and there is no need to replace a member who dies. The majority of Swazi do not know who is on the *Liqoqo* or the special qualifications of each member.

The character of tribal councils is frequently misunderstood because they are regarded as more formally constituted than is actually the case. The *Liqoqo*, for example, is largely informal—and that is one of its major assets. The king may summon any member whom he desires to consult or whose services he requires. He does not hold regular sessions, but discusses matters that arise with members who are available, and only when an important decision on policy is necessary does he call the full *Liqoqo*. A few members are always at or near the royal villages and may advise on everyday routine. When the king travels, one or two of the *Liqoqo* are usually in his entourage. The *Liqoqo* operates, even when it does not meet as a corporate body, through individual members who are in more or less constant attendance on the king and the queen mother.

The functions, like the personnel, are not specialized or precise. The *Liqoqo* may advise, make decisions, and execute them. During my stay in Swaziland, the *Liqoqo* discussed, among other issues, questions of land, education, traditional ritual, court procedure, and transport. The members saw that their decisions were put into effect, but actually very few decisions were taken. Any matter may be referred to the *Liqoqo* but the sanction of the *Liβandla* is required on important matters. The rulers bow before the councils, and if they violate an accepted law the *Liqoqo* may impose a fine. Members of the *Liqoqo* do not fear expulsion if they speak freely, and they openly criticize when they feel that it is necessary.

The *Liβandla* is a larger and more formal council than the *Liqoqo*. Its members include, firstly, all the chiefs and their leading counsellors; secondly, prominent headmen; and, thirdly, any adult male who wishes to attend. The *Liβandla* is not distinguished by the rank of its personnel from the *Liqoqo*, for every prince, chief, and able responsible commoner is a member of the *Liβandla* and a potential member of the *Liqoqo*. But because the *Liβandla* is more representative of all sections of the people, and no one is prohibited from attending and speaking at the meetings, it is less manageable than the *Liqoqo*.

The *Liβandla* is summoned by special messengers sent from the royal villages. The messenger informs the chief, who calls together the headmen in his principality. If the chief cannot attend and speak for his people, he sends a deputy as his 'eye' or his 'mouth'. Informants insist that in former times a chief who ignored the call to a national meeting without good reason was heavily fined. 'Does the king summon for play?' At present, failure to respond is severely criticized, but, as far as I know, is never punished.

The procedure at the meetings is defined by precedent. The people gather in the cattle byre of the capital and sit in a semicircle facing the king, queen mother, their immediate attendants, and a few leading councillors. A leading prince of the *Liqoqo* acts as spokesman on the *Liβandla*. He or the Great Councillor opens the meeting and tells the people why they have been summoned. No agenda is sent out beforehand, so that the matter may be a complete surprise. When it has been explained, any member of the *Liβandla* may speak. Even if an issue has been thrashed out in the *Liqoqo*, the *Liβandla* can still object to the decision. Speakers at the *Liβandla* always begin, 'You people of Ngwane' or 'You Swazi', for this is considered a representative gathering of the nation. The king usually sits silent until the majority opinion is clarified, and then he speaks. He is greeted with the royal applause, '*Bayethe*' and a shower of stereotyped praise. The queen mother rarely speaks. Sometimes she is referred to by a councillor and he reproduces her comment.

The *Liqoqo* may on no occasion override a decision of the *Liβandla*. *Liqoqo* members live scattered among the people, and do not wish to antagonize them. Moreover, there is no sharp cleavage in interest, so that there is a genuine endeavour to reach unanimity. Neither council is divided into parties with specific and conflicting policies; the members are essentially peasants, and only in recent years have different occupational groups arisen and put forward sectional interests.

Recourse to the full *Liqoqo* and *Liβandla* is rare; they developed in a society where communication was slow and where life was sufficiently unchanging not to require many sessions or new decisions. In the years 1934–6 inclusive, the *Liqoqo* was summoned four times and the *Liβandla* three times. A council rarely meets more than once a year; the weakness of the system is apparent in the present period of rapid transition.

6. *The Relationship between the Central and Local Administration*

Within the national political organization are a number of interlocking units varying in size and importance. Government extends from the smallest local unit, the homestead, upwards to the central administration. In each unit of the hierarchy similar principles are at work; the functions of the authorities are roughly similar in kind, though different in degree; the personnel is chosen on similar grounds and, where numbers permit, is subdivided into similar departments. The head of each local unit is described as *umnumzana*; whether this refers to the headman of a homestead or the chief of a principality is evident from the context.

The head of a homestead wields recognized legal and administrative powers. He is responsible for the torts of the inmates, controls their property, and speaks for them before his superiors. If, however, a matter arises which affects members outside of the homestead, he must immediately consult his *lusendvo* (kinship council), presided over by the head of the lineage. The *oyise* (fathers—i.e. family elders) are then summoned.

The *lusendvo* deals with *tiβi tendlu* (dirt of the huts—family affairs which need no intervention from outsiders).

When other families are involved, as in cases of adultery or premarital pregnancy, the respective kinsmen meet to discuss the matter and try to reach a satisfactory conclusion. If they do not succeed, they appeal to the political authorities—'cold people', non-kinsmen. The wider kinship group is not a local group, and is subordinate in legal and administrative matters to political units.

People who live on one ridge or in one valley, or who are literally within shouting distance of each other, co-operate in work, support each other in ceremony and form a distinct local group known as *laβakhelene* (those who build together, i.e. neighbours). They frequently recognize one of their members as a leader—a great person (*umuntfu lomkulu*). He obtains his position in various ways and often with an informality foreign to the European. He may be the first man to receive land from the chief, his overlord, and later arrivals are indebted to him for their gardens; he may be a relative of the chief or of the king and receive homage because of his rank. His position is usually taken over by his heir. The 'great person' may be invited to arbitrate in disputes between families in the neighbour-hood, and he sometimes deals with minor cases—slander, trespass of cattle, trouble over gardens. But he exercises no precise legal authority, and he cannot enforce any fine.

The first local unit which has an *umnumzana* recognized by the central authorities is the *sive* (principality), under a *sikhulu* (chief) or *umtfwanen-kosi* (prince), whose position is usually inherited. He is the head of the area in law, economics and ritual. He mediates between his subjects and the rulers; presides over cases that family councils could not settle; sanctions fines and other punishments inflicted by his court; investigates serious cases before sending them on appeal; exercises rights over land and labour and in brief reflects in miniature the privileges and duties of the king of the nation. If his mother is alive, she shares with him the responsibilities of control and is in charge of the main section of his homestead.

The paternal kinsmen of a chief are spoken of as the 'princes' in the area. Thus in the principality of Mpundla Maziya, the Maziya are 'princes'. A Dlamini is a foreigner, and is not permitted to take part in the private discussions of the Maziya kinsmen. They constitute the family council (*lusendvo*) which takes the place in the principality of the national inner council (*liqoqo*). Non-relatives are represented on it by an *indvuna* appointed by the chief-in-council. The local *liβandla* is consti-tuted by headmen of the area, some of whom are consulted more than others, and form in effect a working committee. The chief discusses with these two councils such matters as the acceptance of new arrivals, the introduction of new regulations, judgements of the court. From these trusted men the chief selects his emissaries if he himself cannot attend national functions.

Each chief has at least one main *indvuna*, to attend to cases, supervise labour, and represent the claims of subjects. In one principality there may be as many as three *tindvuna*, each with specific duties. Thus Chief Dalata had one for cases, another for the age classes and a third to supervise his homesteads. The main *indvuna* is usually assisted by a *liphini*, who, if he proves himself capable, is given the position on the death of the senior. The court of the chief also includes messengers, cooks, attendants, and magicians.

The interaction between local and central authorities is complicated by the system of royal villages. In Chapter III we described how these were graded with the village of the queen mother as the capital, the 'barracks' of the king ranking second, and so on. The various principalities are attached to these villages, and while some are directly subordinate to one of the two main villages, others are attached indirectly via less important royal centres.

The king decides on the alinement of principalities and royal villages. Distance from the monarch may make for independence in local authorities, but there is no evidence that the further a chief or prince is from the capital, the more likely he is to resent control. By being linked directly to one of the main royal villages, the head of a large principality is, moreover, prevented from becoming too autocratic, and yet he exercises greater autonomy in local affairs than if he were attached to a neighbouring royal village under a governor of minor importance.

The arrangement of the political units is therefore not on a simple geographical basis, and the political hierarchy is not to be conceived as a number of concentric circles extending from the homestead to the nation. Diagramatically, the situation can be represented as follows:

ACTUAL ALINEMENT   FORMAL REPRESENTATION OF HIERARCHY

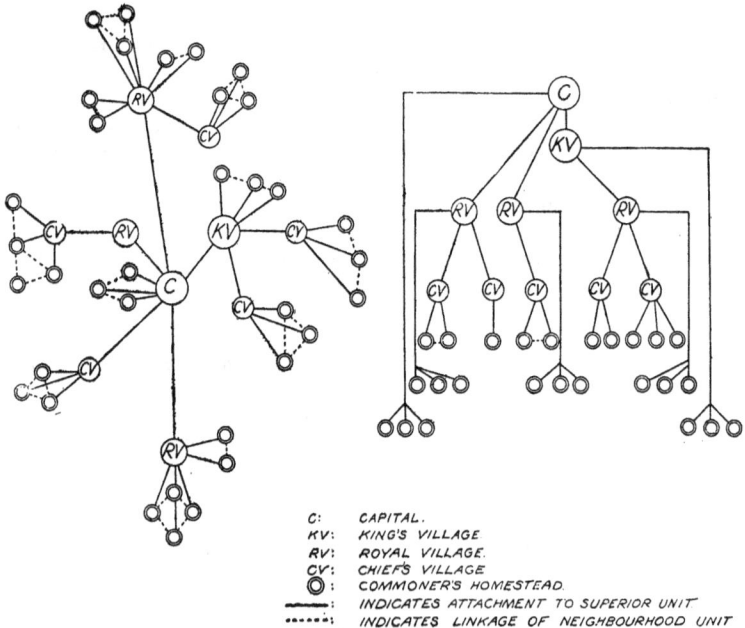

C: CAPITAL.
KV: KING'S VILLAGE.
RV: ROYAL VILLAGE.
CV: CHIEF'S VILLAGE.
◉:   COMMONER'S HOMESTEAD.
——: INDICATES ATTACHMENT TO SUPERIOR UNIT
·····: INDICATES LINKAGE OF NEIGHBOURHOOD UNIT

Irrespective of the limited degree of subordination of some of the powerful local chiefs, no chief possesses autocratic powers within his principality. His councillors, known as *Baniniyo Bake* (his owners), exercise a strong curb and do not hesitate to rebuke him and even fine him if he seriously infringes the rights of subjects. I obtained two instances of fines being inflicted on chiefs by their councils. In the first case, a chief wanted to evict an old-established family from its land without adequate reason. In the second case, a chief was fined for committing adultery with the wife of a subject. If a chief does not accept the advice of his councils, they may always appeal to the central authorities, who will, if they consider it necessary, tell him 'to rest' and appoint another member of the area to act in his place.

7. *Vassalage and Slavery*

Characteristic of the Swazi political structure is the bond of *kukhonta* —the offer of homage and allegiance to a superior. Chiefs *khonta* to the king as a sign of loyalty; commoners *khonta* to chiefs and their wealthier fellow commoners. A number of young men, especially those who are ambitious and have little opportunity in their own families, attach themselves to the villages of rulers and nobles. Some offer allegiance to aristocratic women, more especially to the queen mother and the senior queens, or to the young princes who will later hold State positions. No stereotyped oath of fealty is taken, but the subject asks if he can be the 'person' of the lord, 'his dog', 'his boy'. The custom of offering allegiance is falling away with the introduction of labour for Europeans, and at Loɓamba there were only four men in this position.

Kukhonta is a type of vassalage, involving legal and economic obligations on both parties. The subject accepts the rulings of the lord's court, his claims for service and his right to occasional tribute; the lord recognizes his obligations to give land, protection, economic assistance, the blessings of his ritual and a hearing to the man on his council. He welcomes the 'person' as a labourer and attendant; formerly he was also a warrior.

The nature of the bond varies with the status of the vassal. An important youth does not break his ties with his kin, whereas unimportant men seek from the lord the benefits they cannot obtain from their own kinship groups. The bond of allegiance is extended along lines of fictional kinship—a survival from the time when the nation was organized on a clan basis. While to the outside observer the bond between unrelated lord and man is an important political development from the purely kinship ties uniting members of society, the Swazi themselves do not recognize it as a radical break from the past kinship structure. There appears to be no conflict between the claim of a kinsman and that of a political overlord for the service of the man; and from his point of view, the overlord acts if the kinsmen are unable to assist.

The less wealthy men ask from their lord assistance when they wish to marry, and they occasionally bring their wives to his homestead and not to that of their own kin. They continue to follow the ritual of their clan, and are buried by clansmen, but if they are isolated from kinsmen the lord appoints substitutes; and in law cases the lord as well as the senior kinsmen may be asked for help. The bond is mutually beneficial, and the economic motive that dominates the relationship of master to servant and landlord to tenant is but one of many reciprocal claims. The conditions are understood, even though they are not explicitly defined, and the relationship may be terminated by either party.

In a different category from *tikhonti* (vassals), whose allegiance is voluntary, are the *titfunjwa* and *tigcili*. *Titfunjwa* were captives of war, who were brought as youngsters to the king and distributed by him to his wives or renowned warriors. An old Sotho, Mbadlana, who was seized as a child, is the last of the *titfunjwa* captured in war. *Tigcili* included children of men killed as evildoers (*ßatsakatsi*): the children were occasionally saved, declared free of the taint, and used as servants.

Tigcili is usually translated as 'slaves', but the word 'slave' conveys a false meaning. The concept of slavery, of regarding a person as a thing to be bought and sold on the open market, was, and is, alien to the Swazi. The word *sigcili* (singular) and the abstract quality *bugcili* are sometimes figuratively applied to a wife, and to her status in the husband's home. The *tigcili* of olden days also had very definite rights; to call them *tigcili* or speak of them as *tigcili* in their hearing was an insult and could be punished by the man who had them under his protection. They were described as his 'orphans' or 'children', were fed by his wives, and the girls received as high a *loßola* as his own daughters. The men were entitled to speak on the council and to marry, provided they had the cattle to obtain a wife. A *sigcili* was permitted to hold a national post, and some received responsible positions in the homesteads and grew wealthy from cattle given them for loyal service. The queen mother mentioned *tigcili* who had become *emasoka wendlunkulu* (from *kusoka*—to circumcise; *indlunkulu*—the great hut) and looked after important men and their property.

The *sigcili* could transfer his allegiance from one lord to another. If a *sigcili* were badly treated by anyone else, he could appeal direct to his lord, ignoring intermediary officials, such as the *tindvuna*. A *sigcili* was allowed to lodge a complaint against his master, and no *sigcili* could be killed without the permission of the king. He had the same protection as other subjects in the courts. The main drawbacks of *bugcili* were the absence of own kinsmen, the lack of supporters in ritual, and the limited economic security.

The economic conditions of the traditional society did not allow of a slave group, since every man, irrespective of his status, was required as a warrior and every woman as a worker in the field. At the present time there is no section of the population to which one can point as descendants of *tigcili*. At no time did they form a caste. They have been completely assimilated into the nation, intermarried with 'free' men and women, and no stigma is attached to their children.

8. *The Character of Swazi Authorities*

The relationship between a Swazi chief and his subjects is essentially personal; he knows each family on his land and is related to many of them. He often greets youngsters by the names of their grandfathers, and is acquainted with the family genealogies. Every birth, wedding, and death is reported to him, he assists the people in their troubles and eats at their feasts; he is consulted about illnesses, ploughing, selling of cattle, seeking of work, and the best magicians. One chief discussed for hours whether a herdsman, tossed by a bull and dangerously ill, should be sent to the hospital or be treated by a Swazi herbalist. No important information should be withheld from him. When, in a recent murder case, a chief was said to have no knowledge of the disappearance of the victim, people insisted that, if this were true, he had the right to fine his subjects.

The conservative Swazi chief is not aloof from his people; he practises the same customs, holds the same beliefs, and lives on the same level; his interest in their difficulties is not that of a tolerant superior, but of a fellow sympathizer. Chiefs are trained to 'feel with' their subjects; children of chiefs and of commoners grow up together, the princes' most intimate attendants are recruited from commoners. The idea of educating chiefs in special schools in an attempt to combine hereditary right with European 'efficiency' has sometimes been suggested by members of the British administration, but is opposed by the Swazi. Educational differentiation is discouraged, lest a chief 'forget his people' and adopt European values. Thus Sobhuza was sent to school with a band of comrades from all strata, and those whose parents could not afford the expense were educated with national funds. Sometimes one hears remarks such as: 'It is not evident that So-and-So is a chief; he was well brought up.' A queen told her son not to be conceited and walk looking skywards, thinking that the people would follow him.

A chief is criticized by the majority of Swazi if he is aggressive, domineering, very progressive, independent, or ambitious. Such qualities as ability in debate, efficiency in organizing work, knowledge of law are admired, but are not encouraged, and it is expected that they be contributed by advisers.[1] A chief should always remember that he is 'chief by his people'. He takes his stand from their wishes and is directed by, rather than directs, their opinions. He accepts the decisions of the majority and tries to win over the minority.

Since chieftainship is usually hereditary, it is not possible to choose men who approximate most closely to the ideal chief. Swazi do not delude themselves that noble birth inevitably ensures a noble character; they view their rulers with eyes sharpened by self-interest, but failures and black sheep do not destroy respect for the aristocracy.

A social attitude to superiors is inculcated in all Swazi from childhood by laws of etiquette, by ritual and myth and a range of situations in which superiority is emphasized. This is particularly noticeable in the relationship of subject to chief. No subject stands upright when addressing a chief, or approaches too close. When giving or receiving anything, the subject shuffles forward with bended knee and utters exaggerated praise. No ordinary commoner has free access to the great, nor may he come near with weapons in his hand. Chiefs, be they geniuses or nincompoops,

---

[1] Cf. Machiavelli. 'The first conjecture made of a prince and of his intellectual capacity should be based upon a consideration of the men by whom he surrounds himself, and when these are faithful to him and sufficient for his occasions, he is to be accounted a wise prince for having chosen them sufficient and kept them faithful.'

F

harsh or kind, must receive the overt treatment standardized by their status. They are always accompanied by trusted followers, and wherever they go they usually collect a crowd of servitors. 'Where the king moves, life moves', commented Dr. Seme in his polished English on one occasion when Sobhuza visited the royal village of Entonjeni, in the Peak district, and people from miles around flocked to pay court and bring beer and pumpkins and other tribute.

Homage is not only an indication of a man's rank; it also produces the personality appropriate to that rank. It is effective and, to some extent, conscious, propaganda. 'The homage', Swazi say, 'makes a person big, gives him shadow.' Mpundla lying on his stomach in his hut, while a wife carefully delouses him, appears simply a fat old man. As the hut fills with people, who squat squeezed together rather than disturb or inconvenience him, as voices are respectfully stilled while he speaks, or a chorus of praise is emitted when he suddenly bawls to someone outside to enter and drink from the beer bowl, his *sitfunzi* (shadow: personality) is made apparent. There is then no confusing of chief and subject. The chief usually develops an appearance of self-confidence, a poise and dignity in contrast with the humble and obedient behaviour of the subjects. Swazi do not make the further logical deduction that if the tables were turned, the chief might appear insignificant and the subjects glorious.

Personality is further developed by *imitsi* (medicines) graded according to the status of the individual. 'There are, however, chiefs who can never have personality; even *imitsi* does not help them much. They are very weak.' If a person uses a treatment beyond his or her status, it is dangerous both to himself (or herself) and to those whom he (or she) has tried to equal; the greatest personality medicine is possessed by the king and the queen mother.

Subjects revere their rulers, not for what they are, but for what they, the subjects themselves, project into chieftainship. They grade all men and women in relation to the king and his mother. He is the Lion, the Sun, the Milky Way, Obstacle to the Enemy, Great Wild Animal, etc.; she is Lady Elephant, the Earth, the Beautiful, Mother of the Country, and so forth. Compared with them, the highest officials are likened to 'tiny stars' or 'little ant-heaps'. And compared with these dignitaries, the average man speaks of himself as 'a dog', 'a stick', 'a nothing'.

It is easy to distinguish the queen mother as she sits on the mat in her yard, discussing cases, hearing gossip, organizing work, plaiting rope, or performing other duties associated with women. She is dressed in skins similar to those of any other conservative woman. But on her hair is a crown of wooden pegs topped by a jaunty red flamingo feather set between lucky beans; round her ankles and wrists are tied small pouches of potent medicines. Yet the insignia that she wears are only part of her *sitfunzi*; her status is primarily evidenced by the homage and praises bestowed on her.

The 'personality' of the king is made even more conspicuous. His clothing is almost identical with that of his humblest subjects; he wears no obvious bundles of medicine. But men sit at a distance from him, women do not raise their eyes to his; when he moves, attendants shout his praises and he summons the most powerful chiefs with the imperious command '*Ngemandla*' ('With all power').

People find it a strain to be constantly in the presence of the great. Men with little sense of inferiority or humility complained that when they were long with the king they trembled and shook 'because the medicines he uses together with his royal blood are too strong'. A Swazi woman described how, at the agricultural show in Johannesburg, she suddenly felt her heart beat and her limbs weaken. A few men were coming towards her. She said to her friend: 'Let us move. There is someone there too strong for me. I think he must be my king.' Later she learnt that it was indeed Sobhuza. Her friend was not affected, 'because she was a Sotho and joined with other medicine'.

The status personality of the subject is adjusted to that of the chief. A 'good subject' is a man who is loyal and fully prepared to accept his subordination; in return, he considers himself entitled to respect and consideration. He is prepared to speak up in the council if he considers that his chief is 'wasting the people'—if he calls upon their services too frequently, takes no interest in their troubles, is stingy, or does not look after their families when the men are away on State work.

It is in the chief's interest to behave courteously, generously, to draw people towards him, not to force them to seek the protection of another; not to ignore them, but to recognize their *Budvodza* (manhood value). The rights of a Swazi chief are not so great that subjects can be enslaved in his service, and his powers are limited by the weapons in their hands. The great deterrents to a would-be tyrant are public criticism, loss of subjects, and the fear of murder by poisoning or witchcraft. Subjects do not easily rise against their chiefs, and never in organized parties— political murders are the acts of individual malcontents, not of hostile organizations.

I found most Swazi chiefs men of average ability, performing their duties moderately, within the narrow limits of their present position and training. Over 95 per cent are uneducated and conservative, representing the standards of the majority of their subjects, who are also uneducated and conservative. Europeans stress efficiency and the ability to lead. The traditional activities of the chief are routine, and he relies for their execution largely on their acceptance as habit and custom by the people. Some Europeans criticize the Swazi chiefs and read into their positions qualities not required or desired in the conservative society.

The more defined functions of a ruler do not necessarily add to his position, and may, in fact, detract from it by reducing him to the level of mundane activities and associations. The Swazi king and his mother have as their essential quality something more subtle and more powerful than executive authority—the sanction of sacred knowledge and ritual.

CHAPTER VI

RITUALIZATION OF THE KING

THE Swazi king is the symbol of the nation, the man who is more than man, 'father' and 'son' of the people. His position is vouched for by tradition and myth, and is enhanced by ritual and taboo. His status is reflected in the growth of royal villages. His health and strength are identified with the wellbeing of his subjects and the fertility of nature; his illness brings dread, his death disaster. Ritualization of crises of life, a universal feature of human society, is designed to protect the individual from possible dangers and to give him additional powers. Among the Swazi the ritual depends on status in the political hierarchy, and at each stage of development the king is treated with elaborate and unique rituals that set him apart from ordinary men.

1. *Royal Villages reflect the Development of Kingship*

The growth of the king takes place against a background of royal villages that react to each marked change in his status. In Chapter IV, I described the royal villages as they existed in 1934; but in 1901, when the king was a mere babe and his father Bunu was dead, there were certain important differences in structure as distinct from differences in personnel.

Each king starts a new capital and new royal villages. An heir is not simply taken to an existing royal village and put into the hut of his predecessor. When a king dies, his capital is modified and continues to be in the charge of the queen mother, who becomes the queen regent till the heir and his mother are able to take control from the new capital that has been evolved. Each new capital is usually correlated with the name of the king who inaugurates it; thus precedent dictated that Sobhuza's village be named Loɓamba, after that of his great grandfather Sobhuza I.

The new capital begins with the death of the former king. The hut of his main wife, the future queen mother, is carried by night from out of the harem to a site near a hill a short distance from the old capital. Round the hut selected men build a few essential living and store huts and a cattle byre. The new unit is known as the *umstangala* (stone-walled cattle byre), because the cattle byre is surrounded by stones and not the usual palisade of branches.[1] An *indvuna* (governor) and special attendants are sent to look after the *umstangala* and attend to the mother and child. She is given the title *Naɓomntfwana* (Mother of the Child) and he is the *Umntfwana* (Child—of the nation). Even if the child is still very young, he has separate quarters. The future queen mother spends most of her time in her hut, which is dedicated to her late husband, and into this

---

[1] This is possibly Sotho influence.

72

hut, known as the *liciβa*, the child may not enter. The hut is associated with death, and the king must avoid all contact with death.

In the winter of the third year the mourning period ends. The mourning hut and objects connected with it are destroyed, and the mother and child move to a newly built homestead, the embryonic future capital. Nothing from the *umstangala* is taken there, but certain objects are carried from the old capital to the new, as a material symbol of the continuity of kingship. The old capital is moved a few hundred yards, and rebuilt on the same pattern as before, but it is without the sacred objects and the sanctuary in the cattle byre. The cattle from the *umstangala* are transferred to a small kraal built near the embryonic capital and known as the *ligangadu* (the place of mourning).[1] An *indvuna* is placed in charge, and the *ligangadu* becomes a national sanctuary, to which, in former times, men could flee for safety if condemned to death by local chiefs. The *ligangadu* is associated with the powerful dead. Cattle used in the *umstangala* and *ligangadu* may never be moved to other royal villages, nor may any of the Dlamini eat of the flesh of these animals. When the king reaches full manhood and has many wives, the *ligangadu* is abandoned, and the cattle remain the property of the governor. The *ligangadu* of Bunu, Sobhuza's father, was abandoned in 1934.

The new capital, as can be seen in the diagram (Appendix IV), is divided into two main living sections, one for the young queen mother and the other for her son. Her quarters include living and store huts for herself and her attendants, and the whole section forms the *Indlunkulu*. Her son's quarters are known as the *lusasa* (dense cluster of bush, because of the heavy palisading of the cattle byre). The *lusasa* lies to the right of the cattle byre (looking east), and in the cattle byre is a small sanctuary. The *lusasa* is subdivided into the 'white' and the 'black'. Access to the 'white *lusasa*' is permitted to most people who want to see the young king on State business. There his mother may visit him, but she may not touch him. She is not allowed even to enter the 'black *lusasa*'; the king and special male companions and instructors sleep and eat in this section, and when he is physically mature his lovers visit him there. He is periodically doctored for kingship in the sanctuary and in the 'black *lusasa*'.

The period spent in the embryonic capital varies in length with the age of the heir on his father's death. For Sobhuza it lasted eighteen years. It is a period of training, and during this time the young queen mother visits the queen regent and learns from her the duties of the position, while selected men instruct the youth in his share of government.

The village grows in size as devoted citizens come to live near their king, and barracks for age classes are established. But the village is not yet the completed capital—the *lusasa* must develop into the *sigodlo* (heart, harem). The *Umntfwana* may not yet take the lead in national affairs, nor may his orders be accompanied with the words *Ngemandla* ('With Power').

The transition from the embryo to the full capital takes place when the *Umntfwana* is considered of an age ripe to marry his first recognized

---

[1] According to some informants, the *umstangala* itself becomes the *ligangadu* but Sobhuza insists that a new kraal is built as the *ligangadu*.

wife. Until that time he has been permitted lovers, known as *emaphovela* and not yet *emakhosikati* (queens),[1] but they may not live at his village. When however the *Umntfwana* passes through a ceremony of social maturity known as the *siβimbi sokutfunga*, he marries two queens selected by national councillors, and the *lusasa* gives place to the *sigodlo*. (See diagram, Appendix III.) The *sigodlo* is built by regiments of all the nation. In the entrance is the ritual hut, the *sigodlo* proper, where he celebrates his first recognized marriage. The *Umntfwana* becomes the *Ingwenyama*, and the *Naβomntfwana* becomes the *Indlovukati*. She purchases the secrets of the position from the retiring queen regent. The transaction is described as *ukuloβola umango* (to *loβola* the world).

A new reign is inaugurated on the pattern of the past. The new capital is modelled on traditional lines. Thus Loβamba resembles, albeit on a smaller scale, capitals of kings from the reign of Ngwane. Even the old sites are perpetuated, and Loβamba stands on the site of the former royal village of Enkanini. Evergreen medicinal shrubs (*intseleti*) planted in the reign of Sobhuza's royal ancestor continue to grow in the courtyard of a woman who serves the present queen mother, and in the ritual hut itself are mats and other objects transferred from reign to reign.

Kingship grows with the stages of social development of the king even beyond his first marriage, and receives overt symbolization in the village. The poles of the king's first harem at the capital are built of a special tree, the *luβembetfu*; later on this is replaced by branches of the *intocwane* tree, and when the king builds his separate village or *lilawu*, the new harem which he establishes is surrounded by branches of the *incoto*.

Thus the royal villages reflect the growth of kingship, and no village will ever have associated with it the same ritual as the capital until a new king reaches maturity.

2.   *Childhood of the King*

I have so far given the background, or local setting, of the king's development. It remains to describe his socio-biological growth from birth onwards. The heir to the kingship may not be known until the ruling king is dead, and so his early training may be identical with that of all other sons of the king.

The birth of every royal babe is marked with special rites. The average woman bears her child in her own living hut, assisted by elderly women, more especially by the mother-in-law, senior co-wives (if any), and friendly neighbours. But a queen, when the pains begin, is moved from the harem to a hut in the citizens' quarters and is placed in the care of a woman of that hut. Neither the queen mother nor the first ritual wife of the king may be present; they are closely connected with the king and he must avoid the weakening and polluting influence of woman's blood.

While the news of a birth is always made public and ordinary work is taboo to all the inhabitants of the homestead, additional ceremony marks

---

[1] Lovers of commoners are spoken of as *tingani*; those of the king and of princes as *emaphovela*, and they are more closely bound than *tingani* to enter the harem of their lover.

PLATE I

(a) BUILDING THE SHRINE HUT AT THE CAPITAL: OLD WOMEN LAYING THE FIRST MAT (*Umcengo*)

(b) THE HUT, DECORATED WITH BRANCHES OF *Lugagane*, IN WHICH A WIFE OF THE KING GIVES BIRTH TO HER CHILD

PLATE II

(a) FIXING THE HEAD-RING: LUHOGO MANDZEBELE WAS VERY DEFT WITH HIS FINGERS AND ALSO HELD A HIGH POSITION AS COUNCILLOR

(b) QUEENS BINDING MEALIES: PART OF THE WORK AT HARVEST-TIME

the birth of a king's child. The main *indvuna* summons the royal regiments to gather branches of the *lugagane* (a species of acacia). With these the old men of the village surround the birth hut, and special protective medicines are put over the entrance. In the meantime the child is strengthened in smoke (*kuβunyisela*) from a fire in which are burnt parts of animals considered dangerous to the health of young children. Royalty has special ingredients known only to a limited number of medicine men attached for this purpose to the royal villages.

When the navel cord drops off (on the fourth or fifth day), the medicine man treats the child again with special decoctions of 'the *Malangene*' (Princes) to give it 'power', and he also doctors the mother, who is then permitted to suckle the babe for the first time. Incisions are made on her breasts and charred medicines are rubbed in. The severed navel cord, the observable link between mother and child, is carefully handled and disposed of; the navel remains a symbol of mother-child attachment, a vulnerable point, that strangers should not touch.[1] Queens are particularly careful of the navel cords of their children, 'because', they said to me, 'the king has more powerful enemies than ordinary men'.

Mother and child remain in seclusion for a period that is regulated by status, not by physical needs. Queens stay in the hut until the fourth full moon after the birth; wives of important princes until the third full moon; poor commoners for less than a week. 'Who would cook for them, draw their water, plant their fields, cut their wood?' The longer rest period is therefore possible for noble women because of their greater economic security; it also enables them to take ritual precautions throughout those first months when mother and child are considered particularly weak and susceptible to harm. People in mourning may not enter their hut; menstruating women must perform a minor rite before they do so; and people who have been on long journeys and are likely to carry *mkhondvo* (dangerous influence) must wait a day or two until they are 'cool' and harmless. When the mother goes outside to relieve herself, she covers her head with a blanket, bends her body and may not go into the huts. These precautions can only be taken while the woman is in the hut and does not have to carry on her normal economic and domestic tasks. The royal child receives regular treatment, including the usual daily enema, but everything associated with the babe is specially handled 'in the way of kings'; thus the stools are not thrown outside, but are put into cow dung kept in a special little clay pot.

On the day of the full moon of the fourth month, the queen returns to the harem and again there is special treatment for her and her child. She leaves behind her all the old clothes and utensils used in the birth hut, and they belong to the woman who tended her. The queen mother summons the royal medicine man, who cuts wooden pegs, known as

[1] The navel cord is usually sewn into the band that a woman wears round her waist, and it is kept there till it is completely shrivelled and dry, when the woman lets it blow away beyond the reach of enemies. To lose it before 'life' has gone from it is an evil omen, to be explained by diviners. For a stranger to touch the navel cord or the navel of the child merits severe rebuke: 'It will cause illness.' The link between child and parent is figuratively illustrated in the question, 'Where is your navel?' when inquiring about a Swazi's home and parentage.

ematinta, from trees (the *mbondvo* and *masweti*) believed to have the quality of giving vitality to those who touch them ritually. The pegs are neatly strung together, girded for a few minutes round the loins of the child, and then tied round the neck of the queen, who wears them for the years that she suckles the child. The *ematinta* are an ornament, an indication of status, and a protection against harm. The queen guards them with the greatest care and buries them only when the child is grown into an adult. To lose the *ematinta* is almost as bad an omen as losing the navel cord. Wives of princes of the second generation are also privileged to wear *ematinta*, but the medicines are different and less potent than those used for the children of the ruling king. In addition to the *ematinta*, the royal child is washed in foamy medicines 'to make it shine'. It is given an enema and special ablutions at the entrance of the mother's hut—on the right-hand side for a boy, on the left for a girl. The other queens crowd round to welcome and praise the new arrival. Then it is carried to the *indlunkulu* (great hut) and introduced to the 'chief woman of the homestead'. Sometimes she bestows on it a name, usually selecting the name of an illustrious relative.

That night the child is shown to the moon, and henceforth is no longer a 'thing', but a 'person'. 'Showing to the moon' is practised with variations by all clans; it is usually performed when the moon is waxing or, as by the Dlamini, when it is full. Underlying the rite is the belief that 'as the moon grows' or 'is grown' so the child 'will grow to fullness'.[1]

Until the child can walk, it spends much of its time firmly tied in a sling to its mother's back. For commoners the sling is made from goat-skin, but for the Dlamini the skin of the *umsumphe* (a buck) is used, and once a child is known to be the future king, he is carried in the skin of the silver monkey. This animal provides powerful medicine, for it is admired for its reputed longevity and virility. And whereas ordinary children are cared for by women and little girls, the child king is carried and tended by responsible men. Old Ntshweße Hlophe often described to me how he,

---

[1] Until the child is shown the moon it is described as *luswane*—a noun belonging to the class of miscellaneous objects. It must not be called by name nor sung to in words (it is lulled with the meaningless 's ... s ... s ... s ...' of comfort for someone not quite human), nor held by the father. After it has been shown the moon it is an *umntfwana*, i.e. it is placed in the personal class. The rite of showing the moon is a simple symbolism. Among the Dlamini, on the night of the third full moon after birth, the child is carried by a nurse girl to the cattle byre and the nurse points to the moon, saying: 'There is your friend. La la la.' She sits the child down, waits for it to cry, then runs and picks it up, carries it to the mother, who has re-entered the harem that day, and the mother suckles it.

Among the Maziya near Stegi the rite takes place when the moon is just visible. With the Mahlalela, the rite varies slightly for boy and girl children. A girl is shown the moon when it is still very new, and a boy when it is nearly full. The mother carries the child to an ash heap in the yard. An old woman accompanies her, carrying a lighted brand. The mother puts the child on the ash heap, squeezes a little milk from each breast on to the end of the brand and throws it towards the moon saying, 'There is your friend'. Then she runs away and the old woman picks up the child and carries it to the mother to feed. In all clans the mother marks the change in her status by cutting off the curls that grow in a fringe on her forehead (*kusinga*). The mother is only permitted to cohabit with her husband after she begins to menstruate again, but 'it is usually at the time the child becomes a person'.

and his brother Loshina before him, were chosen by the Queen Mother Gwamile to look after the young Sobhuza.

Royal children grow up with the children of commoners. They join together in work and play, but distinction obtains in rituals. When the same rite is performed for all, the royal children are specially protected. Thus at the rite of 'cutting of the ears', offspring of the king or of leading aristocrats are always preceded in the operation by a commoner's child. Every year at the ceremony of kingship the ruling king, princes, and princesses are doctored separately from commoners. If any mishap befalls either the homestead where they are staying or the nation they rule, they are treated by national *tinyanga* (medicine men).

The puberty of the king, bringing with it the potentialities of full manhood, is a national concern; kingship must be perpetuated through the male line. The puberty ritual for ordinary Swazi had almost entirely disappeared at the time when both an individual and a national ceremony were enacted for Sobhuza. The individual treatment for the boy king is given in private in the seclusion of his hut after the first nocturnal emission, but the national celebration of the event, described as his *siβimbi sokutfomba*, is held publicly with great pomp a few months later.[1] The medicine for the treatment is known only to a lineage of the Maβuzo clan living at Mafutseni. The head of the lineage, Madlinkomo, was fetched for Sobhuza's puberty. The specialist takes the boy king, accompanied by regiments, to a river. The regiments dig a huge stone from the damp earth while the specialist prepares his ingredients. The boy king sits on the stone and receives elaborate treatment. It includes the cutting off of his hair, the enacting in mime by the specialist of the rite of circumcision that had been performed in fact, until the reign of Mbandzeni, and the washing of the king in foamy medicines. A pitch black goat is killed, the head is cut off and the contents are removed. Into the empty space in the goat's head, the specialist puts the king's hair; he then places the goat's head in the hole from which the stone has been dug and rolls the stone back into its place. In olden times the king and a small number of selected followers would have been crowned after this ceremony with the waxen head ring which marked the age of marriage. But the regents for Sobhuza decided that, since he went to school, and new ways of living were entering the country, this should be omitted.

Some Swazi state that the custom of sewing on the head-ring was abandoned because a sinew from the back of a human being was required for this purpose, but other and more reliable informants insist that a sinew was never used for the king. They point out that all things connected with a dead body are taboo to him, and explain the misconception by the fact that after his installation the army is always sent on a military or hunting expedition described as *kulanza lusinga* (to fetch the sinew). But this was a metaphorical expression marking his development; not even the sinew of a captured animal could be used to sew on his head ring. The only sinew considered suitable was one taken from a beast of

[1] The ritual is reconstructed from detailed information given by Sobhuza, Ngolotsheni Motsa, Mandanda Mtsetfwa, and Ntshweße. I extract only the main items and use the present tense as the ritual is an essential basis of the king's position.

the sacred herd, the *mfukwane*. Among the Mahlalela clan, I was told that a human sinew was used for their chiefs, but that 'when the Dlamini overcame us, we gave up our chieftainship'.

After the rite at the stone, the boy king returns with added status to the capital and there is great feasting and dancing in his honour. This is known as the *siβimbi sokutfunga* (the ceremony for sewing on the head-ring), and coincides with his marriage to his first ritual wife. The *Umntfwana* (Child of the nation) is soon to become *Inkosi* (King), *Baβe* (Father), *Ingwenyama* (Lion).

His installation is public. Regiments from the whole country are summoned and gather in the cattle byre. The youth is placed in the centre of the men, and the regent announces, 'Here is your king'. For the first time he is greeted with the royal salute, '*Bayethe*'. Leading men give him advice and wish him prosperity.

He receives a few emblems—an assegai of which the handle is rehafted for each king, and the blade washed in gall (concentrated essence) of a black ox; a wooden staff that is believed to make the holder invisible, and a bracelet of copper. The insignia of a Swazi king are not conspicious: their power lies in their association with past kings.[1]

3. *Transference of the King's Blood*

The ritualization of the king has as one of its essential features the creation of blood ties between the king and certain of his subjects.[2]

The relationship is spoken of as *sihlanganiso* (union), from *kuhlanganisa* (to unite). Until Mswati's time the ritual was practised not only by the Dlamini king, but by heads of other leading clans such as the Mahlalela, Simelane, and Mngometfulu. With the development of the central Dlamini kingship, it seems to me that the blood pact of local chiefs lost importance, and it survives among them now only in attenuated forms. The actual operation is not practised, but special individuals are regarded as being in particularly close association with the chief.

The men with whom the king or chiefs form the relationship are called *tinsila*, from *insila*—a word that means filth, dirt of the body. *Insila* is an essential part of the self which, even when it has been removed by washing or scraping, remains intimately linked with the person, so that, on the principle of contagious magic, whoever obtains possession of the 'filth' can influence the owner. The king or the chief is not spoken of as *insila*; the partners are termed their *tinsila*.

The main features of the ceremony for the king, and it is with him that I deal specifically, were described to me by Sobhuza and the *insila*—Ngolotsheni Motsa. The details of the ritual are unknown to most other Swazi, since 'it is a thing of kingship' from which they are excluded.

---

[1] The position of clan chiefs of the higher ranks is similar in many respects, and the importance of their insignia also lies, not in the objects themselves, but in their association. In 1936 the chief of the Mahlalela was killed by a native policeman on the border. Before his subjects could claim the body it was buried in Portuguese territory. It was difficult to retrieve the body, or even to discover where it was buried. The Swazi were terribly distressed, because they required from it the bracelet of chieftainship, without which, they felt, they could not install his successor.

[2] See Chapter VIII, pp. 105.

When the king is nearing puberty, but still in the *lusasa*, the councillors send to well-known lineages of the Mdluli and Motsa clans to bring back from each a boy of roughly the same age as the heir apparent. 'It is necessary that their blood does not surpass his in strength'. The boys have in no way been prepared for their new rôles, and Ngolotsheni says that in his case it was a terrible shock to find that he had been selected for a post that was known to be onerous and dangerous. The parents of the boys are unable to refuse to give up their sons, and must, moreover, make a show of pleasure in obeying the royal command.

Knowledge of the ingredients that are used is confined to a senior lineage of the Shiбa clan living at the Nkomati river. The Shiba claim to have practised the ceremony for the Dlamini from the days at the first national home, Eshiselweni. The leading *inyanga* is the head of the lineage, but he is assisted, as is usual in national ritual, by other members of his family, who will teach his heir. The organization of the ritual is in the hands of governors (*tindvuna*) of the main royal village.

The ceremony takes place in private. The first operation is performed between the young king and the Mdluli. The *inyanga* makes tiny cuts (verb *kugata*) with a special knife on various parts of the body of the Mdluli. The incisions are made on the right side of the body—right wrist, right ribs, between the big and second toe of the right foot, and so on.[1] Similar cuts are made on the right side of the king. The *inyanga* takes a little blood from the Mdluli and rubs it into the cuts on the king's body, and then he rubs blood from the king into the Mdluli. Into the cuts he also rubs medicines that have been charred and powdered. A similar operation is performed on the left side with the Motsa and the king. The Mdluli is henceforth known as the 'right-hand *insila*' and the Motsa as the 'left-hand *insila*'. The principle in the procedure is that 'danger will first enter into the *tinsila*, danger that was directed against the king will go to them'.

During the operation no oath is taken, but the union is as real as if life had been pledged for 'the medicine and the blood work without words They are with power; they speak in the body.' The making of incisions and the rubbing of burnt and powdered medicines into the blood which oozes forth is very common in Swazi doctoring—the interchange of blood is, however, unusual[2]—and the blood is the most potent of part of the treatment. I was given the names of some of the ingredients on condition that I did not publish them. The names are condensed spells—descriptive of the power the ingredients are believed to contain and hence exert. The names of plants used in the pact between the king and his *tinsila* denote power, strength, and loyalty.

The bond is of so intimate and compulsive a character that it acts automatically. As a result, the king and the *tinsila* are closely identified and whatever happens to the one will, Swazi believe, affect the other. The *tinsila* go with the boy-king through the *siбimbi sokutfomba* (puberty

[1] Marwick writes that the *tinsila* 'are incised on the left arm in the case of the right-hand *insila* and on the right arm in the case of the left-hand *insila*' (p. 260). This is said by all my informants to be incorrect.

[2] It also takes place when widows are ritually handed over to kinsmen of the deceased husbands.

ceremony) and formerly they also had the head ring sewn on at the *siẞimbi sokutfunga* (ceremony for the sewing).

I have already mentioned that the nation provides the king with his first two queens. They are chosen from special clans, the Matseẞula and Motsa, and are known as his 'right-hand queen' and 'left-hand queen' respectively. Each is also described as his *sisulamsiti*, from *ukwesula*—to wipe away, *msiti*—darkness, charred medicines. They remove his boyhood darkness and immaturity, and give him the fullness of manhood; they cleanse him from the darkness of medicines and restore him to normal life.

The marriages of the first two queens, especially of the Matseẞula, are marked with unique ritual, and the bond created between the king and the Matseẞula is in some respects similar to that created with the *tinsila*. National councillors go to a well-known Matseẞula family and ask for 'a daughter for the country'. The parents agree, and before the girl leaves home cattle are sent from the rulers to mark the marriage. The girl must be a virgin, and it is essential that she comes willingly to the king. If she weeps or resists, it is considered a bad sign, and she is abandoned for another Matseẞula. While the bridal parties of other girls consist of female age-mates, sympathetic women, and affectionate 'brothers', the Matseẞula's wedding party is drawn from the regiments which took part in the *siẞimbi sokutfunga* of the king. Leading national councillors hold her by the arms and walk with her to the newly-built harem. The warriors sing a sacred song, the burial song of kings, the song of the annual ceremony of kingship and other major occasions. The warriors hold their spears in their hands; informants likened the ceremony to the moving of an *impi* in battle. Not for Matseẞula the ordinary songs and dances, the weeping and the wailing, the demonstration of reluctance by her family to part with a daughter. She walks slowly and must not weep: 'She is a man, an *inkosi* (ruler); and she should be proud in fulfilling her duty, however difficult.'

She enters the harem with the king and a ceremonial operation is performed in the ritual hut. National doctors make incisions on her right side and do the same to the king. Their blood is then mixed. The king spits potent medicine of fertility through the holes in the walls of the ritual hut, and performs additional ritual symbolic of his enhanced status and manhood. Henceforth the Matseẞula is regarded as part of himself, and he must treat her with respect, and never raise his voice in anger; he addresses her as 'Mother'.

A few weeks after his marriage to the Matseẞula queen, he marries a woman chosen from the Motsa. The ritual is more simple, and there is no transference of blood. But certain ritual is enacted which sets her apart from other wives. Once the Matseẞula and Motsa are in the harem, the lovers (some of whom already have children by the king) are brought in as well, but they are subordinate to the two nationally chosen women.

Soon after the king marries his ritual queens, the *tinsila* must also marry. Other men of the same age are not yet permitted that status, but the ritual obligations of the king and his *tinsila* override the usual restrictions imposed by age. The first wife of each *insila* is usually selected by the queen regent and council, and is married with cattle from the ranches of kingship. These women are settled at the capital, and should be there for important ceremonies. They have free access to the harem, and are under the care of the ritual queens.

The mystical bond between the king and his subjects does not end with the two *tinsila* and the two ritual wives. When the *tinsila* are married, councillors fetch two youngsters, one a Matseбula and the other an Nkambule, to act as junior *tinsila*. No ritual is performed for the juniors, and they are only permitted to undertake the more menial, albeit intimate, tasks connected with doctoring the king. Once an *insila* is married, it is *tila* (taboo) for him to carry anything on his head—a taboo that applies to a number of leading members of the nation for reasons of ritual and/or prestige. The junior *tinsila* fetch water in which to wash the king and assist the senior in various ways, but they are not initiated into the more esoteric duties. The Matseбula is the right-hand junior *insila*, and the Nkambule is the left-hand. They may touch the king's person, clothes, and even eat from his dish when he has finished. But a junior *insila* can never be promoted to the position of senior *insila*: 'he will not have the strength'; he has not gone through the experiences of puberty, marriage and so on with the king and has not absorbed his blood. When the Matseбula and Nkambule *tinsila* marry, two other youths, a Mdluli for the right hand and a Thwala for the left, are appointed in the same way as the Matseбula and the Nkambule. It is unusual for a king to outlive the marriages of more than three pairs of *tinsila*, especially since the junior *tinsila* are not given greater privileges than others of their age. The wives of junior *tinsila* may be married with cattle given by the ruler from the royal herd because of the services that the *tinsila* perform for the nation. The women may be given as attendants to the ritual queens; at present the Matseбula queen has as her special attendant the wife of the junior Nkambule *insila*.

Besides his bonds with the men and the two ritual queens, the king enters into additional protective bonds. The first ten queens in the harem, the senior queens, are spoken of as *emakhosikati 'enhlanga* (queens of the incision). They are specially doctored, but only in the case of the Matseбula is blood part of the treatment. The remaining eight, excluding the Motsa queen, who is in a special category, are inoculated with medicines only. The ten succeeding queens undergo no special treatment, but for the next ten there is again a rubbing of medicines into the bodies of the king and the women. 'It strengthens him.' For the fourth ten wives the rite is not performed, for the fifth ten it should be repeated. Thus the ritual is held for alternate ten queens. The queens themselves do not identify the treatment they receive with that of the first two ritual queens, but both Sobhuza and Ngolotsheni Motsa (left-hand *insila*) mentioned the similarity and thereby gave me a clue to a deeper understanding of the 'blood covenant'.

The death of a senior *insila* or of one of the ritual queens during the lifetime of the king is regarded as a direct attack on the king himself. It is a greater menace to the king than the death of a full brother or any other subject. So close is the identification that should an *insila* predecease the king, he is not recognized sociologically as dead. His widows may not weep for him publicly, nor don mourning robes; his kinsmen may not practise the usual mortuary rites; the burial is unostentatious, and every effort is made to divert any ill effects from the king rather than to give to the deceased a recognition of the important position he held during his lifetime. Shwapa Mdluli, Sobhuza's right-hand *insila*, died many years ago, but his widows will only weep for him when the king himself dies. A senior *insila* cannot be replaced, his position is dependent on his having 'shared life' with the king. He is sometimes described as his twin.

The death of the king puts the *tinsila* out of office. The left-hand *insila* goes with the Matseɓula queen to a special village known as *liɓadse* built for her far from the capital; the right-hand *insila* receives an area over which to rule. The area is named 'Emashoɓeni' from *emashoɓa* (tails of cattle) given as rewards for services. Some Swazi believe that in the past *tinsila* were killed on the death of the king, but my more reliable informants insist that men other than *tinsila* undertook this final pilgrimage.[1] *Tinsila* from the time of Mswati are known to have lived in the country after the death of the king.

The possession of the king's blood raises the status of the *tinsila* above that of other subjects. An *insila* is called '*Ɓaɓe*' (Father) by the people, including the princes, and is recognized as 'standing with the king' in national affairs. The right-hand *insila* is important in warfare, and is described as the 'fighting hand of the nation'. He helped doctor the king before the regiments left, and he accompanied them with special medicines. The left-hand *insila* is primarily important in the annual ceremony of kingship (the *Incwala*), and it is he who, at the death of the king, assists the doctors to handle the corpse and prepare it for burial. The *tinsila* should always be available for the ritual needs of the king, and one of their main duties is to wash the king in medicinal potions, a right-hand *insila* washing the right side, and a left-hand *insila* the left side. They go with him into his sacred enclosure in the cattle byre, and help prepare his medicines and his food.

The *tinsila* act as 'shields' of the king, warding off evil directed against him. The blood, believed to remain in psycho-physical contact with the person from whom it is drawn, enables the *tinsila* to 'feel' when harm threatens the king. Witchcraft directed against him is intercepted without conscious effort by the *tinsila*, and their own lives are endangered in his defence. Ngolotsheni Motsa is always ailing, and he attributes his ill health to his position, pointing out that he is never so ill as when near to Sobhuza. He is also subject to terrible nightmares, which he interprets as witchcraft directed against both Sobhuza and himself by men who are jealous of his power and contact with the king.

The two main ritual wives, Matseɓula and Motsa, are also regarded with special respect by the nation and take a leading part in public affairs. They are the 'mothers' of the people, the women who help the

---

[1] In this the Swazi differ from the Zulu, of whom Shooter writes: 'Of male attendants he [the king] has a sort of valet who appear to wear his cast-off clothes. When he is sick they are obliged to allow themselves to be wounded that a portion of their blood may be introduced into the king's circulation and a portion of his into theirs. They are usually killed at the king's death or escape to a tribe where they are unknown, as no one would willingly accept the *umsiva* of another' (Shooter, *The Kaffirs of Natal*, 1857, p. 117).

king develop from boyhood to manhood, and strengthen him at the annual ceremony of kingship. They are believed to be organically affected by all that happens to him.

The question arises: to what extent can the Swazi blood bond be regarded, as it has hitherto been, as an example of blood brotherhood? The term 'blood brotherhood' implies the creation of a kinship tie, the admission of a stranger into a group through relationship bestowed by blood.

Amongst the Swazi, the ritual transmission of the king's medicated blood brings the *tinsila* into a relationship that is both more intimate than and different in effect from that of full brothers. The *tinsila* alone are permitted to eat from the same dish as the king, wear his clothes, and touch his body. During the period in the *lusasa* few princes are allowed to enter his enclosure, but the *tinsila* are always close to him, and when he is most strongly doctored with national medicines the *tinsila* and special councillors are his sole companions. In boyhood, the king and *tinsila* may call each other *umnakitfu* (our brother), though more usually the king uses their personal names, and, especially in later life, they address him by his royal title. The *tinsila* may not marry into the king's immediate family because of the mystic bond of blood that is over and above the ordinary kinship tie; they are not permitted to marry even distant members of the royal clan. The king, moreover, must marry at least one woman—the Motsa queen—from the clan of the *tinsila*. It is doubtful whether the king would ever marry a full sister of an *insila*, but informants considered that this restriction was imposed more by 'character' and 'decency' than by any rigid prohibition.

The bond between the Swazi king and his *tinsila* must be considered in conjunction with the bond between the king and his ritual wives. The king is not included into the Mdluli or Motsa clans as one of their members, nor are the *tinsila* incorporated into the Dlamini clan. The *tinsila* are identified with the leader of the nation, which is a political and not a kinship unit. The clans that are selected are clans which have been associated with the Dlamini from the early period of national history. But they are not all of the same Embo Nguni stock as the Dlamini: the Motsa, Matseɓula, Nkambule, and Twala were probably originally Sotho. The blood bond between a man and his wives is obviously not analogous to the creation of a kinship tie, for that would be a breach of exogamy—a marriage with artificially created sisters while marriage with real sisters is prohibited.

The artificial blood bond is a ritual act. According to my interpretation, the bond with males protects the king from the danger sent him by possible rivals and enemies; the bond with women protects him from the dangers associated with the act of sex.

Here it is useful to give data from the adjoining Zulu.[1] If a Zulu head-

---

[1] The importance of this relationship has not been perceived by modern workers among the Zulu, probably because the ritual aspects of Zulu kingship have declined. I collected information, however, from Zulu in Johannesburg, and the relationship is briefly mentioned in *Zulu English Dictionary*, Rev. J. W. Colenso, 1905, 4th Ed., p. 553. I have discovered that the ritual exchange of blood among the Southern Bantu is more widely spread than has hitherto been recognized. The only type of exchange that has been recorded in any

man noticed that after cohabiting with one of his wives 'their blood did not agree'—that he felt exhausted and ill—he called a doctor who made incisions on the body of the man and the woman and mixed their blood together with medicines. This treatment could be performed with one wife or several wives. Apart from this, there was one wife known as the *sisulamsiti* or *umsizi*. It was her duty to cohabit with the husband when he had been treated with powerful medicines and he 'threw the darkness to her'. The Zulu *umsizi* is not the first wife or the main wife, but a wife with whom a man has intercourse for personal safety.

Among the Swazi the *sisulamsiti* is the first recognized wife in all important homesteads, but she is not the main wife—mother of the heir. In the king's harem the Matseɓula and Motsa are both *tisulamsiti*; in other words, the first wives of the king and the women to whom he throws the danger of medical treatment (the wipers-away of darkness) are the same people. Neither group can provide the queen mother.

It should now be clear that the Swazi blood transference is not blood brotherhood in the usual sense of the word. The 'blood' creates a mystic bond that is part of the power and personality of kings, and in former times was part of the power and personality of clan leaders. It is an enforced relationship. It does not cement ties already existing between friends.

Whereas in most primitive societies the covenant is open to all tribesmen, among the Swazi it is a prerogative of leading men, more particularly of the king. In other tribes there is a wide range from whom to choose the partner, whereas among the Swazi the choice is delimited by clan membership. Usually it is a voluntary pact, but among the Swazi it is a compulsory bond. Elsewhere an oath is essential, whereas among the Swazi no verbal pledge is taken. It is usually entered into between people of the same sex and status, whereas among the Swazi it is between people of different status and of opposite as well as of the same sex.

Despite these differences, reciprocal obligations are imposed by all the pacts and the varying nature of the obligations depends on the structure of the societies. Unequal obligations are imposed on the Swazi partners who are of different rank. The blood does not equalize the status. The Swazi 'union' is essentially a ritual that protects the king and helps to maintain the hierarchical society that he represents. This is further illustrated by the attenuation of the custom among clan heads. What was originally a widespread cultural element received special emphasis in the case of the king—just as other aspects of the kingship are accentuations of usages relating to clan heads generally.

Polygyny as Part of the Ritualization

The ritualization of Swazi kingship is directly linked with the custom of polygyny and the extension of the harem. The king is expected to have more wives than any of his subjects, not so much for economic as for social and political purposes. In other homesteads the wives are primarily the workers, and hence polygyny is connected directly with wealth.

detail is associated with the marriages of widows and widowers. I find that it also occurs between man and wife, and sometimes between men among Zulu, Venda, and some Tonga.

But the king obtains tribute service when required from any subjects, and his wives are not primarily workers. I have already indicated how polygyny unites various sections of the people, and the queens are of political value in binding the king to his subjects and extending the control of the royal family.

Sometimes the king marries a queen with a ritual which indicates that she will be the main wife. This he usually does when he reaches a ripe age. If he should not marry such a conspicuous queen, there are various difficulties, which are discussed in the following chapter.

National councillors are sent to 'beg' the main-wife-to-be from her people. No parents would refuse this honour, and a young virgin is selected. Such a marriage is usually politically motivated, and her parents are of noble rank, possibly of another tribe.

Whereas other wives of the king (except for the two ritual queens) are brought into the harem with little ceremony, the marriage of the great queen is executed with elaborate display. It resembles in its major items the marriages of other women who have been married specifically as main wives by important men. These marriages emphasize the group aspect of the contract, and may even be performed in the absence of the groom. The marriage of the main wife of the king differs fundamentally from his marriage to the Matseɓula, characterized by the mystic physical bond.

Despite its resemblances to the marriage of other potential main wives, the ceremony for the future queen mother is marked by the use of special ritual objects, including a spear handed down from generation to generation and specially bound. Moreover, instead of being smeared with red clay or ordinary cow dung, she is smeared with dung from the sacred herd, the *mfukwane*.

Though it is considered desirable for the king to marry a conspicuous main wife, such a marriage is not always contracted. It was last performed in the reign of Sobhuza's great-grandfather.

Whether the king marries a main wife or not, the queens are graded for all national purposes by seniority. Only after his death, and in the case of the ritual queens, is the principle of seniority obviously displaced by pedigree. The first ten queens are made conspicuous by special insignia, and take the lead at national festivals. They are not, however, as prominent as the queen mother, and there is little likelihood that the future queen mother will be chosen from among them.

4. *The Health of the King*

Once the king is selected he must be kept strong and virile because the prosperity of the nation is associated with his health. Every new year he is treated with medicines to 'renew' him, and he is always protected from contacts that might weaken him.

A Swazi king must avoid all contact with death.[1] He must neither see

---

[1] In 1940 there was great agitation because the car in which Sobhuza was travelling hit a man and killed him. Swazi kept on telling me what a terrible thing it was that the king should have been so close to the pollution of death. They mentioned as a side issue that the driver of the car, Sobhuza's chauffeur, was being charged with culpable homicide.

G

nor touch a corpse nor approach a grave. Until he has been purified, he may not travel over a road along which the corpse of an important person has been carried, nor may be come near kinsmen of the deceased. No one may die at a royal village, and as soon as any of the inhabitants fall dangerously ill they are removed to homesteads that he will not visit. He may not mourn a death for more than a few days, since mourning is a period of dangerous affiliation with the dead: 'When the king is in black-ness, the whole nation is without strength'. Every death is considered his loss, and he must be guarded against pollution on the death of important subjects. All Dlamini, through the kinship tie, share to some extent in the danger of contact with death and observe certain restrictions, but none of them are subject to such rigorous taboos as the king.

The mystic link, or participation, between the king, the nation, and the external world is shown in many situations. Thus throughout his life he may not drink water, lest, 'by connection with his personality', this bring lightning and destruction. The identification of the king with sun, moon, and vegetation is described fully in Chapter XIII, which deals with the annual ritual of kingship.

When the king dies, his corpse is treated with reverent care and unique ritual. Like all people, the Swazi vary their death ceremonies with the status of the deceased. Mortuary rites as an index of rank will be dis-cussed in a later chapter, but here it is necessary to outline significant items related to the handling of the body of the king. His death is kept secret until his heir is installed. Only the queen mother, governors of the royal village, tinsila, specialists in the death ritual, and a couple of intimate attendants know the truth. Day and night the body is guarded. People are told 'The king is ill' or 'The king is busy'. Swazi believe that if the king's death were known before his successor was appointed, the country would be 'light'—weak and vulnerable to an attack from enemies. Though the people may suspect that he is dead, they will not dare to speak, lest they be accused of 'wishing to kill the country'. Secretly, in the darkness of night, he is moved to the ritual hut in the harem where he celebrated his marriage with his first ritual queen.

For the king, and the king alone, a primitive method of embalming is practised. The specialist, the same Shiba who performed the blood pact between the king and his tinsila, 'squeezes the juices' from the body to prevent too rapid decay; and informants insist that as a result of this treatment the body does not putrefy. This practice is another indication of the symbolic value of the king who is not permitted to suffer the usual physical decomposition.[1] Over the body are rubbed medicines pleasant to the ancestral spirits, and round the body is wrapped the flexible hide of a pitch black ox. On the head, which is left exposed, the magicians place a covering of fatty membrane (umhlehlo) and over the forehead is stuck the inflated bladder of a black goat and a sprig of wild

[1] An interesting analogy is found in the treatment of the corpses of chiefs of some of the independent clans until they became subservient to the Dlamini. Chiefs of the Maseko and Simelane were not buried, but were burnt on flat stones near flowing water, and as the fire reached the head of the deceased chief, it is stated that a bird, the umnguphane, sacred to the clan, rose phoenix-like from the flames. As the Dlamini king became more and more powerful, the ritual of clan chiefs died out.

asparagus (*impunganhlola*). Diviners in their period of training use similar medicines to break down the barrier between this world and the world of the dead. The dead king's fists are closed over twigs of the powerful *masweti*, imbued with the sanctity of national rituals. The body, until burial, lies on a shelf cut from the same wood that supports the national shrine hut. Cattle are slaughtered and roasted 'to keep off the smell of death' and 'to rejoice the dead'. The ancestors must be placated and prepared to accept the newly dead, who becomes the most important link between the two worlds.

The corpse is buried when the heir is announced. Chiefs and subjects from the entire country are summoned, and on a night 'when the moon is black' (when no moon is visible) they carry the corpse on a bier of special wood to the royal caves. The mourners keen the song that marked his marriage to his Matse6ula queen. As dawn breaks, the men leave the cave. He has been settled among the dead with a live black goat and other personal articles for his comfort. Then the men of the nation return and fold their hands behind their backs and sling lion skins as cowls over their shoulders; women, especially those connected with the dead by blood or marriage, cut their hair and wear mourning robes. But mourning may not go on indefinitely: the new heir is alive, and through him the nation will again be strong.

In the following year a day of national mourning is fixed, and the warriors weep and cleanse themselves of the darkness. And in the winter of the third year the queens thrown off their mourning 'ropes'; the queen mother leaves the *umstangala*. When the mourning period is at an end, the nation must, moreover, be reinvigorated. A *lihlambo* is organized, and the men, wearing special clothing, partly military, partly mourning, rally behind their new king. The *lihlambo* is a ritual hunt, and formerly it might also be an attack on another tribe; the unity of the nation is thereby demonstrated and the spears are 'washed' and purified for the new king.

So strongly is the welfare of the people bound up with the life of the king that his death is considered to be a direct attack on the nation, and vengeance is essential. Until Mbandzeni's reign sorcerers were sought and ruthlessly exterminated.

Though the nation mourns its king, it knows that kingship will be continued. The old order does not change. The graded sections of the people receive treatment suitable to their status. The heir to the throne goes through the many ceremonies that his father went through before him. And on his death, the nation weeps anew.

CHAPTER VII

CHOICE OF THE HEIR

EVERY political system has some mechanism whereby officials are replaced and the duties they executed are continued. Peaceful succession according to clear-cut law is the usual method of substituting personnel and maintaining the political structure. Forceful usurpation, however, may be a normal legal form of succession, and the old equilibrium will continue under murderers of former rulers, while unsuccessful attempts will be considered treason punishable by death. The victorious usurper may not aim at revolutionizing the system of government; he may be actuated merely by personal ambition, and backed by supporters who desire only a change of personalities and not of policy.

Among the Swazi, succession to political offices as well as to family estates is regulated by definite laws that to some extent restrain, even if they do not altogether exclude, seizure by force. Sectional loyalties are not based on conflicting ideologies; rival claimants are always from the same social level, usually from the same family, and there is no conception of a political system that might oust the existing one. Swazi describe a conflict over succession as *umbango*—the word for tribal or civil warfare. Tribal warfare consolidates national unity; in civil war, the nation itself is temporarily divided, but different factions are united by their leaders till one victor is recognized by all. Once a dispute over succession is settled, one successor is finally recognized.

The man who succeeds to the political office is called *inkosana* (little chief), and he is also the *indlalifa* (heir: *dla*, eats; *lifa*, inheritance). He becomes the full representative of the family, principality or nation in all situations formerly controlled by his father. The group, afflicted by the loss of the veteran, reintegrates itself round the youth.

1. The Danger of Friction

Swazi laws of succession and inheritance, and the explanation given for these laws, demonstrate a conscious attempt to overcome the lines of fission that are likely to endanger the unity of the group concerned. Swazi criticize the Zulu because seizure by force characterized their line of succession. Swazi kings, in particular, claim their position by birth.

Since most Swazi high officials are polygynous, I discuss succession in polygynous families in greater detail than that in monogamous families. The more wives, the more complications, cannot be taken as the general rule, as laws defining status are fairly clear.

However, except under special circumstances, a successor to a polygynist is not known publicly during his father's lifetime. The Swazi, unlike some other Southern Bantu, do not automatically accept the first wife as the great or main wife. It is usually only after the death of the husband that a council chooses the heir by determining which of the wives of the deceased holds highest rank. In certain cases, one wife is married when the man is well on in years according to a ritual that leaves no doubt as to her superior status in his harem. Prominent men, chiefs, and especially the king, are expected to contract a marriage of this kind, in order, no doubt, that the identity of the heir may be unquestionable. At the same time, he will be too young to challenge his father's powers during the patriarch's lifetime. Even in these cases, however, the child is never publicly announced as successor, and open discussion is discouraged. The fiction of equality is studiously maintained until after the father's death, when the actual appointment is made.

Swazi give cogent reasons for this. The heir's position is coveted, and ambition for the power and wealth it brings often leads to strife—strife in the homestead between father and sons, between brothers, between co-wives, between women and their husbands; strife in the nation between related claimants, each supported by his own loyal followers. Strife is expressed in lawsuits, in acts or accusations of witchcraft, and formerly in armed attack. Although strife for succession often intensifies loyalties within each hostile faction, it weakens the larger unit. Swazi consider that when the heir is not known, the kinship group has greater solidarity: co-wives and their sons are more likely to remain on terms of equality and friendship, and the position of the father is more secure, since there is less likelihood of divided loyalties and a possible attempt to hasten his death. Swazi quote a number of cases in which young men, confident that they would be chosen as heirs, behaved aggressively and presumed on their future status. In a typical instance it was rumoured that the heir apparent doctored himself in his father's cattle byre, an act calculated to cause the death of his father. One day the boy killed a beast from the family herd and sent a portion to his father according to the law of *ukwetfula* (to give tribute). When the old man learned from which herd it had come, he sent it back and ordered the youth to leave the home. The son, although a favourite of the chief, was severely denounced on complaining to him of his father's harshness: 'Is your father still alive? What son complains that he does not rule during the health of his father? Go and beseech his pardon.'

On those rare occasions when there is little or no doubt, the future heir is usually sent away from home for safety and grows up 'hidden' by trusted relatives. These are usually the mother's people, who may benefit from his future honours, or the paternal aunt, whose cattle were used to *loßola* the heir's own mother and who has a recognized responsibility towards the child. During the lifetime of the average Swazi polygynist, therefore, it is rarely known for certain who will be his successor: nor are the possible candidates canvassed in public.

2.   *The Council Responsible for choosing the Heir*

After a man's death, a council of kinsmen (the *lusendvo*) chooses his successor. The responsibility for summoning the council rests on the mother and senior paternal uncle of the deceased. The patrilineal lineage is represented by all full brothers of the father of the deceased; the eldest son of each collateral generation; and, if the deceased is a lesser son, by the main heir to the father's estate. The father's full sisters and oldest daughter, and the oldest full sister of the deceased, are also allowed on this council. The mother of the dead man has a special position; in the case of the king's mother, she is said to 'stand for all the people'—a lone and powerful influence. Great friends of the deceased, or men who are particularly respected, may be referred to, but never form part of the actual kinship council.

The council is a fairly flexible unit. In the absence of full brothers or real mother, classificatory relatives are substituted. The size and structure of the council itself varies with the social position of the deceased. Only the immediate family is interested in the distribution of the property of an insignificant commoner; distant relatives are called to discuss a vacancy in a principality or to review candidates for the posts of royal specialists in the rituals of the nation; and the entire country is combed for leading princes to appoint the successor to kingship. Councillors of the main royal villages also sit on the council which selects the new king; their main duty is to see that 'blood does not become too heated', to advise, and indicate precedent, not to dictate a decision.

The widows and children (apart from the father's first-born son), maternal relatives (except for the mother), and 'cold people' (non-relatives other than officials, who are then included by legal fiction as kinsmen) are not admitted to the discussion, which often takes place in the great hut of the homestead. It is said that 'shame' or 'pain' prevents them from wishing to attend. Widows and children, because of their strong personal interest, should not be present when their merits and demerits are discussed, since it is undignified to 'push oneself forward', and humiliating to be rebuffed or passed over in one's presence. Maternal relatives have no say, because their property and positions go to their own male kin, so that they are deemed uninterested in the intimate affairs of other families, especially those of royal standing. There have been cases where the maternal kinsmen took an active part in pushing the claims of their 'own blood', but as a rule they recognize the legal authority of the paternal relatives in choosing the heir.

An important kinsman who is not summoned to the meeting of the council or even notified of the death, sees in the omission either a slur on his character—a hint that he was considered instrumental in the death —or an attempt by those who exclude him to circumvent the law and appoint their own favourite. It is in his power to take the matter to court, and the choice of the council may be altered. The influence of a woman member of the council is as great as that of any of the men, as was shown in the case of the late Chief Memezi:

His full sister arrived to mourn her brother's death and found that the council had already chosen Pufela as his heir. She claimed that the honour belonged to Joni, son of a woman of a preferential marriage (a woman of the clan name of Memezi's paternal grandmother), while the pedigree of Pufela's mother was, in her opinion, questionable. Though some people contended that Pufela's mother was bestowed on Memezi in marriage by the Zulu king himself, Memezi's sister was convinced that the girl was a 'nobody', given merely as an attendant, not as a wife, and that her wiles had won Memezi's affection. And why, demanded the sister, had Pufela run away when he heard that she had come and would support Joni's claim? And where, when the choice was made, was that other important member of the family council, the heir of

Memezi's oldest brother, the lineage head? Though he was in an asylum in Pretoria (the Union), no one had sought his advice. Perhaps, she hinted, it was they who had driven him mad in order to benefit by his absence. He had been away but a short while, and behold his insignificant juniors snatched his rights and even took his lovers as though he were dead. Some of his 'brothers' who had spoken so loudly and appointed Pufela had not even come to bury Memezi, their 'father'; and she, Memezi's sister, born from one womb, was not married in England that she could not have been fetched for the discussion. So she took Joni and his supporters to Sobhuza, who told the family council to reconsider their decision.

The king and his advisers, the final court in cases of disputed succession, do their utmost to guide the kinsmen to a decision rather than to make it for them. The court listens to the arguments of both sides, poses probing questions on the mode of marriage, pedigree of wives, wishes of the deceased and other legal points. Eventually the leading councillor sums up, indicating the relative merits and guiding the choice by innuendo. He often concludes: 'Return to your homes and appoint the heir; you, not we, select him.' The matter may remain undecided for years, the control in the meantime being vested in the 'mother' of the deceased and his closest 'brother'. The council rediscusses the evidence, the issues are debated in private, subtle propaganda is made; if the members still cannot reach an agreement and there is danger of violence, the king's court 'cuts the case'. The candidate against whom the decision is given and his supporters sometimes accept defeat with good grace, and continue to live in the principality. If they prove recalcitrant, they are moved to another area. There is only one heir, and if they are not prepared to accept him, they must not be near enough to harm him and cause disaffection.

3. The First Wife

The fundamental principle underlying the selection of an heir is that power is inherited from men, and acquired by them; but it is transmitted through women, whose rank, more than any other single factor, determines the choice of successor. 'Nkosi ngunina' ('a ruler [is ruler] by his mother').

In monogamous homesteads the wife and her eldest son automatically take charge when the headman dies. When a man has only two or three wives, all daughters of commoners, it is not unusual for the first to be recognized as the main wife. But it is very difficult to determine precedence in a large polygynous homestead, and for this reason candidates are 'strained' through a mesh of complicated laws and precedents.

The idiom of succession states that 'A first wife does not dispute the homestead', i.e. she is not a claimant for the position of main wife. Among people of high rank the first wife is more important in ritual. She is known as sisulamsiti (wiper-away of darkness), the woman who raises a man from immaturity to maturity, and with whom he cohabits at certain crises in his life. Her pedigree is unimportant, but she is specially honoured as the woman who gives her husband the power and privilege of full 'man-hood'. In the harem she is important because of seniority, and she co-operates with the 'mother' in the domestic arrangements, the distribu-tion of food, and the maintenance of order. But she does not bear the main heir.

In every polygynous homestead, except that of the king, the first wife is expected to bear her husband his first son. This boy receives the name of *Lisokancanti* (First Circumcised), a verbal survival from the time when circumcision—*kusoka*—was practised. Even if she bears a son after other wives, her son is still the *Lisokancanti*. Should she bear no sons, the headman usually gives her a boy from another wife 'to put in her womb', and that boy is considered First Circumcised.

We have already mentioned that the first two recognized wives of the king, the Matseβula and Motsa queens, are each known as a *sisulamsiti* (Chapter VI). But they do not bear either the First Circumcised or the Little Chief. On this point there is much secrecy, and I am unfortunately not permitted to publish certain information. The First Circumcised of the king is the son of a woman whom he made pregnant before he married the Matseβula or Motsa wives, but she is only subsequently brought into the harem.

A balance is established between seniority and pedigree in the harems of important men. The first wife is dominant during her husband's life-time, the main wife is dominant after his death. The position of the children is similarly regulated. First Circumcised is his father's confidant: he is told how the family property is distributed and who his father considers should be the heir, or Little Chief. Little Chief is subordinate until, after his father's death, he is publicly installed. First Circumcised, as a member of the council that chooses the heir, is partly responsible for the honour bestowed on him, and acts as his adviser. In return, it is incumbent on Little Chief, once he is established, to reward First Circumcised with cattle, and to treat him with great deference, requesting his presence at every important function and giving him a place of honour. The two men are considered to have complementary roles in lineage affairs, for First Circumcised is trained as impartial adviser, while Little Chief holds the threads of the executive power in his hands. This arrangement originated, I am told, from the fear that if the functions were combined and controlled by one and the same person, family interests might be subordinated to self-interest. In one case on my records, the rank of the first wife was indisputably higher than that of any subsequent wife. The dual rôle could not be avoided, and the First Circumcised-cum-Little Chief was nicknamed 'He who skinned both' It was necessary for him to act very cautiously in order to avoid rousing family criticism.

4. *The Main Wife*

When the family council selects the main wife, it pays special attention to the mode of marriage of the wives and the rank of their parents. These factors are interrelated, since the nobler the birth, the more elaborate as a rule is the marriage ritual. Two types of marriage, each with various subdivisions, receive special consideration. They can be classified as (a) arranged marriages; (b) preferential marriages.

(a) *Arranged marriages* are primarily the concern of the families of the future man and wife; the individuals are relatively unimportant and in extreme cases are not even consulted. Sometimes negotiations are started by the kinsmen of the girl, and less often by the kinsmen of the boy. In either case the girl has a special claim to the status of main wife. If the initiative is taken by the man or his family, they 'beg' the girl from her group with a special beast 'to open the mouth', and her position as Great Wife is almost definitely assured. Arranged marriages are known as *ukwenzisa* (to make marry), and when the man's group takes the lead the procedure is sometimes described as 'to beg' or 'to dip up' (as of water from a river). The ceremonies for arranged marriages vary slightly according to locality and clan, but in all cases the *ukwenzisa* bestows special privilages. In some instances the ceremony dramatizes a woman's position as future main wife, but in spite of that her son is not publicly spoken of as successor till her husband dies. The legal fiction of not knowing the identity of the heir is maintained as far as possible. *Ukwenzisa* matches are usually contracted for the children of aristocrats and less frequently for commoners.

The motives underlying arranged marriages are complex. They depend partly on the social standing of the two families, on economic considerations and on the character of the parents and children. All informants stress the point that parents like to choose partners for their children because they want them to be well looked after and secure. Parents consider their own judgements to be wiser, and marriage is a kinship affair, not an individual matter. Aristocrats, moreover, seek men of equal rank for their daughters, in order that the girls may retain a high social status, and they ask for more marriage cattle than do commoners as a mark of rank and wealth. The economic motive is most obvious in the case of poor commoners, who occasionally—even at the present time—betroth their girl children to men of substance in settlement of debts. Apart from socio-economic considerations, great friends may plight their children 'to strengthen friendship'. In former times, a warrior occasionally gave his daughter to a man who assisted him in battle. A man, anxious to win the king's favour, may send a daughter as wife. This technique was once favoured by chiefs and led to diplomatic unions. The custom of arranging marriages is steadily falling away under the pressure, legal and moral, of Government and missionary respectively. It remains most firmly entrenched among the conservative aristocrats.

Irrespective of motive, the family of the groom recognizes the marriage as an honour, and sends a beast known as *inkomo yokuɓonga* (beast to praise) to the parents of the girl. If she is very young, the boy's people often send a cow as *isondlo* (maintenance, from *kumondla*—to feed). Once the cattle are accepted by the girl's parents she is considered betrothed to the man, although not yet his wife. Betrothals are usually made by parents when the girl is still young, in the hope that she will grow accustomed to the position and be wise enough when mature to appreciate the benefits it bestows. Princesses are trained to realize that the only marriage befitting their rank is with men of national standing chosen by the royal family. Even if a princess falls deeply in love with a commoner, she is not permitted, as a rule, to marry him. Her marriage may not be arranged till she is fully grown-up, but her premarital experiences are not publicly discussed. Even if she becomes pregnant and bears a child, she is *loßola'd* as a virgin by a man who is considered of sufficiently high status to be chosen as her husband.

If a man marries more than one princess, the council grades them according to the status their respective mothers held in the harem. Sometimes the daughter of an important queen has a child of a lesser queen sent with her as *inhlanti* (subordinate co-wife); should the senior wife be barren, a son of the junior woman is 'put in the stomach' (*faka esiswini*) of the 'big mother', i.e. given to the senior woman as her child. Obviously marriages with more than one princess of equal standing are not 'arranged' for the same man, since this would lead to unnecessary friction over succession. As the number of chiefs, however, is limited, daughters of the king by different wives sometimes wed the same husband. More frequently, daughters of a past king by the levirate and daughters of the reigning king are co-wives. On the death of their husband there is often difficulty in choosing the leading princess from among them, and the council discusses at great length the ritual of marriage, the rank of maternal relatives, the seniority of the women in the harem and the individual characters of the women.

The king and the princes do not allow a leading princess to be ignored in favour of another woman. On one occasion when this was attempted, a prince is reported to have said: 'Can a ruler eat from the floor while the dog eats from the dish?' But blood prerogatives are weakened with distance from the main spring of royalty. The more remote relatives of the king, women whose fathers could not trace direct descent from the ruling lineage, have been passed by; the claim of distant and diluted royal blood was overruled by other considerations.

The main wife of a king may be selected by the royal family council from the family of a leading chief, and married with the ritual mentioned in the preceding chapter. But if a king dies before he has taken a conspicuous main wife, the tests of parentage, mode of marriage and, finally, of character are applied. There are many legends of kings who possessed some extraordinary quality which marked them at the time of selection as the rightful heirs to kingship. One such legend is given at the end of the book (Appendix V). In these myths kings are kings 'by nature'. They weep tears of blood, or their spittle is lightning or they remain invulnerable though many enemies plot their death. Many Swazi are still convinced that the marriage of a woman destined to be the queen mother is heralded by a heavy fall of rain.

In former times some of the clans practised supernatural tests to select the main heir. Thus it was customary for candidates to the chieftainship of the Mnisi to dive into the pool Mantsholo, near Mbabane, each bearing a lighted brand. The youth whose flame was not extinguished by the water was regarded as heir. An alternative test was for each of the disputants to throw a goat into the pool, and the owner of the goat that lived was 'destined by the ancestors' to rule. The growth of the ritual and power of the central government of the Dlamini overshadowed the customs associated with clan chiefs, and, finally, unique local rituals for selecting main heirs dropped away. The more general principles of grading wives by their parentage and mode of marriage are now applied throughout the nation.

(b) *Preferential Marriages.* Arranged marriages sometimes coincide with preferential marriages—marriages between special classes of relatives.[1]

First comes the woman addressed as *gogo* (grandmother), a term extended to any woman with the clan name of a paternal or maternal grandfather or grandmother. Marriage is not permitted with all these classes of grandparent, nor are the 'grandparents' with whom marriage is allowed considered to be of equal social value. The 'grandparent' preferential marriage applies, moreover, only to men, for a woman is not encouraged to marry a man with the clan name of her grandparents. In addition, whereas exogamy prohibits a man from marrying a girl with the clan name of his father's father (i.e. his own clan name), marriage with a woman of his father's mother's clan gives the highest status to the woman; the woman 'wakens the home' (*vusa indlu yekake*) of the husband's maternal line, and reunites the alternate generations as can be seen in the following diagram:

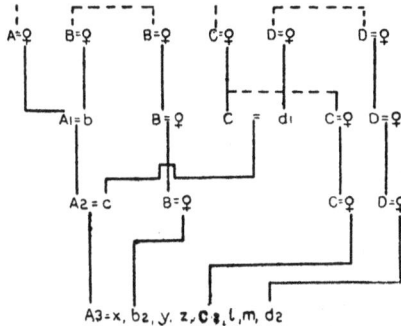

Key

−−−−·Clan connections ———DIRECT DESCENT

ALPHABETICAL LETTERS REPRESENT CLAN NAMES

CAPITAL LETTERS REPRESENT MALE MEMBERS eg A.

SMALL LETTERS and SYMBOL ♀ REPRESENT FEMALES

Order of preference of wives of A_3: b_2, d_2, c_2, x, y, z, l, m

A_2, son of the woman *b*, is made the father-in-law of the woman b_2 (his mother's relative) by the marriage of his son, A_3. Because kinship terms are extended to all the members of the mother's clan, A_2 still calls b_2 'mother', even though he is unable to link her with his real mother in a

[1] This preferential marriage is yet another social feature indicating the extent of Sotho influence among the Swazi. 'The Nguni . . . rigidly prohibit marriage or sexual relations of any kind with people related through any of the four grandparents' (p. 74). 'The Sotho tribes all allow certain types of kin to marry' (p. 86). A. W. Hoernlé, in *The Bantu-speaking Tribes of South Africa*. edited I. Schapera. Routledge, 1937.

genealogical relationship. The cattle that left A's lineage for the woman *b*, made A2 legitimate. The transference of these cattle creates a bond with the B lineage to legitimize A1's own grandchild. It is not necessary to trace further repercussions of the preferential grandmother–grandson marriage here.

Marriage with a woman bearing the clan name of either maternal grandparent is approved. A3 is encouraged to marry a woman of the *siβongo* C (i.e. of his maternal grandfather), including his mother's classificatory brother's daughter (i.e. his maternal cross-cousin). Marriage with the daughter of a full maternal uncle is discouraged on the grounds that it verges on incest. The man A3 calls the woman of the *siβongo* C 'mother', and she, if his own mother is dead, is said to 'waken the hut of the mother', i.e. the bride of the maternal line is put into the great hut of the man's homestead and exercises special rights associated with the mother in the economic and domestic life of her son. Swazi also approve of a man marrying a girl with the *siβongo* of the maternal grandmother, D, thus 'wakening the huts of the mother's kin'.

The social and economic benefits derived from a marriage of A1 and *b*, of C and *d1*, entitle A3, as the meeting point of the four lineages, A, B, C, and D, to obtain his main wife from B or D, the groups to whom cattle were initially given by A and C. The men of B and D have no reciprocal claim to the sisters of A3, though, if they should marry, everyone rejoices that 'the cattle returned home'.

These preferential marriages are summed up in the idiom, 'The seed is begged from kinsmen' (*inhlanyelo iyacelwa esinini*).

Preferential marriages are usually undertaken to honour one or other parent and incidentally to keep the marriage cattle in circulation in the kinship group. Since no Swazi desires to create unnecessary conflict, few of them marry both a paternal and maternal *gogo*. Where however this happens, the paternal *gogo* usually receives preference, though, if the mother is alive, she sometimes attempts to persuade the council to favour her own mother's clanswoman.[1] Marriage with a paternal cross-cousin is allowed, but does not bring any benefits, and it is sometimes discouraged, because a man's sister is a suitable co-wife for the husband of the paternal aunt. This is because the brother benefits from the sister's marriage cattle, and therefore, especially if the sister is childless, he is expected to give her one of his daughters as junior wife (see Appendix VI).

As a result of these preferential marriages, relatives by marriage are not strictly marked off from relatives by blood, and power circulates among already related kinship groups.

5. *Women of Little Importance*

A girl who *utiganela* (makes love for herself) and chooses her own husband stands little chance of selection as main wife in homesteads where there is a wife whose marriage has been arranged by family elders or who belongs to a 'preferred' category. The lover relationship, known as *kugana*, is public. The girl goes together with a group of her girl

---

[1] The outstanding case of this was the way in which the Queen Mother Gwamile influenced the choice of main wife in the homesteads of her sons.

friends, all dressed in special raiment, to the barracks of the boy, where a spokeswoman announces in loud and boasting fashion that So-and-So has selected a particular suitor. The boy, even if he is at home, does not reply, but one of his friends accepts for him, and lauds him as a man of virtue and good family. The girls return, singing and showing-off. About a month later the girl is summoned to her lover, and the premarital relationship of *ukujuma* begins. At the present time, the *gana* is not often inaugurated with full ceremony, but once a girl accepts the overtures of a boy, she does not hesitate to claim him as her lover and enter into an open alliance.

Where the attachment ripens into a desire for marriage, the girl informs her parents that she is 'grown up'. They question her on the boy's position as if they knew nothing of the existing relationship: the fact that they accepted the youth as their daughter's lover does not imply that they will welcome him as a son-in-law. Mothers in particular sympathize with their daughters having lovers of their own age, but are often as insistent as their husbands that girls should take in marriage men who are old, responsible, and well able to provide for them. If the girl's choice is accepted, her parents arrange the necessary preliminaries, and send her forth with recognized tokens of consent.

Sometimes the girl's parents are not prepared to give their consent, and she 'forces through', 'steals herself', and flees to the man's home. His people, always pleased to receive another worker and bearer of children, may rush through the ceremonies by which her acceptance by their group is shown; they smear her with the red clay (*liβovu*) of wifehood and have her dance in the cattle byre to bid farewell to her own people. In addition, they may send cattle to her own people in the hope that this will thaw their opposition. If they accept the cattle and slaughter the *lugege*, a beast essential to validate a marriage, the girl is recognized as a full wife. Her status, however, is low, and, except in a monogamous homestead, she will not, as a rule, be chosen as the mother of the heir. If her people refuse the cattle, the marriage is endangered, and the man's group can be sued in court for 'smearing the girl with red'. Moreover, her father is entitled to marry her to someone else. Her past is never forgotten; her waywardness is condemned, since 'such women break up homes'.

6. *Loβola*

Swazi pay special attention to the question of *loβola* when determining the status of women in the harem. The council inquires into the source from which the cattle were provided and the number given or promised.

It is the duty of the father or his heir to *loβola* the first wife of a son, and if possible to assist the boy to obtain additional wives. If the father is dead, and the man is himself the main heir, he must not *loβola* his wives, more particularly his first wife or main wife, without the consent of the family council that negotiates for him. A man distributes his cattle among the huts of his wives, keeping the greater portion in the hut of his 'mother', and it is from this main stock that he takes cattle for independent wives. The cattle for a main wife are never drawn from the herd allotted to a subordinate wife. Cattle for a main wife of a chief are usually contributed by the headmen in his principality. Among the Swazi round Namahasha she is *loβola'd* with cattle obtained on the marriage of the chief's full sister, and if he has no full sister a classificatory sister is adopted for this purpose. Cattle for the queen mother come from leading men in the nation, and if the queen mother is chosen after her husband's death, these cattle are given retrospectively.

The factor of number is important, since it is generally accepted that the more important a woman the higher her *loβola* value. For the Queen Mother Lomawa, 150 cattle were sent to her brother at Esikoteni, her home; for Tonga Tonga, full sister of King Bunu, 100 cattle were given. For less important princesses, 15–20 cattle are the rule; the average commoner's daughter commands 'ten plus two' cattle. The ten are known as the *emabeka*, and the two have special names—the *lugege* and *msulamnyembeti*. If a man has not the ten, he must still provide the two animals, which in fact seal a marriage. The *lugege* (from *kugega*—to make a deviation) is slaughtered by a representative of the girl's parents and divided into equal portions between the two groups to show that they accept the marriage. The *msulamnyembeti* (the wiper-away of tears) or *inhlanga* (reed—used by a mother to give a child an enema) is given to the mother of the girl as a recognition of all that she has suffered in bringing up her daughter. The *msulamnyembeti* is not killed. Once the *lugege* and *msulamnyembeti* are accepted, a claim can still be made for additional cattle, but nothing can dissolve the marriage except a special ritual known as *kuβukula sisu* (to break the stomach).

In cases where the marriage is approved by both families, late payment of cattle is relatively unimportant, but when there is antagonism, suspicion, perhaps even a rival suitor, the cattle are the *pièce de résistance*, and are emphasized in the law courts as indisputable evidence of marriage. The essentials of Swazi marriage can therefore be regarded as (1) the consent of the parents or guardians of the young people; (2) the killing of the *lugege*.

The general consensus of opinion is that a clever and self-respecting woman will not remain long with a man who has given no cattle for her. She herself does not ask for them, but her father or guardian demands them, taking the girl back to her own home and holding her as hostage if the animals are not forthcoming. Some devoted women have returned to their men despite protests, threats, and even beatings. In the early days '*loβola* did not end'—a few cattle were paid after marriage, and demands continued throughout the marriage. Even at the present time, the parents of the girl, to reinforce their demands, sometimes take her home after she has borne a child and thereby induce the husband to give a beast to fetch her back. A woman who leaves her home against her parents' wishes and is not *loβola'd* is taunted in moments of anger and jealousy as being 'a wife of no importance'. However, her status will be redeemed whenever cattle are given, and it is a recognized custom for sons to '*loβola* their mothers' even though the mothers are dead by the time the sons possess cattle.

7. *Death of a Main Wife*

The death of a woman does not affect the rights of her children to succeed to the position of their father. When a Swazi is asked how many wives he has, he gives the total number he married, qualifying the reply with the number of wives who are still alive and the number of those who are dead. The status of the wives during lifetime is continued after death by their children.

Swazi law provides for the contingency of a real mother dying during the lifetime of her son. The most suitable mother substitute is usually an *inhlanti* (subordinate co-wife). Swazi marriage ritual provides, subject to certain conditions, for a wife receiving as *inhlanti* a younger member of her family. Whether this potential claim be effective or not depends on the attitude of the wife's parents to the number of *loβola* cattle. If they consider the number adequate, the most suitable *inhlanti* is a younger sister of the bride by the same mother and father. If no full sister is available, a half-sister by the same father is sought. But no man would force his wife to send her daughter as *inhlanti* to a half-sister without the consent of all the women affected, lest any mischance befall either of the wives and he be held responsible.

When there is no full sister, a full brother is sometimes pointed out at the marriage of his sister, even if he himself be as yet unmarried, as the potential father of a girl child suitable as *inhlanti*. This claim operates because the brother will benefit by the marriage cattle of his sister, who therefore has a right over the offspring of the marriage she has made possible.

The king has a recognized right to any of his *βalamu* (sisters-in-law). This right is exercised within what Swazi consider reasonable limits. He is not permitted to tamper with any *βalamu* who are already married. His anger, however, is considered legitimate if anyone interferes with the younger unmarried full sisters of his queens—classificatory sisters have greater freedom. Most senior queens with no full sisters in the harem have either half-sisters (by the same father) or clan sisters (of the same clan name) attached to them as subordinate co-wives.

The necessity for a mother substitute if the queen mother dies before the king is specially provided for. In other homesteads, if the mother dies, a classificatory mother—usually a junior co-wife—is put in her place; and if the son is full-grown it is possible to raise a wife to the status of 'mother'. Not so with the rulers: the dual monarchy must be divided between two people of different generations who stand to each other in the mother-son relationship. Once a queen is installed as queen mother, one of her full sisters is usually incorporated into the harem of the late king, even after his death, and is spoken of as the 'Little *Indlovukati*'. Again, if there is no full sister, the family provides a half-sister. She helps to run the royal homestead, but is excluded from the secret rites unless the older sister dies, in which case she is the most likely substitute.

Swazi consider that the relationship between a king and his mother is likely to be strained if she is his classificatory and not his full mother, and the danger of friction is further aggravated if she also has a son of her own. Thus the late Lomawa's sister, Nukwase, was still a child when Bunu died, but she was brought into his harem and bore two sons and two daughters in his name by his brother Malunge, the Regent. When Lomawa died, Nukwase, who for many years had assisted her, was appointed to rule in her stead with Lomawa's own son Sobhuza. Before the final decision was reached there was a lengthy palaver, since some people feared she might favour one of her own beloved sons more than the rightful king.

8. *Failure of the Main Issue*

Provision must also be made against failure of male issue to the main wife. If she is barren or bears only daughters or if her son dies before he reaches manhood, the son of a co-wife is 'put in her stomach' (*faka esiswini*).

Owing to antagonism between co-wives, and the affection of a son for his own mother, the council chooses if possible the son of a co-wife whose subordination is recognized or a child whose own mother is dead. In addition to subordinate co-wives who are relatives, important women sometimes have as *tinhlanti* unrelated women. For example, princesses and daughters of local chiefs are accompanied on their marriage by young girls, usually of plebeian descent, who act as handmaidens and, if their mistresses agree and the husband wishes, as subordinate wives. The right to grant these girls in marriage is controlled by the aristocratic women, who also receive any cattle given for the marriage. Since polygyny is the ideal, it is usual for the husband to take the girls as wives and they are almost automatically attached to their mistresses' huts as *tinhlanti*. The king and his mother may give a young unrelated queen to one of the established 'big queens' as *inhlanti*.

When the main widow has no sons, but is still young, the 'blood' rights of her husband are protected. Swazi say the heir must be the son of his own father. Only in the absence of a physiological son can a boy by the levirate be made main heir, but even in this circumstance Swazi sometimes prefer to appoint a boy in whom the blood of the male line is most pure. Thus Prince L—— died without male issue. His main wife bore a son by the levirate, but the royal council is not sure whether to appoint him, since it appears that when L—— was still 'a child' he impregnated a girl. He did not marry her, but she bore a son who has practically grown up in Johannesburg. He may be fetched back to Swaziland and 'put in the womb' of the main wife. Other members of the kingship council suggest that one of Sobhuza's own sons by a junior wife be given to the main woman to perpetuate her husband's line, since he was so important a member of the royal family. L—— died more than ten years ago, but no decision has yet been reached. Another illuminating case occurred in the immediate royal family on the death of the heir-apparent, Ludvonga, when the council chose the motherless Mbandzeni as heir. Mbandzeni's regiments executed Ludvonga's mother, with whom the nation hoped he would rule harmoniously, because he found her plotting against him. Mbandzeni-in-council appointed a woman of the clan of his own dead mother to rule in stead. The dramatic case of Princess Sencaɓaphi is described in Appendix VI.

If the main heir dies before he is married, but after he has already taken a recognized lover, his family seek to perpetuate his line through her. If she is willing, she is married with cattle from the herd of the deceased and is 'entered by' (cohabits with) one of his brothers, either real or classificatory. The children they produce are held to be the legal offspring of the deceased, and the first son of such a union is usually accepted as the main heir.

The position with regard to people of high rank is less clear. The issue arose in the case of Ludvonga, the boy king who died before he reached maturity. His people had fetched for him in marriage the daughter of the distant chief, Langalibalele, who was a maternal relative. When Mbandzeni was 'put in the stomach' of Ludvonga's mother, wise councillors warned him not to become intimate with the girl, lest he be regarded merely as regent continuing the line of Ludvonga through the levirate. Mbandzeni ignored the warning and the girl bore a son. The queen mother supported the claims of this child because the mother was related to her, but one section of the councillors opposed the claims on the grounds that the father of a king must be a king and not a prince or even a regent, and that the physiological mother of a king must be the wife of a king and not his brother's betrothed. The issue remained unsolved, however, for the child died in mysterious circumstances.[1]

9. *Guardianship and Regency*

The heir to a polygynous homestead is frequently a minor. This is no coincidence, but the inevitable result of the fact that (a) a man usually marries the woman who will be appointed his main wife only when he is well on in years, and (b) Swazi insist that '*Inkosi inonopa kufa*' (a chief dies young). He does not live long enough for his heir to dispute the position. Jealousy and witchcraft are directed against political leaders. Guardianship is consequently recognized as part of the machinery of succession; in the case of the king, a period of regency is essential even if only for the years during which the new rulers are segregated in the mourning village and embryo capital (see Chapter VI, 1).

In all but the ruling family the guardian (*umpatseli*) is the oldest full brother of the deceased and, failing a full brother, a classificatory brother appointed by the council. Only in very exceptional cases is the guardian the oldest classificatory brother of the heir, while under no circumstances is a stranger appointed.

The choice of a full brother awakens ambivalent reactions. Some Swazi state that the full brother will rarely steal the possessions of his 'own blood's child', and will protect him against rivals. On the other hand there is recognized the danger that a full brother, because he too is the offspring of the main wife, will be ambitious for his own promotion. The antagonism may not be publicly articulated, even if it is strong, since to show it is 'outside the law'. Two cases of conflict were brought to my notice: in one, the older man had tried by medicines to secure his position, and in the other he refused to hand over control of ritual knowledge though

[1] This example appears to contradict the principle that important men marry their main wives late in life and that the heir is not known till the father is dead. Swazi explained that the *fiction* would have been maintained.

H

the heir was mature. But in most cases there seems to be no trouble, especially if the older man receives due deference from the youth.

Principles different from those that govern guardianship in ordinary families were evolved for the heir apparent. Because of the decree that 'A king is not followed by blood brothers', a regent is normally a classificatory brother and not a full brother of the deceased. The danger of usurpation is thereby decreased, and the mother is not tempted to supplant an older by a younger son—in theory and frequently in practice, the youngest son is a mother's favourite. Swazi prefer a woman married as queen mother to bear daughters before a son, for if a son were followed by a girl, people would not be relieved of their anxiety until the end of the period of pregnancy. If it happens that another son is born, some informants said it would be best for one of them to die before the position of kingship fell vacant. The limitation on the number of sons is only possible where the queen mother is known from the time of her marriage, otherwise, as is shown in the case of Gwamile, who had three sons, there is no safeguard. On the death of Bunu, his younger brother Malunge acted as regent.

A logical corollary of the above law is that the queen mother may have no sexual relations after the death of the king, and while all other queens —and widows of other men—are carefully allotted to relatives of the deceased to raise children in his name, the queen mother must remain chaste. There is the danger that a son born of such a union may threaten kingship. Ritual beliefs sanction the enforced abstinence: the queen mother is 'the earth' from which the king drew life, and were she to 'mix the blood of kingship' the forces of Nature would react.

Human emotions sometimes violate ritual dictates. Thus LaZidze was a young girl on the death of her royal husband, and his half-brother Ndwandwe, the regent, is said to have desired her. When her son died suddenly, senior councillors accused Ndwandwe of treason and he was executed. Then Nature itself reacted, and the rain would not fall.

An heir does not usually appear to resent the delay in obtaining full control. He realizes his inexperience and the value of the support of the guardian who remains a strong influence in the family council. In one instance, when Sobhuza asked a guardian how his ward was progressing and how big he was, the guardian replied: 'Oh Lion, he is still under the hearth.' A few weeks later a group of young men came to do tribute labour and the king, on asking the name of the leader, was informed that he was the ward. He commented that it was time the boy was installed; the boy himself had made no move to obtain power. Occasionally, however, the youth grows impatient and jealous of his guardian. Thus on the death of a certain chief, the first-born son of the deceased was appointed to hold the place of his young half-brother. The guardian was a trustworthy and responsible man, but the heir believed that he was gaining too much influence, and one night he fired the hut where he thought his guardian was sleeping. Fortunately, he was in another hut and escaped. The family council denounced the youth, and appointed another son as heir. The youth and his mother left the district. My informant commented: 'This might not have happened if the guardian had been a "father" of the boy.'

Thus, while guardianship is an integral link in succession, it is a source of danger and temporary instability. In some cases it works well and smoothly, and in others it leads to acts of violence. As usual, the final determinant is individual character.

10. *Character*

Inevitably in systems governed by the hereditary principle, character is a subordinate factor. But in certain cases 'good character'—defined primarily as kindness and generosity—may win for individuals who would otherwise remain insignificant the positions of main wife and heir. In two recent instances brothers and subjects of a chief supported a woman 'who shared with them the beer she brewed and the food she cooked, who never lacked in respect nor raised her voice in anger. The other women were arrogant and mean; they thought they were already raised to power.' The Queen Mother Gwamile was appointed primarily because of her exceptional personality. Her father was a minor chief, and she, moreover, was a child by the levirate. Occasionally an outstanding son has won for himself such affection that he is appointed with his own mother over a child whose mother is of nobler birth. But this is not put forward as a general principle by any family council.

When the choice lies between two candidates who are closely matched in all respects, character may be a decisive factor. But Swazi try to give to the one who is not selected some compensation in the form of wealth and power in order to prevent antagonism and trouble in the future. This man is known as 'one who nearly ruled' or 'one who ate the back of the neck' (a prized part of the meat of the beast). The heir, on the advice of the elders, allots him a few cattle in addition to those of his mother's hut, sends him meat when he slaughters a beast, invites him to drink when there is beer in his house, and relies on his co-operation in any enterprise. At the same time, he usually sees that the other does not become an effective rival with an independent following. An able man has his more wealthy and intelligent kinsmen as useful allies; one who is less diplomatic finds in them a powerful opposition.

Good character usually carries most weight when the legal position is not very clear; bad character, on the other hand, may cause a woman to lose the position to which she is entitled by pedigree or mode of marriage. Irrespective of her credentials, for example, she is disqualified if found guilty of murdering her husband by witchcraft or sorcery. She and her supporters invariably seek to reverse the judgement, but if the majority of the kinsmen remain dissatisfied, even the king will not force her selection upon them. Witchcraft directed outside the homestead, however, does not debar a candidate.

An adulteress is not excluded from appointment as a main wife, but if found guilty more than once she is suspected of having murderous designs on her husband, i.e. of being a potential sorcerer. The wives of two prominent chiefs, dismissed by their husbands for adultery, were recalled when the chieftainship fell vacant, and were installed with full honours. The more 'respectable' section of the people openly voiced their disapproval; others took the view that by discreet and productive adultery a woman 'hits birds for her husband'. Informants also referred to a chief significantly named 'Appeared-through-a-stranger'.

It is unlikely that a divorcée or widow who remarries will ever become a main wife. Such women are regarded with distinct disapproval, since marriage, particularly for a woman, is considered a permanent union which even the death of the husband should not dissolve. Women who leave their husbands or refuse on his death to accept one of his relatives rarely perform the ritual (known as 'to break the stomach') which makes remarriage possible. They enter into clandestine liaisons and the children they bear have little standing either in the homestead of the deceased or of the physiological father. 'To break the stomach' also meets with censure, and a divorcée or widow for whom cattle were given by a second husband is sometimes passed over in favour of a wife for whom no cattle were transferred. In such cases, fidelity, companionship, children, and length of marriage are more highly valued than the legal document of cattle.

Swazi laws of succession are primarily designed to counteract tendencies to fission created by rival personalities. Political allegiance is a personal bond and all aspects of government are identified with the personality of the rulers. Swazi realize that men are strongly motivated by ambition. Ambition leads, as countless instances have proved, to ruptures that begin in the family and homestead and then spread and threaten the stability of the nation. The higher the post, the stricter the laws of succession, although even so conflict is not always avoidable. The mechanism of hereditary succession is that best adapted to perpetuating the past. It ensures a smooth change-over in personnel and a continuity of function on the principle epitomized in 'The king is dead. Long live the king.' In a society in which tradition is all-important and in which the sanction of precedent assumes ritual expression in the ancestral cult, hereditary rights are a characteristic political feature.

CHAPTER VIII

BLOOD, KINSHIP AND LOCALITY

SWAZI believe that a king is born, not made. A man without 'the blood' cannot be king, and the magic of kingship would 'not agree with the blood' of a man of another tribe. A man who usurped the kingdom, but who was not of the royal clan, would put the entire nation in danger by 'killing the blood of kingship'. Defeat of another tribe and its consequent subservience is, conveniently, not equated with usurpation.

This dogma requires an investigation into Swazi beliefs concerning heredity, which is, of course, closely allied to kinship affiliation and its extension, the clan. The clan in turn must be examined as a political unit in the nation.

One of the first questions to consider is: to what extent is the western concept of consanguinity present in Swazi society?

1. *Blood and Kinship*

The nucleus of each homestead is the biological family, established by marriage, but dependent for its continuity on the concept of 'one blood'. Swazi say that a child is 'one blood with its father and its mother'.

Although the primary relationship in kinship can be expressed in terms of perpetuation through consanguinity, the blood tie is not an inevitable kinship relationship, nor does the same degree of consanguinity with different kinsmen receive the same social recognition. This is evident in that (1) among people with whom blood bonds can be traced, some are excluded from kinship relationship (e.g. a child who is born by a woman, during the period of marriage, to a man other than her husband, is treated like all her other children unless the husband breaks up the marriage); (2) the same degree of consanguinity is given different social emphasis (e.g. a mother's brother is put in a different category from a father's brother); and (3) certain people unrelated by blood are treated as, and are called, kinsmen (e.g. mother's co-wives are called 'mothers').

The blood group is extended, by the so-called classificatory kinship system, from the immediate biological family to maternal and paternal groups, the largest of which is the clan. The father's brothers (real and classificatory) are called 'fathers', the mother's sisters (real and classificatory) 'mothers', and their children 'brothers' and 'sisters'. The mother's brother is 'male mother' and the father's sister 'female father'. The classificatory system is not, however, an automatic, logical extension, according to generation and sex, of the initial relationship of the biological family. Other considerations, especially laws relating to marriage and inheritance, cut across it. For example, a classificatory mother's brother's child is an especially suitable wife for a man, though marriage is forbidden with a classificatory father's brother's daughter, who is described as being of 'one blood'. Again, marriage in the paternal clan is prohibited to commoners because of 'the blood'; on the other hand, marriage with a woman of the maternal clan is allowed, and as we have shown in Chapter VII, marriage with a woman of the paternal grandmother's clan is highly commended and brings her definite privileges.

Daily contact and custom rather than blood ties determine the kinship system, and actual blood kinship is only one type of kinship, not necessarily the most active.

All people with whom a genealogical tie, real or fictional, can be traced, are, however, described as being of 'one blood', and the relationship of 'one blood' is a strong social compulsive. 'No person can throw away his blood' is the Swazi equivalent of 'Blood is thicker than water'. A man cannot abandon a kinsman in trouble (i.e. 'refuse his blood') or 'the blood' will react, and the family ancestors, often the equivalent of our 'con-science', will trouble him. Blood is particularly sensitive to outside influ-ences and events, and people claim that they 'feel by the blood' or 'by the stomach', where blood is concentrated, if any mishap befalls a kinsman, no matter how far away. The physical bond between a man and his children does not impose the sociological pattern of paternal behaviour, but may conflict with it. Yet, though a man may be denied the right of social paternity over a child, the child is said to be impelled by the 'call of the blood' to seek him out in later life.

These views are particularly interesting, in view of the different schools of thought concerning the nature of the kinship tie and its relation to, or divorce from, the blood tie. Briefly, there are two schools of thought, one of which (Robertson Smith, Frazer, Levy Bruhl, etc.)[1] holds that kinship is based on community of blood, whereas the other (Evans-Pritchard, Westermarck, Crawley) maintains that this is a Western con-cept. 'The theory that primitive kinship is welded by a conception of the blood tie is, in its legal pedantry, unprimitive' (Crawley). In an article on 'Zande Blood Brotherhood',[2] Evans-Pritchard states: 'Azande speak of members of the same clan as having sprung from the same seed, but the filiation is not spoken of as one of blood. A Zande thinks of his clan rather in terms of sociological function than of physiological affinity.' 'To argue that kin are people with one blood', he remarks further, 'would be, as far as Zande society is concerned, a white man's interpretation of the facts based on his mode of thinking about kinship primarily in terms of blood relationship.'

The Swazi data appear, superficially, to support the second school of thought, but there are indications that the facts, as so often, are rather too complex to be accounted for exclusively by either theory. The use of the term 'one blood' to cover those with whom there is no physiological tie, and also to exclude some with whom there is, implies that the Swazi, like the Zande, think of kinship primarily in terms of sociological function; but, on the other hand, they express kinship relationship in terms of physiological identity, even though they do not base their particular behaviour patterns on the facts of physical relationship. Kinship obliga-tions depend chiefly on contiguity, on day-to-day relationships, but are fictionalized as blood ties.

The question is not merely academic, for on it turns not only the

[1] 'To be of the same blood is to possess the same vital principle, and in this sense all who are of like blood make but one single living being. It is in this that the clan relationship really consists.' Levy Bruhl, *Primitives and the Supernatural*, Allen and Unwin, 1936, p. 267.

[2] *Africa*, Vol. VI, No. 4, p. 397.

mechanism of kinship and hereditary succession and such phenomena as blood-brotherhood, but also many of the allied mystical or supra-secular values of kingship, and the principle of hereditary rank.

Before considering Swazi ideas concerning hereditary character traits and the superiority of certain clans, it is necessary to analyse some of their beliefs concerning blood.

2. *Blood and Social Situations*

The significance of blood depends entirely on its context. In ordinary situations it has no special significance; in ritual it acquires specific attributes. When an animal is slaughtered the blood is a favourite portion, a food like other foods, and is taboo to no one. The blood of a menstruating woman, however, is considered capable of destroying the fertility of cattle and the production of crops, and it may bring illness on men. During menstruation a woman may not walk through a herd, for, it is said, the cattle would grow thin, nor may she eat curdled milk lest the future milk yield be tinged with red; should she walk through a garden, the 'fruits in the earth'—monkey-nuts, sweet potatoes, ground beans—and 'those fruits with seeds embedded in pulp'—pumpkins and gourds—will wither, and this disaster can only be avoided by special ritual precautions. The illness her blood causes to men is named *lugolo*, and is described as a wasting illness that leads to coughing of blood. Menstrual blood is also considered part of the foetus that grows within the womb—its discharge is analogous to a miscarriage, though less terrifying and polluting—and menstruating women are subject to treatment and restrictions similar to, but not quite as stringent as, those imposed on women who miscarry. In both cases they must avoid all physical contact with the opposite sex, they may neither cook for men, nor touch their clothes, and the women themselves are in a state of danger as well as being a source of danger to others.

In certain situations, however, menstrual blood is not destructive, but is considered a life symbol or rather a life force: thus the recurrence of menstruation after a woman gives birth 'washes her' and enables her to cohabit again with her husband, and after a death in the family circle, a man should not cohabit with his wife until she has menstruated.

The Swazi reaction to loss of blood depends on circumstances. A man who cuts himself slightly when working might take little notice of the trickle of blood, and would not necessarily 'feel himself in danger', or think 'that it is his life that is slipping away',[1] but if someone whom he distrusts or dislikes takes even a drop of that blood, then indeed he feels himself lost. It is no longer just blood, but something that was part of himself, and that has now come into the control of an enemy. Thus when a man, who in a fight drew blood with his stick, wished to show that he did not want to kill his opponent, he left the blood-stained weapon behind to be doctored by the kin of the patient, 'for if he took the blood with him he could work sorcery on it and stop the wound from healing'. The spilling of royal blood is believed to bring danger to the whole nation, and in the past a Dlamini found guilty of a crime meriting death was

[1] Levy Bruhl, op. cit., p. 274.

clubbed or strangled, but never stabbed. Old Swazi insist that if human blood is spilt at the royal villages the country will be polluted. On the other hand, a diviner, both during and after training, should lose a great amount of blood, and nose-bleeding especially is regarded as a sign of ancestral goodwill, the spirits then being able to enter into the space left by the blood.

Many rites are directed to 'purify the blood' and 'make it shine' (i.e. to endow someone with an attractive personality), while unpopularity is attributed to the work of sorcerers who 'kill the blood'. Though blood, like bone and flesh and other parts of the body, is believed to contain the essence of life, neither it nor bone and flesh, etc., are necessarily treated as sacred.

Where, however, blood or its symbolic substitute is used in ceremonies, mystical properties are attributed to it. *Liβovu* (red ochre) is associated with blood and has 'great power', so that a young child, more especially if sickly, is often smeared with red ochre to 'strengthen' and fortify it, and a novice to the office of diviner has his or her head smeared with *liβovu* till fully qualified and powerful. A bride on arrival at her husband's home, on the main day of the marriage ceremonies, is smeared with red ochre, and while some informants say that this signifies the end of her virginity and others that it marks her incorporation into the kinship group of the husband, most agree that it is connected with 'blood'.

These few examples suffice to show that, so far as the Swazi are concerned, it is impossible to make a single cultural abstraction of the significance of blood: its significance depends entirely on varying social situations. Blood *per se* has no special mystic significance; and blood ties are ignored and kinship ties are artificially created.

The transfusion of blood from one person to another imposes sociological obligations distinct from those associated with kinship, as was described in the section on blood brotherhood in Chapter VI. As Crawley stated, blood 'is only one of the many vehicles by which contact influences relation'.[1]

3. *Heredity*

The next question that arises is the extent to which blood is associated with inherited characteristics in a society where rank by pedigree is emphasized. What specific innate qualifications, if any, are claimed by the aristocracy of birth? To answer this it is necessary to state briefly the Swazi theory of procreation, and the shaping of personal character by external influences.

Swazi know that a child is the result of intercourse between a man and a woman. They believe that in intercourse the semen (*isikhanuko*, from *kukhanuka*, 'to long for') of the male 'joins' with the fluid (also called *isikhanuko*) of the woman, and that this leads on certain occasions to conception. The fluids then enter the womb (*sisu*, the word for stomach) and join with the menstrual blood, growing from a *lihlwili* (clot of blood) to a person animated by the *umoya* (life spirit). Transmitted to the child are features of both male and female parent. Swazi are interested in the process of conception, but are not curious about it, and direct their efforts

---

[1] Crawley, *The Mystic Rose*, 2nd edition, Vol. 1, p. 258.

to protecting the child from harmful external influences by various taboos on the pregant woman.

Unlike those peoples who attribute physical characteristics to one parent and mental to another, or flesh and blood to one and bone to the other, the Swazi consider that both parents contribute to the make-up of the child. It may resemble either parent, or may bear physical likeness to a more distant relative, while in character it 'follows' one or both of its parents. If it 'follows' the father's side more than the mother's, people say his 'blood overpowered' (infinitive, *kwehlula*) hers, and if the mother's side is predominant, that her 'blood' overpowered his,[1] but in the same family the children are often 'mixed'.

On the question of inherited character traits, which is still vexing Western biologists, Swazi recognize that children need not necessarily inherit the virtues of either parent. A child may be inferior to both its parents and exhibit defects which neither possesses, or it may be superior to both. A child usually takes after one of its parents, but there is no guarantee that it will resemble the 'better'. Many a good, generous man has a corrupt and mean son, just as a patient, industrious woman may have quarrelsome, lazy children. On the whole, members of one family bear a stronger physical and mental resemblance to each other than to anyone else.

There is a clear recognition of innate differences between individuals: the superiority of some in intelligence and character, and, at the other end of the scale, the defective people, madmen and idiots, who 'were born not-people'. These individual characteristics are attributed partly to *intfalo* (nature), partly to upbringing and training, and partly to the action of supernatural agencies. The belief that external influences can affect 'nature' even from the time of conception is reflected in the food and behaviour taboos imposed on pregnant women and their husbands. The value of education and training is also insisted upon, and many characteristics of later life, such as meanness, disrespect, and pride, are partly accounted for by 'bad training'. It is consequently not enough to be born great, and the training of a king is especially important. Nevertheless, without the claim of heredity, a Swazi has very limited opportunity for acquiring any position of privilege.

That privilege is inherited and not dependent on any primitive eugenic considerations is clear. True there is a ruling stock, the Dlamini, but their distinction does not derive from any of those ideas of intrinsic 'racial' superiority, and consequent allegations of inferiority, with which we are so familiar to-day. The superiority of the Dlamini is based on conquest, and is perpetuated by accepted tradition and laws of hereditary succession. Pedigree and privilege interact mutually so that the desiderata of both are fused and, in the person of the king especially, attach to themselves countless other values, both secular and mystic. The 'blood' of a king, becomes, therefore, a widely connotative symbol.

[1] For similar beliefs among the Kxatla, see I. Schapera, *Married Life in an African Tribe*, Faber and Faber, 1940, p. 218.

4. *The Clan Hierarchy*

Clanship, the legal emphasis of one group of kin, operates on a non-physiological basis, but is expressed in terms of 'one blood'. The clan is the widest group with whom kinship is claimed. Every Swazi, male and female, retains throughout life the *siβongo* (clan name) of his or her father. A woman cannot transmit to her children her clan name and the legal filiation that it implies. Most clans are named after their first founder, e.g. Mamba, Mnisi, etc. The names of other clans refer to an episode in their history: for example, two brothers were in the veld when one killed a bird and ate it all, while the other hàd nothing; so they quarrelled and formed two groups, the Sifunza (*kufunza*, to gobble) and Masilela (*kusilela*, to lack).

In addition to the clan name, there is the extended praise name (*sinanatelo*, from *kwenana*, to borrow with the intention of returning). The *sinanatelo* refers to important episodes in clan history, national offices held by clan members, and unique characteristics such as the possession of special medicines. It is often a clue to the single origin of two clans now spatially separated. Thus we get the Maseko and Ndlovu, the Gweβu and Shaβalala, and many others, linked by references in the *sinanatelo*.

Fission was a characteristic of the clan in the days when it was the local political unit; it usually occurred through quarrels between brothers, or the wish of one group for independence or new lands. The following clan history illustrates the process of sub-division:

A woman of the Motsa clan, married to a Shaβalala man, bore two sons; the elder was named Maladla, the younger Mnisi. Mnisi was living with his mother's family at Mhlogavula (near Wakkerstroom). The Motsa worked the rain. The ritual was in the hands of the male head of the clan, and when he died his mother took over. She performed the rites in the hut where she slept with her grandchild, Mnisi. He was very astute and used to watch, pretending to be asleep. His mother's people suspected him, and one night, during the work, one of them took a burning log and put it between his big and second toe. He lay motionless, even when they asked if he did not feel his flesh burning. In the morning he simulated surprise and asked 'Who has burnt me?' and he wept. The flesh grew together, but by that time he knew the full ritual and he stole the medicines and fled. When the elder brother Maladla, who had succeeded his father as head of a Shaβalala lineage, came to beg his mother's people for rain, they told him what had happened. He went to Mnisi, who promised to make rain for him as it had been done at the Motsa homestead. This he did, whereupon the Motsa came and fought the brothers and they fled. After an exciting period of wandering, Mnisi arrived at the Mdzimba hills (Central Swaziland) and built the Umhlangwane kraal near the Mbuluzi. Maladla went to his mother's people on a visit and was killed. Mnisi became the founder of the Mnisi sub-clan, and grew in power. In the reign of his grandson, Kuwela, Sobhuza I arrived. Kuwela sent a beast with the humble words, 'Now I am your person', and he was allowed to remain in peace. His was a 'big' name in the country; the stories of his knowledge of medicine were told everywhere, and the king knew the praise: 'The Mnisi, the Rainmakers, one with the People of Motsa.' Henceforth every Mnisi must, as part of the clan ritual, burn himself or herself even slightly, or there would be death in the homestead. Mnisi and Motsa do not intermarry, though they live in areas far apart.

Subdivision or fission was part of the political growth of the nation. The sub-clan became autonomous, had its own land, and controlled its own wealth and fortune. Fission occurred in most clans, and more particularly in the ruling clan. The Nkosi Gininza, Nkosi Mamba, Nkosi Dvu, Nkosi Ngwenya, were all originally of the royal Nkosi Dlamini *siɓongo*, Gininza, Mamba, Ngwenya being the names of princes who were given local autonomy. Mamba received special privileges and the right to practise certain semi-royal rituals because of services he rendered to King Mswati.

As the nation consolidated, fission in the clan became less important politically. It is now continued in the royal clan only, and no longer for direct political purposes, but ostensibly to enable the king to marry women who are otherwise forbidden by the law of exogamy. Indirectly it serves to keep the real nobility a numerical minority and restricts the aristocracy to the closer relatives of the king. The king should not marry a clan sister more nearly related to him than through a common grandfather. Under no circumstances whatsoever could this girl be considered a candidate for the position of his main wife and the future queen mother. When the relationship between the king and the father of a clan sister he wishes to marry is remote—when 'kingship in his (the clansman's) blood is already weakened'—the title Nkosi is sometimes, and without any specific ritual, abandoned: the Mabuza, Ndlela, and Magutfulela were all originally Nkosi.

While in the royal clan fission extends the range of potential wives, in commoner clans sub-divisions are not permitted to intermarry. In the same way as no Motsa may marry a Mnisi, no Gweɓu may marry a Shaɓangu, no Matseɓula a Mkabele, etc.

The clans are graded into a rough hierarchy, and the rank of a clan is measured by its position in the national structure. The entire clan as such does not hold the position, but only certain lineages of the clan that are regarded as representative. The lineage (a unilateral line of kinsmen between whom genealogical relationship can be traced) extends among most commoners only four or five generations back, but among aristocrats sometimes as far as ten generations. In every large clan there are a number of parallel lineages, unable at the present time to trace exact genealogical connection, but linked up with the senior lineage at irregular points of the family tree. Not every member of a clan has an equal chance of being the 'fount' or 'spring' of a new lineage, since bachelors are naturally ruled out and unimportant men are forgotten.

At the apex of the hierarchy is the Dlamini clan, in which the lineage of the ruling king is pre-eminent. In each lineage members are roughly graded by their distance from the head, just as the lineages are graded by closeness to the senior branch. We have shown that the Dlamini closel related to the king hold important administrative and army posts; the same principle applies to direct descendants of founders of collateral lineages. The more remote Dlamini of all lineages are described as 'just of the *siɓongo*' and merge, for practical purposes, with the masses. They participate in and enact in attenuated form the Dlamini ritual, and enjoy a certain social prestige. The royal clan, though limited by periodic sub-division, is still the largest because of the extent to which polygyny is practised by the king and by princes. The king may *goma* (seize by force) any unmarried girl, and his officials have as one of their duties to bring him any maidens of exceptional beauty. Leading princes practise polygyny as one of their privileges, and usually have sufficient cattle to maintain a large harem.

Next in rank come the clans that have provided queen mothers, and which are described as *ematalenkosi* (*kutala*—to bear, *Nkosi*—a ruler). Until the reign of Bunu these clans were limited in number to once independent chiefs—the Mndzeɓele, Simelane, Nkambule, Ndwandwe, and others—but on Mbandzeni's death the nation chose as his main wife a woman of the Mdluli clan, daughter of a commoner. The innovation was due to the outstanding ability of this woman, and to the chaos that existed at the time through conflict with, and between, the Europeans. With each reign the number of *ematalenkosi* clans may increase, but there is a tendency to repeat marriages with a clan that has provided an outstanding queen mother. Thus LaNgolotsheni, Sobhuza's mother, was selected because she belonged to the Ndwandwe clan, the clan of the famous LaZidze. On the classificatory principle the king's maternal relatives are all those who bear the clan names of his father's numerous wives, since all are called his 'mothers', but only the clan name of his real mother, the woman who assumes political control with the young king, attains national status. Unilateral transmission of the privileges of name, property, and ritual through the paternal line does not exclude the maternal kin from playing an important role in social, economic, and political activities.

Third in rank are clans 'with their own kingship', each with an area ruled by a well-defined senior lineage, and possessing a ritual for its leader that makes it dangerous for him to come into close contact with the Dlamini head. The ritual and medicine of the heads of these senior lineages of non-Dlamini clans cause them to be considered a potential menace to the king, and they are excluded from the great annual ceremony performed by him for the nation, although they are obliged to send representatives and tribute to his court to demonstrate their loyalty. From these semi-independent clans a queen mother may be drawn and the clan thus be raised to the class of *ematalenkosi*. The Magagule, Mngometfulu, and Mahlalela are among the foremost of the clans 'with their own kingship'.

Slightly lower in the scale are clans that were once powerful, but have been reduced by the Dlamini conquerors, though still allowed to retain certain functions of national importance. The once independent Gweɓu, for example, are the national war doctors. Responsible national officials of clans associated with, but not necessarily conquered by, the Dlamini lend prestige to their clan names, and their offices give an opportunity for boasting and sometimes for special economic and social privileges to all members of their clan. The Zwane, Fakudze, Hlophe, and others are in this category.

Lowest in the hierarchy are clans with no local centre, no recognized national representative, no claim to national ritual, and no effective relationship with any powerful groups. Somewhat contemptuously labelled *emathonga* (aliens), they are excluded from the sacred acts in the annual national ceremony, although they are otherwise given the full status of nationals, and individuals through merit may receive positions of trust.

There is some connection between the rank of a clan and the period at which it was incorporated into the nation; association with the Dlamini from the period of Eshiselweni, the national home, is usually recognized as an advantage in the selection of officers and the granting of other privileges. Ranking on this basis is not inevitable, however, and groups (like the Ndwandwe and one group of Simelane) who were not incorporated until much later are considered politically, economically, and socially superior to groups of indigenous peoples who were incorporated at an earlier date. Originally there was discrimination on the basis of parent stock, the Nguni applying the term *Msuthu* with contempt, but intermarriages obliterated the evaluational distinction.

Clan customs are not used as a basis of grading; no special clan rules, taboos on food or behaviour, are considered superior or inferior to others. Special clan practices are followed at birth and death, and sometimes at puberty and marriage; in ordinary living, certain behaviour characterizes all those with the same clan name. It is accepted, for example, that the Simelane avoid a bird connected with the death ritual of their chiefs; the Dlamini abstain from eating the sheep, the Dvuɓa from eating the dove; infants of the Gamedze, Maɓasa and Lushaba clans are suckled on the first day, Maseko babes on the fourth, the Simelane, Dlamini, and others on the day that the navel cord drops off.

'Marrying-up' is a well-known practice among the Swazi. Though a person without rank or substance cannot aspire to the daughter of a prince or chief, a wealthy commoner is sometimes accepted as a son-in-law. If he has many wives and children 'his name grows', and his aristocratic wife, who is recognized as his main wife, gives standing to the family Nevertheless, he cannot change his clan name, nor can he ever become a prince.

An outstanding man may 'elevate the clan name' and his lesser clansmen will enjoy reflected glory. This becomes more noticeable if his position is passed on to his son. Thus Josiaha Vilakati, of fairly humble parentage, became, because of his education, secretary to the Queen Mother Gwamile and established the Vilakati as an important group in the country.

The clan hierarchy is therefore neither precise nor static. While some clans have risen in rank through diplomacy or loyalty, others have been degraded through conquest or the treachery of their representatives. Grading of clans is in no way analogous to the caste system. Clan exogamy is an essential part of the political structure; there is no monopoly of occupations; and a certain degree of social mobility is recognized amongst the élite.

5. *Kinship and Locality*

By Mbandzeni's reign the clan was subordinate in the political structure to the nation. The king was king by virtue of his position in the
conquering clan. From being a society in which a number of small clans
of relatively equal status were the political units, the nation had developed
its hierarchical structure of graded clans and lineages. The growth of the
nation, orientated towards rank and military conquest, had broken down
the territorial basis of the clan. At present many clans are without local
centres and only retain functions useful to the royal clan. Thus the
Matse6ula and Motsa provide officials for special rituals; from the
Hlophe are drawn tutors of the young princes; the Mndze6ele are
admitted to rain ritual, and so on. Clan myths have given way to national
sagas.

I counted twelve clans that have a local and political centre, whilst
scattered clans under officials chosen by the Dlamini ruler numbered
over forty.

Evidence of the original local basis of the clan is to be found in the
changing meaning of the word *sifunza*. It seems that in former times the
sifunza was a local unit occupied by a patrilineal clan or lineage. At
present the two factors, locality and kinship, can be separated. In reply
to the question, 'What is your *sifunza*?' Swazi usually give their *si6ongo*
(clan name) but when asked, 'Who is the chief of the *sifunza*?' some give
the name of their political chief, though his clan name is different from
their own, and others give the name of the man whom they consider the
direct heir of the founder of their clan, though he does not live in the
same locality. When litigants appear before a court of appeal, they are
asked; 'Are you one *sifunza*?' If they have the same clan name and also
the same political leader, they reply 'Yes'; otherwise they explain their
kinship and political allegiance, and a representative both of the kinship
and of the political group may be required.

A distinction is thus drawn between the *si6ongo*, which may be scattered
in a number of principalities, and the *sifunza* as a local unit.

The point can be clarified by an example. On asking Mbonyo Si6andze
for his *sifunza*, he replied: 'Si6andze'. He then continued that the
source or centre of the Si6andze kinship group was Ecembeni, under
Nguni Si6andze, his grandfather. Men with the clan name 'Si6andze',
who live far from Ecembeni, but who are subordinate to Nguni's lineage,
give Ecembeni as the centre of their clan group. Nguni also has a
number of families with clan names other than Si6andze under his
jurisdiction; they describe themselves as members of his *sifunza*. They
give their kinship affiliations with lineages of the same *si6ongo* in other
localities. If one of these men has a lawsuit, Nguni sends him to report
to the representative of his (the subject's) senior lineage. As each non-
related family increases in number it may develop into a lineage, and if it
has sufficient land to accept non-kinsmen the head of the lineage becomes
in addition the overlord of a *sifunza*. The *sifunza* has thus become essentially a local political group with a kinship nucleus.

With the weakening of the territorial basis of the clan, the tie between
clansmen has loosened. The word *lusendvo* that formerly implied all

members of the clan, is now used more especially for a council drawn
from within the clan or lineage. In theory representatives of the entire
clan are required to discuss such matters as marriage, inheritance, and
family disputes, but in point of fact only small sections take part, and are
described as the *lusendvo*.

When the head of a senior lineage of a clan lives in a political district
away from junior members, he is without the strongest of all political
sanctions—the power to allot to them their land. His kinsmen may turn
to him when harassed by their political overlords, or when they want
assistance in ritual or economic affairs, but he is not a powerful influence
in their lives. In everyday economic, legal, and social activities the
alliance is with the district chief, and only occasional visits are paid to the
senior kinsman to show respect, attend ceremonies and discussions, and
to ask for advice or help.

Though the political head, the land-giver and protector, has super-
seded the clan head, clan, and especially lineage, ties remain emotionally
effective. As one informant explained: 'If my chief were not of my
siɓongo and I heard he was going to send someone to kill a clansman, I
would have to go by night and warn him, my blood.' At the national and
district courts, men often keep a watchful eye on the interests of clansmen,
and particularly of clansmen whom they know personally.

The position of hereditary chiefs who have been in one area for a
lengthy period is strengthened by the presence of men of their lineage
and clan. They predominate over any other clan, and the senior kinsmen
of the lineage are known as the princes of the district. This situation
is clearly seen among the Mahlalela of Namahasha, the Simelane of
Hlatikulu, the Ndwandwe of Eɓulandzeni, the Maziya of Stegi, and
others. The chief cannot, however, compel members of his clan or
lineage to live under his control.

While the bond is strongest with the paternal lineage, individuals
sometimes move to areas controlled by maternal kin, establishing the
relationship of *umlanzakati* (follower of the female side). They receive
good land and sometimes become minor chiefs (e.g. the Matse of Stegi
started off in this way).

It is thus clear that, in the heterogeneous nation, clan membership has
different meanings for different clans and sections of the people. To the
Dlamini, or to men who belong to other 'clans with kingship', the clan
is a much more effective and real unit than it is to isolated members of
scattered, defeated, or immigrant clans. Clan ritual is retained in clans
that have hereditary political significance in definite localities, and
weakens in clans that are politically unimportant. The clan is then an
exogamous group with a common name and certain common customs,
but without effective loyalty or organization.

Though the nation has outgrown the stage in which clans were the
dominant political units, the kinship basis of the political structure is
still important. Because of the distribution of royal blood throughout the
nation, and the importance of the royal lineage in national affairs, Swazi
maintain the concept of the nation as a kinship group with the aristocracy
as the core of the wider kin. The nation can, with some justification, be
described as the 'family writ large', for, though this ignores the local

divisions that do not coincide with kinship units, it stresses the fiction of kinship and the personal bond extended to political leaders along patterns of kinship behaviour. On the other hand, the type of structure in a nation built on conquest is fundamentally different from that in a society composed of small clans, each with a local centre, and each with roughly equal status. The clan structure was broken by the rise of military age classes owing allegiance to the head of the Dlamini clan.

CHAPTER IX

THE AGE-CLASS SYSTEM

THE Swazi nation is essentially a military unit, held together by *emaButfo* (regiments) that stretch beyond the boundaries of the clan and the principality. Every *liButfo* (regiment) includes men of roughly the same age, the same training, and the same ambitions. Sons are separated from fathers, and brothers from brothers. The scope of the individual is defined by the opportunities thrown open to the age class into which he automatically falls. Only the aristocrats hold special privileges and may lead units to which they would not otherwise belong.

The age-class system is an elaboration and formalization of the age stages—the division on biological grounds into childhood, maturity and old age. The emphasis on age, typical of a homogeneous and slowly developing society, weakens as the society becomes more complex. Together with the stress on age we find a distinction on the basis of sex, the age system of the patriarchal and military society giving to men the positions of prestige and glory.

1. *The Attitude to Age*

'Respect and obey your elders.' This oft-repeated and trite phrase is put into action in Swazi homesteads. Its meaning is, when necessary, beaten into the young, but usually less drastic teaching is sufficient. The young ones, observant, ever ready to imitate, see the older brother demand deference from the younger and in turn submit to the father; they notice seniority operating in the harem where the oldest woman takes precedence at the distribution of food and beer, and the remaining wives follow in order of age; the young are made aware of their own physical and mental dependence on their seniors.

With increasing age the inferiority of women is lessened. Old women, especially those with married sons, take control in activities from which young and unmarried men are excluded. They sit on the family council, deal with domestic disputes, distribute property, and assist in ceremonial.

Children are taught to follow the ways of their parents. The training of boys is directed towards hardening them physically and disciplining them mentally. When not more than four or five years old they herd calves, help with the milking, and learn to set traps for birds. As they grow older they spend most of their time in the veld, and when at home they associate mainly with the men for whom they cook and fetch and carry. Swazi are contemptuous of boys who are brought up 'beneath the apron' of the womenfolk. Sobhuza selected a special tutor from the royal warriors to teach his sons manly behaviour. Boys must become self-reliant: they learn how to use a spear and build a shelter; how to slaughter, skin, and divide an animal. They are trained to fence and wrestle; and are instructed in the 'correct method' of argument. They form local groups for economic enterprises—hunting and herding—and for social amusements—love-making parties, and mock battles with neighbouring groups. Steadily they break away from the homestead and join wider units.

The girls are educated in domestic duties and their routine remains almost unvaried from childhood onwards. They steadily acquire the arts and skills considered necessary for women and desired in them.

The play world of Swazi children is based on imitation more than imagination. It is the adult world copied without being experienced. As experience and knowledge grow, there is no sharp disillusionment or sudden awakening from a world of fantasy. The things that children 'should not know' are limited mainly to ceremonial, and they are encouraged to participate in other activities in so far as their physical development permits.

Their development is not reckoned in years, but in age stages, which are socially emphasized, as shown in the chart (p. 134). Physical potentialities must receive social sanction before they may be legitimately fulfilled. The enjoyment of full sexual intercourse, the right to bear children, the establishment of an independent homestead are status privileges which must be socially accorded. No *libungu* (youth) may become an *indvodza* (adult man) until the king accords his age class the right to marry; no *intfombi* (girl) may behave as an *umfati* (wife) until the marriage ceremony is enacted. When individual desires run counter to social conventions that attempt to control and standardize self-expression, the offender incurs the penalty of fine, mockery, and loss of status. Behind the power of age loom the legal sanctions of society.

The respect claimed by age must, however, be reconciled with the emphasis on pedigree. In polygynous homesteads the heir is frequently younger than the sons of women married before the main wife. While, on the one hand, his position is superior to theirs and overrides the disabilities of youth, on the other hand, he is considered less experienced and should defer to them before taking any action. If not, he may find himself isolated and may even be fined. Again, because of the extension of kinship a boy may be the classificatory 'father' of a man twice his age.[1] Seniority in the kinship structure is considered the more dominant relationship, but the elders have the power to fine the youth if he abuses his position.

The behaviour enforced in the kinship group is extended to non-kinsmen. Old men are regarded as 'fathers' of the law and their words carry great weight in the council. They may send any young man on a message, and he should not refuse without good reason. They do not hesitate to dismiss opposition somewhat arbitrarily with a 'Be quiet. You are still young and know nothing'. Their age entitles them to organize work and distribute the reward of food, keeping special portions for themselves. They pronounce judgement on the younger generation by

[1] It is fascinating to watch the way the correct adjustment is inculcated into the young. Thus one day a group of children were playing and a domineering little girl of about eight turned in anger on a little boy of about five. A friend rebuked her 'Don't speak to him like that; though he is younger than you, he is your "father".' And on another occasion, when playing 'house', the girl acting the role of 'mother' instructed her 'child': 'So-and-So is your female father; you must respect her exceedingly. You may even be her subsidiary wife, though she is younger than you.' It is more usual, however, to hear an order clinched with the comment 'I am older than you. You must listen to me.'

standards of value derived from the past, and condemn divergence of opinion and new ideas as 'European ways'.

In national as well as domestic situations, the privileges of birth are limited by the authority of age. Quite often the heir to a national post is a young man without experience. His friends advise him: 'A wise man does not oppose the head-rings (the aged).' If he is wayward, he arouses criticism and may be fined. The structure of the councils hallows tradition.

It is true, however, that young aristocrats exercise privileges denied to their plebeian contemporaries. They may marry at an earlier age and enjoy greater economic and political benefits (see Chapters V and X). Princes receive marked deference from aged men, and have them as attendants. They may even join an age class to which their years do not entitle them, and act as leaders. But whether they belong to a class of their contemporaries or of their seniors, they are identified with that class and are finally kept in check by the class.

2. The Organization of Men's Age Classes

The strength of the national system lies in the integration of the principles of age, local solidarity, and noble birth. They form overlapping bonds joined together in the person of the king, who is considered to be the direct descendant of the first conqueror of the land.

The king, no matter how young he may be, is at the head of the *emaɓutfo wemadodza* (men's age classes). Under him are a series of officials who frequently also hold responsible posts in the civil administration.

The king publicly appoints an *indvuna yemaɓutfo* (commander of the age classes), who lives at the capital, leads in national expeditions, assumes control of all local contingents when they are mobilized, attends the national court, and stops fights between the men. He is chosen from among the commoners for his ability to maintain discipline, his knowledge of military organization, his trustworthiness and loyalty; but since major decisions are taken by the civil governors in council, it is not thought necessary that he be outstandingly intelligent.

Assisting the *indvuna yemaɓutfo* is an *umntfwana wenkosi* (prince), who serves as the king's representative. He does not live at the capital, but comes there for special occasions. He is a man of considerable importance, usually a classificatory father of the king, and a member of the Inner Council. Within the national army, each age class has its own *indvnua* and prince, who, naturally, are subordinate to the commander-in-chief and leading prince.

In addition, there are minor officials chosen for trustworthiness and personal ability. Some, known as *emaphini* (handles of the spears), supervise labour and execute commands. Capable organizers and wise strategists are known as *itilomo* (from *umlomo*, a mouth) and they advise the senior officers. Finally, in order to keep traditional knowledge alive, the king may select at least one *umuntfu lomdzala* (old person) to act as exemplar and tutor.

The age-class organization was more elaborate and precise in the days of inter-tribal warfare than at present. In Mbandzeni's reign the *itilomo* were prominent public figures, but when I asked for the names of modern *itilomo* I was given names of the *tindvuna* and *emaphini* of the various age classes. Nor is a specific *umuntfu lomdzala* recognized; any responsible old man is consulted if a question of precedent arises, and little instruction is given on ancient military lore. Moreover, since inter-tribal warfare has been stopped, the officers of the regiments have become subordinate to the civil administration.

A similarly constituted staff organizes local contingents, but, because of clan pride, a chief who is not a Dlamini appoints a member of his own clan as 'prince' of the units. When summoned to the capital, he accepts his subordination in the national scheme.

Within the age classes are units of varying size. The smallest group consists of the four to six inmates sharing a single hut in the barracks of their age class. Each hut has a recognized owner, frequently the man primarily responsible for its erection, and his permission must be obtained by anyone who wishes to stay there. If men from a certain locality come constantly to the capital, they usually build their own hut in the enclosure of their age class. Ties of friendship are very strong between hut mates: they work together, share food, tend each other in sickness, and rely on each other for favours.

But the basic functioning unit of the age class is the *siceme* (squad), a group of eight to twenty men who stand together for drilling and danc-ing, though they do not necessarily share the same hut. Within the *siceme* the men are graded by length of service and by skill in the dance. The leading men stand towards the outermost end of the row in the *hlehla* (parade) and the least experienced are farthest from them. Veterans jealously uphold their rank, and drive away an upstart who tries to push his way into a place to which his time of service does not entitle him. The *siceme* may or may not have a specific name, but every man knows with whom he stands, and the squad is a recognized working team within the *liβutfo*.

An indefinite number of *ticeme* form a *lichiβa* (platoon), which is usually organized round an important youth, more especially a son of the king, or, in the district, the son of a chief. An age class may include as many as eight *emachiβa*, each with its own name, war cry, and insignia. When the *emaβutfo* were more numerous, each *lichiβa* had its own central meeting hut, but now there is only one central hut in each barracks.

The *emachiβa* differ in one important respect from the *emaβutfo*—the *emachiβa* reflect local divisions while the *emaβutfo* are nation-wide units. Thus the age class known as the Balondoloze extends throughout the nation, but the Balondoloze of Loβamba, Lozita, and other centres embrace differently named *emachiβa*. On national occasions, however, the *emachiβa* of each locality fit into the national *liβutfo*, and form the *emakhandza* (plural—local contingent).

Sometimes there is conflict between the *emachiβa* within a single *liβutfo*, but as a rule the *liβutfo* is sufficiently strong to control hostilities. Each regiment obeys its own leader chosen by the king, flourishes an emblem of its unity, and shouts its own formulae of response to com-mands. The regiment is the conspicuous unit on national occasions. Then age mates from all the country collect in one *sihonca* (enclosure) and

practise song and dance. Men of other age classes are treated as tres-
passers, and driven off with blows and jeers. Between contemporaries
there is expressed a camaraderie and loyalty; they address each other as
intsanga yetfu (our age mate) or *umfowetfu* (our brother), and treat each
other as equals. They eat together, smoke hemp from the long pipe
which is part of the equipment of each age class, and work together.
They share a central meeting place or clubhouse in the barracks. This is
known as the *lilawu lenkosi* (hut of the king) and is the largest hut, distinguished from ordinary living huts by horns over the doorway as
tokens of food received from the rulers. Carriers accompanying a local
contingent sleep in this hut, and friendless strangers receive accommoda-
tion and partake of food cooked on the communal hearth. When a newcomer wants to be admitted to an established barracks, he stays in the
central hut till one of the warriors takes pity on him and asks him to
share a living hut. When beer is brought for a warrior, though most of it
may be drunk with special friends in his own room, one pot is always
carried to the communal hut.

Thus each regiment has a strong corporate life, and is distinct from
other regiments. But within each, the tie is closest between contemporaries of one locality, and particularly between those who are more or less
permanently together in the barracks. This is seen most clearly when a
fight breaks out: if it is between two age mates living together in the
barracks, their friends try to separate them, but if the combatants belong
to two different localities, their friends usually join in the fray.

Between the various age classes, there is often rivalry and resentment.
A senior regiment commands preference in the distribution of food, has
first right to the women and leads in ritual. The younger men do not
accept subordination willingly, and may take up arms. They are, however, usually restrained by loyalty to the same chief and a local solidarity.

A new regiment should be inaugurated when a senior regiment is
ripe for marriage, as it is necessary always to have a number of young and
unmarried (ritually pure) men for purposes of national ritual. The
regimental cycle is roughly five to seven years, and the new class includes
boys who are about to mature and those who have recently matured. The
class liberated for marriage covers men of roughly twenty-five to thirty-
five years of age. Marriage, which marks the fullness of manhood,
removes men to some extent from ritual services to national leaders. But
the number of regiments remains more or less constant and the duties
of the members fall into two marked phases, pre-marital and post-
marital, associated in the first case with ceremonial and in the second
with political responsibilities.[1]

The king may decide for himself when a new regiment should be
organized, and mention it to his counsellors; or, if they consider the time
overdue, they bring the matter to his notice. In either case he must

[1] Sobhuza formed the last regiment in 1934 and named it the Sikonyane
(Locusts). It included youngsters from about ten to over twenty and was
divided into two sub-sections: The Sukasambe (Hoppers) from roughly ten to
fifteen years, and the Sikonyane (full-grown Locusts). A third intervening
regiment may develop as the Emakasa (Voetganger stage). The class above the
Sikonyane, the Emasotsha, had not yet received permission to marry, but many,
despite the fine as penalty, had taken wives and made girls pregnant.

sanction the formation. The announcement of the new regiment is made by leading counsellors before a representative gathering at the capital, and everyone is expected to rejoice when the new batch of men is permitted to marry, and the new batch of youths is initiated into national service. On returning to their homes, the men who were present inform the youngsters. Of course the nucleus of each new regiment already exists among the children living at the royal villages.

Some time later the king mobilizes the youths into barracks. He may do this by sending forth the summons, '*Lukani tinsambo*' (plait the ropes), and boys who wish to live at the royal villages prepare the requisite building material. On a specified day they arrive, singing and decked in finery, and begin to build their huts on a site allocated by the king. Should he not issue the call, boys may build of their own accord in a clear space behind the barracks of an established regiment. As others join them and the huts increase in number, the king may either allow them to surround their huts with a fence, making a separate barracks, or order them to 'carry their huts' to an established unit. However, the regiment always retains its own identity.[1]

Now it is important to notice the effect of the age-class system on individual Swazi. While every man is automatically a member, the extent to which they are affected by the organization varies considerably. The determining factor is whether or not a youth lives in the barracks of a royal village, or remains most of his life in the homestead of his father. Only a limited number of *emaßutfo* are stationed throughout the year at the main royal villages and at villages of the more important chiefs.

Men in residence at royal villages have a higher status than those of local contingents, and are known by the special title of *imißutfo* (sing., *umßutfo*), in addition to the general term *emajaha*, which is applied to all members of the age classes. *Imißutfo* are distinguished by special ornaments, songs and dances, indeed so great is the pride of the *imißutfo* that no matter how sincerely they may admire the marching song of a local contingent, they will not adopt it into their repertoire. From the *imißutfo* the king selects his trusted messengers, who receive recognition from all sections of the people. Formerly, in wartime the *imißutfo* were privileged to lead the attack of their age classes, for 'Those who serve the king must be the first to receive the stab.' *Emajaha* stationed at homesteads of chiefs hold a higher status than the casual members of the district, but not the honoured position of the *imißutfo*.

Any man may become an *umßutfo*, and this is one instance in which the consent of a father or guardian need not be first obtained. No one can stop a man working for the king, the father of the nation. As a rule a man, especially an important man, is eager that at least one of his sons should stay for some years at headquarters and the family councils often send the heir to be educated as an *umßutfo*. In this way the rulers come into close touch with prominent men of the country and they, in turn, are trained in service. No one is compelled to serve for any defined period,

---

[1] Thus the present Emasotsha built their huts behind the Emagavu who were few in number and older in years. Later the Emasotsha were told to join the Emagavu. They adopted the same insignia, but retain their own section eader and form their own platoons.

and the relationship is purely voluntary; many Swazi, discussing 'joining the European army' and becoming an *umßutfo*, emphasized the more personal nature of the Swazi organization, the relative freedom of its members, and the status of the royal regiments.

3. *Orientation to Warfare*

Warfare was essential to maintain the type of society that developed with the consolidation of kingship, and it became the main avenue whereby commoners could achieve power, wealth, and fame.

The one duty that the age classes are no longer allowed to perform is the key to their former importance and present impotence. Inter-tribal warfare has been suppressed and for war against Europeans, the traditional weapons are out of date.[1]

The king symbolized the nation as the major war-making unit; no other man represented the people or could send the regiments to fight. Even a regent did not have the power: the defeat of the Nyatse regiment during the minority of Mswati's heir was attributed largely to the fact that the regent Ndwandwe had exceeded his authority. The nation as a whole never went to war; the king always selected certain regiments, usually drawn from both the married and unmarried classes. A residue of men remained behind to look after the women, children, aged, and the king himself. Minor forays and raids conducted by local chiefs against each other or against small groups of aliens on the borders were not regarded as war. The local chief could not, for this purpose, summon any of his men serving at the capital.

Inter-tribal wars were waged for many purposes. In the reign of Sobhuza I they were primarily to obtain new territory and to retain national independence; by Mswati's reign the war aims had changed, and wars were largely for wealth or excitement. The change in aim can probably be accounted for by the difficulty that was already experienced in enforcing order over a wide area.

War was sometimes initiated by the warriors to display their courage, loyalty, and strength. The prize was glory and booty, more especially cattle. Swazi point out that it is usually the young and unmarried men who are anxious to fight, for 'The old men remember their wives and children, while the young are eager for praise.' Veterans were usually sent to keep the reckless youths in check. One group of young bloods would boast to the king: 'Let us show you what we can do. Let us show you that we are better than Such-and-Such regiment.' The king would agree; it was not wise to have a turbulent army without an external foe, and an enemy rich in cattle would be selected. A typical case of rivalry occurred in Mbandzeni's reign when the Mtshindi platoon of the Indlavela regiment derided the Timdjodjosi platoon, so Mbandzeni sent out all the platoons of the Indlavela to attack the Sotho; the Sibetshane won for themselves the greatest honour and brought back most cattle. The names of many great warriors are still remembered; among the foremost are Mbovana Fakudze, the fighting general, who led the Swazi

---

[1] But it is significant that in the present war the men were organized on the traditional basis under European control.

in the Mshatse war against the people of Sikukiku; and Sandlana Zwane, fighter and diplomat, in the reign of Mbandzeni.

The Swazi, like the Zulu, often attacked in a semicircle with the young men at the 'horns' and the veterans as the 'chest'. If the terrain did not admit of such tactics, the commander-in-chief and his staff would decide which group should move forward and from where. Some sections were always kept in reserve and sent out when their mates were hard pressed, or the enemy was in flight.

The *emaqawe* (heroes) obtained part of the spoil they brought home to the king. Mbandzeni gave one man eight cows and let him keep a little girl whom he had seized in a raid. This was a liberal reward; more usually one beast was given. Each hero also received *tiqu* (a necklace of wooden pegs) that was both a decoration and a magical protection against bad dreams and the vengeful spirits of the dead. On future occasions, after taking part in the parade of the age classes, the braves would perform solos (*kugiya*), repeating their grand achievements in mime before an admiring audience.

Apart from inter-tribal wars, fights broke out between older and younger age classes and between age mates in different localities. The usual cause was a dispute over women. The older men had the majority of the women, and this the young men resented. Thus in Mbandzeni's reign there was a bitter feud between the Giba and the Mgadlela regiments, and in one fight twelve men were seriously injured and one killed outright. The leader of the attacking regiment 'urged his men to score the faces of the young men so that the young girls would no longer admire them'.[1] Sometimes the boys of one locality were considered too successful with women of another locality, and the jealousy of the 'home-town men' was aroused. Swazi cite cases to show that local solidarity prevented men from fighting elders living in the same area, but the age bond was stronger than the local bond when the age classes came together at the royal villages.

The weapons of warfare were limited in type, but effective for their purpose. They consisted of the *sikhali sokujijimeta* or *sijula* (throwing spear) which had a small lanceolate head and long handle; two types of stabbing spear: the *lidjozi* with a broad head, and the *umdlundlu* with a long narrow head; two kinds of battle axe: the *sizeze* with straight points, and the *intsanga* with flanged tips; a wooden knobkerry—the *indvuku*—with notches cut in the head to make blows more effective; and the *sihlangu* (oxhide shield) rounder and slightly smaller than that used by the Zulu.[2] The men prided themselves on their weapons, and the king sometimes gave a shield or spear as a special mark of favour. Fighting was largely at close quarters, and the short stabbing spear, adopted from Shaka's Zulu in the reign of Mswati, was the most effective weapon. To return without it from a fray was a sign of defeat, if not of cowardice.

Swazi, as well as many Europeans, are of the opinion that the Swazi were not as militant as the Zulu. This can be accounted for by the more

---

[1] Letter from Theophilus Shepstone to the British Commissioner, 20 February 1891. Cmd. 7,212, p. 18.

[2] The *sihlangu*, or battle shield, must not be confused with the *lihau*, or dancing shield, used when walking the countryside or courting.

aggressive character of the Zulu rulers and also by the more hostile nature of their contact with Europeans. Shaka and Dingane, the great Zulu military despots, were notorious for cruelty and egoism (neither would allow any of their male children to survive), while Sobhuza I and Mswati, their Swazi contemporaries, were relatively benevolent.

Death on the battle field was a hero's death which could not be mourned by the kinsmen. Every man was an asset of the nation, a *sihlangu senkosi* (shield of the king), and his death in defence of the nation was placed in a different category from death by any other cause. Actually the number of Swazi who died in warfare does not appear, from discussions and genealogies, to have been very high. In the genealogies of twelve important families, going back four generations, nine out of 220 men died violent deaths: three were killed in war, five were destroyed as wizards (the justness of the accusation was of course hotly denied by the descendants), and one was killed in a brawl. A Swazi with whom I discussed these deaths commented: 'Those who were killed in war died well; the others just wasted themselves.'

Wars were accompanied by elaborate ritual. The old war medicine was, and still is, in the hands of a special clan, the Gwe6u, who were forbidden to use it for private individuals or for civil strife. The ritual before the men went on the warpath included the capture by the warriors of a fierce bull, the skinning and removal of the right foreleg while the animal was still alive, and the treatment of its flesh which the men ate to give them strength and resistance. The warriors were also lined up with their shields touching, and then the war doctor walked along the lines poking medical roots against the shields and chanting a spell.[1] Before they attacked the men were again fortified.

But treatment for the army as a whole did not satisfy the ambition of individuals to whom warfare was largely a personal matter in which they hoped to win fame and wealth, and for this reason ambitious warriors also armed themselves with medicines obtained from private doctors.

Swazi believed that an important condition of success was the behaviour of those who remained behind. The king, together with the national doctor, performed destructive rites against the enemy, and many taboos were imposed on the behaviour of the civil population, more especially the wives of the absent warriors. Infidelity in particular was condemned, and the women tied heavy ropes round their waists while their men were away. Warfare was dangerous, not only because of the obvious physical risk, but because of the power of dead enemies. The men who killed on the field, more especially the brave, who drew first blood, received elaborate public treatment. The medicines used were very similar to those still applied to protect people when a close relative is killed by lightning. Vengeance of slain men was feared, and the medicines to guard against it were not always effective. Thus *Emanzawe*

---

[1] Obviously this is not the place to discuss ritual, but it is relevant to point out that a type of spell is usually contained in the name of the material substance. Thus the war doctor says, 'Here is *ngununu*', 'Here is *mpishimpishi*'. The name of the substance *ngununu* is derived from the word *ngunyile*—to be stabbed, but not seriously injured though the enemy believe I am killed and will leave without inflicting a mortal blow. *Mpishimpishi* brings darkness before the eyes of the enemy, it 'makes one invisible' (*unempishi mpishi*) and able to escape.

are the spirits of men slain in the battle against Mzila, son of Soshangane, which have 'possessed' the Swazi since the reign of Mswati. Efforts were also directed to prevent harm coming from booty affected by the quality of enmity.[1]

Warfare was an intermittent activity. The regiments usually left when the fields were ripening and were back for the threshing season, when their labour was needed at home. No war continued more than a year, and many raids lasted less than a month, while the actual fighting sometimes lasted only a few days. The men took with them insufficient food for a long campaign, and relied mainly on obtaining cereals and meat by plundering *en route*. The army could plunder with impunity: 'there is no case against an army' is a Swazi maxim. Sometimes the king gave a few head of cattle to slaughter on the way and each man had with him a little food for the road. But warfare did not involve any radical change in the economy or the technology of the people.

4. *Labour*

When the *emaβutfo* were not at war, they served as labour battalions for the aristocrats throughout the country, and that is their main function at the present time. Their most intensive work is related to the agricultural routine, and they plough, weed, guard the millet from the birds, reap, and thresh. They are also summoned to gather wood, cut laths and poles, help build and move huts, drive locusts from the fields, skin animals, run messages, and fetch and carry. Some of the *imiβutfo* act as guardians and escorts of the royal women and others serve as the personal attendants of royalty.

Labour is irregular. Sometimes a royal regiment will be summoned six days in succession.[2] At other times a whole week may elapse without the rulers requiring their services. In 1934-5, the warriors at Loβamba were summoned on an average less than three times a week. Local contingents are called upon less frequently and perform most of their work for their local chiefs. At Nkaba, in 1935, the men came six times to work for their chief, Mnisi, and twice they went to the capital. At Gwegwe the men worked eight days in 1936 for their chieftainess, Sencaβaphi, and were not once sent to the capital.

No man is ever fined by the national court for not obeying a call to labour. If, however, anyone consistently disobeys without good reason, the other workers rebuke him and sometimes belabour him with sticks. He may lodge no complaint. It rarely happens that a chief removes a subject from his area for laziness alone, but continued laziness leads to a suspicion of the graver fault of insubordination. Moreover, an *umβutfo* can go home or go to work for the Europeans when he pleases, but his age mates resent it if he is always absenting himself when there is much work to be done.

---

[1] Thus when the booty included cattle, the *inyanga* doctored them with a lighted brand both to prevent them from returning to their former owners, and also to destroy the *lupahlo* (evil power) they might carry.

[2] Nowadays, Sunday is generally accepted as a day of rest.

When not occupied in tribal labour, the men are free to do as they like, though they are expected to listen to the discussion of cases, which takes place almost every day at the tribal courts. They also spend some time in the barracks, where they are entirely self-dependent. They cook, build, smear the floors, they even thatch and bind the grass down with ropes, tasks that are normally performed by women. When for any purpose, such as the building or repairing of the ritual hut at the capital, male experts are required, there are always a few men available who became famous for their technical ability in the days when they worked in the barracks.

It is the duty of rulers to provide the regiments with a portion of their food in return for labour,[1] and in addition many a man has accumulated a few beasts, the nucleus of a herd, as a reward for special services. The rulers naturally take a greater interest in warriors stationed in royal villages than in men with whom they have slighter contact, and they help trusted labourers loɓola their wives, pay taxes, or buy clothes. These are also the types of rewards which permanent members of a local contingent can ask of a local chief. An umɓutfo is also used as messenger (and later as witness) in court cases, and if he acts for the winning side he receives a beast as his fee.

Some of the permanent labourers have come to the royal village because they could derive few benefits from their own parents. Of forty-five men at Loɓamba in 1935, thirty were either second or third sons or else children of unimportant wives. Eight of the thirty gave as their reason for staying at the capital their poverty and expressed the pious hope that the king would remedy it. Four men were children of important chiefs, and three were princes. One prince explained: 'I am a brother of the king. We must teach the people to respect him. We do that by doing his work—you must never just spend breath.' There were three orphans and one said: 'The king is my father and my mother.' Love of, or loyalty to, the king, which really means co-operation for mutual benefit, is a fairly glib and common answer to a direct question: 'What are the advantages of living in the barracks?' Among other reasons given for joining are enjoyment of the parade; dislike of working for Europeans; 'just to see what it is like'; a desire for friendship and companionship, and national pride in 'work of a Swazi'. All informants agree that an umɓutfo receives a lower monetary remuneration than the average Swazi employed by a European, but point out that the umɓutfo has a freer life and a position of prestige.

5. Education

Little formal education is given in the regiment, but it is the main training school of conservatives. It continues and extends the work of kinsmen who enforce the authority of age and seniority. Throughout life the position of a man is fixed in, and by, his age class, which defines his rights over those who are junior to him and his obligations to those who are senior.

[1] The economic basis is more fully discussed in my article, 'The Military Organization in Swaziland', *Africa*, Vol. X, No. 2, pp. 181–4.

The age class regulates to a considerable extent economic opportunities, political duties, and the moral code. The main distinction obtains between age classes that are permitted to marry and those in which the men are obliged to remain single. The unmarried group leads a more free and easy life than the married. The change in status was formerly symbolized by the putting on of the head-ring, and it is interesting to note that some men wept when this was done, or tried to run away, because 'it was hard to leave *Bujaha* (youth) and enter *Budvodza* (full manhood)'. Apart from an increase in responsibilities, age carries privileges: control of a homestead, ownership of land, and prominence on the council are the rights of the marriageable classes.

A man who violates the marriage regulation is fined a beast known as 'the beast of deception' which goes to the national revenue. His act is judged to be an offence against the king and the 'beast of deception' is claimed over and above any fine for impregnation, which goes to the girl's kinsmen. A youth may have lovers, and this is an open and honourable relationship, but he must not make them pregnant.

The rigid control of the age of marriage is explicable in the context of the military and aristocractic society. A supply of physically mature but reckless warriors was required, and we have already mentioned that the unmarried are considered the best fighters. Moreover, 'pure men' who 'have not wasted their strength in children' are required to doctor the king at the annual national ceremony (see Chapter XIII).

Within the age class the individual is trained to share and co-operate, to practise generosity, bravery, and loyalty. He is taught to condemn selfishness, cowardice, and independent action. Age gives no special group in the society permanent privileges denied to other citizens, since every individual can anticipate that, in the normal span of life, he will pass through every phase of social activity. But it is only among his contemporaries that the average Swazi can gain leadership; all his life he is curbed by his age mates. This is one of the negative aspects of the system from the point of view of the individualistic European. It is probable that from the time of its inception there were cases of maladjustment—ambitious men who would not be checked, or men whose ideals were not those of the rulers and the masses. In the past these created personal difficulties and conflicts; there were no organized groups with opposing aims and methods. With the arrival of missionaries, the sex code of the regiment was given undue prominence over other aspects, and a number of converts follow the lead of their teachers in opposing the entire regimental system.

Within the age classes the political leaders, who derive their rank by virtue of birth, continue as the elite. Their position is not challenged by the plebeians, who attain recognition in the age classes, and the prospect of advancement for such people is, moreover, dependent on the will of the established aristocracy. The emphasis on age therefore strengthens rather than weakens the hierarchy built on pedigree, and provides an effective military, labour, and educational machine for maintaining it.

6. *The Organization of Women's Age Classes*

Women also have their age classes, but these are not as formal or rigid as the regiments for men. This is because women are bound to domestic and local, rather than national duties; they spend their time housekeeping and providing food for their families, not in warfare and cultivating royal fields to support national enterprise.

Women's age classes are not formed with any regularity, and they coincide directly with physiological stages of development (see chart, pp. 135, 136). Throughout the country there are three major working divisions: girls before puberty, between puberty and marriage, and married women. The pre-puberty class includes young undeveloped girls and girls reaching puberty; the class after puberty includes girls permitted to have lovers and girls prepared for marriage; the class of married women distinguishes between the young wife not yet with child, the married woman of longer standing, and the old woman. In olden times clothing and style of hair marked age status throughout the nation; to-day, even in conservative homes, the division is less obvious. But only marriageable and married women wear their hair in a high bun, and only married women wear the *sidwaɓa* (skin skirt) and *sidziya* (skin apron).

There are no women's regiments extending under a single name throughout the nation. Within each principality the three major age divisions, and more especially the second and third, usually have their own names and sets of songs. At Loɓamba only the married women have a name, *Emadvonda*; the others are simply labelled *tintfombatana* (girls). At Nkaɓa each class is named. The name is usually given by the leading woman (the mother of the chief), or by a prominent member of the class.

Membership for women is not as definite as for men. Each woman is expected of her own accord to co-operate with her local contemporaries. Moreover, whereas men retain the same age-class affiliation throughout their lives, women, because of patrilocal marriage and the local limits of their age classes, change their membership on marriage. Girls who once formed one local subdivision are scattered as wives through many areas, each with its own married age class. No women stay in barracks separated from their families. A woman is above all a member of a kinship rather than a national group.

The divisions into squads and platoons are known, but have little significance; sometimes in the *liɓutfo* of married women, wives of a polygynist form their own sub-section, some calling it a *siceme* (squad) and others a *lichiɓa* (platoon) under a special name; similarly in the girls' class, half-sisters or girls living close by may form a small unit, but it is more in the nature of an informal club than an essential and formal age-class subdivision.

The official personnel of the women's classes is vague. The position of the queen mother in the women's age classes is by no means as powerful as that of the king in the men's regiments. Only when women come to the capital for work are they under the queen mother's direct control. As her representative she appoints the wife of the main civil governor spoken of as *incusakati*. If there is a princess or a daughter of the local aristocracy in a woman's age-class unit, she is treated with the respect considered to be due to her birth, but there is also always a women's councillor (*indvuna*) of common stock in charge of the work. There may be an *indvuna* for each age-class subdivision, but when old and young co-operate the senior automatically takes precedence. Chosen for her character and energy, her task is to see that the women perform their work, to find out why some have absented themselves, and to stop any quarrelling. When many local subdivisions of the same age class come together at the capital or other royal villages, they retain very markedly their local character, but recognize the *incusakati* as chief organizer.

7. *Activities*

The women's age classes are essentially working teams; they weed, thresh, winnow, brew beer, shell mealies, cut grass, and plait ropes. Most of their work is for the head of the local unit, and they may be summoned even more often than the men, as happened at Nkaba in 1935, when the women worked nine days and the men eight.

The *emaβutfo waβafati* do not give women particular political, economic, religious, or social power; they are primarily the units through which commands for service are executed. At the same time the age class is a background against which exceptional women stand out for their industry, skill, and organizational ability.

The educational influence of the women's classes is not obvious and direct, but subtle and indirect. Young girls, in particular, are strongly influenced by their membership. As among men, the term 'our age mate' implies comradeship and mutual help. The local age class is the unit in which friendships develop and instruction is received. Breaches of the sex code standardized for a particular age are effectively punished by the mockery and even ostracism of contemporaries. Formerly, if a girl became pregnant before marriage, her age mates seized a beast from her parents, killed it in a special way and ate it. Songs of ridicule were, and occasionally still are, composed to humiliate such a girl.

On the whole, the age classes play a relatively small part in a woman's life compared with the influence of the regiment on a man, more especially if he stays in barracks for months on end. The group activities of the women in their organization are the same as in the homestead, and do not, as in the case of men, include opportunities of a different order. The nature of the women's *emaβutfo* reflects the subordinate rôle of women, and the extent to which they are bound by domestic tasks and local interests.

8. *The Umcwasho*

Apart from age classes, unmarried girls occasionally join together in a strong unit under the patronage of a princess or daughter of a chief. This organization is spoken of as the *umcwasho*; I participated in what may be, because of opposition from various Europeans, the last national *umcwasho*.

The *umcwasho* is distinct from the puberty ceremony which ended in the reign of Mbandzeni. The puberty ceremony for princesses had as its main characteristics a period of seclusion, sex instruction, feasting, doctoring, and the preparation of girls for motherhood. The *umcwasho* is mainly a celebration to honour an important young lady, and is spoken of as *sika saɓantfwana* (a custom of children) or *kuɓakhulisa* (to make them grow up). Adults treat it with a mixture of pride and amusement, like fond parents at a birthday party.

The movement is inaugurated by a group of girls living in the same principality, who choose from among themselves a daughter of the local chief to be their *inkosatana* (princess). Permission for the holding of the ceremony is then obtained from her father and the most important of his womenfolk. These older women, who have themselves been through the organization, form the advisers, and direct the work of the new group. The main responsibility, however, is in the hands of the girls who 'carry the *umcwasho*'—that is, who wear the *umcwasho* uniform. The princess is assisted by an *indvuna*—a young commoner chosen for her intelligence—and by a select few who form the *liɓandla* (council).

The *umcwasho* has been held on a minor scale in various principalities, but in 1935 it was a national affair to honour Sobhuza's four elder daughters and the child of his most important sister. Ɓethusile, a girl of fifteen years, was the senior princess.

In March 1935, runners were sent to summon girls from different parts of the country to the capital, and on a specified day between 400 and 500 girls arrived in local contingents, each under the leadership of a daughter of the local chief and her *indvuna*. They became subordinate to the staff at the capital.

The ceremony was inaugurated by tribute labour. Very early in the morning the girls collected in their age and locality groups, paraded, and went to gather wood. On their return they flung down their bundles with a flourish and, with Ɓethusile in their midst, danced before the inhabitants of the capital.

On the following day they were given the 'laws of the *umcwasho*' regulating clothing, food, language, morals, and general behaviour. The organizers distinguished between the young and immature and those of an age to take lovers. The junior group had its own colours, food abstentions, and passwords. Having received the laws, the girls sang, danced, feasted, and then returned to their own homes.

Obedience to the laws was enforced by the whole group, which ruthlessly ferreted out offenders and punished them with fines which, if not immediately produced, rapidly increased in amount. Throughout the period of the *umcwasho* no physical contact whatever was permitted between the sexes, and a fine of one head of cattle was inflicted on a man —even the king—who made love to an *umcwasho* girl. The shame of breaking the law was heightened by a grandiloquent ritual of mockery.

In July the girls were again summoned for service to the capital.[1] They

---

[1] Between the inauguration and the second summons, the *umcwasho* came to the notice of the missionaries. Though Sobhuza had made it clear that the *umcwasho* was not compulsory, some chiefs had coerced parents to send their daughters, some parents had forced their daughters without pressure from the chiefs, and girls had left school of their own free will. The missionaries criticized the ceremony as immoral and reactionary, and appealed to the Administration. The Administration said it was not prepared to interfere as long as there was no coercion.

came in the *umcwasho* uniform and were sent to cut reeds for the wind-
screen of the queen mother's hut. On their return they gave a grand
display of singing and dancing, and were rewarded with five animals
provided by the rulers.

The ceremony ended the following winter. In the meantime the girls
had constantly practised group songs and dances and had made for themselves new dancing dresses. At the capital they removed the old *umcwasho*
uniform, and appeared in the provocative finery associated with courtship
—diminutive skirts, bodies bare to the waist. They carried large knives
and ornaments of ingenious design. The princesses were distinguished
by the red feather of the *ligwalagwala* bird in their hair.

Dancing was held every afternoon for five days, and proved an attraction to Europeans as well as Swazi. The Resident Commissioner and his
wife were invited to the party on the first day and, in the company of the
five young princesses, inspected the dancers. At least 800 people took
part in the performance. The royal women of the nation danced their
recognition of the growing up of the children, and the king, surrounded
by his attendants, later took part in the festivity. Every now and then he
rushed out with a few of his companions to whoop in front of the girls and
proudly strike his shield on the ground at the feet of his daughters and
sisters, shouting spontaneous praise and encouragement. His mother, a
little wearied by the excitement, rested on the ground and criticized the
dancers.

On the last day the girls again fetched reeds and then went to Sobhuza's
village to be dismissed. On their return to their own homes, the girls of
each principality danced at the village of the local 'princess', and her
father, assisted by his subjects, provided a last feast.

The celebrations, held in the autumn and winter months so as not to
interfere with the agricultural work of the women, were expensive. To
feed the girls cost the rulers thirty-one animals, more than three bags of
grain, and a number of pumpkins. The food was provided at irregular
periods during their stay at the capital. It is doubtful whether it covered
even half the amount that was actually consumed. The rulers were not
expected, however, to bear the total cost, and some girls brought pro-
vender with them from their own homes, while others were looked after
by the citizens on whom they were billeted. But an impression of royal
generosity was created by the fact that when the rulers gave, all the
umcwasho members were called together to eat in local and age groups and
the display was obvious and lavish. Each feast ended with praises of the
royal family expressed in song and dance.

Having passed through the *umcwasho*, the girls remain in the unmarried
age class of their localities, until they are separated by marriage. The
umcwasho group never again appears as a social unit. The *umcwasho* for
girls is, however, one of the few female organizations; hence its interest.
Occasionally a chief has held an '*umcwasho*' for his sons, but in their case
it is recognized as a festive, rather than an educational, gathering. It is
insignificant in comparison with the regimental organization.

The age classes, whether formally proclaimed as among the men or
informally organized as for women, are adapted to a homogeneous
peasantry. They force the individual to march in time with a group

represented by the conservative aristocracy. They also inhibit the development of an hereditary class with permanent privileges, since every individual can anticipate that, in the normal span of life, he or she will pass through every age class and its associated status activities.

K

STAGES OF GROWTH OF MALES

Age (approx.)	Swazi Name	Activities	Ritual	Outward signs
3 months.	*Luswane.*	Kept in hut.	Stage ends when child is shown the moon. Receives name.	Wears only protective medicines.
In third year.	*Umntfwana* or *Ingane.*	Carried in a sling. Taught to walk and talk.	Weaned.	Wears nothing or string of beads.
3–8 years.	*Umfana.*	Plays a great deal. Herds goats. Plays house.	*Kusika tindlebe*—ears cut.	Wears tiny *lidjoba*—loin skin.
8–17 years.	*Lijele.*	Herds cattle. Responsible messenger.	Puberty ceremony.	Wears loin skin and begins to wear penis cap.
17–27 years.	*Lijaha* or *Libungu.*	Seeks lovers. Enters age class as *lijaha.* Fighter, hunter. Carefree.	Acceptance of lovers.	Takes pride in appearance. Wears bead ornaments made by lovers.
27–60 years.	*Indvodza.*	Married man. Attends councils. Has many responsibilities.	Putting on of head-ring.	Head-ring.
Over 60.	*Lichegu* or *Umhlaba.*	Grandfather. Works less.	Supervises ritual of his sons. Receives great respect.	Head-ring.

STAGES OF GROWTH OF FEMALES

Age (approx.)	Swazi Name	Activities	Ritual	Outward Signs
3 months.	*Luswane.*	Kept in hut.	Stage ends when child is shown the moon. Receives name.	Wears only protective medicines.
In third year.	*Umntfwana* or *Ingane.*	Carried in a sling. Taught to walk and talk.	Weaned—bitter aloe rubbed on mother's breast.	Wears nothing or string of beads.
6–8 years.	*Sidzanzane.*	Plays a good deal. Helps mother. Smears floor, learns to grind, plays house (*emandlwane*).	*Ukusika tindlebe*—ears cut.	String of beads and sometimes little skirt of grass or cloth.
8–15 years.	*Litshitshana.*	Nurse-maid. Helps in home and in fields.	Ends with puberty ritual.	Skirt of grass or skirt and short toga of cloth. Hair in many styles. Never long. Decorations—bead necklaces.
15–17 years.	*Lichikiza.*	Has a lover. Visits his home. Knows a woman's job.	Public selection of *singani* (lover) in his barracks.	Dresses carefully in *mahiya* (cloth).

Age (approx.)	Swazi Name	Activities	Ritual	Outward Signs
17–22 years.	*Ingcugce.*	Ready for marriage. Last fling.	Putting up of hair into high bun. Ends with marriage ceremony.	Though hair is up, bun is still small. Wears dress of cloth.
21–24 years.	*Makoti* or *Umlobokati.*	Bride at husband's home. Works for mother-in-law.	Ritually given permission to behave as wife.	Wears skin apron and skin skirt. Apron worn under armpits (*ukwencaya*).
24–55 years.	*Umfati.*	Wife and mother, tied to home.	Given increasing participation in family ritual.	After birth of first child, raises apron over one shoulder.
55–65 years.	*Isalukati.*	Grandmother. Less work in home : helped by daughters - in - law and grandchildren.	Aids married sons in family ritual.	Less careful of personal appearance.
65 upwards	*Umhlaba* (earth) or *Lidloti* (ancestral spirit).	Can do no active work.	Treated with respect due an ancestral spirit.	Usually wears any old clothing.

CHAPTER X

WEALTH IN THE PEASANT SOCIETY

THE aristocrats who hold their positions by birth, and the age-class officials recognized within the group of their contemporaries for individual merit are usually, but not always, the more wealthy members of the conservative society. But though differences of wealth exist, no class structure similar to that of industrialized European society has developed. There is no capitalist class with the monopoly of the means of production, no proletariat from whom these means are debarred, and no self-conscious, leisured class that maintains itself on the labour of others

1. *Technical Limitations*

Swazi technology is crude and unable to support permanently a large number of people in activities that do not contribute directly to the food supply. The homestead makes most of the articles that it needs; even the great men do manual work in the intervals between hunting and attending public discussions; princes build the framework of their homes and palisade their cattle byres; queens spend days toiling in the fields. The material equipment is shaped by hand directly from the environment; it is usually of limited durability and requires frequent repairs.

Swazi rely for their subsistence primarily on the crops that they cultivate, yet they have little agricultural science, and do not produce sufficient for their needs. Until the plough was accepted (in 1890 in the central area), the chief implement was the hand hoe made by native smiths. Hoes were scarce, and it appears that many a family did not have sufficient for all the workers. Those without hoes used digging sticks of very hard wood (such as *umhohlo*—elephant wood; *impondvowendlovu—Combretum imbere*) pointed at one end, or heated and shaped like hoes, but so short that workers were obliged to squat in order to handle them effectively. With so cumbersome a tool, little soil could be prepared. At the present time, hoes, differently shaped from the traditional implements, are bought at stores, and in addition ploughs are used for the larger fields by even the most conservative Swazi; but improvement in equipment has not usually resulted in an increase in yield, since the necessary subsidiary knowledge has not been acquired.

The varied nature of the country is imperfectly utilized. Swazi have observed that certain soils 'feel for' certain crops, but they have no scientific understanding of soil deficiencies. Crops are not rotated; the gardener waits till the harvest is poor and the earth visibly 'tired', then he lets the field lie fallow till it again bears the species of grass and shrub known to require 'strong soil'. Cow-dung and rubbish are seen to make land fertile (*vundzile*), and for that reason old village sites become treasured family garden lands, yet no effort is made to manure the fields. Swazi do not terrace, nor, apart from digging narrow furrows a short distance inland from the rivers, do they irrigate; they transfer responsibility for the essential water supply to the rulers as rain-makers. No efficient method of control over pests is known, and pests are indeed many,[1] though every gardener attempts to safeguard himself by magical ritual. When a crop is finally harvested, the underground granaries are neither waterproof nor airtight, and though they are carefully fired and covered, a certain amount of rot is inevitable.

Similarly, in other economic undertakings, Swazi possess a body of effective, empirical knowledge, but its range is restricted. The circular hut, with its neat framework of bent saplings, fine waterproof thatching, beaten dung floor, and low arched doorway, is a pleasant enough shelter. But Swazi, with their limited knowledge of construction, cannot increase the size beyond a restricted circle—the dome is beyond their ken. The nature of the building material does not permit of any permanent structures—the grass rarely lasts for more than five or six years and the wood is not treated to withstand ants or weather. Moreover, when a fire is lit in the centre of the hut in the slight depression that serves as the hearth, smoke can only escape through the door or the interstices of the rounded walls.

If we examine the utensils—pots, spoons, meat dishes, milk pails, beer strainers, and baskets—or the furniture which consists entirely of sleeping and sitting mats; or the clothing of skin, hide, and feather, the characteristics of Swazi technology are again evident. Clay, wood, grass, skins are skilfully worked and serve the purposes to which they are put, but the material soon breaks or perishes or tears, and every new article is laboriously made by hand. Only the grinding stones outlive the human span, but the slow and arduous process of grinding grain, the essential of every meal, illustrates a further simplicity in the technology of the Swazi.

The tools distributed in every homestead are not sufficiently varied or complex to permit of developed specialization. An essential condition of economic classes is therefore absent.

Conservative Swazi do not attempt to improve their existing techniques, and over the course of many years the methods of agriculture, hut-building, production of utensils and clothing remained fundamentally the same. Perhaps a new shape in baskets and a new fashion in mats were introduced, but little else changed. This stabilization, or conservatism, cannot be considered the result of an inherent inability to change, because under the stimulus of urban conditions the Swazi, like other Africans, have become men of many new trades. Conservatism results from the interplay of numerous social factors: the limitations of the accepted implements, the narrow bases of associated knowledge, and more especially from the nature of the economic and political organization and ritual practices.

Peasant life in a difficult country, isolated from intimate contact with the processes rather than the products of industrialism, does not produce rapid development. The partial control achieved over environment satisfies the fundamental needs of food and shelter. The existing technology is sanctioned by custom and convention, by the ethics of the ancestral cult, and by taboos. Thus the activities of the most enterprising agriculturalist are curbed by the shortage of land, absence of individual

[1] For example, *umgundzatshane*—army worm; *isihlavana*—stock borer; *mcobolonjwane*—bagrada bug; *umswenya*—cut worm; *usincencane*—aphis, etc.

tenure, restriction on the period of planting, absence of markets, and the fear of evoking an accusation of witchcraft from his fellow men.

When new articles are adopted it is in accordance with certain principles of the general structure of the society. Articles are introduced or sanctioned ultimately by the aristocrats. This was obvious from the days of Mbandzeni, when the concessionaires brought their goods to the king. In all the instances that I have investigated, the plough was first accepted among conservatives by the chief or a leading councillor after its utility had been demonstrated, usually by a missionary. At present, imitation of the Europeans gives a certain prestige value, but is regarded with suspicion by the traditional leaders. The foreign articles that they are prepared to accept do not disturb the existing pattern nor oust old artefacts; thus the petrol drum is used for carrying water in mundane activities, but the calabash and clay pot are necessary for sacred occasions; similarly, the plough has not fully displaced the hoe either in economics or ritual.

Like all people, Swazi need strong incentives of prestige or utility to accept innovations that will affect deeply-entrenched attitudes and behaviour. Because the leaders hold their position by pedigree, they need not, and frequently do not, encourage innovations unless their own prestige is enhanced. The chiefs would not agree with this statement; the process is not deliberate. They do not consciously retard new developments; their behaviour is the result of the support they receive from the mass of their subjects who are anxious to continue the existing system.

2. Division of Labour

Every Swazi participates to some extent in the production of food. 'People hunger, therefore they work', 'no chicken scratches for another', express the Swazi attitude to manual labour. Laziness is heavily censured. When men discuss qualities desired in wives they always stress diligence (*kutsele*) and deftness (*nakile*).

As in other primitive societies, the major division of labour is based on sex. Different psychological and physiological qualities are attributed to men and women as *intalo yaßo* (their nature) to explain the allocation of particular occupations. Instilled in Swazi from childhood is the theory that 'the strength of woman does not equal that of man'. The male is considered to be born 'hard' and 'firm', a leader in the fight and council, while the 'nature' of woman is 'weak' and 'soft'. Certain tasks are therefore considered 'to equal manliness' and others behove women; a few activities are open to either sex.

To those activities in which one or the other sex has a monopoly based on psycho-physical attributes, Swazi attach judgements of value. The work of man is superior to that of woman. It is therefore not the type of work, or its productivity value, but the sex of the workers that gives rating to labour. The specific duties of men are warfare, hunting, cattle-keeping, and sporadic, energetic labour in gardens and building. The work of the women is primarily domestic and agricultural, and is more monotonous and continuous. The man clears virgin fields of trees and rock, the woman then does most of the hoeing and planting; he cuts the timber from the forests for palisading the cattle byre and supporting the hut, she cuts the grass for thatching and plaiting. He stands and argues in the council, but she may only discuss family affairs. While he seeks doctors or diviners, and goes on long journeys, which once were dangerous and tests of manhood, she tends the home and rears her children. He herds and milks the cattle, the main index of wealth, while she is often considered a menace to their health and, during menstruation in particular, must make long detours so as not to pollute the animals by contact. The specific duties of men are those commemorated in song and dance, and in tales told to the children. 'Women do not dance their work.'

Most work is performed by men working with men, or by women assisted by women. When members of both sexes co-operate in the same activity, they divide into sex groups. Swazi always stress sex differences and attraction; they consider sex a potentially disruptive force which, if controlled, becomes an incentive to harmonious co-operation. Usually in joint labour the men and women pass insinuating remarks and compete with each other on a sex basis. 'To work close to a woman kills your work. You see that she is female and you male. When you stand with men and she is with women, you rival each other. It awakens your manhood.'

Swazi recognize that in some activities the division of labour is conventional, and then it is not correlated with specific sex traits. Local variations exist through historical contacts. Thus in the Namahasha district, where Ronga influence is strong, men thatch, bray, sew the skin skirts for women, and plait the fine beer strainers, while in the rest of the country similar tasks are normally allotted to women. Even within a local subdivision, the allocation of duties is not as rigid as a mere listing of 'Men's and Women's Occupations' might suggest, since necessity sometimes makes members of one sex perform work associated with the other. An old princess, daughter of Mswati, expounded the position of women in her father's day: 'Women did hard work. They often were left alone because the men, with the boys as carriers, went to the royal villages. Sometimes the girls had to look after the cattle. No, not the mothers, because they were of other blood (groups).' An old man added: 'If the father were away and there were no sons at the homestead, who would do the milking? The daughters, of course. Such daughters would be praised.' In conservative homes of modern times the overlapping in the intermediate occupations is often marked, but at the extremes—hunting and warfare at one end, and tending the children and cooking for the family at the other—rigid division and rating remain.

In addition to division of work between men and women, age influences the labour supply. Children are not encouraged to undertake strenuous work. Thus a mother refused to allow her young son to chop wooden poles with the men, saying: 'It is heavy. He is still a child and he is not strong. Let him rather stay with the children.' The most tiring work is normally undertaken by the full-grown men and women. To the immature and the very aged, Swazi relegate duties that do not require strength, but physical purity. Old people usually continue active work as long as possible, however, for they are aware of the precariousness of their economy. Only old men and women with many sons and strong and energetic daughters-in-law can take life easily.

Rank by birth cuts across distinctions of sex and age; every Swazi does not participate to the same extent in manual labour. The aristocrats and their leading councillors are responsible for providing suitable conditions for successful effort rather than contributing their own labour. They arrange that ritual specialists treat the land, the seed, the growing fields; they regulate the times of the various stages of garden work; they summon men and women for communal parties in district and national enterprises; and they supervise the feeding and entertainment of workers when a task is completed. The time taken up in these tasks inevitably leads to the aristocrats performing less manual labour than their subjects, and some of the older princes allow their nails to grow into long talons to show that they need not exert themselves, and can afford to supervise and talk.

They are not, however, exempt from working with their subjects, and most of the food in their homesteads is the fruit of their own efforts. The extent to which the king, princes, chiefs, and noble-born men and women, including the queen mother, take part in the ordinary routine of work, in addition to performing specific organizational and ritual duties, depends partly on personal character and partly on social restrictions. Sobhuza dances and parades with his men, but does not accompany them to the fields because he must devote so much time to other duties. The late Queen Mother Lomawa was sickly and performed the minimum of garden work required by ritual; Nukwase, her successor, has always been an energetic gardener and goes early in the morning to a vegetable plot she started near the capital. Princes and princesses join with other men and women in local work parties, but there is less necessity for them to work constantly.

Although the aristocrats are expected to participate in the productive activities of their homesteads, certain magico-religious restrictions are imposed by rank. The king, his *tinsila*, some of the leading chiefs and magicians, the queen mother, and the two ritual queens are not permitted to carry burdens on their heads. It is taboo, and Swazi believe that to break the prohibition would lead to national disaster. The queen mother is also prohibited from using the grinding stones for grain, and her food must therefore be prepared for her.

Senior princes and chiefs may do little work in their own principalities, and yet stand shoulder to shoulder with their subjects when they serve at the royal villages. Participation by aristocrats in communal parties indicates that tribute labour is not directed to the specific holder of a position, but to the position itself: kingship receives recognition and not the temporary incumbents of office. Moreover, at the capital men, plebeian and aristocratic, often undertake tasks such as plaiting rope and thatching, which in their own homes they leave to their women folk. Discussing this, men have said simply: 'It is at the capital' or 'We work for the *Inkosi*'.

3. *Specialization*

As a result of the economic homogeneity of Swazi society, each individual plies a number of crafts. Every man is able to build, hoe, tend cattle, sew skins, and cut shields; every woman is able to thatch, garden, make mats and other domestic utensils.

But recognition of individual aptitude has led to a limited specialization within the general skills expected of each man and woman. Men able to bray hide with the jagged metal scraper, and leave the skin pliable and whole, or to cut shields of good shape and balance, or to carve dishes that neither crack nor wobble, are commissioned by their less deft and sometimes less patient fellows. Similarly, women whose mats and baskets are firmly and neatly bound, whose hut pinnacles are strong and regular, and more especially women who can make strong pots, are *tinyanga* (specialists) in the industries of the society. But they work at these subsidiary tasks in odd hours—at beer drinks, after work in the fields, on days when agriculture is taboo for ritual reasons—and Swazi specialization is more of a hobby than a full-time occupation.

While certain crafts are practised primarily or even solely by individuals with particular skills, local environmental features also contribute to specialization. The best carvers live in the well-wooded bush veld, where the finest timbers are found. There grows the *umvangate* (wild syringa: *Baukea africana*), *umnguma* (wild olive: *Olea verrucosa*), *umhohlo* (elephant wood: *Bolusanthus speciosus*), and *umtoma* (Transvaal ebony: *Diospyras mespiliformis*). A few carvers work in the middle veld and one or two in the high veld, but there good wood is rare. The people of the uplands tend to barter mats and grain for articles made by the skilled carvers of the bush country. Again the finest pots are made by women who live near *liɓumba* (clay deposits) scattered over the country, often near river beds of the middle and low veld. Salt was formerly only obtainable from the plant *sishephelu* and from two types of soil, *munyu* and *voyizane*, which were not widespread. The salt was worked by the people in the vicinity of these areas and exchanged for other articles. For no commodities is there, however, organized inter-district exchange comparable to that found in East Africa and Melanesia, nor is there a recognized class of traders. The craftsmen who ply their local hobbies trade their goods haphazard at irregular intervals: occasionally a man from the low veld gathers together a few articles and, accompanied by a wife or a *lubziɓi* (young carrier), sallies forth to the higher areas, or a man from the high veld, when on a visit to the low veld, takes the opportunity to acquire articles needed in his home. There are no fixed partners, no trade routes, no definite middlemen.

As the homestead is the basic economic unit, crafts tend to be inherited. A man usually uses his sons and a woman her daughters as chief assistants. In a sample of eleven wood carvers, nine had been taught by kinsmen, and of eight potteresses seven had learnt from their 'mother'. But these crafts do not carry sufficient prestige or profit to be jealously monopolized.

The two occupations that are most exclusive are those of the specialist in ritual and the smith. With the specialist in ritual I deal in the following chapter.

The work of the smith requires a long apprenticeship, skill, and, formerly, self-discipline in maintaining the taboos. The early Swazi both smelted ore from the matrix and turned it into various articles— hoes, knives, pincers, and spears. It is important to stress the distinction between smelting and smithing. Smelting is 'a chemical process in which the ore is separated into the metal and the slag', and smithing is a physical process 'in which the metal does not change materially in composition but in shape'.[1] No deep mining was undertaken, partly because of the simplicity of the smelting technique and partly because of the nature of the ore (haematite and malachite). The ore was carried by hand to the forge for smelting. Apart from a few pockets of iron in the country, the main supply was obtained from the coast. The number of men who were able to smith always outnumbered those who could also smelt.

The smiths hold a high position in Swazi society. Their implements have a definite scarcity value. Iron implements are never buried with their owners, but form part of the treasured inheritance of the heirs.[2] Sobhuza was anxious that the old craft should not be lost when European metals became available at shops, and he sought and found the son of a smith of his father's reign. This man, Mahutfulo Gininza, combines his work as smith with the post of governor of the royal village of Nsuka. He does not extract ore from the ground, but he uses the same technique as his fathers in his primitive forge. Formerly the work was associated with many taboos, but these have largely fallen away, and Mahutfulo was amused at the idea that the success of his work could depend on such things as nakedness or abstention from sex before entering the forge. At the same time, the workshop, a dilapidated hut, is still placed some distance from the living huts, and menstruating women do not enter.

Swazi claim that at one time they also had specialists in copper and brass. The queens of Mbandzeni wore heavy necklaces and arm-rings of copper. Sobhuza's first ten wives have on their skin aprons beads of brass. Perhaps these came into Swaziland from the Pedi, or, if the Swazi did possess knowledge of these metals, it has completely disappeared.

The simple working of metal obviously does not give an industrial character to Swazi culture any more than the limited specialization of other crafts. Swazi 'specialized' work is executed by a few individuals who have no contact with each other and no guilds to protect their interests; regular markets are absent; there is no control of supply to meet the demand; the output is limited and apparently there is no competition.

Smiths, potters, wood-carvers, and other craftsmen have no rigid price for their goods, but a rough scale of measurement obtains. Arguments, however, are rare; the first offer frequently comes from the would-be buyer, and the final price is reached by friendly discussion. The price

---

[1] L. G. Maingard: Paper read to the South African Association for the Advancement of Science, *South African Journal of Science*, Vol. XXX.

[2] Compare this with the reason given by the Tonga for not burying iron and copper articles. Junod writes that 'Iron is dangerous to the deceased because it does not decay as quickly as the corpse, the rugs, and the mats. It must not be buried. Copper and brass still less because they do not even change colour.' *Life of a South African Tribe*, 2nd Edition, Vol. I, p. 140.

may vary with the status relationship of maker and recipient. An aristocrat or kinsman who admires a piece of work is often given it freely, 'to rejoice him', 'to praise him', and the donor waits for an occasion when he will receive a return for his generosity. Although specialists derive economic benefit from their work and the more successful become wealthy, they do not attempt to free themselves entirely from the land.

4. *Work Parties and Communal Enterprises*

It is impossible for the homestead to satisfy its labour requirements at all times, and, apart from the assistance obtained from specialists, Swazi rely on sporadic communal work for a number of activities. Since there is no special class from which to draw, kinsmen and neighbours help each other, and the aristocrats are specially privileged in obtaining labour. The king and his mother obtain tribute labour from the entire nation, the princes and chiefs from subjects in their area; moreover, they may summon workers, not only for themselves, but also for relatives.

Communal parties are organized on a local basis and reflect the status of the organizer. Commoners may not demand assistance, they may merely *cela* (beg) or *ncusa* (call for) help; political authorities may *memeta* (shout) for it. A commoner holds a *lilima* (from *kulima*, to hoe), a chief holds an *umemo* (from *kumema*, to carry on the back; or *kumemeta*, to shout?). A *lilima* is communal labour, an *umeno* is essentially tribute labour. A commoner cannot request help from non-relatives living in other principalities without informing his chief; the chief controls the work of subjects and may negotiate with neighbouring chiefs if he requires extra workers or material. When a commoner decides to hold a *lilima*, he sends someone, usually a child, to invite the neighbours the day before; when a chief holds an *umemo*, he sends his warriors to shout at the cattle byre of subjects; when the king or his mother require workers, a herald walks between the rows of huts at the royal villages and issues the order three or four times in loud penetrating tones, ending with a flourish of royal praise songs.

The number of work parties held by a Swazi depends on status and to a lesser extent on the nature of the undertaking. Thus when the wealthy chief of the Mahlalela moved his homestead, he summoned the local regiments and provided beer at each stage of the activities: when the cattle byre was erected; when the first huts were carried to the new site; when they were thatched; when the floors were beaten; and, finally, when the great hut was established. But when Sifuba Twala moved his miserable abode, he could not afford to provide food for extra help at any stage and the only workers were his wife, her sister, and her sister's husband, who lived nearby. The task, which with a few extra helpers might have taken two or at the most three days, took twelve days to complete.

Rulers and chiefs encourage subjects to assist each other; no man's gardens should be ruined because he is unable to afford a *lilima*. Prince Mnisi told me that he was anxious to see that 'the poor' did not suffer, and cited the case of a woman who was ill and whose husband was away at the time that the corn was ripe for picking. Mnisi asked a neighbour to have his wives brew beer, and gave some grain himself: 'Is she a witch', he said, 'that she should be killed?' Similar instances were noted in the principalities of Nzaβankulu and the Simelane chief. But, despite these examples, poor people undoubtedly suffer sometimes because they cannot afford to reward workers.

A work party is approached from different angles by the organizer and by the workers. For the organizer it is primarily an economic venture, and secondarily an occasion for the enhancement of prestige. The cultivating of large fields and the building of large homesteads necessitate joint labour. Formerly most work parties were required for hoeing, but since the plough has been introduced and more land is cultivated, most work parties are for weeding. The first fields must be weeded when the last gardens are planted, and delay in weeding chokes a crop. Only by communal effort can the owner of large fields clear his early plots on time, and later he is confronted with the task of weeding and harvesting at the same time. The economic urgency for co-operation is also evident in building or moving homesteads. These tasks take place in winter-time, huge quantities of grass, rope, and reeds are required, and the routine activities of the homestead cannot be neglected. How can this be done without outside assistance?

The organizer is interested in having the work completed on time; to him or her (for women often organize these ventures) a work party is an economic enterprise that requires careful handling. The organizer calculates whether the stores are sufficient to stand the strain of rewarding the workers. Women are severely criticized by their husbands if they hold a party when food is low. The average Swazi does not embark on a *lilima* merely to lord it (*kuβusa*)—that position he could enjoy as fully by giving an ordinary beer party. A *lilima* is a necessity and men go to considerable trouble to obtain grain on credit, and thrifty women are careful to save grain for *emalima*. The chart on p. 146 illustrates the type of communal work party and the reward.

The reward for communal work in conservative homes is always a feast, eaten at the home of the host. This is as integral a part of Swazi economy as money payment in European service. But the feast is not regarded as a wage and is not a means whereby people support themselves. The hosts offer sporadic hospitality, not permanent employment, and work is voluntary, not compulsory. The reward is sometimes a beast, and sometimes beer. It is divided among the workers according to rank, age, sex, and locality. The larger the group, the larger its portion, is the basic principle in distribution. Individual effort or piece-work is not considered. The host calculates the amount that will be required beforehand, although the number of workers who will respond to the call is uncertain. Then, some workers come early, others late; a few people stroll along for the feast and sit expectantly on the outskirts of the throng. When beer is plentiful, the workers do not resent the guests, and only once did I see a man receive so hostile a reception that he walked away in shame. He was a man who never assisted others and was notorious for his meanness. Some hosts give non-workers a separate bowl of beer or dish of meat. At one *lilima* a very unpleasant fellow grumbled about the meagreness of the reward; the host's son turned to him angrily: 'What are you saying? Beer is to rejoice, not to pay.' An old man dismissed the grouser:

EXAMPLES OF *LILIMA* AND *UMEMO*

Status of Organizer	Work	Days	Workers		Reward
			Men	Women	
Queen Mother	Threshing	1	30 (approx.)	—	24 gallon bowls of beer
	Cutting grass	2	—	40 per day	4 gallon bowls of beer 2 large pumpkins and mealie meal
Chief	'Work party of oxen' (*lilima letinkabi*) for ploughing				Small ox
	Weeding	1	18	31 first day,	Beer made from one whole bag of *mabele*
		2	22	34 second day	
	Building reed fences	3	—	Approx. 20 each day	Beer made from half bag *mabele* and quarter bag mealies (i.e. between 10 and 12 gallons)
Rich Headman	Moving and Rebuilding	14	27 men and 14 women helped him at various periods		Gave beer from half bag *mabele* at various stages and also killed a goat
	Weeding	1	12	24	About 8 gallons of beer and pumpkins for converts
Poor Headman	Weeding	1	—	18	1 gallon beer
	Grass for thatching	1	—	12	2 gallons of beer

'*Uyanuka silungu*' (He smells European). In theory the rulers need not reward workers, but they usually provide a beast or two when a big job is completed, and generosity, not payment on any fixed scale, is expected of them.

In addition to the economic benefits, a host derives a great deal of personal prestige from a large *lilima*. The social aspects of a work party are more particularly marked when the host is an important man. Dancing, singing, boasting, and display are as essential as the feast. Before a task begins for political leaders, workers gather together and sing and dance at the host's home. When the work is over, the feast is enjoyed at leisure; if the work ends late, the feast is postponed till the following day. Then the entertainment begins: men and women sit in their separate groups chanting old national songs, and every now and then an individual rises and flaunts his or her dancing skill to honour the host and rejoice the spectators. The host sits on his mat or sheepskin rug apart from the rest of the people. He keeps the workers under control, distributes the food, and calls any man whom he wishes specially to honour to drink from his own pot of beer.

The worker in a communal party does not give his services from purely philanthropic motives. He is aware that, if he does not assist others, he, in his turn, will not receive assistance. Individuals engaged in joint effort are expected to concentrate and work seriously. I have watched them sweat in the fields for hours on end, hardly pausing to rest. To relax after a short spell of work is an admission of inferiority and of laziness. Each worker tries to keep up with the others in the line. When he feels he has shown his stamina, he may relax, look around, pass remarks, comment on someone who is obviously slacking, or who is chopping wildly with the hoe, or merely pushing the earth back over the weeds. The right time to rest and talk is when the task is complete, and the whole crowd gathers round the food. Sometimes work by a *lilima* is very bad, but usually it is satisfactory. A Swazi knows that if he does not work as well as others, he will be criticized and lose support for his own endeavours.

Apart from the motives of economic interest and self-respect, Swazi enjoy the feasting and general conviviality that mark the end of the work. They occasionally discuss the generosity of the host before they respond to his call, and I know one woman who was said to be so mean that no one wanted to work in her gardens. Poverty is regarded very differently from meanness. Conservatives express scorn of the *emalima* of those Christians who do not 'thank' helpers with a feast, but 'pay' each individual worker a separate reward—a candle, a piece of soap, a little salt, or even a small sum of money. 'They are like Europeans. They buy people', is quite a common comment.

The chief of a principality is always notified of a big *lilima* and is invited to the feast. He does not participate in the work. If he arrives he receives a lavish welcome and communal parties are an effective means of establishing personal contact between chief and subject. Gudumane Mahlalela, a relatively unimportant chief, told me that he was extremely popular 'because he always visited his subjects at their beer parties!' If the chief cannot come, a bowl of beer or some meat may be sent as tribute to him.

A *lilima* establishes contact between chief and subject; an *umemo* may bring together chief and chief. Thus when Prince Nzaβankulu held his *umemo*, some of Princess Sencaβaphi's subjects drifted along to help, and the Prince sent to Sencaβaphi (who is his classificatory sister) three huge bowls of beer. She reciprocated later with the side of a goat. The inter-principality effect of an *umemo* depends on the state of feeling already existing between the chiefs.

A few enterprises require a more elaborate organization than a single *umemo*: a number of workers may be needed to perform separate tasks for a common end. The outstanding examples of this are the building of a new royal village, the moving of an old village to a new site, the repair of the *indlunkulu* of the capital. In these national enterprises, the rulers draw on the resources of different localities for the supply of essential materials: reeds from the marshes, long grass from the midlands for thatching and plaiting, and sturdy wooden poles and saplings from the low veld. Materials are supplied by the chiefs of principalities who call upon the services of their own subjects, male or female, according to the nature of the work. Men and women expert in different stages of building are summoned, and within the sex division there is further particularization on the basis of age.[1]

Large-scale enterprises requiring planning, foresight, and the ability to control as many as 1,000 workers on specific days, are always connected with the king or his mother. The important fact emerges that, although each homestead is more or less self-sufficient and economically independent, the political system creates a widespread economic interdependence and a specialization of tasks, even if of a temporary nature.

5. *The Distribution of Wealth*

A Swazi is considered rich if he has many cattle, a large harem, and fields productive enough to feed his family and disburse hospitality. Without any one of these he is often labelled 'poor': without cattle he cannot obtain wives, without wives he cannot provide hospitality (the demonstration of wealth), without fields he cannot support his family.

Swazi are materialists, not mystics. Too much stress has been laid on the ritual value of the possessions of primitive people, too little on the material uses. Swazi desire *impahla* (goods) to satisfy their earthly needs for food, sex, shelter, and status privileges; the goods which satisfy these purposes acquire ritual and æsthetic values.

The sentimental attachment between men and the things that they make and use exists to a greater or lesser degree in every society, and in primitive peasant societies the attachment may go farther than in industrial centres, leading to identification between men and things. Thus the Swazi identify the milk of cattle with the tie of kinship, and a Swazi may not drink milk in a homestead where he or she intends to marry; or, again, intimate personal possessions are regarded as containing the essence of a person and must be buried with the body to which they belong. The identification, or mystic participation, is always limited by socio-economic

[1] See Appendix VII for an example.

considerations: we find, for example, that not everything associated with the dead must accompany them to the next world.

Wealth is unevenly distributed, as one would expect in a peasantry organized under a hereditary and military system. Wealth can be discussed under the headings of land, cattle, and women. All are described as *impahla* (goods) and over each category the *umnikati* (owner) has various rights, which must be reconciled with the rights of others, for it is never the individual, but the individual in his group, who exercises recognized economic claims.

Land

Land, the basis of the economic system, is held by the rulers. The power that they wield over subjects is usually referred back to the control they exercise over the distribution of land. Land is valued according to the various purposes for which it is required, and though its area be vast, its quality may be poor. In Swaziland, it is the scarcity of good arable land which makes its distribution a major index of status.

The king, as 'herder of the people', is said to 'serve out' the land. Within the principalities this prerogative is vested in the chiefs, subject always to an appeal to the king's court. And within the principalities, the headmen divide the fields among their dependents in proportion to the status of their wives and the age and sex of their children.

Swazi say: 'Of course a chief has fat lands; he does the cutting for others.' The gardens of the rulers are more extensive than those of any subject, and throughout the country are *emasimi wenkosi* (royal fields) from which they receive the harvest from the crops cultivated by kinsmen and subjects. Some of the royal fields lie on the fertile sites of old royal villages (e.g. Emfabantu and Shayaze); others are unused plots selected by councillors. And a few chiefs, anxious to win royal favour and show respect, set aside a field and plant it 'for the *Inkosi*'. Within the principality the size of the chief's gardens depends largely on the size of his own family, and in addition he has a large field cultivated under his direction by his people. A chief with a very small family may have less land than some of his wealthy polygynous subjects.[1]

Within the homestead, the largest field always belongs to the headman and his mother and is worked by all the inmates. The rest of the land is distributed among the wives, and adjustment is made between the demands of seniority and the economic needs of junior wives with more children than their seniors. To give one wife fertile soil protected from sharp winds and to give another poor, stony, exposed ground may disrupt a homestead.

As long as the land is used, and the subject does not violate any major law of citizenship, his rights to the land are recognized; but if for various reasons the land is abandoned or the subject banished, the land reverts to

[1] Thus Chief Gudumane Mahlalela, who has only one wife and no adult children, cultivates two gardens of under 2 acres each; and his subjects cultivate for him a large field of about 4 acres. His more successful half-brother, Makwedla, has ten wives and many grown children, and claimed 14 fields of which four were over 2 acres.

L

the overlord. The old system of land tenure depended on adequate land being available for chiefs and subjects; at present, there is a rigid delimitation of land, and this has had important consequences.

Indebtedness for garden land and other privileges is commuted in service and also in tribute from the products of the land. The amount is neither regular nor specificed, and depends on the wish of the subject. The custom, spoken of as *ukwetfula*, is basically part of the relationship of son to father and indicates respectful subordination. This was extended to political lords, and Swazi tell me that formerly chiefs vied with each other in the magnitude of their gifts to the king, but to-day the custom is falling away.

Pasture land is more widely shared than garden lands, but, at the same time, grazing rights are controlled by political allegiances. A Swazi cannot pasture his cattle wherever he pleases. Rulers have recognized areas near their large cattle posts to which subjects do not take their cattle. Within each principality there are exclusive pastures for the use of cattle of the local inhabitants, and herdboys co-operate on a local basis against others who bring cattle to their watering holes or pasture. A headman, moreover, may drive away stray cattle which come too close to the immediate environs of his homestead, where his own animals graze when they are not taken to a common field.

The political overlord also exercises control over such natural resources as reeds and indigenous timbers. While the king and his mother may call on any chief for a supply, local chiefs (sometimes acting on behalf of their subjects) must obtain permission from their colleagues. In some of the middle-veld and bush-veld areas chiefs also set aside special hunting grounds, and for others to infringe this preserve invites trouble. The spoils of the hunt are carefully divided with reference to the status of the organizer, the rights of the men who first wounded the animals, and the age and local affiliations of the other participants.

Cattle

The distribution of livestock further illustrates the correlation of rank and economic privileges. Swazi own sheep, goats, and dogs, but cattle are the *sine qua non* of wealth. 'A beast is the head of a person.' 'Cattle are our life, our bank, the property which establishes us.' 'Cattle do not rot like corn, and they multiply with time.' Their uses are multifarious: they provide food and clothing, they are the most desired reward for loyal service, the medium by which ancestral goodwill is ensured for health and prosperity, the closest approximation to currency, the means of ratifying marriage, the modern beasts of burden and essential draught animals. They are required on occasions of national and family importance, and a man without cattle is indeed poor and insignificant—'he is like an orphan without kinsmen'.

The Swazi express the emotional attitude typical of so many African tribes to their herds. Epigrams, symbolism, riddles are built around them; a rich vocabulary exists to describe animals of different colours and horns of various shapes, and men are referred to in terms of cattle and cattle are praised with the praises of men. Each beast in the byre is known by name, colour, and temperament; some have well-known genealogies, and the age of cows is gauged by accurate enumeration of their calves. Children model clay oxen and play games with herding, milking, and cattle raiding as the central themes; folk tales and national legends extol cattle blessed with human characteristics. Sometimes in the evening, when the cattle are brought home to be milked, spontaneous praise songs by the herdboys will mingle with the lowing. Elaborate ritual provides for almost every condition of the herd, and aims at improving their health and fertility, and at neutralizing evil influences emanating from mourners, menstruating women, or other sources of dangerous power. The king is praised as the 'Bull' of the nation.

Now whereas every man has a claim to land, he has no such claim to cattle. While a few Swazi own several hundred head, others possess none at all. Because cattle are not counted, and because wealthy men place their herds in more than one homestead, it is difficult to obtain accurate figures of their distribution. In former times cattle were concentrated largely in the kraals of national leaders, but at present any man able to earn enough money can buy a beast and gradually accumulate a herd.

To say that the king and his mother are the wealthiest cattle owners in Swaziland gives a false impression. It is more accurate to state that the cattle of kingship, the cattle of the nation, exceed those of any individual. In 1936, Ngolotsheni Motsa was sent to look at these herds and estimated that there were over 3,000 in royal ranches in the bush veld and nearly 1,000 in other royal villages. The sources from which the cattle of kingship are derived have been restricted with the abolition of inter-tribal raids, and of the practice of 'eating up the byre' of men condemned as traitors or wizards. The bulk of the herd remains part of the inheritance of each king and to this nucleus are added cattle from fines, tribute, death dues, and loβola. At present, cattle given in marriage for women attached to the royal line is possibly the largest single source of revenue. Senior princesses command up to 100 beasts, and the juniors are never considered to be worth less than twenty-five. Moreover, male subjects anxious to marry may obtain one or two beasts for this purpose from the 'cattle of kingship', and in return refund the full loβola of the first daughter of the union. Any girls absorbed into the royal villages as attendants of the queens are rated more highly than other children of their fathers, and, in the same way as female war captives, are regarded for purposes of national economy as royalty and often loβola'd as such.

Each royal cattle post has its own name, history, and place in government. The king cannot sell the animals for his own benefit. Some are used to feed the people at national gatherings, others to obtain wives for royalty, and some for national sacrifice. The most sacred herd is the *mfukwane*, which numbers a couple of hundred head and may not be used for ploughing or other mundane purposes.

Within the principalities chiefs usually, but not inevitably, own larger herds than their subjects. The nucleus of their wealth is the inheritance, but I have heard of three cases in which this was dissipated during the minority of the chiefs by their guardians. At the same time, under the conservative régime, a chief can recuperate his fortunes more rapidly than a commoner, wealth is a potentiality of his position. He receives cattle in fines,[1] tribute, and high *loɓola* for his daughters.

There are an increasing number of commoners who possess as many cattle as their chiefs, or even more. The following figures from the Matsapha district indicate the variation between different homesteads:

No. of Cattle									
0	0–5	5–10	10–20	20–30	30–40	40–50	50–60	60–70	Over 70
No. of owners									
6	0	2	7	9	4	3	2	3	1

These figures do not include cattle owned by headmen, and kept at other homesteads.

Within the family itself there is a further inequality of wealth as a result of the mode of inheritance. This is particularly the case in polygynous homesteads where the oldest son of the main wife receives all the cattle of the main hut, any cattle not otherwise allotted: and also the marriage cattle of the first daughter of each of the other huts. His share far exceeds the inheritance of his brothers and half-brothers. Girls may be given property, but may not inherit it; if there is no son the property may, however, be kept for the first male grandchild. The youngest brother always receives the *insulamnyembeti* beast of his sisters, but a middle brother may inherit nothing. Oldest sons of the remaining wives inherit the cattle allotted to their own mothers' huts, and the cattle of all daughters other than the first. Their younger brothers are in a relatively worse position. To even up the position, a man may *sikela lupawu* (cut a portion for) any child, male or female, but inequality of wealth is sanctioned to buttress authority. Similarly, definite provision may be made for each wife separately, and there is the custom of giving a woman after many years of marriage a beast (or beasts) known as *liphakelo*. This animal entitles her to partake of milk in her husband's home, and in the event of his death the *liphakelo* is an insurance for herself and her children. But the main stock remains the property of the main wife, and she and her son are supposed to look after the other members of the family.

Wives

Cattle, the main goods in circulation, are exchanged primarily through marriage. In certain contexts, Swazi tend to speak of wives in much the same way as they speak of cattle, and together they mark status. One day when I remarked to Mnisi that his daughter was beautiful, he replied: 'That she is female is enough. A cow is a cow, no matter how thin.'

Since the aristocrats usually have most wives, they control the major flow of wealth. Cattle come to aristocrats rather than go from them on the marriage market. The king himself need not give any cattle for his queens (Sobhuza is the first king to *loɓola* his wives); while commoners rarely receive more than twelve head of cattle for their daughters, princes and chiefs demand from fifteen upwards. On the debit side, the expense is again less for aristocrats. The aristocrats may expend more in obtain-

---

[1] For example, Chief Nzaɓankulu received seventeen beasts in fines during 1935; Chief Mnisi received eleven.

ing their wives, but their subjects contribute some of the cattle for the main and most expensive wife. I calculated that marriages of Sobhuza's female relatives brought into the immediate Dlamini family over 300 head of cattle in the years 1934–7, and his own daughters were not yet mature. The number disbursed to acquire wives for the leading Dlamini men is impossible to ascertain. Whether expenditure for women equals income from women depends on the ratio of the sexes.

While polygyny is the ideal of conservatives, the accumulation of wives is restricted by social and political motives. Even if a man has adequate land and enough cattle to increase his harem, he may prefer not to obtain more women. This restraint is imposed by the fact that too many wives often leads to jealousy and witchcraft, and—even more important —by the fact that a commoner who has more than five or six wives wakens the enmity of less successful men. Cattle can be, and are distributed in other homesteads if they make an owner too conspicuous, but wives cannot be so conveniently kept in the background. Thus polygyny, despite the prestige that it brings, involves certain disadvantages and is kept within the limits imposed by status. Only the king may increase his harem without fear of censure, and conflict between the queens is mitigated by their distribution at many royal centres.

Women may be described as an investment of the Swazi; whether or not they are a profitable investment depends on their physical strength and fertility. A monogamist may become wealthy if his wife bears many children, especially girls, and, on the other hand, the wealth of a polygynist decreases in the absence of offspring. Swazi consider that both the birth and the sex of children are largely due to luck and ritual. This is important in considering wealth among the Swazi: the objects they prize most—women and cattle—are subject to accidents outside man's control. Wealth can fluctuate considerably in a man's lifetime, not through the artificial manipulation of an exchange, nor as a result of concentration and industry, but through *inhlanhla lenthle* (good luck) and *inhlanhla lembi* (bad luck). Death of young children, disease, sterility, and other disasters threaten the economic security of all Swazi, but the political leaders have greater opportunity than their subjects to recover from these misfortunes.

Summing up this section, we see that wealth and political power usually coincide, political power creating wealth. Political power is vested primarily in the aristocracy of birth, and wealth is therefore largely a privilege of pedigree. Even those aristocrats who do not hold political power have more chance than the average commoner to gain wealth. Some commoners are very wealthy, but their wealth is limited by social considerations, and is, as it were, held on sufferance. Wealth, in fact, is relative—the standard is the property possessed by political authorities, and for a commoner to own more than his chief is condemned among conservatives.

6. *Prestige and Generosity*

Swazi accept economic and social inequality, and approve of wealth as the privilege of men of noble birth. But obligations as well as benefits accrue from wealth: rich men gain prestige and security, not by hoarding, but by judicious distribution.

There is a limited competition for material possessions, largely because of their prestige value. The competition is primarily expressed through ritual, which is over and above the general technical effort. Swazi have a large body of productive ritual, and there are various practices designed to steal the fruits of another's labour and to protect one's own property from theft. The correlation between theft and ritual is shown in the attitude towards the thief, who is despised as a wizard.[1] But the man who uses ritual only to produce abundance and to protect his own efforts is socially approved. To derive full benefit from his goods, however, he must use them partly for the benefit of others. This follows to some extent from the perishable nature of most Swazi products and the absence of desirable alternatives: what else can be done with large stores of grain, beer, or meat?

Generosity, moreover, is inculcated from childhood. Women beat children who are greedy and take too large a portion of food from the common pot; the children themselves enforce the rule of sharing; a woman found to hide food in her hut was jibed at by co-wives. A good person gives, a bad person is stingy and eats in secret—'like Europeans', is often added. In the model and rich homes of Prince Nzaßankulu and the diviner Mahube an extra dish was usually set aside for the unexpected guest. Generous hospitality is a law: every traveller is shown a hut, and receives food and a sleeping mat for the night. Aristocrats and men connected with national duties are particularly well entertained, but no one, however insignificant or disreputable, should be turned away from a home. A host belittles his gifts, the recipient exaggerates them and accepts even the smallest article with both hands.

A Swazi is constrained to use gifts in a definite manner. Thus if a beast is slaughtered in his honour, he divides it according to strict measure, apportioning the liver and one side to the women, the entrails and tail to the boys who skinned the beast, the head to the men of the homestead, and the hide to whom he chooses, and so on. Umnyakaza instructed me in the etiquette of accepting gifts: 'Things like pumpkins, monkey-nuts, even chickens, don't count, but be careful with meat and beer. Divide exactly and don't show favouritism. A man must not grow fat on presents. Remember that the people who made the gifts see how you use them.' The elaborate ritual of giving provisions far above the needs of the traveller is most obvious when the king is the guest, and he, through his officials, redistributes the major portion of the tribute he receives. Thus at a dance in the Peak district, fifty-four pots of beer were brought on one afternoon from eight different centres. Each group of carriers received a pot, known as *intfutfu* (smoke), for their labour, three bowls were sent to the harem, and the remainder was distributed among the dancers and onlookers according to rank, sex, and locality.

Generosity is distinct from waste. Waste occurs mainly in societies

---

[1] The usual technique for catching a thief is to treat an object or spot with *ithophomnwane* (*kuthopha*—to grab; *mnwane*—the toe). The medicine, in Swazi belief, causes the hand or foot of the thief to swell or his body to break into foul sores.

where people produce more than they require, or where the means of production are monopolized by a privileged few who are under no obligation to level up possessions. Waste is rare in Swazi society, since no surplus is produced and the privileges of aristocrats depend on the goodwill of commoners. I never saw food thrown away or destroyed in Swaziland, except for specific ritual purposes. Vast quantities of food are consumed at ceremonies, especially at weddings, even though later in the year food may be scarce, but there is no waste. The distribution, imposed by recognized obligations, both expresses and forms social ties.

While generosity is admired, the accumulation of wealth is not conspicuous. Rich and poor live in the same type of home, have the same meagre furnishings, the same style of clothing, and similar occupations. Rich men divide their homesteads, and loan out their surplus cattle; they bury their stores of grain in pits that are not easily noticed—and hide their money in the ground or the thatching of their huts. Display and boasting meet with social disapproval unless directed towards an approved social end. People of rank have greater licence, and commoners consider that they have a stake in their wealth, since it should be expended to obtain and retain dependents. In the same way as the size of a family indicates the status of a headman, so the number of subjects is an index of political power and generosity.

In order not to awaken jealousy in overlords or fellow subjects, and indirectly to ensure that epidemics in one locality will not destroy his entire herd, a wealthy man often places out (verb, *kusisa*) cattle among poor families. The *isisiwe* (temporary keeper) benefits by having the cows for milk and the oxen for ploughing. If an animal dies, he takes the meat, but, to show that he did not kill the beast, he should always carry the skin and the tail to the owner. The *isisiwe* may not treat the cattle as though they were his own and use them to pay fines or take wives. In return for honest service, however, the owner may advance animals for marriage or other purposes. Goats are also loaned out, and as they bring less return to the keeper he is usually rewarded annually with one goat, called *sisinga*. In those instances where the *isisiwe* abuses his trust, the owners usually have no redress, since the *isisiwe* possesses little. Occasionally a poor man or a bachelor, because he has no one to herd for him, places his few head of livestock with a friend. But the *sisa* relationship is essentially associated with the distribution of goods by the wealthy to the poor. It was impossible to estimate the extent to which the custom mitigated poverty throughout the country.

The king and his mother do not *sisa* cattle; in addition to the herd at each of the main royal villages, they establish *tinhlonhla* (cattle posts) under trusted men of aristocratic or plebeian families. I have the names of six royal cattle posts in the middle veld and the bush veld, and there may be others. A keeper of 'king's cattle' derives advantages similar to those of the *isisiwe*. Moreover, he distributes the milk that he himself does not require, and divides the meat of any animal that dies among the people of the neighbourhood. He is also directly dependent on the rulers, brings them his cases, and may ask them for marriage cattle and other favours. The keepers have a high standing in the nation; as Ngwaβadla Dvuβa of the Empolonjeni ranch stated: 'This is a work for the king for which a reason is clear.' In olden days disputes sometimes arose because a man in charge misappropriated the cattle. To avoid this, he is not allowed to have his homestead at the post and build 'as though the cattle of the king were his own'. At the post he may erect only a living and store hut; his main homestead is usually close by.

With the attitude to wealth that I have outlined, borrowing (*kuɓoleka*) and begging (*kucela*) have connotations different from those they possess in a European milieu. No shame attaches to either. They enhance the status of the rich, and are necessary for the poor. Begging, in particular, confers an honour—it is a sign of deference. Only if the request is refused is there a certain awkwardness, and to avoid this intermediaries are usually employed. At first, not understanding the Swazi approach, I resented the way favours were always asked through a third person. Then someone explained: 'It would shame you to refuse and me to be refused. A boy does not ask for a bride; he sends someone as his mouth.' If a request cannot be accorded, the refusal should always be courteously phrased. The Swazi have the attitude expressed by the Moroccans: 'Say to me, "O my lord", and strip me naked; don't say "O dog", even though you make me rich.'

A gift obtained by begging need not be reciprocated, but a loan should always be repaid. Payment of a father's debt can be enforced against sons in the chief's court, but such action is seldom necessary, for, as European traders will tell you, most Swazi are scrupulous in repaying loans.

Sisa and generosity are thus recognized means of reducing economic disparity. The redistribution, far from humiliating the receiver, is praised and brings prestige to the giver. The property privileges of rank are thus on a secure basis.

At the same time, the absence of an economic class structure is evident. Accurate figures of income and expenditure are unknown, and this is typical of a society where goods are limited and not regularly assessed: land is not surveyed, crops are not measured on a fixed scale, and regular wages are not paid. The basis of prestige and power is primarily birth, not the accumulation of property. The figures that I give in relation to property were obtained by laborious effort. Whereas my questions on law, politics, and ritual were grasped even when they met with opposition, most uneducated Swazi could not understand my efforts to measure fields, estimate harvests, count cattle, and define standards of living. I do not consider that their attitude was due to hostility and suspicion. Some of the people were undoubtedly afraid that 'when the white man counts your goods he taxes them', but the main difficulty was that the approach to property is different in European and Swazi milieus and different factors are emphasized. Swazi do not discuss the exact size of a herd, the number of workers, the hours of work, and the acreage that a chief has under cultivation. They are interested in whether the cattle come from *loɓola*, fines, or raids, the composition of a work party, and whether the chief is a generous man.

The administration of the people involves heavy expenditure that must be met from national and local revenue. The political leaders provide food for periodic meetings of councillors and of labourers, reward specialists in ritual and messengers (whose duties sometimes keep them from their homes for weeks and even months), and perform ritual that involves the slaughter of many sacrificial beasts and the brewing of great quantities of beer. The king and certain chiefs also support orphans and destitute aged as well as their own extensive families. No sharp distinction is drawn between public and private income. The king or chief, as main heir to his father's estate, inherits the property allocated to the main hut, and as the eldest son of his mother inherits the property allocated specifically to her hut. But once he is appointed 'king' or 'chief' the two inheritances become fused, and in a government as personal as that of the Swazi, the difference between a man acting in his public and in his private capacity is not recognized. 'If the king gives me a beast, do I know from where it comes? Does he say, "The nation would not like me to give it to you; so I will take it from my own secret herd"? No, the goods of the king are the goods of the nation.'

CHAPTER XI

INDIVIDUAL VARIABILITY AND RITUAL

THE main specialists are the so-called 'magicians', who operate in different departments of the homogeneously occupied society. Some concentrate on agriculture, others on war, others on cattle-keeping, others on specific illnesses, and so forth. Because of the recognition accorded to their claims to exceptional powers and a readiness to accept their pronouncements, they have the best opportunity, next to the king and his mother, to sponsor new ideas. But men are original only in relation to local contemporaries, and only develop their ideas against a receptive social background. The purpose and direction of the magicians, or specialists in ritual, lie in the social conditions of their times. Their advice is followed because of the promise it offers of immediate advantage, and it requires the perspective of history and a comparison with other cultures to judge the real effect. The efforts of the Swazi specialists in ritual stand condemned by European standards of science; to the conservative Swazi these people remain the honoured representatives of law and knowledge.

1. *Recognition of Individual Variability*

Swazi discuss explicitly the diversity of human qualities and use a rich vocabulary to describe recognized psychological types. No Swazi ever accepts the doctrine that all men are born equal or identical. They judge from behaviour in particular situations, and always with an egocentric bias, whether a man is mean or generous, good or evil, patient or hasty, brave or cowardly, stupid or intelligent, tractable or obstinate, thieving or honest, credulous or sceptical. 'The hearts of people are not alike', they say; and judge their fellows, as men do in every country, with such comments as 'he has no brains'; 'he is skilled with his fingers'; 'he is trustworthy'; 'he always asks questions'. They are aware of human frailties, of fickleness and deceit, and they often ascribe actions to anger, jealousy, love, and other such emotions.

Judgements of character depend on the standards of culture, and these standards change. Thus a convert said, 'It is bad to fight and to kill. It would be better if we all lived together peacefully and tilled our fields. Any army destroys its own people.' An old man, who accepted the canons of a military culture, remarked: 'He is mad. I knew another madman. When his wife committed adultery, he did not hit her or even fine her lover; he gave her much food and let her take with her whatever she liked.' Then there are the real idiots of all places and times, and among the Swazi they are tolerated and fed, and sometimes teased by the children. Swazi never treat these unfortunates with cruelty or open contempt, not because of the sensitivity of their feelings, but because of fear and anxiety for self-protection. 'It will come back on you or your children if you mock a cripple or an idiot.' Somewhat akin to the idiots are the dreamers who think they are inspired by spirits, and yet fail to achieve the success of true diviners.

The psychic attributes that affect a man's success or failure are regarded from one standard by the people concerned and receive a different interpretation from the European sociologist. Swazi consider many qualities innate, so that certain individuals are born for happiness and others are doomed to misfortune. It is the old tale of the evil eye, or the child with the caul. I was told sad stories of men and women with *sitozi*, a quality which brings misfortune and unpopularity with ruthless inevitability. One man complained sadly that it had dogged him from childhood. It had first manifested itself when, as a very young boy, he had stabbed a goat in a fit of temper, and when the owners cut up the animal they found one whole side filled with water. In addition to facing a claim for having stabbed the beast, the boy was suspected of witchcraft, till the diviner confirmed the plea of the boy's parents that it was *sitozi*. The next time he killed an animal, the precious blood spurted out like a fountain and was all spilt. His *sitozi* was again to blame. He fears that if he were to hit anyone, even lightly, he would kill him. 'It is like thorns, some make great sores if they just touch you and others are longer and go deeper, and yet do no harm.' Another man, through his *sitozi*, fell out of favour with his chief and finally left the district. 'Whatever he did was wrong, but he was not a wizard.'

Allied to *sitozi* is *luqunga*, the passion that is roused in men, particularly those in authority, when their position is threatened. They tremble like the *luqunga* (reed). 'They are like hollow things moved by the angry wind.' They cannot be blamed for the crimes they commit. *Luqunga* rises in a chief when someone else wins the loyalty of his subjects, or in a man who is treated cruelly and has no redress: he talks of suicide or murder. It is the same uncontrollable lust to kill that enters a man when once he has slain and against which he must be purified; it is a power that pervades the very weapons that he has used so that they too need to be tempered and cooled.

Then there are men who speak in anger and their words automatically have a destructive effect; they have brought on a curse without intending to harm. Sometimes a man shouts: '*Ngitiyela utlodliwa yini*' ('I don't know what will eat you'), and those present try to bring about a reconciliation lest 'the tongue' have an effect; or a rejected woman declaims, 'You will die a bachelor' or 'You will die on the veld'. Though she does nothing, turns to no witchcraft, the man dies. Then she repents bitterly, but in vain. Some informants say that the curse gives real sorcerers an opportunity to operate without bringing suspicion on themselves; others insist that the curse itself has the harmful effect.

There are also people with *lihlumbi* (bad blood) in their bodies, who weaken and injure those whom they touch. Women who have it devitalize their men, and a man who strikes another lightly might kill him because of the power that is in his, the striker's, blood.

These attributes are considered to be innate, but not necessarily inherited from either father or mother. Some verge on witchcraft, but witchcraft is only partly innate and must be developed by special treatment. The qualities of *sitozi* and *luqunga* are in the body. They afflict automatically, and though they can to some extent be eradicated by treatment, they can never be totally removed.

The Swazi have developed an elaborate system of personality treatment which aims at making men 'shine', beloved, and successful. Personality ritual is always graded; it varies for child and adult, male and female, commoner and aristocrat. Formerly, it was a crime punishable by death to use the personality treatment of a status to which one should not aspire.

The concept of innate characteristics that can only be combated by ritual induces an attitude akin to fatalism; will power is relatively unimportant, because ritual alone is efficacious. Ritual, from the viewpoint of the European observer, may reintegrate a person and give him self-confidence, but it does not drive him to seek new channels of social expression. Personality treatment is a psychological adjustment to a socially standardized situation; it may be effective if unchallenged by strong opposition. It is essentially a sanction of conservatism.

On the other hand, individual variability affects all classes of society, irrespective of social stratification. This recognition of the oneness of mankind allows for tolerance of weakness in the aristocracy, and praise for outstanding commoners. The emphasis on the social hierarchy is not expressed in claims of ethically superior qualities by the aristocrats.

Within the social framework, buttressed by ritual, individual ambition can still operate. Competition and jealousy are regarded as 'the nature of men', and while these qualities are deplored, they explain and even justify certain actions. 'We Swazi have too much jealousy' is a phrase frequently heard in discussions between themselves. Men want not merely enough for their needs, but more than their fellows. There is ritual to produce bountiful crops in one's own fields, and there is also ritual to steal grain from neighbours. There is ritual to make one's own dogs keen of scent and swift in the hunt, and ritual to throw the dogs of others off the trail.

With all this recognition of the diversity of types, no effort is made to be original, and originality is in fact condemned and avoided. Originality is associated with arrogance, and Swazi say: 'No man should push himself forward. That is why it is good to take a position through birth.' In practical work experimentation is almost non-existent, the aesthetic side of the culture is narrowly stereotyped, and new ideas are not encouraged. Swazi should not, and usually do not wish to, cultivate temperamental differences.

The ideal personality of the Swazi varies with position, age, and sex, and to some extent with specialized occupation. Probably the greatest distinction is between the sexes. Thus the man described as 'good' or 'respected' is a man of courage in face of physical danger, acumen in the council, firmness in the home, and who is generous to all. Aggression and self-display are required on specific occasions—in warfare and in the dance—but otherwise are severely criticized. 'A bad man has greed and jealousy; he wants always to make himself great.' In a woman Swazi admire above all else industry and obedience; a bad woman is argumentative, obstinate, and a poor, slovenly worker. Those individuals who diverge too widely from the ideal, lay themselves open to mockery, ostracism, and finally to the accusation of witchcraft or sorcery.

These ideal qualities reflect the institutional activities of Swazi society, the mould by which individuals are conditioned. Swazi society is relatively simple, and the interests of institutions do not conflict. In our society, the economic structure stresses competition and aggression, religion emphasizes brotherhood, and while one political party aims at totalitarianism, another fights for individual liberty. Swazi society has a more co-ordinated and harmonious pattern. Economics, politics, law, religion, and leisure occupations inculcate, and are based on, recognition of the privileges of birth, the reciprocal duties of superiors and inferiors. They stress the dominance of the male, the dependence of women and the respect due to age. This has already been indicated in previous chapters, and will become still more evident in an analysis of the rôle of the specialist in ritual, the individual who diverges most from the ideal and yet follows a stereotyped pattern.

2.   Why and how People become Specialists in Ritual

The Swazi have a generic term, *inyanga*, which they apply to a specialist in any handicraft or profession. Thus we find the smith (*inyanga yokukhandza insimbi*, i.e. one skilled in iron work), the professional herbalist (*inyanga yemitsi*), and the expert potteress (*inyanga yokuɓumba tidziwo*). Among the specialists are also classed various types of doctors and priests, who are named according to the techniques or the speciality that they practise: the one who smites (*inyanga yokuɓula*), the corn specialist (*inyanga yokukhandza emaɓele*) the one with the bones (*inyanga eyamatsambo*), and so on. The term *inyanga* is used in a general sense for any specialist in ritual.[1]

To the Swazi ritual knowledge is 'deep', 'heavy knowledge', a powerful tool used in most private and communal undertakings. It gives success in war, good crops, rainfall, health, prosperity, and security. It is used to bring to life the fullness that it promises and so rarely yields. It bridges the gulf between the probable and the improbable (between our concepts of reality and unreality). Swazi reality is full of wonder. Men play with lightning and fly invisible through space, turn into animals or steal the souls of enemies by uttering their names. Unreality scarcely exists, and since actual disproof of ritual efficacy is lacking, doubt is the limit of Swazi disbelief. There is no rigid dichotomy of nature into the natural and supernatural; supernatural powers are all-pervasive. This does not mean that the Swazi lack pragmatic knowledge; indeed, such is obviously essential for the continuance of all human societies. But everything to them has two aspects, the ordinary and the potentially extraordinary, and the two overlap and interact.[2]

The power of ritual lies in the owner as well as in the objects he uses. 'Everything', Ngolotsheni Motsa explained in English, 'goes by connection with people. If a potteress fires a pot during menstruation it will crack. A human body is more than flesh and bone and blood. It has the

[1] I prefer to use the more neutral, less ethnocentric term, 'specialist in ritual', in place of the more usual label, 'magician', and to use 'ritual' where others might use the word 'magic'.

[2] Obviously this is not the place to discuss theories of 'magic' and religion and their relation to science, but I wish to point out that none of the recognized theories can be applied without modification to Swazi data

spirit that joins with things the body touches.' Specialists in ritual are respected, admired and feared because of the greater 'power' that is part of their deeper knowledge. Unlike certain Southern Bantu, mere knowledge of the substances is insufficient; 'things must unite with the power of the person who applies them'. The more serious the situation, the more obvious this becomes. A specialist's equipment sometimes lies unused when there is no son having the quality to endow it with success. Specialists are imbued with this 'power' by direct contact with the supernatural through the ancestors or with their sanction.

Swazi recognize two main types of ritual specialist: *inyanga yemitsi* (the herbalist) who works primarily with material ingredients, generally referred to as *imitsi*, and the *isangoma* (diviner), who relies mainly on inspiration. The two categories are mutually dependent, and the practitioners co-operate in much the same way as the general practitioner and the specialist in Western society. Swazi specialists in ritual reflect the general hierarchical tendency in Swazi society and are graded from the diviner downwards. Their grading depends on the type of ritual they perform, the people with whom it is associated, the way they obtain their knowledge and the technique they use, and, within these categories, on the successes they achieve.

Every Swazi has some knowledge of medicines, and the lowest grade of specialist is the person who has picked up a larger stock of recipes than his friends and is not prepared to distribute them without some reward. He claims no inspiration from the ancestors and no tradition of belonging to a family of specialists. He is spoken of contemptuously behind his back as a *lihumushi* (a mountebank, a shark), a man who came to his profession through ambition and shrewd business sense and extended his stock by outright purchase. Such practitioners, said to be few in Mbandzeni's reign, are definitely on the increase at present, since they have the opportunity of buying medicines from men outside the country and from European drug stores. Some specialize very intensively and will treat only one or two illnesses or misfortunes, while the cures attempted by others compare not unfavourably with the panaceas of some of our own patent medicine vendors. Informants say that some of the self-taught herbalists are skilful enough, but insist that 'the ancestors must subsequently have agreed that the work meet with success'.

Occasionally a Swazi who does not come of a 'medical' family desires to become a reputable herbalist and approaches a respected practitioner who, after consulting with prayers and libations his own ancestral teachers, usually agrees to accept the man as an apprentice. His training lasts from a few months to several years, depending on the range of knowledge of the master, the aptitude of the pupil, and the attitude of the ancestors who may show in devious ways whether or not they are satisfied. Once the apprentice qualifies, he calls on his own and on his master's spirits for success and, like other ancestrally qualified *tinyanga*, periodically renews the power of his 'bags of medicine' in an elaborate ritual reaffirming his dependence on the dead. Men who acquire expert knowledge in the above-mentioned fashion are usually motivated initially not so much by greed as by interest in their own illnesses or the illnesses of relatives. Curiosity alone is rarely considered an adequate reason for further study and is not encouraged. A layman who shows too great an interest in *imitsi* is suspected of evil intentions, and most men are therefore unwilling to appear eager to interfere in the lives of others without the backing of tradition or supernatural compulsion.

Swazi place their trust in those *tinyanga* whose careers are destined from birth and sanctioned by the dead. Knowledge of ritual and 'the medicine bags' are retained in a family and are an important part of the inheritance. The holder of the secrets imparts them to a favourite son, a younger brother, or other close kinsman, who, when the 'real owner' dies, is obliged to instruct the heir. If he does not wish to practise, another son or relative found acceptable to the dead may learn the secrets. A man is 'pushed by the heart', or 'his head takes readily' and by various signs the ancestors recognize 'their child'.

Ritual used specifically for national purposes is limited to certain loyal families. The practitioner must be acceptable to the rulers, who may deprive him and his family of the birthright if their work is considered unsatisfactory. No one may purchase or otherwise acquire the esoteric knowledge considered essential for national well-being.

Operating in both individual and national situations are the diviners (*isangoma*; plur: *isanusi*), the most powerful and respected specialists. They form a separate and significant group, and to enter the fraternity a lengthy initiation is essential. Swazi describe a diviner as *umuntfu loβoβokile* (person with hole in the head), an expression applied to anyone of outstanding intelligence. 'From the beginning' ancestral spirits are believed to have entered the bodies of some of their earthly descendants, thus giving them wisdom to foretell the future and discover the causes of misfortune and death, and imbuing them with power to show the way to security, health, and prosperity. Possession is not a metaphysical concept of the spirit world; it is the spirits themselves in a most obvious manifestation.

The initial qualities of all classes of diviners are similar, and though it is not necessary to describe these in detail, mention of some of the more striking features will illustrate the type of person who obtains power over other members in his society.

Certain types of sickness indicate possession. A man who is apparently robust and healthy falls ill. The illness sometimes follows on a terrible physical experience, but there may be no visible symptom of disease. A man becomes fastidious about his food, eats little and complains of pains in various parts of his body: his arms, his head 'that splits like a twig', his shoulder blades. He is tormented by fearful dreams of snakes encircling his body, of drowning in a flooded river, of being torn to pieces by enemies; indeed, he becomes 'a house of dreams'. These dreams must be interpreted; they are omens that can be useful in guarding against misfortune or in anticipating benefits.

It is not immediately evident that a sufferer is about to be a diviner, for many people fall ill, whereas the spirits come to few. Only after sacrifices and medicines have proved useless does some specialist diagnose that 'the patient is troubled by a spirit'. This spirit was, till Mswati's reign, always that of a kinsman, but after the war against the Mshatse (Sotho), spirits of non-relatives and of foreigners and also spirits of wild animals (snakes, crocodiles, lions, birds) came to possess men. Possession has links, on the one hand, with the ancestral cult and on the other with disease. In all cases the possessed suffers mentally and physically, but it is only if the possessing spirit is one that can be made to conform to an accepted social code that the disease is approved in ritual and the possessed becomes a diviner; otherwise the treatment is directed to 'close the spirit'. Possession by friendly human beings, most frequently kinsmen, is usually considered socially beneficial.

When the case has been diagnosed as possession, the spirit is encouraged to manifest itself. The patient is placed under the care of a recognized diviner, who may have quite a number of novices to train at one time, and they live at his village or with relatives close by. The possessed are moody and restless; sometimes they weep and brood alone, or they yawn, take snuff continually and sneeze. (The two latter are not associated —the sneeze being considered a manifestation of the spirit, 'as when a man sneezes after he has been dead' i.e. fainted.) In addition to these physical peculiarities, each novice composes a song. He rushes out, usually at night, and dances and chants his own composition, while the villagers gather around, join in the refrain and beat their hands. Eventually the nature of the spirit becomes clear, and if human it mentions its name. Should the spirit be socially acceptable, it is carefully developed over a long period of treatment.

The master diviner doctors the novice with special concoctions to put him into harmony with the spirit world. He is washed in foaming liquids and eats special herbs; he is given unique regalia and red ochre is rubbed on his hair; in all ways he is made to realize that he is different from ordinary men. Sometimes he roams the countryside gathering roots and herbs pointed out in dreams, and thus accumulates a stock of medicines. He often goes to the sea, where he collects strange shells and submerges himself in deep pools. Finally, he undergoes the ceremony of *ukuphotula*, the end of all ritual treatment, and many people come to see him dance and sing and demonstrate his power. The spectators hide odds and ends for the young diviner to discover and he throws out hints to members of the audience about their various predicaments. He is *thwasile* (reborn),[1] and is honoured with gifts of goats, assegais, and beads, because he is a man with 'the spirit in him', a man of great power and special prestige.

Despite the honoured position of diviners, men do not wish to be 'entered' by the spirits. They often fight against possession, especially in the early stages, and the reasons given express the socially inculcated attitude to greatness. It is considered best to be normal, not to be limited all one's life by special taboos on sex, food, and general behaviour; not to be exhausted by the demands of someone stronger than oneself; not to have to shoulder responsibility for the life and death of others. There are men, therefore, who try to stop the spirits, 'close the way', 'drive away the dreams' by the use of special medicines taken in accordance with rigid rites. But on the whole, this tampering with the ancestors is considered dangerous, since it may leave the person permanently delicate and deranged, an object of spite by the spirit he has thrust from

The same verb *ukuthwasa*, is used for the appearance of the new moon.

PLATE III

(*a*) WARRIORS DANCING

(*b*) AN *Inyanga* STIRRING FROTHY MEDICINES USED TO TREAT PATIENTS
SUFFERING FROM *mfufunyane*, A TYPE OF SPIRIT POSSESSION

PLATE IV

(a) PRINCESSES IN THEIR *Incwala* DRESS

(b) SOBHUZA II ON THE FIRST DAY OF THE LITTLE *Incwala*

him and of neglect by others angered at the reception given to one of their kind.

Though the diviner does not obtain his position by birth, there are certain families famous for producing diviners, and Swazi recognize that the peculiar mental quality, the disposition to see visions and dreams, lies in 'the blood'.

People of high birth and responsible political positions are not encouraged to practise as medicine men, far less to become diviners; nor do they wish to do so. Their duty is primarily to administrate and to perform national ritual. Should the affliction of possession fall on a Dlamini, the verdict is 'it came from the mother's family'. I know of only one important Dlamini, a woman, who was possessed and developed into a fully-fledged diviner. I could find no case of a leading prince or chief who was recognized as possessed. Some informants stated that if this were to happen the spirit should be closed at all costs, but others denied the necessity. One thing, however, was clear, Swazi want their leaders to represent them, to be guided by them, and not to be impelled by the wayward will of a possessing spirit. Without training, the king is acknowledged to be able to divine, to 'feel' evildoers when evildoers are near him, but power of divination is given for his own protection and for the safety of the nation: it is not developed for other purposes.

The fact that the one Dlamini who was possessed was a woman raises an interesting point. For convenience, I have written of specialists in ritual in the masculine. Actually ritual is one of the main outlets for women as well as men.[1] But whereas few women are herbalists, many are diviners. What is the reason? I think it lies in the relative status and occupations of the sexes in Swazi society. A woman's duty is at home, looking after her children. To acquire potions and to practise, the herbalist must scour the country, and the independent wandering and intimate contact with the homes of strangers is more in keeping with the behaviour of men than of women. A woman who is curious about *imitsi* runs the risk of being suspected as a sorcerer in the patriarchal, polygynous homestead; she is in a worse position than a man who acquires medicines without permission from the ancestors. Moreover, girls are rarely taught medicine by their fathers, and the heir designed for the 'bags', like the inheritor of national ritual, should be a male. Again, women are without the strong stimulus of economic ambition that drives certain men to become specialists, since it is in the power of a woman herbalist's husband to pay one beast to her parents and thereafter control all her earnings. Finally, it is difficult for a woman to fulfil her other obligations in addition to practising medicine. 'If a husband doesn't hoe, his wives will feed him; but if a woman doesn't, who will look after her and her children?'

Possession, however, is in a different category. A woman cannot fight against the spirit of an ancestor that wishes to 'change her head' and make her a diviner. All other considerations fall away and her family and her

---

[1] It is impossible to give accurate figures of the ratio of herbalists to diviners, and of men to women in either profession. I was told that the numbers of women who were 'possessed' and of men who bought medicines were increasing, while the number of men possessed was decreasing.

M

husband and his kin must accept the spirit's sway. When during a séance a woman diviner is inspired, she has control over her husband as well as all other inmates of the homestead. As a diviner, she brings them prestige, wealth, and promise of security.

3   Specialists at Work

The sophisticated European, often unaware of his own irrationalities in thought and in action, is fascinated by the ritual practices and beliefs of other people and labels them 'magic'. Ritual flourishes in Swaziland: specialists make porous rolls of dough from medicated grain crushed by a pregnant woman, to give the fields full crops; they doctor stones to drive away the hail; they catch little birds, slit their tongues and rub in medicines to stop the birds eating the corn; they boil wooden pegs in frothy potions and stick them in the pinnacles of the huts to keep off the lightning. There is ritual for every dangerous situation, and ritual must be performed when the situations arise. I remember a sultry night in the bush veld when lightning flashed and crackled and the inmates of the homestead covered everything that was white and shiny with a dark cloth; then they sat quietly on the floor, having rolled up the mats, and threw me suspicious looks because I had brought some *imitsi* into my hut. Near the door the headman placed a broken potsherd on which he burnt anti-storm medicines, and an old woman occasionally rushed to the doorway brandishing a broom to sweep away the lightning. That night a child living next door was struck and killed 'by the heaven'. For several days the whole homestead was treated; every inmate was scarified and had anti-lightning soot rubbed into the cuts; they dipped their fingers into boiling brew, sucked a little, then spat it out east and west. No one was allowed to wash for three days, and the huts were sprinkled with medicines. The child was buried some distance from its home.

I spent three months at Namahasha studying divination. Namahasha is on the frontier of three administrations, Swaziland, Portuguese East Africa, and the Transvaal, and there the diviners still practise their ancient rites. Specialists of other types are to be found in all parts of the country, but the diviners, the smellers-out of wizards, operate primarily in isolated areas remote from police control; when they suspect that they may be discovered in Swaziland, they hold their séances in a district under another administration.

In the midst of a world of inexplicable happenings, with people living and dying in strange ways, it is hard to reject Swazi beliefs in ritual and witchcraft. In conservative homes there is no challenge from empirical experiment, and the dividing line between scientist and specialist in ritual, and hence between science and ritual, does not exist for the Swazi.

Some techniques are superficially similar to those of Western science and might be classed as such by the Western observer, but they, as well as those that would be considered 'magic', are based on premises that he could not accept. To the Swazi both techniques are modes of control or attempts to control. The herbalist gives enemas, purges, poultices, steam baths, sets broken limbs, and lets blood; at the same time, he chants spells, sucks out objects from the patient's body and performs numerous rites of the type common to every primitive culture. His most prosaic treatments are often directed to ends that could not be correlated by us with real causes; enemas are given to babies to protect them from attack by malignant animals; purges are used to bestow on men radiant personalities, and steam baths to destroy evil possessing spirits. The herbalist works with laws formulated on the principles that like produces like and that participation continues between objects which have once been in contact, albeit later separated by space. The fat of the lion induces courage in men. The hair of a loved one can be used to obtain full possession of the beloved.

The position of the specialist in ritual is essentially determined by his acceptance of the standards of the group among whom he works; it is from the group that he obtains the sanction to practise and the technique. He organizes and directs attitudes already in existence towards accepted ends; he does not create new attitudes or ends.

Herbalists wander over the countryside spreading stories of their own successes and developing a belief in their particular ritual. They wear their 'bags'—pouches, calabash containers, and charms—as signs of their profession, and when they undo their kit and display the odd assortment of roots, branches, tufts of animal skins, bones, stones, powders, and all manner of curious objects, they elaborate skilfully on the powers of each and tell how effective it has proved on previous occasions. Treatment is not secret, but private or rather limited to the homesteads, for rarely is a patient treated without those who are in close contact also receiving treatment. By their words, their work and also their mode of living, specialists advertise their ability. The *inyanga* who claims to have medicine that will make women bear, or crops give a good yield, must be able to point to the fertility of his own wives and to an abundance of grain in his own fields. He is a successful man in the community, and this is a guarantee of his medicine.

Diviners demonstrate their power most dramatically in the *umhlahlo* (séance) to discover evildoers. Many diviners have certain physical abnormalities—a squint, a nervous twitch, a limp—and even when they appear normal in ordinary life they change under the influence of the possessing spirit. I have seldom met such a quietly-spoken man, or a man who appeared so sane and balanced, as Mantshomane, but when possessed his exhibitions were particularly violent; his eyes rolled and shone, his lips quivered, his body writhed and twitched. Diviners dress their part. They wear fantastic clothing of skins and plumes, and in their hands they clutch a *lishoβa* (switch). This is usually the tail of a kudu or wildebeest, the strange animal whose young are said by some Swazi to have horns while still in the womb, and whose tail is considered to be full of power and of a sensitivity able to 'feel' the approach of an enemy. The switch is rendered more potent by being dipped in concoctions made from the wet spot on the nose of the hyaena, the fat of the elusive hardbacked armadillo, the eye of a lion, the nose of a dog, the beak of a hawk, believed to scent a carcase from afar, and similar powerful ingredients.

Early diviners used few techniques, but many have been added in recent years. The most admired of the conservative type of diviner divines without any conversation with the audience. The famous

Mahuße described his sensations and perceptions: 'I think. I eat medicines that work in my body like matches to dry wood. Behind the shoulder blades I feel a shiver. I do not open my eyes. It is not with my eyes that I see. My ancestors see for me. I see in a dream. I speak as in sleep.' Sometimes the consultants chant songs and clap their hands, while the diviner dances himself into a high pitch of excitement, then stops and speaks. Many diviners expect indicative responses from their consultants; in the middle of a dance they throw out a statement and add 'shaya' (strike); the chorus replies 'Siyavuma' (we agree). Each announcement is a feeler, a clue whereby the possessed builds up his case, piecing together the evidence from the emotion behind the replies and finally he gives the information that is sought. The accompaniment of drums in séances, the technique of sniffing (kufemba), the use of calabashes from which a high voice speaks, the rattle that shakes of its own accord, all these are modes of Swazi divination.

The ultimate mode of divination is the umbondvo ordeal, which is still practised occasionally. Umbondvo is a poisonous mixture that is believed to have no effect on the innocent, but which intoxicates the guilty into a confession. It is administered by diviners fetched from Portuguese territory, and I came across one case in which umbondvo was used during my stay in Namahasha. The taking of umbondvo is recognized as a tense, nerve-racking experience. It is usually conducted on days when the sun blazes from a clear sky and the suspects are told to sit with legs stretched in front of them from early morning till late afternoon. The women may wear only their skin skirts and the men their loin skins, so that they cannot hide protective medicines. They 'burn in the sun', they 'feel the umbondvo'. Sometimes it is given as a liquid, sometimes as a powder. The guilty writhe, crawl, and make terrible noises and confess why they acted as they did, even though they are often unable to explain exactly how they accomplished their purpose. They publicly express their hatred of the victim.

Swazi are permitted to consult more than one diviner, especially in serious cases, and informants stated that diviners rarely disagreed. I have the impression that there is a strong esprit de corps among diviners whose confirmation of each other's verdicts sanctions their powers. Swazi, however, will not accept this. I suggest that, given the same consultants and techniques, the diagnosis will almost invariably tally; but, given other consultants with a different interest in the same situation, the decision may easily be reversed. An interesting example came from Umnyakaza's family. His grandmother was accused by co-wives of witchcraft, and though her husband did not believe the accusation, it was confirmed by a number of diviners, and he was driven finally to accept it. She and those of her children who were with her were killed one night. However, two of her children were elsewhere and escaped, and after many years one of them went to the king and asked him to clear the mother's name. Other diviners were consulted, the whole situation had changed, and they pronounced the dead woman innocent and her children uncontaminated. The king asked the youth if he wanted to 'bring back the hand' against those who had caused his mother's death, but he replied: 'No. We are all your people.'

The more successful practitioners are among the most wealthy commoners in the society. They receive payment according to the nature and success of the treatment and the status of the patient or client. Thus a herbalist receives an initial gift of a goat, spear, or other article to 'open the bag' (*kuvula sikwama*), and a further payment, equally flexible, to 'make the medicine shine' (*inkanyiso*—from *kukanyisa*: to make shine). Portions of animals—sheep or cattle—are frequently required as ingredients, and the herbalist is liberally provided with meat of any beast that is slaughtered, and he usually also receives the skin. Umnyakaza commented cynically: 'An *inyanga* can always say he needs a cow to help a man, but he often means to help himself.' If the treatment is for sickness and the patient recovers, he pays a 'cow to praise', but if he is not cured there is no final fee. The cow entitles the patient and also any member of his homestead to free treatment, except for gifts of food to the doctor, for subsequent illnesses. For work that is regularly performed, such as doctoring a homestead against lightning, a fee of a beast also constrains the *inyanga* to make free periodic visits. Some *tinyanga* are avaricious; others accept tokens if the patient is poor. For minor cases, the diviner may receive from a commoner a basket of grain or a few shillings, but a chief usually rewards him with a beast. In theory, the more serious cases are conducted with the sanction of the king, and the reward is high. For an *umhlahlo* to discover the 'real murderer' of the young chief Sidloko Mahlalela, eight head of cattle and a sum of money (some say £20 and others £30) were paid to diviners by the Mahlalela family.

Refusal to pay a specialist in ritual may lead to a threat that powerful medicine will be used to extort the fee. Three cases were cited of men who were 'beaten by lightning' because 'they thought they could play with an *inyanga*'. Sometimes, but not often, specialists in ritual sue for their fees at court. A specialist who claims more than his due, or who troubles a man who is extremely poor, is severely criticized, and Swazi insist that in olden times chiefs kept avaricious specialists in check.

As a result of their propaganda and the powerful influence they exert by their activities, *tinyanga* are greatly respected and feared. They are recognized leaders, organizers, and protectors. Even when they pay casual visits to homes, they receive preferential treatment and people pander to their opinions. Hostility towards them is controlled, and quarrels with them avoided. As one man commented: 'A quarrel between ordinary people has less likelihood of being implemented by poison'; and again: 'What a specialist gives, he can take away.' The status of specialists in ritual is, moreover, buttressed by their relationship with the political authorities—a relationship that is mutually beneficial.

4. *Rulers and Specialists*

Ritual sanctions, and is in turn sanctioned by, the political hierarchy. In theory the king controls the ritual used by his subjects, and may call on any specialist to display his knowledge. Formerly, if the king thought specialists were withholding vital secrets, or that their knowledge was dangerous, they were killed; to-day moral pressure is put on them. But

one man whom Sobhuza tracked down as claiming to possess the secrets
of flying witches said to him openly: 'Do you think that two of us with
this knowledge could live?'

Political authorities rely on specialists in difficult situations: when a
case is particularly baffling, the diviner is called in as a legal expert; when
famine threatens the country, other doctors are summoned to prepare
fields for prosperity; when the army leaves for war, national specialists
cover the men with weapons stronger than the shield. If the desired end
is not achieved, the specialists serve as convenient scapegoats. In turn
they offer plausible defences: they were frustrated by the wrath of the
ancestors, strong counter-ritual, or breach of taboos. Given the opportunity, the specialist shifts responsibility for failure from himself and from
the political leader without detracting from the power of ritual or the
prestige of authority. Lightning struck the barracks of a royal village a
few days after it had been fortified against such disaster, but the specialist
in ritual was not discredited. He 'proved' that a very powerful and unexpected counter-ritual had caused one of the warriors to drop his candle
against the thatch!

Tinyanga bolster up the powers of rulers by treatment to make them
'overshadow' subjects, potential rivals, and neighbouring chiefs. The
ingredients used vary considerably. It is mainly in connection with the
doctoring of chiefs that gruesome ritual murders have taken place.[1]
Portions of the human anatomy, more especially the sex organs, were
required for the potency of the medicines. In most cases, however, an
animal, not a human being, is used, and informants insist that doctoring
with a person was introduced by the Sotho element and is rejected by the
majority of Dlamini, who avoid contact with corpses. For a subject to
use human flesh in his 'personality ritual' is condemned as sorcery by all
political authorities.

At the same time that specialists are the support of the people in
highest authority, they are considered to be the allies of the poorest
commoner. They fulfil this dual rôle by expressing the desires of all to
obtain the things they value, while in effect they stabilize the *status quo*.
The people themselves accept a social stratification, and the specialists
maintain it, both by pointing out as evildoers those who break through
the barriers and by giving each member of the nation the promise of
individual security. In the district the diviner 'smells out' the enemies of
the chief, and, when consulted by the king, purges the nation of rivals to
kingship. No man may 'smell out' a witch without reporting it to his chief,
and no chief without informing the king. Chiefs sometimes break this
law and apparently have always done so.[2] The chief knows that no diviner
will 'smell him out' in his own principality, and the diviner realizes that
his prestige depends largely on the favour of a political patron. The
district chief is only afraid of diviners summoned by a higher political

[1] For examples that came before the European Administration, see B. A.
Marwick, *The Swazi*, Cambridge University Press, pp. 207–12.

[2] According to Prince Msuduka, son of Mbandzeni, it was because of this
usurpation of royal power that rulers made certain spots, especially at royal
villages, into sanctuaries for men fleeing from the wrath of local chiefs. It is
interesting to note that sanctuaries served the same purpose in medieval Europe.

authority. 'Where they (the chiefs) are themselves the great, they do not need to tremble.'

Swazi specialists do not rival the chief's established authority, or usurp the privileges attached thereto. If a chief sees a specialist becoming too wealthy or powerful, he may curtail his land and even banish him, or he may employ another specialist in ritual and so lower the status of the erstwhile favourite. Thus, while the chief and the specialist co-operate, and the specialist exercises great power, the chief is paramount. The specialist may lead in a particular enterprise, and during the rite the chief may be subordinate to his commands, but the ritual specialist holds his power by grace of the chief.

The most important national ritual, the making of rain, is the prerogative of the king and his mother. Like other ingredients, the rain medicines only become effective 'by connection' with the body 'power' of the rightful users. Full knowledge of the ritual is confined to the queen mother, her son, and three other people in the nation.[1] One of the three is a very old man, appointed in the reign of Mbandzeni, the second acted with Bunu, and the third is the special servant of the present rulers. So secret is the work that Sobhuza requested me not to publish the names of these men. Two other functionaries have an important rôle, but they may not be present when the most esoteric rites are performed. Two little girls, chosen because they are light in colour and gentle of disposition, play a minor part and are replaced on reaching puberty.

Rain ritual is worked when required on the initiative of the rulers or at the request of subjects from distant principalities. Sometimes they bring cattle known as *tinkomo tomdvumezulu* (cattle to thunder the heavens) as a supplication, a tribute, and a sign of faith. The pilgrims anticipate rain on their return journey.

The technique of rain-making can be varied, going from strength to strength, till finally rain falls. The rulers may begin with a ritual that is little more than a washing in foamy medicines; if the heavens remain 'firm', a pregnant ewe is treated and rain may fall on part of the country; if rain is required for the entire country, a pitch black cow in calf is needed. The nature of the other medicines and the modes of manipulating the rain stone, the most precious ingredient, can also be developed. People at the capital, where rain rites are always performed, contribute towards the success of the work by obeying definite instructions: for example, they must not fight, be rowdy, or cover their heads when walking past the ritual hut. But they take no part in the actual work, and to attempt to pry into the secrets is tantamount to attempting to usurp the power the secrets give.

If, despite weeks of seclusion and labour, rain still does not fall, the rulers seek the advice of diviners, who may attribute the drought to the anger of royal ancestors or to a breach of taboos. In 1935, the hostility of the ancestors was roused because of the 'bitterness in the hearts' of the main officiants, a lack of harmony that threatened to 'kill' the country. Driven to desperation by the dry earth and dying cattle, subjects came to scold (infinitive—*kutsetsisa*) the rulers with stereotyped reproaches: 'We

[1] See article by P. J. Schoeman, 'The Swazi Rain Ceremony', *Bantu Studies*, Vol. IX, pp. 169–77, and my article in the same volume, pp. 273–81.

are rotted; and what wrong have we done? Tell us what you blame. If you are angry, speak. You witch! You queen! You are killing us. You have no heart. We die, killed by your son. Ruler! Why do you hate us?' (verbatim text). The queen mother replied mildly: 'It is not me; it is *Unkulunkulu* (God).' On another occasion she blamed the people because they no longer obeyed the old law. Then she blamed them because they did not listen to God, and, finally, she blamed the Europeans. Explanations for failure of ritual are as endless as hope is undying. Rulers, like subjects, accept the efficacy of ritual techniques.

The rain medicines used by the Dlamini were taken from chiefs of conquered clans, more especially the Mnisi and the Magagule. The founder of the Mnisi had stolen it from his maternal relatives, the Motsa, and the Magagule had stolen it from the Mngometfulu. When, in the reign of Mswati, the power of the Mnisi was completely destroyed, they lost the ritual, but the Magagule retain a large principality and a hereditary chief who, Swazi believe, still works 'local rains'. Sometimes he is consulted by the Dlamini, but he does not know the full ritual.

A few other clan chiefs also have specific medicines which they use in their own principalities and which they may be asked to contribute for the sake of national well-being. Thus the Maziya of Stegi have powerful protective medicines to sprinkle over (*kupunga*) a village; hence their praise name, Maziya Mapungwane. The medicine is known only to the chief and one of his brothers, and they periodically apply it to royal villages as well as to their own main homestead. Or, again, the Ndwandwe near Bremersdorp control medicines used for the great annual ceremony. But the majority of clan chiefs do not contribute to national ritual, and the isolated medicines of specific chiefs dwindle into insignificance compared with the ritual of the king and his mother and their power to command all other specialists.

5. *Sorcery, Witchcraft, and the Status Quo*

The work of the *inyanga* is largely to combat the acts of the sorcerer or witch (*umtsakatsi*). Between the *inyanga* and the *umtsakatsi* there is perpetual battle, and at the same time a mutual necessity. Swazi contrast them on the grounds that 'the *umtsakatsi* destroys people', and 'the *inyanga* helps'; one is bad, the other is good. But not all destructive ritual is condemned as the work of the *umtsakatsi*, nor do all constructive rites receive social approval. Judgement of good and bad depends on the situation, and the standards of social behaviour. When a family learns from a diviner that someone motivated by hatred or malice has killed their kinsman, they are legally entitled to set in motion *lizekwa*, retaliatory ritual, to destroy the 'murderer'; when a husband suspects his wife of adultery and injects into her, without her knowledge, medicine, known as *likuβalo*, to bring a devastating disease on the lover, he is approved for defending his marital rights. On the other hand, medicine that destroys the *status quo* is condemned as the *βutsi* (poison) of the *umtsakatsi*, and the man who is too successful is also accused of using evil medicine. Thus the term *umtsakatsi* is applied, not to every person who employs ritual in order to inflict injury or death, but to those people who are judged by the canons of the society, expressed in the hierarchy based primarily on blood, to be acting anti-socially.

The term *umtsakatsi* is applied to both witches and sorcerers. Some African people distinguish sharply between these two categories according to the means by which they become evildoers.[1] A witch is usually born with the evil or is injected with it, so that witchcraft is a physiological and often an unconscious quality. The sorcerer acquires the technique from others and uses sorcery only occasionally, and with conscious purpose. Among the Swazi the difference is recognized, but the term *umtsakatsi* or *umloyi* is applied to both witch and sorcerer. Witchcraft is usually transmitted by a woman to her children, and it may also be injected into anyone in later life. It is not necessarily inherited. A woman who is herself a witch may inoculate one or all of her children with the *inhlanga* (virus) when the child is still at the breast. She will take a boy child and make an incision in the anus, or a girl child and make the incision in the vagina (spoken of for politeness as the bladder), and rub in the special medicines of witchcraft. The child will naturally be unaware of its fate. The inoculation is not, however, sufficient to convert a normal human being into a witch. The witch potentiality must receive direction and training, and if the child is separated from its mother before this is complete, it will wander about aimlessly, it will be mischievous, but fairly harmless. The initial medicine actuates evil; the teaching directs it into effective channels. The young witch is introduced gradually into the foul society of witches and finally buys acceptance by destroying with witchcraft somebody dear and of the same flesh and blood. In addition to individuals doomed from childhood, others become witches of their own free will under the tuition of a self-confessed witch. Occasionally a husband teaches a favourite wife, and less often, a wife gives her knowledge to the husband, or a friend demonstrates his friendship by confessing his power. To share the secret is tantamount to handing over control of one's own life, and it is rare for adults to show such trust in each other. The majority of witches are, therefore, believed to be primarily connected with a family of witches through the female line.

Witches come together at night, discuss past achievements and plan further horrors. Swazi say that witches are fully conscious of their power, and though they only meet at night they are aware of each other during the day and gloat over the effects of their nefarious activities. Within the fraternity there is the inevitable hierarchy of leaders and subjects, organizers and labourers, local groups under their own chiefs, the skilled, who can become invisible and fly through air, the less skilled, who ride animal familiars, and the novices, who only walk. Promotion depends on destruction of property and life, and between the witches there is competition in evil prowess and anxiety to ascend the witchcraft ladder. The witches are therefore a group permanently organized for anti-social activities.

Swazi sorcerers, on the other hand, are men and women whose anti-social acts are evoked by specific situations and who, often after lengthy

[1] See, for example, H. Stayt, *The BaVenda*, Oxford University Press, 1931. For the clearest exposition on witchcraft, the reader is referred to *Witchcraft among the Azande* by E. Evans Pritchard, Oxford University Press, 1938.

deliberation with their better selves, seek the assistance of an *inyanga* to work destruction. Then he and his client both become, temporarily, sorcerers.

Every Swazi is considered a potential witch or sorcerer, and at any particular time no one is quite certain who is and who is not an *umtsakatsi*. Kinsmen of an accused always support a plea of innocence, lest they should be thought to share the taint. 'Even if they know that he has practised evil, they are not certain whether he has become a witch.' They hope that, removed from the situation that evoked the evil action, he will again be a useful citizen.

Whereas in some African societies the techniques of witchcraft are distinct from those of sorcery, among the Swazi they overlap. Witches and sorcerers, like other specialists, work primarily with material substances, the names of which are esoteric and sum up the intrinsic qualities of the ingredients or the effects to be achieved. The *ɓatsakatsi* may work in a variety of ways, either through direct contact with the person or thing they wish to destroy or from a distance. If an *umtsakatsi* wishes to kill a man he either 'causes him to eat' (verb—*kudlisa*) by treating his food, especially his beer, or he 'throws' (verb—*kuphosa*) death from afar. He uses portions of the clothing, excreta, hair, or some other part of the body containing the 'essence' of the person, and the name of the victim is a most important ingredient.

Swazi believe that nothing is beyond the power of the *umtsakatsi*: he draws an invisible medicated line across an enemy's path and calls his name, and when the man walks over the line he is struck down; he flies invisible through the air, enters a hut, casts a heavy sleep over the occupants and steals the *umoya* (breath); he strikes with lightning or concentrates sun's rays to burn his rival's body; he is the master of animal familiars which he sends to kill and injure innocent men and women; he has sex intercourse with the baboon and produces the ghastly half-man, half-animal, called *imfakaɓili*; he raises the dead from their graves in the form of tiny shadow men, and sends them to do his work. Men who kill by open force (*kusondza*) are also called *ɓatsakatsi*, and in olden days there were feared *ɓatsakatsi*, known as *tinswelaɓoya* (*kuswela*—to need; *uɓoya*—hair), who seized lonely travellers, robbed them, and sometimes mutilated their bodies for the potent organs of life. The crimes of the *ɓatsakatsi* are therefore manifold, and attack every aspect of social life, threatening political and economic security, ancestral benevolence, justice in the courts, the essentials of bodily health and mental ease.

The existence of witchcraft and sorcery is considered self-evident: they are manifested in the unaccountable death of good and young chiefs; in barren fields, empty granaries, cattle that die from no apparent cause; they are proven by the criminal's evasion of justice; by unbridgeable quarrels in the family, inexplicable accidents, homes struck by lightning and other disasters. Interpretations of such acts are supported by an understanding of individual differences and human passions; the acts themselves are confirmed by confessions made at séances and ordeals, and by a current mythology. *Ɓatsakatsi*, wearing only a white girdle of witchcraft paint round their loins, are described as having been seen transfixed by powerful good medicine for all to gaze upon. Moreover, at the end of every life, sorcery or witchcraft turns up the trump card of death.

Because of the similarity of principles and techniques, based on belief in ritual, the greatest *tinyanga* are sometimes feared as the greatest sorcerers; those who have the highest power to combat evil have also the strongest means to achieve it. The attitude to leading specialists is therefore a mixture of fear as well as of admiration, of suspicion as well as of trust. Only diviners who work primarily through the inspiration of the ethical ancestors are beyond doubt.

While in normal times Swazi do not worry much about sorcery, and perform their daily routine with prosaic efficiency, fear of sorcery overwhelms them in periods of stress. Then they turn to the 'good' specialist as representing the constructive active interest of the society, to enable them to continue the struggle of living. Sometimes the *tinyanga* pronounce themselves unable to contend with sorcery. I have on record two cases, one of a man and one of a young woman, who were thus abandoned. They went to the European hospital, where they were pronounced healthy, but were kept under observation. Slowly they died.

Witchcraft and sorcery know no limits: they can be directed against anyone and everyone, but at the same time they are usually selective, and take toll of people between whom social bonds already exist. There is good reason for a diviner pointing out to consultants a person whom they suspect as their enemy. Enmity and dislike are usually mutual, and as often as not when the victim hates a man so much that he is prepared to regard him as an *umtsakatsi* the feeling is reciprocated even if it has not been expressed in action. Moreover, friction is postulated in certain relationships and the 'smelt out' falls within the relationship. The 'smelt out' person reflects lines of anticipated conflict in the society, actual conflict is not necessary.

The social context of sorcery and witchcraft is stereotyped by the alinements of Swazi society: they are alternative explanations of a conflict, real or potential. In a polygynous homestead the *umtsakatsi* is usually (*a*) a jealous co-wife, (*b*) an unscrupulous half-brother ambitious for the inheritance. Outside of the homestead, sorcery is manipulated usually by (*a*) commoners jealous of their more successful fellow men, (*b*) princes against each other, against chiefs, and against the king, and (*c*) chiefs against princes and other chiefs. A great man does not need to use *batsakatsi* against someone very inferior in status, nor is he suspected of wasting his time in this manner. Sorcery is an indication of status, and of the ambitions for improvement of status, which operate within the limits of the stratified Swazi society.

The main theme of this chapter, the relationship between ritual and rank, can now be summarized. Ritual, 'good' and 'bad', sanctions the structure of Swazi society. The 'good' specialist is the ally of the chief, and welfare officer to the commoner; he represents to the nation conservatism, harmony, and stability, in contrast with the *umtsakatsi*, the dangerous malcontent, the ambitious rebel.

No individual is ever free from social compulsion, yet he never conforms absolutely to type: obviously, if he did there would be no specialists, 'good' or 'bad'. They diverge from the average and from the ideal personality. The 'good' specialist is expected to be more intelligent, self-confident and aggressive than laymen; he is encouraged to interfere in the affairs of others and expose their most hidden secrets; he may boast and display his powers; he is required to pit himself against all hostile forces. Because of his dependence on the chief, he is restrained from developing into a powerful political leader and also from exercising his abilities to the full. In any society where the scope of individuals is dependent on the sanction accorded by an aristocracy of birth, commoners of great individuality are penalized. Wedged between the chief and the *tinyanga*, on the one hand, and the *ßatsakatsi*, on the other, the ideal for the masses becomes a relatively unenterprising mediocrity.

CHAPTER XII

DEATH AS AN INDEX OF RANK

EVERY Swazi is the meeting point of the different principles—pedigree, age, sex, individual variation—underlying his social life. At any time and in any activity one or other principle is dominant, and occasionally principles overlap and conflict. These principles express themselves in social behaviour, and the social personality[1] of each individual is the sum total of relationships determined by their interaction. Rarely—indeed, never—in life does the social personality as a whole appear, since the situations constantly change and demand a shifting of ties. In one activity a man is father; in the next he may be a son, a doctor, or a councillor. But at death the social personality, the full status, is exposed; death breaks existing bonds and shapes new ones. Death ceremonies in every culture indicate status, and the world of the dead is modelled on the organizations of the living.

1. *Explanations of Death*

Death is accepted as part of social life, but interpretations accounting for death vary from one society to the next. In a well-known myth that the Swazi share with other South-eastern Bantu death is imposed on man by the arbitrary and fickle nature of *Umkhulumcandi* or *Umvelamcandi* (the First Being) and the laziness and greed of an animal. *Umkhulumcandi* sent the chameleon to tell mankind that they would live for ever, and the chameleon went to deliver the message. A little later the First Being changed his mind and sent the lizard to tell men that they would die. The lizard glided off, and on the way he passed the chameleon, who had stopped to eat the tasty berries of the *kweßeletana*. The lizard delivered his message of inevitable death, and when finally the chameleon arrived men would not listen to his words.

Death is not considered an abstract power: death is personified in sorcerers. The immediate physical cause is often obvious—lightning, snake-bite, illness, a fall from a height—but any of these are regarded as secondary factors, not primary ones; as the means and not the agent. Thus when the young Chief Sidloko Mahlalela was murdered by a policeman, every Swazi believed that the policeman had been worked upon by sorcery (*lunjiwa*) to do the bad deed of Sidloko's real enemy. A séance was held to discover the 'real murderer'.

Only in the case of very old people is death sometimes accepted as both natural and desirable, and in former times, men and women who were completely helpless, mentally and physically, were already called 'ancestors' and occasionally assisted by younger kinsmen into the world of ancestors. The killing of ancients, usually by putting a hard lump in the food to choke them, was not considered murder, nor was it done for economic motives. The very old had become socially useless on earth,

---

[1] This chapter owes much to A. R. Radcliffe-Brown's discussion of ritual in *The Andaman Islanders*, Cambridge, 1922, Chap. V.

MORTUARY RITUAL AND RANK

Rank of deceased	Time of burial	Place of burial	Clothing of deceased	Goods in grave	Mourners	Period of Mourning for status groups
King	Lies in state till spring. (Primitive embalming keeps b o d y from decay.)	Royal Groves.	Skin of black ox and special insignia.	Formerly live men. Live black goat. Many personal possessions and *incwala* clothing.	Nation.	Men mourn one year. (Remove head-rings, wear loin-skins over shoulders.) Widows mourn three years. Other kin as much as one year with gradually decreasing intensity.
Queen Mother	About one week after death.	Cattle byre of Royal Village.	Skin of black ox. Bladder of sheep on forehead, and other insignia.	Personal possessions.	Nation.	Representatives of Nation mourn one month. King one week. Relations one year or less, decreasing with age and closeness of relationship.
Princes	Few days after after death.	Mountain Caves.	Black ox skin.	Live black goat. Personal possessions.	Subjects, National leaders, family.	Widows mourn longest. King one day. Subjects—men only—one month.
National Officials (irrespective of clan)	Few days after death.	Royal Cave.	Black ox skin.	Personal belongings.	Other National officials. Family.	As above.
Tinsila	In Special Category Described in Text.					

Rank of deceased	Time of Burial	Place of burial	Clothing of deceased	Goods in grave	Mourners	Period of mourning for status groups
Headman	Next day or a few days after death.	Cattle byre of his village.	Black ox skin.	Personal possessions.	King. Political overlord and local inhabitants. Family.	Non-relatives mourn one day. Widows three years. Other kinsmen less.
Wife (main)	Usually day after death.	If own homestead, at entrance of cattle byre, otherwise at back of homestead.	Skin skirt and apron.	Personal possessions.	Family — hers and her husband's.	Husband removes head-ring, mourns one year. Grown children one year. Little children less. Co-wives one month.
Wife (junior)	Day after death.	Behind her hut.	do.	do.	do.	Husband does not remove head-ring, mourns one month. Children as above. Co-wives as above.
Child of Commoner	Day after death.	Behind mother's hut unless heir who is buried in cattle byre.	Wrapped in mats.	Few personal belongings.	Family, especially mother and own brothers and sisters.	Depends on age of deceased, whether only child, etc. Real mother mourns longest.
Miscarriage	That night.	Depends on clan—most Nguni in ant-heap or at cross-roads.	Body placed in pot.	—	Parents and brothers and sisters.	Mother up to 3 months if royal wife, otherwise one month. Father a few days.

but they would be valuable in the world of the dead, where they would again possess their full faculties. They were mourned with due ritual by their kinsmen.

2. *Gradation of Mortuary Ritual*

Swazi burial rites reflect: (1) the status of the individual in the nation (2) his position in the homestead, and (3) his clan membership. It is probable that before the clans were welded into the nation, mortuary ritual varied mainly from clan to clan, but nowadays national officials receive special treatment. The main stress is on the distinction between aristocrat and commoner in a hierarchical political structure.

The death of a Swazi interrupts his relationships in both the national and the domestic spheres; the two do not necessarily coincide. Among the mourners there are often non-kinsmen as well as kinsmen, and these groups look at the dead from different angles. The child of a commoner is mourned with little ostentation and only by his immediate family; the child of a king is buried by the governors of the royal villages. The community, through its legal authorities, may judge a man a wizard and condemn him to a brutal death; but his own family may weep for him, albeit in silence, bring back his spirit in secrecy, and even try to clear his name posthumously.

The overt reaction to death is stereotyped and permits of little deviation. Swazi who do not conform are suspected of having been instrumental in causing the death. The ceremony depends on the status, and not the character, of the deceased and of the mourners. A king, no matter how unpopular, is buried with special ritual, and the whole nation weeps for him. A woman may not be buried at the entrance of the cattle byre while her husband is still alive; one of twins, no matter how dearly loved, must not be wept for in public during the lifetime of the surviving twin, and he is not said to have died, but to 'have gone away', or to 'have married'. The artificial blood-brothers of the king may not be mourned till the king himself is dead.

Each death awakens its own emotions, and is treated with its specific rituals; for the emotions there is no measure, whereas the ritual is laid down for each status relationship. Two wives died: for the main wife the husband took off his waxen head-ring and mourned one year, but for the young wife he could mourn publicly for only one month, though he said: 'With her I always stayed sweetly; I wanted no other woman.' At one funeral a sister of the deceased was crying very lustily, but interrupted herself to whisper to me before I left: 'Don't forget the sixpence you promised me for beer. I'll send Totwa back with you to fetch it.'

Status differences are made obvious in the treatment of the corpse and in the behaviour, clothing, period of seclusion, cutting of hair, and other such acts of the mourners. Thus the ceremonies are simplest for a child that dies before it has yet received a name, and most elaborate for the king of the nation.

The corpse is prepared for the grave by special personnel. Among Dlamini and important chiefs the duty devolves on non-relatives; among ordinary families the work is performed by kinsmen, and if an outsider assists he is entitled to demand a special beast to 'wash him from the pollution'. Men prepare the corpse of a man, and women that of a woman. The people who carry the corpse are usually relatives. Inevitably the rôle of members participating in any funeral depends on the quota of relatives available; thus if a grown son dies in one family, the father may have to take an active part, and in another he may have brothers, or even maternal kinsmen, to relieve him. Swazi say 'a corpse exhausts one' and by touching it 'the strength of a man is drained'.

A male aristocrat mourns the same loss for a shorter period than a commoner, while women married to aristocrats often mourn longer than wives of ordinary men. Thus a queen mourns the death of a baby for three months, and other women mourn for one month. Women often mourn longer than men for the same loss, a mother longer than a father, a wife longer than a husband.

Women are expected to show their grief more obviously, and must even force themselves to shed tears while men are expected to control themselves. It is not surprising in this society to find that daughters are mourned less than sons of the same age, and that the young and the very old are less lamented than those who are full-grown and strong and active. Young and immature children are always cleansed and fortified quickly, while adults must adhere to a lengthier and more rigid mourning. Indeed, in the rules of mourning are reflected the principles we now know well: the privileges of the aristocrats, the dominance and active strength of the men, the subordination of the women destined to spend most of their lives with people of another family, the ignorance and vulnerability of children who understand nothing and who, in the weakness induced by mourning, would be good targets for evildoers.

Practically every Swazi has experienced the death of relatives; some Swazi have mourned for many and others for few. The ritual cannot be extended to cover more than one death. Each mourning involves abstention from sex, and this explains the shorter period of mourning by men than by women in polygynous society. The king mourns his losses for a relatively shorter time than do any of his people. Were he to mourn the death of every wife, child, kinsman, and subject for more than a few days, he would be in a state of constant taboo and vulnerability.

It would be tedious and unnecessary to recount in detail the variations for each individual, and these are roughly indicated on the chart (pp. 178–9). There I have shown how the status of the deceased determines the time and place of burial, the treatment of the corpse, the number of mourners, and the periods of mourning by the status groups affected by the loss.

The reaction of men and women to death depends on their status relationship to the deceased in both the national and kinship circle, and the manner in which they will have to reorientate their status behaviour to each other. They must recognize the gap created by the loss, but a web of new living relationships must cover it so that social life can continue. An infant dies, and the mother is bitterly sad. She often weeps when she is alone, and she must weep when people come to pity her. Because she is judged to be 'without strength' and in danger from the death, she is medicinally treated; but the *inyanga* does not look at her subjective sorrow —he sees if she has other children, if it is the first child, a middle child, or the youngest; he sees too if she is the first wife, or if she has co-wives;

N

he notes the status of the man. On these facts depends his treatment, both in quality and in the number of people to be treated. These, too, are the facts expressed at the burial, and they are mentioned by the mourners and people who come to condole.

Death can abruptly increase or decrease the status of surviving kinsmen. The average wife deprived of her only son, her promise of security in the future, has as little standing as a childless woman; while an insignificant youngster becomes a man of importance if, on the death of his father, the council selects him as main heir.

Death, more than any other event, brings together kinsmen from various localities, and hence observers have sometimes regarded mortuary rites as a means of creating family solidarity and stressing family unity. Among the Swazi, family antagonisms and jealousy frequently come into the open through death, though it is considered wicked to fight during the mourning ritual itself. Kinsmen come many miles to make their peace, not with the living, but with the dead, as it is his angry spirit that they fear. If kinsmen quarrel, the breach may remain unhealed until one of them falls ill and then every effort is made to patch up the dispute, 'to cleanse the heart'; if it is too late and the man dies, his burial might be delayed, as happened in one case I knew, to give a brother with whom he had quarrelled a chance to bid farewell to the corpse and so secure his own well-being. But the quarrels with other healthy kinsmen are not made up; there is no general reconciliation.

3. *The Social Meaning of Death*

The way that death affects the social status of the survivors can well be seen by considering from this angle the death of a headman, the most important figure in a homestead.[1] His death alters the position of his wives, his mother, and his children, all of whom were dependent on him; his paternal kin, who aided him in family matters, his maternal relatives, who had definite obligations towards him, his in-laws anxious to protect their own interests, his chief, to whom he owed local allegiance, and, finally, the king, who accepted him as a Swazi citizen.

When a man falls ill the above-mentioned people are expected to help him, to a greater or lesser degree according to their status orientation to the patient, to resist death. The kinsmen should inquire frequently how he is getting on, express sympathy with him, and some may even recommend their own doctors. As the illness grows, and it becomes obvious that he cannot live, all close relatives must be informed. Those who can should come and bid him farewell, and this is particularly necessary for any relative with whom he has quarrelled. He must die at peace with 'his blood'.

The death itself is made public in a long-drawn wail uttered by the close kinsmen who have sat and watched him in his last hours. Some of them, in apparent anguish, rush outside, others beat their bodies on the floor, and each expresses the loss from his or her standpoint. So the mother keens 'my son'; the wives 'my husband', 'my lord'; the brothers

[1] This approach was first indicated by A. R. Radcliffe-Brown, op. cit., Chap. V.

weep for a brother, and the children for a father. The stereotyped out-
burst may not last long, for the full wailing will be uttered after the body
is buried. Messengers are again sent to inform the kinsmen who will be
most affected and now it is even more imperative that they should arrive,
for it is essential that they be medically treated and strengthened. Death
is contagious; the deceased seeks companionship. Those who cannot
possibly be present and those who are more distantly related and hear of
the death by accident obtain medicines for themselves. Most Swazi use
siβaha and *likhatsatfo* (tough barks, hard to break), and *maluleka* (from
kululeka, to free (from memory)). If people are not able to procure the
right medicines, they drop ash into water before they eat or drink.

It may be many months, even years, after burial before some relatives
are able to 'weep' at the grave and put a stone on it. But if they have
known the deceased at all well, they always try to come sooner or later,
lest they be suspected of having caused the death, or lest the spirit be angry
at the apparent neglect, and also because it is a way of expressing genuine
sorrow.

The widows are considered to be those most adversely affected by the
death of the headman, and their overt behaviour is dictated by their
status in his harem. He breathes his last in the hut of the main wife, or,
if she is not known, in the hut of the first wife. The ritual is primarily
directed at showing which son will succeed, through the rank of his
mother, to the status of the deceased. After death the council may tell
one of the women that her child will be the first to throw the sod on the
grave, a sign of his status as main heir. Soon after the burial, the widows,
accompanied by elderly women, go in sad procession of seniority to the
river. An old woman in charge approaches the main widow and cuts off
her hair with a spear belonging to the deceased. An ordinary knife may
be used on the other widows. If the main widow has not been decided
upon, this is made clear by the use of the same implement for all. Sitting
at the river, they plait rough caps of grass to cover their shorn heads,
make ropes for their necks and waists, turn their skirts inside out, and in
other ways indicate their status as widows. They mourn for the longest
period and vocalize their grief the most. For about one month after the
burial they may not wash, sleep on mats, appear in public, or eat from
ordinary utensils. At night they sleep together in the hut of the main
widow, at the back of which is built a small fender where heirlooms and
offerings to the deceased are placed. The sole occupation during this
month is weeping and plaiting fine mourning caps to replace the rough-
and-ready ones they are already wearing.

After the first month the spirit of the deceased is brought back to the
home and the mourning of the widows is to some extent relaxed. They
wash at the river with medicine known as *emagucu* (from *kugucula*, to
reverse), they turn their skirts the right way round, smear themselves
with fat, and put on their new caps. A widow with sons leaves a hole in
her cap; one without sons leaves no cavity—her mourning is all-extensive.
Till the winter of the third year the widows remain in mourning, less
rigid, it is true, than during the first month, but still inhibiting. They
must not sing, dance, or indulge in sex or lewdities. They avoid all contact with the brothers of the deceased, their future consorts. Finally, in

a public ritual, the widows throw away their mourning and are brought
back into normal life. They are praised if they have behaved themselves
with due restraint, and the main widow is allotted to the brother chosen
by the senior kinsmen as the 'thighs', the procreator of children to perpetuate the name of the deceased. The other women are free to choose
him or another of his kinsmen, and spend the rest of their lives in the
condition, frequently an unhappy one, of widows attached to a man
who has his own wives. They have to change their mode of living. Their
own homestead no longer exists, and they are distributed in other homes.

The mother of a headman is in some respects as adversely affected as
the widows by the loss. Her son gave her security and prestige. She goes
into deep mourning on his death; she tears down her cone and leaves it
wild and unkempt; she does not wash for a month and wears coils of rope
round neck and waist. A classificatory mother is purified soon after the
burial, but the real mother mourns publicly for a year. If the deceased is
her only son and there is no grown heir, she is in a sorry plight, and it
may be necessary for her to seek a new home. To go to a married daughter
is 'too heavy' for a conservative woman who practises son-in-law avoidance. She sometimes goes to a co-wife and is the classificatory mother to
this woman's own son. Or she returns to her own people, a lonely woman,
aware of the antagonism of her brother's wives if he shows her particular
friendliness.

The children lose a father, and from among them one is chosen as the
heir, their superior, a father substitute. He is specially treated and the
goods he will inherit are also doctored. His period of mourning depends
on his age, his ripeness for his new duties. A child can understand little.
He has his head shaved, receives special medicine, and may be sent away
from his home for many years, so that jealous older brothers and their
mothers will not be able to harm him. A grown boy is given stronger
medicines, and is introduced to his new duties as soon as the father's
spirit is brought home. Sometimes the sons must bury their father, and
the heir in particular takes a prominent place. He holds the head when the
corpse is carried from the hut; if another were to do so, Swazi insist that
the body would become too heavy to lift.

Married daughters called to mourn their father's death cut off their
curls, eat medicines, and wear mourning ropes for a month. As for
younger daughters, the question sometimes arises as to whether they
should, as a sign of mourning and suddenly inflicted maturity, put up
their hair and become marriageable, or cut it short like the young girls
who are relatively carefree and whose marriages are still far off.

Brothers of the deceased are deeply affected, because they continue his
homestead. This duty does not devolve equally on all the brothers, and
they are not all equally important in the ritual. The younger full brother
is usually selected to take over the main widow; an older brother is
regarded by the widows with too much respect and fear. He, together
with other senior kinsmen, controls the mourning ritual, supervises the
killing of the sacrificial beasts, arranges the moving of the village when the
mourning is over, and advises the heir.

The maternal kin always send a representative to the burial, and a
special animal is killed when they come to 'weep'. It is to them that the

heir is often sent for safe keeping till he is old enough to assume control, and they may be called in to discuss various matters at the funeral. The men sometimes help to dig the grave and even prepare the corpse, taking instructions from the paternal relatives, who know the ritual required for the clan of the deceased.

While the maternal relatives receive a very warm welcome and are never regarded with suspicion, the blood relatives of the wives are treated with respect and no intimacy. They weep with the daughters who come from their homes, and with the wives who are so often suspected of having killed the man either out of resentment for neglect, or, what is perhaps worse, ambition for their sons and themselves. The mothers of these women help them make their mourning caps and ropes, but do not stay for any length of time. They come again when the widows remove their weeds to see the man who will take over the sexual duties of the husband. Each wife has her own kinsmen; it is to them that she is most closely bound; they claim her and her children if the deceased died without having paid marriage cattle; and they will defend her against a charge of sorcery or witchcraft.

Apart from kinsmen, the death affects neighbours and friends. During the first month of mourning, the adult members of the principality come to the headman's home to condole. They arrive in groups according to sex and neighbourhood. As soon as they are within earshot, they raise a penetrating shriek, 'Hi hihi', and the bereaved kinsmen are stirred to respond and to call on the dead, and elaborate on the loss. The mother shouts: 'Oh my child! Why did you die? What will I be now? I am just a thing, just a dog. Who will bury me?' The widow weeps: 'Now I am an orphan, my father, my husband, has left me.' A sister bemoans the loss of a guardian for herself and her offspring. After wailing in this way for some time, a responsible person, the mother or senior widow, describes graphically the course of the illness. Perhaps in the middle of a visit the penetrating wail is again heard in the veld, and the bereaved begin to weep afresh.

The final status adjustment is made by the political authorities. The chief, attached to the deceased by a political bond assimilated to a kinship tie, wails: 'My child is gone, my enemies are killing me.' But in reality he suffers the loss of a councillor, a labourer, perhaps a friend. The chief always purifies himself by eating medicines when an important subject dies, but he does not undergo the same rites as on the death of one of his 'real blood'. It is with his consent that the bereaved kin seek the sorcerers. Everything of importance, the name of the heir, the allocation of the widows, the settlement of debts, the movements of individual members from his land, must be reported to him.

The king himself is informed and is ritually purified. The heir of the deceased or another kinsman who was in contact with the corpse touches a beast from the herd of the deceased, or, if he was poor, a head of mealies from his storehouse. This is taken to the king, and at the gateway of his village the messengers shout the mournful news of death. Early the next morning the king's attendants take the beast or the mealies to the king in the byre, and he bites ritually (*kuluna*) with a red root, the *mdzambane*, which he spits out on the objects belonging to the dead.

Mdzambane is derived from the word *kudzamba*—disappoint or weaken—and is extended to the dead man's goods used in the purification of the king. If the *mdzambane* is an animal, it is taken to a nearby village and slaughtered, and neither the king nor any other Dlamini may eat of it. Only when the king is purified may relatives of the deceased come near him. The *mdzambane* rite is performed for every adult male except the warrior on the battlefield—in Swazi phraseology, it is for every 'person of the king destroyed by sorcerers'. The announcement of death is also made at the village of the queen mother. She undergoes no purification, but condoles with the kinsmen, and in turn they mourn with her the loss of a 'shield of the nation'.

4. *The Power of the Dead*

Mourning does not lessen the attention directed to the dead. Underlying the ritual performed for every individual is the emphasis on the continuation of life after death. Each man, woman, and child is believed to possess a *lidloti* (spirit) that enters into the child in the womb and later shows itself in the *umoya* (breath). The spirit grows with the person, but when death comes and the corpse is laid in the grave, though the flesh decays and is eaten by ants, the spirit remains. The Swazi theory of spirit, breath and body, is vague and contradictory and need not be discussed here, except in so far as it affects the status of the living and the dead.

The Swazi approach to the spirit is essentially practical. The spirit is powerful for good and ill and must be correctly handled. Some time after burial, when the moon is full, it is brought back to the home in a ritual that varies in publicity with the status of the deceased. The spirit of a commoner's child is fetched unostentatiously: in the evening the father puts an offering of beer at the back of the mother's hut and speaks to the dead in the presence of the immediate family circle. The beer is drunk the next day by old women and immature children, and the rest of the brew is taken by relatives, friends, and acquaintances. When the spirit of a chief is brought home the whole area is affected. In some principalities (e.g. Ebulanzini of the Mkwatshwa) the male subjects go to the grave at twilight; the *indvuna* makes a libation and praises the deceased, exhorting him to come and look after the affairs of the 'orphans'. As they return, they sing the song of the clan. The next day there is heavy drinking and feasting. A spirit that is not properly brought home would, Swazi believe, make its anger felt in illness or other misfortunes.

Swazi are also vague in their pictures of the ancestral world. The dead are described as being very happy, drinking beer, dancing, and smoking hemp; round them are dead kinsmen. They own cattle and dogs and their activities are similar to those of the living, but the spirits do not marry or reproduce. It is a static life. Moreover, the picture is blurred, and obviously could not be a logical duplication of life on earth. It is occasionally described by diviners privileged to be in contact with individual dead, but concerned primarily, not with the life of the dead, but of the living. Swazi usually say that the *emadloti* live below the ground in kinship groups, but are not limited by space. For a while the *lidloti* hovers near its own grave, then, when brought into the homestead, it is at the same time in the company of dead kinsmen whose graves are scattered over the country. The ancestors in fact are everywhere at the same time, and hear and see everything that is said and done. Their most active period is between sunset and sunrise, the correct time for important burials and for appealing to the dead. The ceremony performed to bring the spirits from the grave to the home is clearly not intended to bind them to any locality, but to show them that they are remembered, missed and respected, and to direct their attention to their descendants.

Ancestors make themselves seen and felt in divers ways. Sometimes they come to a person in his sleep, and one of the definite aims of medicinal treatment for mourners is to prevent them dreaming excessively of the dead. Some dreams are stereotyped and their interpretation is obvious; others are complicated and need the diviners' skill to unravel. Sometimes a dream is interpreted as a warning against specific enemies and impending misfortune. To see a dead person frequently in one's dreams is weakening, even if it portends no harm or protects against the evil of others. Sometimes ancestors appear in the guise of snakes, a belief linked with the Swazi concept of the human anatomy. Swazi are convinced that a snake lives in the stomach and changes food into the form that it takes as excreta, and produces small snakes like worms that often appear in the stools.[1]

There is, however, no clearly formulated or consistent doctrine of transformation from the human to the snake; the emphasis is on the end, not the becoming—different men, different snakes. An ordinary man or an unmarried woman usually appears as a harmless green snake, a married woman as a quiet lizard or a snake that stays in dark secluded nooks, the king as a mamba. Certain snakes are excluded from human associations because 'they never come quietly'. The *imfete* (puff-adder), for example, is never considered a *lidloti*. Occasionally snakes indicate characteristics, such as physical blemishes, scars, or particular colouring that their human counterparts possessed on earth. Thus Cebisa, the miscarriage of one of Mswati's wives, is said to be a tiny snake of brilliant red. The behaviour of a snake is carefully noted to detect whether it is an ancestral spirit or an ordinary reptile. The ancestral snakes do not show fear, and move with familiar sureness around the huts. If such a snake comes into a hut and quickly leaves it again, it is taken as a bad omen, a sign of death or fever.

The power exercised by a *lidloti* varies with his or her status on earth; the spirit is the essence of the person and the greater the person the greater the *lidloti*. In the world of the dead, chief and commoners, young and old, men and women, continue the patterns of superiority and inferiority prescribed on earth. The ancestral cult is extended to the nation by the fiction of kinship round the king father, and the dead kings and the queen mothers must sanction all national enterprises.

Despite the hierarchy of the spirit world, the mere fact of being a

---

[1] Swazi suffer greatly from worms. There is also an illness spoken of as *inkunzi* (literally—bull), in which Swazi insist that a snake emerges from the anus and the patient dies.

lidloti gives power over people on earth, and even children are occasionally believed to exert a strong influence. The most outstanding example
was the case of Cebisa, who was diagnosed as the cause of a drought in
the reign of Mbandzeni. The rulers sacrificed a beast to her at the royal
home where her mother had lived, and the custom is repeated when
considered necessary. The unexpected obtrusion of insignificant *emadloti*
may be regarded as a good explanation of otherwise unaccountable
disaster.

Unlike some of the neighbouring Bantu, who believe that death works
no change in character, Swazi consider that ancestors are only bad fellows
when neglected. The ancestors are the ideal, not the actual personality.
The mourning ritual has stripped off the inessentials and it is the
elemental social personality that operates in the spirit world. The mean
and selfish father, the ambitious brother, the disobedient son, may
become after death the guardians of peace and reprimanders of licenti-
ousness, arrogance, intolerance, and meanness.

But the ancestors are also believed to show human emotions in their
reactions to each other and to the men on earth; one of the most frequent
causes of illness is that a particular *lidloti* considers that he has been
slighted. Moreover, the spirit of a man who has been attached to a person
expects greater consideration and is often more trouble than one who was
indifferent. This brings out a very important point: Swazi talk of what
the *emadloti* feel and demand from the living, but obviously this is based
on what the descendants feel and demand from the *emadloti*. Swazi have
more affection for some relatives than others; therefore they dream of
them and think of them more frequently. This interest is explained as
emanating from the dead, and not from the loss suffered by the living.

The ancestral cult is primarily a domestic cult in which the two sets of
relatives, paternal and maternal, exercise complementary and slightly
overlapping rôles as spirits in much the same way as they do on earth.
The paternal are particularly sensitive to family friction over property,
while the maternal are largely protective and tender. Often when a
Swazi escapes from danger the diviner diagnoses that it was averted by
the intervention of the spirit of the mother, mother's brother, or maternal
grandparent.

The existence of the ancestors depends, in Swazi dogma, on the continuation of the family, and their well-being depends on family prosperity.
I have two examples of men who, after recovering from serious illnesses,
stated that they had actually returned from the dead to take wives and
produce children and leave the family name on earth. 'The time of their
death had not yet come', informants commented.

Ancestors usually intervene only in matters concerning themselves and
relatives. Swazi believe that they can help or hinder, give or withhold
health, happiness, and prosperity. Their reaction varies with the type of
treatment they receive and the extent to which they wish to inflict pain
and suffering. A few typical examples will illustrate the domestic issues
in which ancestors are interested and the principles they proclaim. A wife
who did not receive proper burial nursed bitter feelings and sent sickness
to one of the neglectful brothers-in-law. A widow who committed the
heinous crime of intercourse with a brother of the deceased during the

mourning period was punished with madness by the outraged dead. The *emadloti* were not acting out of malice; they were enforcing correct behaviour to themselves.

They protect weaker kinsmen against unjust aggression from more powerful seniors. Chief Solowako accused his half-brother Makontolo of adultery with one of his wives and banished Makontolo from the area; most of the people considered Makontolo to be innocent and were against this drastic punishment. A few weeks later Solowako's mother died and then a paternal uncle (who had looked after him when a boy) fell very ill. The Zionists, a dissident sect of Christians who claim prophetic gifts and act like diviners, diagnosed that the dead mother was criticizing Solowako and that unless Makontolo was allowed to return the uncle would not recover. Makontolo was brought home. Again, ancestors intervene if a man breaks away from the family and lives his own selfish life. Mzululeki had not been home for many years, and lived independently on his earnings as a teacher. He bought a new motor-cycle. Though he rode carefully, he frequently fell off the cycle, and it cost him a great deal in repairs. So finally he went to a diviner and was told that the *emadloti* resented his independence and that unless he made a sacrifice to them he would meet with a terrible accident. He went home and his elder brother sacrificed for him. On his return journey his cycle suddenly skidded, though there was no mud and the sand was not deep. Neither he nor the cycle were damaged, but he said: 'I saw indeed that I would have been killed if I had not recognized my kinsmen'; ever after that incident he was very careful to make periodic visits home and *jokotela* (placate) the *emadloti*.

A woman must not forget her husband, even when he is dead. Mita's husband died before he had paid *loßola* and his posthumous child was left with her parents while she went to work. She bore a son to a man she met about three years later. A messenger came to tell her that her first child was very ill because the father resented her neglect. She said he had no right to resent it, because he had not completed her marriage payment, but eventually she returned home to see what she could do.

The ancestors resent meanness. A man refused to give his younger brother seed mealies and nearly lost his child as a result. Again, a son who did not treat his mother well was made to sacrifice a beast to his father's sister's *lidloti*.

Reciprocity is demanded between men who were 'as close as brothers'. A man always killed a beast for a certain friend when he came to stay at his home, but once he went to the friend and nothing was killed for him. The guest fell ill. The diviner said it was because his *emadloti* were grieved and wished to punish the ungrateful friend, who was obliged to make amends.

Occasionally the ancestors regulate the behaviour of chief and subject. A man insulted his chief and the next day he found a beast dead in his cattle byre, but the skin was not pierced and there was no sign of disease. The chief's ancestors had 'hated' his behaviour. I could find no instance where a chief was punished by his ancestors for an injustice towards a subject, but informants stated that this was possible, and it may be one of the sanctions enforcing consideration towards subordinates.

The ancestors do not aim to kill, but death is their ultimate weapon.

Illnesses sent by the ancestors are distinct from those sent by sorcerers and witches. The ancestors send illnesses that are curable and sometimes end as soon as propitiation to an offended *lidloti* has been made. Other illnesses sent by the *emadloti* require medicines, and may overlap, but do not coincide with the illness of sorcery. Ancestors make a man faint, or send shooting pains all over his person, or choke him, but not to death, in his sleep; they do not make him cough blood, or cause open wounds, or make limbs fester, or gnaw like snakes at a person's entrails, and finally they do not kill. The danger of the diseases sent by the *emadloti*, however, is that *ßatsakatsi* then step in and seize the opportunity to kill. Hence it is essential, if the bitterness of the dead (*lidjoya emavondo*) is diagnosed, that the living sufferers cleanse their hearts immediately to avoid further trouble which might be beyond the power of the ancestors to neutralize. The will to destroy is absent from the ancestors; they punish in order to teach the 'good life'.

The ancestors are not prepared to accept all and sundry into their fold: they reject ('close the road to') the undiscovered murderer, the woman who has a child by a secret lover, and the man who commits incest. The belief in punishment after death is, however, not very highly developed, and this, I think, is because the stress is on social sin and not on individual conscience.

Emadloti reinforce the status of the political hierarchy, but do not exercise the same sanctions as political officers, nor deal with the same crimes. Theft, murder, treason are offences tried in the courts. On the other hand, incest—a 'sin' that arouses intense horror—falls outside of legal action and the *emadloti* take control. A man wanted to sleep with his daughter-in-law and she did her best to resist, pleading that were she to succumb she would be 'bitten' by the dead. The 'bite' of the dead is described as the infliction of unbearable physical pain.

The ancestral cult does not induce a passive acceptance of conditions on earth: 'The ancestors help those who help themselves' (*lidloti liyaßonelwa*). If a man wants to move to a different area, start a new venture, enter into a doubtful case, he should obtain approval from his *emadloti*, but even if this has been secured, he in turn must do his best to make the work a success. Only if he fails is he provided with excuses other than his own incompetence.

Swazi religion is a practical religion. Between the ethics of the ancestral cult and the mundane desires of life there is no conflict. Swazi desire the ends they say the *emadloti* desire for them. Swazi are not concerned with the life led by the dead, but with the way the ancestors influence their lives on earth. No one inquires from a diviner if the *emadloti* are happy and satisfied till they show that they are unhappy and dissatisfied. Ancestral spirits, like witches and sorcerers (*ßatsakatsi*), are thought of most when comforts are few and troubles are many.

Emadloti thus serve as one of a number of alternatives in the explanation of failure or unhappiness, and hence in maintaining the *status quo*. Responsibility can always be shifted to them and from them to the *ßatsakatsi*. The *emadloti* are not all-powerful. The qualities ascribed to them do not lead to the dilemma faced by questioning Christians aware of misery on earth, who are told to believe that God is All-Good, All-Wise, and All-Powerful. The *emadloti* have more wisdom, foresight, and power than men, but the hierarchy of earth itself is maintained and no one ancestor ever reaches complete deification.

5. *Approaching the Ancestors*

On earth it is against the law to approach a grandfather direct if the father is alive, or to appeal to the king without first speaking to his *indvuna*. In the world of the dead, the hierarchy of age and authority is similarly respected. Requests are made to the father, and he forwards the message to the next above him unless a specific ancestor is demanding attention. Direct references are usually made to the *emadloti* reaching only two or three generations back, for, especially in commoners' families, the genealogy is vague beyond the great-great-grandfather; it is unnecessary to know all one's antecedents in a society where each man is primarily responsible to the kinsmen immediately senior to him. Swazi believe in the unbroken continuity of kinship after death and vaguely assume that eventually the wishes of men reach *Umkhulumcandi* (the First Being).

Umkhulumcandi is an otiose Great Ancestor (*Lidloti lelikhulu*). He is never specifically mentioned in prayer or sacrifice, nor does he intervene in enforcing the ethics of the culture. Swazi are not interested in him, just as he is not interested in them. Having 'broken off' all things on earth, the trees, mountains, and people, and having sent death to man, there gradually intervened between him and mankind the immediate dead, bound more closely with the living. He had a messenger, *Umlenzengamunye* (One Leg) who occasionally descended from the skies in a thick mist and was visible only to women and children. His appearance heralded fever, and it was customary to propitiate him. When he was seen (the last time was in Mbandzeni's reign), the news was shouted over the countryside, and people plaited themselves protective amulets and mothers made symbolic offerings of their children. They buried the little ones up to their necks in the river sand for a few minutes, then dug them up and, without looking back, hurried them home. At their homesteads they burnt goats and fat and cattle and made an *umnikelo* (offering). Both *Umkhulumcandi* and *Umlenzengamunye* may once have been more positive influences for good or evil, but at the present time they do not intervene in human affairs.

Ritual, to be effective, must be correctly executed through the socially accepted performers or priests officiating at the right place, at the right time. The enactment of ancestral rites stresses the status of the senior male in the patrilineal society. An heir appeals to his father on behalf of his kinsmen, an older brother supports the request of the younger, and women are 'spoken for' by guardians. In an ancestral cult there is no need for a class of ordained priests; the duties devolve upon the head of a lineage or family. Most rites take place in the cattle byre of his homestead, before the sun rises or soon after it has set. There is no special regalia unless a beast is to be slaughtered, when the officiator wears on his back a sling similar to that in which a woman carries her baby. The appeals are made to the dead through offerings of meat or beer. The offering is laid at dusk at the back of the shrine hut, spoken over and left for the night. Since the ancestors are linked with the paternal hearth and possessions, offerings may not be made to a woman's ancestors at her husband's home nor to his relatives at her home. Only when a man or woman has no senior kinsmen living nearby, and some appeasement of the *emadloti* is essential, are the rules of religious procedure not absolutely and rigidly obeyed. I have come across cases where young men and once even a young woman officiated; once, when beer was not available, uncooked grain was used. It is when the correct conditions could be, but are not attained, that efforts to win over the *emadloti* prove fruitless.

Every family priest has in his homestead one beast dedicated to the ancestors. It is known as *licaβi* (probably from *kucaβa*—to offer) and is usually a particularly fine beast. The *licaβi* is not killed unless it becomes 'too old', and then it is replaced by a younger animal. When the headman speaks to the dead in his byre, the *licaβi*, together with the other cattle, is driven in. If a beast is sacrificed, the real victim is shepherded near the *licaβi* so that by proxy the best goes to the dead. The rulers sacrifice on a scale that is beyond the means of other Swazi, and the *licaβi* is not so prominent. They are, so to speak, able to pay a higher premium for national insurance, since they control the stocks.

Priests of the ancestral cult derive social prestige, but no direct fee for their intercessions. It is, however, important to remember that the Swazi religion does not create a class of priests who live on the contributions of the people; the family priest is also main heir and successor to the deceased, and the provision of libations and offerings is his concern. The religious office sanctions secular duties and gives an additional hold over kinsmen and subjects.

Sometimes the demands of the dead are felt as a heavy burden by the living. Though Swazi believe that the ancestors are eager for their descendants to live in comfort, the wishes of the dead are interpreted by an outsider, the diviner. In 1936, of eight conservative families that I questioned on this matter, four had slaughtered a goat each and two a head of cattle during the past year. One man said he had killed three beasts in the past two years to pacify the dead. One of many examples will suffice to show the economic strain of this religion. An old woman was ill, and suddenly her legs swelled so that she could no longer walk. The diviner diagnosed that there had been bad feeling between her and her son and that the *emadloti* required a white ox. There was no white ox at the home, and, though it was the ploughing season, the son went to seek one. In the meantime a child fell ill because of the dispute and the ancestors were said to demand a goat. This was given by a half-brother and slaughtered; medicines were also required, and finally the son returned with a small light-coloured ox. The sacrifice of this beast had no effect. The son killed the only other animal he possessed, and still the 'bitterness of the dead' was not appeased. Another diviner was consulted. He diagnosed that witchcraft had set in as a result of the delay. Finally, the old lady died.

Ancestral spirits are not worshipped. Swazi address them in much the same way as they speak to the living, and the word *tsetisa* (to scold) is frequently used to describe the manner of approach. Swazi rarely express gratitude when they think the ancestors are blessing them, and they are more indignant than humble when they find they are being punished.[1]

The ancestors should be commemorated (verb—*dvudvuta*) at every important enterprise, so that they will give willing and active help. They are treated as a group—'the ancestors'—on certain occasions and individually on others; and even when not specifically addressed, their presence is implied.

The cult is directed both to the ancestors of each family for the welfare of the family, and to the ancestors of the rulers on behalf of the nation.[2] Domestic ancestors are recognized at the birth of a child, at marriage, in sickness, at death, on the moving of a homestead, and when some untoward occurrence interrupts the family routine. The political deities, ancestors of local chiefs and of the king, are commemorated at similar events in the lives of their descendants, and in addition receive attention on more public occasions. Thus an hereditary chief appeals to his dead kinsmen on behalf of all his subjects if there is a drought, an epidemic, or a particularly bad crop. The king appeals to his ancestors for general prosperity and security.

The most specific recognition accorded to national ancestors is the annual sacrifice of cattle at the royal graves. The king and his mother select special men, mainly *tindvuna* of royal villages and their carriers, to make the pilgrimage of *tinkomo temadloti* (cattle of the ancestors). On an appointed day they come to the capital, and the leaders go into the shrine hut with the king and his mother to discuss their mission. There is no direct appeal to the dead, 'but they are in the hut, hearing everything that is said. We feel them with us'. Then the living partake of snuff and beer specially prepared, and thank the spirits of kingship, past and present, '*Bayethe*'. As the sun sets, the pilgrims come out of the shrine hut, go through the little gateway used for ritual occasions, and walk to the byre. The cattle have been brought in especially, and with their musical lowing mingle the praise songs of kingship shouted by an *indvuna*. To show that they are on national service, the leading pilgrims wear special ornamental head-bands. The group pauses for a short while in the byre; the cattle going to the ancestors stand separated from the rest of the herds.[3] The *indvuna* shouts: 'Here are the cattle. Let them return with good things.' More praises flow forth, the sun drops, the rulers escort the pilgrims through the eastern gate of the byre and, having bidden them 'a beautiful road', go back to their respective villages to await the return of the pilgrims.

The *embilini* (royal groves) are said to be very fearful. Graves of ordinary people become part of the homestead where they died, beacons

---

[1] 'You, son of So-and-So. Why do you kill your children? Why do you turn your back on us? Here is your beast. Take it. Look after us, for we are looking after you. Why did you send illness on this child? You are greedy, you are always ready to find fault.' Extract from a typical address to the *emadloti*.

[2] For a very full description of domestic and national occasions of ancestral recognition among the Bantu, see W. C. Willoughby, *The Soul of the Bantu*, Doubleday Doran, 1933.

[3] In 1935, there was difficulty about moving cattle because of East coast fever, and the cattle had to be sent from the capital 'by mouth'. It required most complicated readjustments, but these were considered successful, since rain fell soon after the pilgrims' return.

by which claims can be staked in land, but kings are buried in caves far from their villages. Round the caves are dense forests with impenetrable undergrowth broken by narrow footpaths. The air is full of noises. The royal command 'With all power' comes from invisible beings. Huge snakes glide through the trees and are praised as kings. The groves can only be entered in safety with the assistance of the keepers, trusted men appointed as chiefs over the surrounding locality. There are three royal groves, two in the south and one in the central area, and each has its own guardian. Woe betide the man who stumbles unaware into the grove, for he will not be able to get out unless the keeper hears his call and releases him with the sacrifice of a beast to the powerful captors.

The pilgrims wait till after sunset before they enter the homestead of the keeper, and when within hearing distance shout: 'Silence all noise'. They sing a sacred chant as they walk in through the byre. The keeper gives them beer and shows them their sleeping hut. Before dawn he wakes them and leads them to the graves, announcing them: 'They have come, the people of Ngwane.' The *indvuna* in charge speaks to the dead. He informs them of all that has happened in the past year and asks for health, strength, and fertility for the coming year. The groves are meeting places of all the powerful *emadloti* of the nation, and the appeal reaches the kings and queen mothers, and important princes even though they are not all specifically mentioned by name and do not all lie buried there. After the *indvuna* has spoken, the pilgrims take of snuff brought from the capital.

On their return to the keeper's homestead two animals are killed—one as a sacrifice from the herd of the pilgrims, while the other is provided as food by the keeper and is known as their 'mat'. From the sacrificial beast the pilgrims receive the right side and foreleg, from the other animal they take all but the head. They cook a little of the meat, and the rest is for the road. Once they have left the keeper's homestead they may not under any circumstances return on their tracks. The remaining cattle are sanctified, and may not be hit or roughly treated on the journey.

The pilgrimage to the three groves is co-ordinated by messengers, and its movements are closely followed at the capital. The pilgrimage lasts roughly three weeks, and during that time the capital is 'under the *emadloti*'. Inhabitants are subject to special taboos. No cattle may be killed in the cattle byre; meat may only be boiled and not roasted; court cases are postponed; and the young queens, 'respecting' the presence of the great dead, wear their best clothes and are not permitted to enter certain sections of the queen mother's enclosure. Beer is prepared for the returning pilgrims.

Their arrival is treated with deep solemnity, for they are believed to bring back with them the *emadloti*. They enter the capital after sunset, and their approach is heralded by the command: 'Silence all noise.' Slowly, and at first softly, a sacred song of kings reaches the people in their huts. It is very impressive. There are no interruptions, no curious spectators. (I was the only onlooker, and was hidden in the shadows of the palisade.) The pilgrims, leading the sacred herd, walk slowly through the byre, and above is a waxing moon that gives to all things a fantastic and unearthly quality. The leaders go to the shrine hut, where the rulers await them with beer and snuff, and receive a report of the journey. The ancestral cattle mingle with the herd of the ruling king, and the gateways of the byre are left open so that if they wish they may meander round the village. Since they are spirit cattle, not to be rudely disturbed, they may even eat the maize stored on the open platforms.

On the following day the animals are apportioned to different royal villages and sacrificed. Each beast is dedicated to a specific ancestor, and may only be eaten by descendants in specific kinship categories. The victim is taboo to those kinsmen, who, during the lifetime of the deceased, were, or would have been, inhibited in their conduct to him or her by laws of avoidance. The animal is identified with the substance of the dead in a new holy communion. Thus the animal identified with King Bunu is eaten by his wives and children, but not by his daughters-in-law, and the beast identified with the late Queen Mother Gwamile is food for her sons and daughters, but not for her sons-in-law. People from the surrounding homesteads share in the feast. The largest number of animals (three to six) is sacrificed at the capital. Some of the meat is roasted that day for the smoke to reach the spirit world; the rest is kept in the shrine hut overnight and eaten the following day. Each animal is, as is usual, divided into portions allotted to specific sex and age groups within the circle permitted intimate association with the particular dead.

At sunset, when the final meal is over, the men place the empty skulls on the hides in the cattle byre; then they form a circle with the chief *indvuna* in their midst, and sing an ancient war song, a song of strength and conquest. The men stamp their feet to the martial rhythm, and as it ends, shout, '*Bayethe*'. When the sun sets the *indvuna* praises the great dead.

It is interesting to note that the king himself does not partake of the holy meat till he is symbolically given permission to do so. When he is well on in years, leading councillors and senior princes take cattle from the herd of an old man, separate the cows from the calves, and place some of the cattle dedicated to the ancestors with the calves. A beast from this herd, from the stock of the old man, is killed; the meat is doctored and the king eats of this ritually. The idea of the perpetuation of the royal line seems fairly obvious in this rite, and the animals of the herd are known as *emashawula* (from *lishawula*—the hemp-pipe, container of the revitalizing smoke).

In addition to the annual sacrifice, there is an annual winter ceremony known as 'the burning of the royal groves'. Warriors from the royal villages and local contingents come in festive clothing to the home of the keepers. A ring of fire is made round the grove, and the flames are controlled before they reach the sanctuary. The reason for this is not known; one keeper said it was 'to stop the graves from being burnt accidentally when the winter grass is fired; the homes of the *emadloti* must not be destroyed'. Fire is a purifying agent among the Swazi, and the rite may be a symbolic protection against harm. After the fire is extinguished, the men sing and dance, and feast on beer and meat provided by the keepers.

The influence of the royal ancestors on the nation is by no means limited to regular sacrifices and ritual. They are believed to be always active and ready to control breaches of traditional conduct. As in the domestic cult, the mediation of the senior descendant is essential to placate the family dead, so the power of the national ancestors can only be tapped through the king.

The dogma of the Swazi ancestral cult outlined in this chapter emerged from descriptions of mortuary and other rituals, and is not formulated by the Swazi in general terms. In Swazi religion, as in all religions, there are inconsistencies and contradictions, but it serves to maintain the ethics and the structure of the culture. The after-life is a static replica of life on earth; the individual dead continue as members of a wide kinship circle with definite status obligations and privileges. The 'spirit' is never free from social ties, never liberated by the promise of immortality. The cult itself condemns new behaviour and new ideas; it makes the living, who cherish themselves in the dead, imitate the dead.

CHAPTER XIII

THE DRAMA OF KINGSHIP

EACH year that I was in Swaziland, Swazi from the Protectorate and from beyond its borders came to the home of the *Indlovukati* to take part in the dominant national ceremony, the *Incwala*. I will analyse this in some detail from the angle of social stratification. Cook, Schoeman, and Marwick have described the *Incwala*,[1] but their accounts are very incomplete; nor can I accept their interpretations.

The *Incwala* can be abstracted from Swazi culture, in the same way as any other situation—a marriage, a court case, a business agreement, the building of a hut, etc.—but it has a wider and more representative personnel, and Swazi recognize it as the most important of all national ceremonies, and the most essential event of the year. Personal joys and tragedies, the birth of a child or the death of a loved one, affect individual men and women, but the *Incwala* 'is the heavy play of all the people'.

The Actors

The first and foremost actor in this drama is the king; when there is no king, there is no *Incwala*. If, after the death of a king, his successor is a minor, the ceremony is not held. Throughout the whole period of regency there is no *Incwala*; the prince and queen regent have not the full status of a king and queen mother. During the twenty-one years of the minority of Sobhuza, the *Incwala* was in abeyance. While the king is a minor, however, embryonic annual ceremonies are held and the ritual develops in potency and complexity as the king himself grows in social strength. The king is, as the Swazi say, the 'owner of the *Incwala*', and it is treason, punishable by death, for anyone else to attempt to hold it. The two occasions on which powerful princes started *Incwala* ceremonies, and the disasters which resulted, are still recounted. When I was in Swaziland the king was at the height of his power and the *Incwala* at its peak. It does not decline if the king shows signs of waning strength, but it appears that such an eventuality is unusual. Kings for five generations have died in their prime. They are said to have died by sorcery; Swazi believe that no one dies a natural death.[2]

The rôle of the other performers varies with their national status. Important participators are jealous of their position and no layman who might know the secret rites would dare to say so. The part played by the

[1] P. A. W. Cook, 'The First Fruits Ceremony', *Bantu Studies*, Vol. IV, 1930, pp. 205–10. P. J. Schoeman, 'Die Swazis se Jaarlikse Seremonie van die Eerste Vrugte', *Annale van die Universiteit van Stellenbosch*, Julie, 1937. Marwick, *The Swazi*, Cambridge, 1940, pp. 182–95.

[2] In my original draft I wrote 'Swazi believe that no king dies a natural death.' Sobhuza criticized this: 'No one, not only the king, is believed to die a natural death.' When I appeared sceptical, he called in some people from the village and put the questions: 'Do people die from sickness? Do they die without being bewitched? Do they die from old age?' One after another, the informants said that without sorcery no one died! (December, 1941.)

royal women, especially by the queen mother, is conspicuous. The queen, the other royal wives, the king's sisters and daughters stand, during the ceremony, with the queen mother. At the climax of the drama the two ritual wives, the Matseßula and the Motsa, strengthen the king.

Incwala ritual is controlled by national priests known as *Ɓemanti* (people of the water), or *Ɓelwandle* (people of the sea), because they fetch river and sea water to strengthen the king. These men may not perform any other than the *Incwala* ritual, but through this they have national status, and the head priest ranks as a leading chief. He was formerly a man of the Mtsetfwa clan; later, he was deprived of his power and a member of the Ndwandwe clan was appointed instead. The present leader is Mgwedjeza, son of Vanyane and grandson of the first Ndwandwe priest for the *Incwala*. The master priest, who is assisted by older male relatives, more especially his father's brothers, is one of the most prominent men in Swaziland, and when he dies is buried with the ritual accorded to a Dlamini prince. His village, known as Elwandle, is a royal village with the taboos of royal villages, and must be protected from the contamination of death. Subordinate to him and his assistants is a group whose leader is chosen for honesty and reliability. The present leader, Ngwabadla Duba, is a member of the queen mother's council and supervisor of a royal cattle post.

The *tinsila* (artificial blood-brothers of the king), and especially the left-hand *insila*, shadow the king throughout the performance. On the other hand, the princes and hereditary chiefs who do not belong to the royal (Dlamini) clan are never in close contact with him. The princes should, however, be present, although they cannot enter the sanctuary at the crucial moment of the ritual. Certain chiefs, other than Dlamini, may not attend the *Incwala*, for they are 'so powerful that their personality might fight that of the king and injure him'.[1] By their exclusion they accept the supremacy of the Dlamini and show their relative independence in their own local ceremonies. Some of their subjects, however, must attend.

The regiments stationed in the three main royal villages play a major part in the public ceremonies and are quartered in barracks in the capital for the duration of the *Incwala*. The rank and file of the nation, the majority of the participants, arrive in local contingents led by their chief or his representative. They come 'to support kingship'. Practically every male Swazi has participated in the *Incwala*; whether once or many times depends on such factors as distance, interest, economic security, health, sociability and, nowadays, Christianity.

The duty of organizing the whole ceremony, seeing that it is held on the correct date, preparing the utensils, providing the requisite ingredients, and informing the nation, devolves on the governors of the royal villages, and the mobilizing for each scene of the drama is the duty of regimental officials.

---

[1] E.g. Chiefs of the Mngometfulu, NKosi Mamba, and Mahlalela. They have special medicines which are considered very strong and dangerous to the king, who is also heavily doctored.

Preparations

Various ingredients must be obtained and prepared before the ceremony opens. The councillors make discreet inquires about a pitch black ox required to decorate the vessels in which the priests will carry the sacred water. The animal is stolen from the herd of a subject not of the Dlamini clan, and the emotions of the owner when he discovers the theft 'help the medicine'. 'He is angry and also proud'. Since it is taken for the benefit of the nation, he receives no compensation if it is the first time; on subsequent occasions he may be compensated. The councillors' henchmen drive the beast into the cattle byre and it is slaughtered with a special spear, and carefully dismembered by warriors accustomed to this work. The tail and skin are taken into the sacred enclosure (*inhlambelo*) and the priests cut the hide into strips and twine it like wickerwork round two calabashes kept in the sacred store hut in the harem. The same calabashes are used year after year till they crack, and the hide decoration is taken off and burnt on a sacred pyre at the end of the ceremony. The tail of the slaughtered beast is tied round the neck of the vessel used by the *Belwandle*, to distinguish it from the vessel carried by the subordinates. The contents of the gall bladder are poured over the mouths of both calabashes. Each is then spoken of as '*inkosatana*' (princess) and is no longer an ordinary calabash, but a sacred vessel. The name seems also to be connected with the *Inkosatana*, a sky deity whose footprint is the rainbow, and of whose mood lightning is an expression.

The *Bemanti* set out with the sacred vessels, one group going to the sea, a little south of Lourenço Marques, and the other to the rivers Lusaba (the old boundary between the Sotho and Swazi), Komati, and Mbuluzi. The departure is a festive occasion. The meat of the 'beast of the calabash' is given to the people at the capital. Special beer and snuff are prepared for the journey in the queen mother's enclosure and in the harem. In the afternoon the king arrives to 'cause to go out the vessels'.

The ancestors must witness the exodus. The king, his mother, leading councillors and *tinsila* go together into the shrine hut and discuss the journey over a large pot of beer, for which due praise of royal generosity is given. Then the vessels are brought in and carefully placed on special black shields; they must not touch the earth on the entire journey. As the sun dips slowly behind the hills the carriers lift the precious burdens and, followed by the rulers and their attendants, walk through a special opening used only on ritual occasions, and enter the cattle byre. Stirred by a praiser shouting the paeans of the great dead, the people of the capital congregate to watch the departure. Meanwhile the cattle have been driven into the byre. Their presence is essential and their lowing is mellow music to the Swazi. For a few minutes the priests and their helpers squat on the ground and inhale the snuff provided by the queen mother. Then, the procession sets forth in single file, serious and quiet, accompanied for a short distance by the rulers 'to put them on a good pathway'.

Sobhuza has introduced a few minor innovations into these preliminary rites, though innovations must not be too radical. Thus, since the master

of the *Belwandle*, the late Vanyane, was too old and sickly to undertake
the long, wearying journey to the sea, Sobhuza sent him and his helpers
to Lourenço Marques by motor car, though the subordinate group, under
the leadership of the slightly more active Ngwabadla, still goes on foot to
the big rivers of the north. In the old days the journey through foreign
country was a perilous undertaking for the benefit of the king and
country. Now that there is no danger from attack and Sobhuza gives
the men money to cover their expenses, it is quite an exhilarating
jaunt.

When the *Bemanti* meet any Swazi on the journey, they behave in a
most unusual way. They are normally responsible men, dignified and
courteous, but when they carry the sacred vessel, the *Inkosatana*, they
behave with a studied arrogance. They accost anyone who crosses their
path, saying, 'You trod on the *Inkosatana*', and demand a fine. They
pillage (*kuhlamahlama*) the countryside and take any beer they find in the
huts. The fines are very light: a pin, grass bracelet, small coin, or other
trifle that has been in contact with the person can be offered. Any tendency to exact exorbitant fines, such as a new hat or jacket, is discouraged.
If a man has no small object with him, he may later bring an exchange
for the first offering. Wherever they go the *Bemanti* are treated with the
utmost respect. At each home where they sleep a beast is killed and the
tail tied round the vessel. To the Swazi who live in outlying districts,
their visit is a sign that the *Incwala* is close at hand, and chiefs often
give money and see that the *Bemanti* receive large bowls of beer,
since they are anxious to help 'support the work of kings'. Many
people, and in theory the whole nation, thus have an opportunity,
through contact with the *Inkosatana*, of participating in the national
ritual.

The goal of the pilgrimage is to fill the vessels and collect special
medicines. The leading *Belwandle* fetch sea-water. They describe the
sea as fearful, magnificent, powerful, a source of new life and unknown
mysteries. They take off their clothes so as not to wet them and wade
waist deep into the water. 'The waves are in rows and we fight them.
They rush up and down like an army, and the mouth of the calabash is
small and it takes a long time to fill. We do not dip it; we want to catch
the foam at the top, for that is the strength of the sea. We chase the waves
as they roll back and then we run forward again to catch them as they
break on the shore, and we are tired by the time the *Inkosatana* is full.'
This accomplished, they go to collect plant medicines. Most of these
medicines grow in the tangled forests of the Lubombo, where inter-
twining undergrowth hampers movement, and it is hard to find the plants
that are needed for the king. The priests squat and rest, inhaling the
snuff given by the queen mother for their journey and sometimes praising
the royal family, till after a while, and partly, it is believed, with the aid
of the snuff, the leaders 'see and remember' where the plants are to be
found and the young men dig them out, cut them, and wrap them
securely in bundles of grass.

In the meanwhile the subordinate group has filled its vessel from the
rivers swelled by tributaries. It is the middle of the rainy season and the
rivers are usually full and rush 'stronger than a strong swimmer'. 'The

waters of the world are fetched to give strength and purity to the king'.[1]

The *Bemanti* then return, pillaging on the way, and wait at an old royal village near the capital till they are summoned to bring the medicines for the first *Incwala* ceremony, the Little *Incwala*.

Now that the material ingredients of the ritual have been obtained, one thing only delays the ceremony; that is, the position of the sun and moon.

The Sun and the Moon

Throughout the whole country there is one main topic of conversation: 'When will the moon and sun be right?' Every morning aged councillors stand in the cattle byre and watch the sun as it rises, judging its position by certain fixed landmarks, and every evening they scan the sky, discussing the size of the moon and the position of the stars.

The importance of the sun and moon in relation to the *Incwala* ceremony hinges on their Swazi correlates. The sun is the more important, for the date of the ceremony is fixed by observation of the solstices. In Swazi cosmology, based on the assumption that the earth is flat and stationary, the sun crosses the heavens in a more or less regular path twice a year, and rises and sets in its northernmost position in the moon of *Kolwane* or *Intlaba* (June or July), and in its southernmost position, when it reaches its 'hut' in the south, in the moon of *Lweti* or *Inkosi encane* (November or December). The actual dates of the solstices are June 21st and December 21st. The sun is considered to rest in its 'hut' in the south, and then to leap out to start its journey anew, and the *Incwala* should begin the day after the sun has reached its hut and is 'resting', i.e. on the longest day. The Swazi, however, correlate the lunar with the solar year, though inevitably there is confusion and 'a moon is lost'. The moon, as in nearly all mythology, is thought of as a woman who follows her male lord, the sun, and when she 'dies' she is hidden by him and then reappears. The *Incwala* should begin when the moon is 'dark', though the Swazi appreciate that the coincidence of the December solstice with the wane of the moon is rare. They therefore decide on the moon before December 22nd and have the ceremony end after the sun has reached its southernmost point. 'The king races the sun.'

It is terrible for the ceremony to be over before the sun starts its journey, and even worse for it to begin afterwards. Either would be a national calamity, requiring special ritual to rectify. In the first eventuality, a doctor of the Maɓuzo clan, the clan which treats the king after a royal death, gives him medicines similar to those used when he has suffered the pollution of the loss of a queen. Unless this is done, the king will not be sufficiently strong to bear the development of the coming year and to withstand kings of other nations who apparently have the 'strength of the sun' with them. In the second eventuality, if the ceremony begins after the sun has started its journey, a special beast without horns must be

---

[1] Since the publication of *The Golden Bough*, it is scarcely necessary to emphasize the importance of water to those peoples especially who live in countries where rain is scarce and the land scorched by a tropical sun. The analogies with the Veda hymns are obvious, and it will be seen that the *Incwala* embodies all the familiar elements of the well-known culture dramas.

used at one stage of the ritual to effect the 'breaking through' from the old to the new year.

The position of the sun and the moon is significant because of their connection with human destiny. Here the moon is the more important, for the size of the moon determines many major events: the removal of an infant from the hut where it is born, the day a king is 'shown to the people', the end of a widow's mourning period, the moving of royal villages. When the moon is round and full, the human beings on whom it is operative will be healthy and shining, but in the darkness of the waning period man is weak and puny. Consequently a ceremony to introduce someone into the fullness of a new status always takes place as the moon is growing or when it is full; one which temporarily isolates a man from his fellows is held in the period of decline and darkness. The moon is also correlated with the mating of certain birds and animals, the flowering of some shrubs and trees, and the growth of new grass. The sun, on the other hand, always appears the same, varying only with the time of the day. Its connexion with human destiny is closest at dawn and dusk: kings and Dlamini nobles should die at sunset or dawn and the caves in which they are buried should be closed at dawn, and these are the times to speak to the powerful ancestors.

The right timing of the ceremony is the responsibility of the councillors, and serious miscalculation is punishable by a fine and even dismissal, since it is judged as treason rather than incompetence; for the king is not only connected but even identified with the sun and the moon. Ordinary subjects are, however, intensely interested and freely offer advice, and the king and his mother may make suggestions, though they are not held responsible for wrong timing.

The Little Incwala

On the day the councillors agree that the moon will 'be black', they send messengers to summon the *Bemanti* for the Little *Incwala*. Those who are in closest contact with the king--his mother, the queens, the *tinsila*, and the main royal regiments—must also participate in the Little *Incwala*.

The *Bemanti* come to Loɓamba, the capital. The children stand on top of high ant-hills, which are always used as look-outs, and watch the road. As soon as they appear the people close themselves in their huts, because the *Belwandle* are permitted to seize any article they like from them and grab any food that they find. The king and the *Bemanti* meet in the cattle byre, where only a few intrepid children and one or two Christian converts follow them. The sacred vessels and medicines are carried into the *inhlambelo* (sacred enclosure) and put into the care of the councillors. The senior *Bemanti* squat on the ground, but the subordinate group go off on the pillaging foray. Special beer for them to seize has been brewed in the queen mother's enclosure and in the harem, and they carry it out to the leaders. They can enter any hut except the sacred store huts, the shrine hut, and the club-house in each of the barracks. These were the sanctuaries, or asylums, in which men fleeing from execution were safe in the old days, but I could find no reason why they should be taboo to the *Belwandle*, and people did not go there especially to avoid being fined. When the raid is over the people come out of their huts to take part in the ceremony.

The honour of opening the *Incwala* (*kugwaβula Incwala*) belongs to the *Indvuna* of the king's grandmother's village. These regiments in 1937 covered the age grades of *Inguluβe* and *Indlavela*, membership roughly from fifty to sixty-five years. They wear semi-*Incwala* dress; graceful cloaks of cattle-tails hang from the shoulders to the waist, flowing tails are tied to the right arms, while feathers and magnificent black plumes shine in their hair; their loin coverings are of leopard skin. The costume resembles war dress, but at the *Incwala* men may only carry plain sticks instead of spears and clubs (although these are occasionally concealed behind their shields). The restriction on dangerous weapons is to guard against the possibility that fighting might break out, since excitement runs high.

The regimental herald shouts a praise song; then the leader commands silence. The only sound is the moaning of the cattle, whose presence is necessary in this as in most rituals. The veterans slowly sing the first of the sacred songs known as the 'hand song'.[1] They hold their shields and sticks in the left hand, leaving the right hand free for the movement which characterizes this dance-song:

> Uye uye oyeha—you hate the child king mu u u oyeha,
> You hate the child king (*repeated*).
> I would depart with my Father (the king),
> I fear we would be recalled.
> mm m u oyeha—they put him on the stone:
> mm m u oyeha he—sleeps with his sister:
> mm m u u u he—sleeps with Lozithupa (Princess):
> uye uye oyeha—you hate the child king.

The words are repeated in varying order over and over again, and finally the song ends:

> Shiyo ihi hi hi shiyo ihi hi hi (four times)
> Hi Hi Hi.

During the song the men of Loβamba and Lozita whoop into the amphitheatre in their feathers and finery and the commander-in-chief arranges the regiments into a crescent. The women come through the upper entrance of the cattle byre to join in the singing and dancing. The wives of the king stand in order of seniority in the front row. They flaunt new shawls and newly-blackened skirts. Behind them are grouped the queen mother with her retainers and the co-wives of the late king. Further back come women of less importance and children of commoners. The princesses form a separate line, again in ranked formation- Each woman holds a long thin wand (*umqusho*) in her hand.

---

[1] Only full photographic and sound recording could convey a real idea of the dance-songs. I am very dissatisfied with my rather free translations of the words and sounds.

After some time, a second sacred chant is started. The men take their sticks in their right hands, and point them forward slowly to the rhythm; the women raise their wands and by skilful movements of the fingers make the wands quiver in time.

> Shi shi ishi ishi—you hate him,
> ishi ishi ishi—mother, the enemies are the people.
> ishi ishi ishi—you hate him,
> Mother—the people are wizards.
> Admit the treason of Mabedla
> ishi ishi ishi—you hate him,
> you have wronged,
> ishi ishi—bend great neck,
> those and those they hate him,
> ishi ishi—they hate the king.

After a long time the song ends:

> awoshi awoshi
> Hi Hi Hi.

The sacred songs of the Little *Incwala* are followed by a number of solemn but not sacred chants known as *imiguƁo*, which are rich in historical allusions and moral precepts. *ImiguƁo* are sung at other gatherings at the capital or the homesteads of chiefs. The following will indicate the theme:

UmguƁo of Bunu's time, urging revenge on those who are believed to have killed the king.

> Come let us arm, men of the capital,
> the harem is burnt,
> the shield of the lion has disappeared.
> Dji o.
> Come let us arm, etc.

While the people are thus occupied, the *Ɓelwandle* treat the king. They fetch medicines and utensils from the store hut in the harem. As they bring these into the *inhlambelo*, the women whom they pass avert their eyes, for there is the belief that to look on the medicine of the king can make one mad. An assistant of the *Ɓelwandle* drives a few cattle into the *inhlambelo* and a little later there is a death bellow. All the animals but one, a pitch black ox, come out. Dancers near the fence hear the thudding of poles and know that the beast is being skinned and prepared for doctoring the king. As the sun sets in moonless night, the king goes into the *inhlambelo* and the formation of the dancers changes from a crescent to a circle, from the partial to the full moon. The commander of the regiments orders a young regiment to leave the cattle byre and stand outside the *inhlambelo*, and the other regiments move upwards, so that the king in his sanctuary is surrounded by his subjects.

The *Indvuna* starts the *simemo*.

(refrain.)
Jjiya oh o o King, alas for your fate
(refrain)
Jjiya oh o o King, they reject thee
Jjiya oh o o King, they hate thee.

This song is repeated again and again.

The *simemo* is connected with important episodes in the life of every king. It is sung on his marriage to his main ritual wife, when the ancestral cattle are brought back from the royal graves, and, finally, when the king himself dies and is carried for burial to the mountain cave. The *simemo* is abruptly stilled by one of the ßelwandle in the *inhlambelo* shouting, 'Out, foreigners!' This applies to all who do not owe allegiance to the king, and in former days to certain groups that were considered alien. All who belong to the Dlamini, including women pregnant by Dlamini men, must also leave. It appears to me that the king at the height of his ritual treatment must be surrounded only by his loyal and unrelated supporters. The ßelwandle leader then shouts: 'Eh eh. He stabs it with both horns. Our Bull.' The people know that the king in his enclosure has spat medicine to break the old year and prepare for the new. First he spits to the east and then he spits to the west, and each time the crowd applauds: 'He stabs it.' This means that what he has done has produced the desired effect, he has triumphed and is strengthening the earth. This marks the climax of the day. Thereafter, the people sing the final anthem, entitled *Ingcaßa Kangcovula*:

> Here is the Inexplicable,
> Our Bull! Lion! Descend.
> Descend, Being of heaven,
> Unconquerable.
> Play like tides of the sea,
> You Inexplicable, Great Mountain.
> Our Bull ye ye, etc.

This is known as the *Lihußo* and is regarded as a national anthem. It is said by some to be very old, but by others to be fairly recent. It is the main *umgußo*. The regiments and the women disperse. The ßemanti remain a while treating the king and preparing for the morrow. The fire burns all night in the *inhlambelo*.

Long before the dawn, the people are awakened by the praiser, who strides backwards and forwards outside the harem where the king slept. The commander of the regiments shouts to the men to dress, a warrior proudly blows his trumpet and the men dance into the cattle byre in their *Incwala* clothes and sing the songs of yesterday. Now and then a voice rings out, 'Come, Lion, awake, the sun is leaving you'; 'They hate him, the son of Bunu'; and hurls other insults to stir the king to activity.

The women take their places, and the king enters the *inhlambelo* with the rising run. The young regiment is again sent to close the circle, the older ones move up, the *simemo* is sung, the 'foreigners' and Dlamini are dismissed, and as the king surrounded by loyal subjects spits to east and west, everyone rejoices: 'He has bitten for the passing year.'

The main ritual of the Little *Incwala* is over, but there still remains an essential 'work of the people for kingship'. The warriors sing a special march song and then weed the queen mother's gardens. On this occasion tribute labour has a special name—*kuɓungula*—a term usually used when one works with little energy, when one plays and dawdles. At the *Incwala*, the *tindvuna* urge the men to strenuous effort, and scold those who slack, but 'it is to ɓungula all the same, for it is *Incwala* time'. About midday the men return and dance again in the byre.

The king, his mother, and his wives distribute huge quantities of beer to the regiments, important visitors and *ɓelwandle* before they return to their own villages. The king, whose beer has been brewed separately in the harem, caters for the warriors, the *ɓelwandle*, and any special friends; the queen mother for princes and princesses, co-wives, and her own regiments; the queens for favoured royalty and individual commoners. The actual quantity varies from year to year, and aristocrats always receive a major share. Sometimes a beast is slaughtered and meat circulates from the yard in the queen mother's enclosure to the people squatting in local and status groups. Each receives a part of the beast defined by the sex and age of the eaters and their relationship to the donor. When the feasting is over the people return to their homes till the moon grows full and the big *Incwala* begins.

The Interim Period

The interim period, fourteen days in 1934 and 1935 and fifteen days in 1936, is part of the *Incwala*, and during that time the ritual is extended to the four corners of the Protectorate. Every day at the royal villages and at the homes of chiefs the *Incwala* songs are rehearsed. Perfect performance of the *Incwala* songs and dances is acquired by long hours of practice. Swazi derive real pleasure from graceful and harmonious movement; the beautiful singers and dancers are admired, and the clumsy are mocked.[1] The *Incwala* songs and *imiguɓo* are rehearsed; the *simemo* is reserved for future climaxes; other *Incwala* songs are not yet 'opened'.

The words of the *Incwala* songs are surprising to the European, accustomed, at national celebrations, to hear royalty blatantly extolled, the virtues of the nation magnified, and the country glorified. The theme of the *Incwala* songs is hatred of the king and his rejection by the people. The actual words of the song are few, mournful, and tremendously moving. The songs are repeated again and again, 'and once heard, no one can

---

[1] In 1935 Sobhuza sent his four eldest daughters together with two other royal maidens to his kraal at Entonjeni in the Peak to have some lessons in the *Incwala* tunes from two very ancient princesses, daughters of the king Mswati. He explained to me that the queens of Loɓamba had not grown up in the royal atmosphere, but had come there on marriage, and the *Incwala* was relatively new to them. I accompanied the young princesses; we found the old women most exacting teachers, contemptuous of the singing and general lack of knowledge of the younger generation, and one old lady was so disgusted at a rehearsal with the warriors that she walked away and vowed she would not listen to them again. The king himself went to the Peak that year, so that it was a period of hectic festivity and enthusiastic singing and dancing.

ever forget'. It is impossible to give a true idea of the *Incwala* performance from the words alone. Very often the apparently meaningless refrain

dji a o o or shi shi shi

dominates the song.

The songs are sacred, not secret. Their sacredness is impressed on the youngest children, and it is a more than ordinary breach of law to sing them at times other than during the weeks of *Incwala*: 'It is as though you wanted to bring trouble on the nation.' In Johannesburg I asked a great friend of mine, a teacher, to check through the words and tune with me. He did so in a whisper; then suddenly exclaimed, 'I fear. Better send this to the owner (Sobhuza) to see.'

The songs indicate the growth and difficult position of the king. Selby Msimang, in an unpublished description of the *Incwala*, writes of the song 'shi shi': 'The song or hymn is an indirect allusion to the king's enemies, not necessarily from outside, but may be from members of the royal family, or among the tribesmen. The line "he hates him! ahoshi, ahoshi ahoshi"—is intended as a thrust against all who may not join in the *Incwala*, whose non-participation is regarded as an act of rebellion, hostility and personal hatred of the king.' Of the *simemo* he writes *inter alia*: 'It is a national expression of sympathy for the king, who, by reason of the manner of his choice, necessarily provokes enemies within the family. The king may be one of the very youngest sons of his father, and older brothers or half-brothers (as they are called in English) must needs be offended at a mere child of their father becoming their king, as indeed was the case in the affair of Joseph, the son of Jacob. The songs show the hatred evoked by the king, but they also demonstrate the loyalty of his supporters. The people who sing the songs sing with pain and suffering, they hate his enemies and denounce them.' One informant said: 'I think these songs are magical preventatives against harm coming to the king.'

A great deal is contributed by the dancing. The movement at the Little *Incwala* is dignified and restrained. There is no abandoned sorrow, no uncontrolled gaiety in the movements to the rhythm. In the 'hand song' men and women put stick and wand under the left arm and keep the right free. They curve it slowly inwards; the body sways slightly, the hand pauses and moves out, and in the pause the right foot bears slowly down. Men and women have slightly different steps, sing different parts, and have different words, but there is perfect harmony and co-ordination. Every now and then in each dance a few women glide forward to 'excite' the warriors. They move in their status groups, no princess steps forth with a queen, no child with a group of adults, no commoner with royalty.

The dances and songs are more than entertainment. They are part of the ritual strength of the Swazi as opposed to other nations. People talk of 'playing the *Incwala*', of dancing it; they emphasize that the dance itself strengthens the king and the earth.

During the interim period, much time is also devoted to putting the costumes in order. There is always danger that the feathers and furs will be destroyed by moths. Some men put on special scents, others frequently take their clothes out and shake them, a few buy 'medicine' from the shops. The costume is expensive—if each article were to be purchased it would cost over £6, but as a rule the men have the cloak from the tails of cattle they themselves have slaughtered and there is barter for the feathers, leopard skins, etc.

Sometimes warriors appeal to the king to assist them to obtain their costumes. During a dance a man will rush towards the king, bang his shield with a flourish on the ground, make his request in a flood of praise, and run back to his line. If the monarch grants the favour, he is loudly extolled, and if he ignores it the man bears no grudge. The king is honoured by the begging, the man by the receiving. Clothing at the *Incwala* indicates rank: only princes may wear the red feather of the *ligwalagwala* in their hair, only princesses a necklace of giraffe hair adorned with shells. The clothing worn at the *Incwala* is more than adornment or sign of rank; it too is ritually potent, and many of the animals whose skins are used are powerful and dangerous.

Representatives from the entire country prepare to move to Loɓamba, and at the capital itself there is tremendous activity; warriors and groups of women summoned by the queen mother bring reed for the fences and grass for thatching in an attempt to fix huts to accommodate the numerous guests; warriors cut down logs for boiling the beer and the meat. The women in the civilian population prepare beer for their own visitors, aware that this is the best opportunity of showing hospitality to friends and of making a profit from beer sales to strangers. Christmas usually falls during the *Incwala* period, and converts come in their congregation to see the queen mother. Almost every day a service is held in her court-yard. The Christians talk of the *Incwala* as 'Christmas of the heathens', and the pagans docilely agree: 'Yes. It is our Christmas, the Christmas of our king, the beginning of the New Year.'

The moon overhead is called *inkosi enkulu*, the moon of the main ceremony of the *Incwala*. As the moon grows the exact date on which the Big *Incwala* should open is feverishly discussed. There are two con-troversial issues: when will the moon be full, and should the *Incwala* open on that or the following day? The old advisers insist that when the king is still only the *Umntfwana*, heir apparent, the ritual should com-mence the day before the full moon, and that when the king reaches maturity it should open with the full moon, and when he has a full harem the ceremony should open the day after the full moon. Sobhuza disagrees, but has obeyed the decision of the majority of his councillors. In 1934, 1935, and 1936, the Big *Incwala* opened one day past full moon.

5. Fetching the Sacred Tree

Swazi name each of the days of the Big *Incwala* by its main event or events, and the first day is to fetch the *lusekwane*, the sacred tree. The *lusekwane* is a species of acacia that grows somewhat sparsely in a few areas in Swaziland and near the coast. It is sometimes known as *ludziwo lwendlovu*, the elephant's pot. It grows with amazing rapidity. Although for many years it has been fetched from the same spot (the Egundwini kraal near the Bulunga mountains) and large quantities have been chopped for the ceremony, the area is not yet denuded. Another significant char-acteristic is that the leaves remain green for many months, even when plucked. Quick growth, greenness, ever-recurring fertility characterize most of the ritual ingredients of the *Incwala*.

As in the medieval legends knights without stain set forth in quest of the grail, so only pure youths may fetch the *lusekwane*. Indeed, the Swazi say the tree was made expressly to distinguish the 'pure' from the 'impure'; a distinction that is drawn between men 'who have spent their strength in children' or have intrigued with married women, and youths who, though they have had love affairs, have not made any woman pregnant. This cleavage usually coincides with the regimental organization, since the king gives a regiment as a whole permission to marry, and most men take the opportunity. It is considered more reprehensible to be a married man in a regiment not yet permitted to marry than a bachelor in an old regiment. If anyone 'impure' were to pick the *lusekwane*, its leaves would shrivel. Each branch is a divining rod of purity.

Early in the morning of the day on which the tree must be fetched there is a rush on the beer in the huts of the residents at the capital; the warriors know they have a long and tiring day ahead of them, and that no food need be provided for them by the rulers. At about 9 a.m. the command rings out in some such grandiose phraseology: 'Hear! Listen that I might tell you matters that come from Shaka the black; he who wraps himself in the skin of a lion. Go out! With all powers! At once! At once to the *Lusekwane*!' 'As you say', respond the men dressing in the barracks, and, with a flourish of sticks and shouting regimental cries, they enter the cattle byre to sing and dance—'to rejoice and work and strengthen the country'—before they depart on their mission. Then they move to Lozita and join with the king's regiments, whom they find already dancing outside his cattle byre. Many local contingents have swelled the permanent regiments and others are still arriving. It is a magnificent sight. The queens of Lozita and nearby royal homesteads and a number of other women face the vast crescent of warriors. Standing somewhat shamefacedly in the background in the women's section are the men in European clothes.

On this occasion the king himself is expected to dance and when he appears there is tremendous excitement. The officials urge the people: 'Dance! Dance! The *Incwala* is not a thing of play. Dance!'

As the king and his special attendants take their stand in the centre of the front row of the warriors, the men greet him with a long shrill whistle. The king dances with his men for nearly two hours in the blazing midsummer heat and everyone 'thanks him by dancing well'. Although he wears the same fantastic costume as the men, people say there is no mistaking him, for he stands out clearly by his 'personality' even among the princes. At last a councillor stops the dancing and appoints responsible men to take charge of the expedition; exhorting them to see that the warriors neither fight nor stray and that they return well and safe.

The journey to the *lusekwane* is a hard test of endurance and also a sign of manhood. Youngsters are intensely anxious to go, and boast once they have been. The distance there and back is about forty-five miles, most of it over rough footpaths. No food is provided. The men must reach the trees by dusk to select their branches, and they must be back at Loɓamba before dawn. When Logcogco, brother of King Mbandzeni, was Prince of Egundwini, he always had food to refresh the pilgrims, but his successor is less thoughtful or generous. Usually a few boys drop out along the roadside, and sympathetic friends carry them back a branch.

They reach the trees, and as the moon rises round and red, each youth hacks down a branch with a knife or with the sharpened edge of a spear. A man in charge starts a new sacred song, a lullaby, the third *Incwala* song:

> We lull him, shiyawo, shiyawo,
> The Child grows, we rock him, shiyawo, shiyawo,
> He who is as big as the world, shiyawo, shiyawo.

The men beat their shields against their sides, and Swazi say that it is the same rhythm which a woman uses to rock a child to sleep. This song is said by some to have been sung by a queen in exile to her babe, who later became the king. The song indicates clearly what the *lusekwane* will do for the king. The *lusekwane*, as we shall see, is used to cover the sacred enclosure where the king will be doctored and born again with new strength and vitality. According to Ngolotsheni Motsa, 'the lullaby sums up the whole of that part of the *Incwala* which affects the status and the person of the king. When the king is surrounded by the *lusekwane* we believe he is being reborn, revitalized, and that he will grow in prestige.' Msimang explains it in almost identical words, and continues: 'The nation's life, soul, and well-being hang in the faith and belief that the rebirth, rejuvenation, and purification of the king ushers in a new life, added virtue and strength and national unity, bound up in the life of the national figure-head and sovereign.' As soon as everyone has picked his branch, the pilgrims leave, singing the song all the while, beating their shields and moving forward with a rhythmic hop. To add to the hardships of these young 'knights', so strong in virtue, rain, the blessing of the ancestors, is considered a good omen on the return journey. Late in the night they reach Lancibana, the resting place near Lozita where, if the king is in a generous mood, he sends a beast for the men to slaughter and eat. Here they remain the rest of the night, for the *lusekwane* must not be contaminated by the sex life of the village; it must be kept pure and fresh. The carrier himself may go into a village for a while, but he must leave the branch outside, and no youth would think of breaking the law, fearing the anger of his friends and the possible harm it might bring on his people. The 'impure' join the company, and towards dawn the entire army marches to Loɓamba, the youths in front bearing their green branches. From the high sandheaps of Loɓamba, the people see them as they rest awaiting the dawn and the king. Their cloaks glisten in the dim light 'like the wings of flying ants' (Sobhuza's analogy). Friends bring them porridge, roasted mealies, and beer, and some seek food for themselves; but they leave the branches far from possible pollution.

As the sun rises on this, the second day of the Big *Incwala*, a group of men fetch the king from the harem to greet the expedition, and lead it to the cattle byre of the capital. The commander of the regiments divides the men into age classes, and the pilgrims, lustily singing the lullaby and holding the branches like wands, push through the narrow gateway, circle along the right wing towards the *inhlambelo*, pass in front of the entrance and drop the branches one on top of the other into a high, sacred heap. They caper off to join the men waiting outside, and then all re-enter. They are organized into a semicircle, and sing *Incwala* songs and *imiguβo*. The king and the women join in, the sun blazes down, the youths seem to have overcome their weariness. The dancing after the return from the pilgrimage appears to be a tremendously powerful mass experience.

In thirty-six hours (counting from the time they started dancing at Loβamba before leaving for the *lusekwane*) the pilgrims have danced six to ten hours, walked roughly fifty miles, cut the tough and thorny branches of the tree, eaten little food (a leader of each age class always carries a hemp pipe to stave off hunger), and slept a couple of hours in the open veld, perhaps in the rain. Only when eventually the regiments are dismissed do the youths seem to realize their utter exhaustion, and most of them sleep the rest of the day. Their services are again commanded for the morrow.

6. *The Bull*

The third day is spoken of as the day of 'leaves' (*emacembe*) and of the 'bull' (*inkunzi*), the two outstanding ritual acts of the day. The leaves are really whole branches of a hardy shrub, the *mbondvo*, that grows profusely on the flats near the capital. Its characteristics are its tough branches (they make excellent switches), and its thick, strong, green foliage. The *mbondvo* is used for other occasions of royal doctoring; from it are cut some of the wooden pegs in the queen mother's crown, and the necklace worn by a queen while her royal baby is suckling. The youths who plucked the *lusekwane* and those who were too weak or young to travel so far are summoned early in the morning to gather the *emacembe*. The branches of the *mbondvo* are thrown near those of the *lusekwane* to the lullaby tune and the old men cover the *inhlambelo* completely with the *lusekwane* at the top and the *emacembe* at the bottom. Only a small arched doorway, wide enough for a beast to squeeze through, is left uncovered, and this is later closed with heavy logs to 'hide the secrets of kingship'. Then all is ready for the major act, the catching of the 'bull'.

Europeans usually arrive during the day, anxious to watch a 'grand bull-fight', 'native life in the raw'. There are few who see in it anything but a barbaric display of courage and cruelty. The whites bring gifts to the queen mother—tobacco, cloth, sweets, cigarettes. A few bottles of Commando brandy or White Horse whisky (Tears of the King of England!) find their way to the princes.

The *βemanti* come, crossing the veld towards the cattle byre—a company of about twenty men, walking without songs, some in *Incwala* clothing, others in ragged European jackets and shirts. They have come to stay till the end of the ceremony, and carriers bring their blankets, mats, and headrests. In the centre are the men with plants for the ritual, and these are taken into the *inhlambelo* and guarded. A few of the party pillage, as on the first visit at the Little *Incwala*.

Again the veterans of Zombodze open the ceremony with the 'hand song', the cattle of the capital are brought in for the occasion, the regiments, now from the entire nation, rush in and take their places in the crescent, and the women play their part. Only the costume is different: on their heads the men have tight-fitting caps of black ostrich feathers magnificently adorned with clumps of *sakaßula* (widow bird); the queen mother and her co-wives wear coronets of *umhlangala* (?) skin, long cloaks of brayed hide, and their skin skirts are drawn up under their armpits, hiding the breasts, instead of toga-wise over the shoulder. The men's cap is for adornment. The dress of the women is of greater significance: the style of headdress is that worn when women are entitled to great respect— the respect of a mother-in-law—and the way the apron lies is the style enforced for a woman in early wifehood and first pregnancy. The 'mothers of the king' are selected for special notice on this day; they are respected by all the nation because of their relationship to the king.

In his covered enclosure, the king is treated by the priests. Utensils are again brought from the store hut in the harem—a native hammer of iron, pincers with which the king will eat of powerful medicine, grinding stones, a bundle of wands. A young *insila* goes with a calabash to fetch water from any nearby big river to mix with the powerful liquid fetched by the *Belwandle*.

Meanwhile, the councillors point out to the *Belwandle* a large black beast, the *umdvutshulwa*. People talk of it as *inkunzi*, a bull, but actually it is an ox. Reliable informants state that at present it is called a bull because it is being confused with the *inkunzi yombenge*, the bull of the strips, which was indeed a bull and was used to doctor the regiments before they went to battle. Other informants say that it is called a bull because it is made strong as a bull by medicines and that the king is ritually identified with it, the strongest beast in the herd. The beast is stolen from a commoner's herd—'such a fine beast; the owner is always angry, but what can he say—a thing of kingship'.

The beast must be caught in the hands of the youths who fetched the sacred tree. Councillors drive it along with the other beasts to make it tractable, through the narrow doorway of the *inhlambelo*, and all the other animals come out after a few seconds. The 'pure' stand tense, ready to pounce as the *umdvutshulwa* emerges and to pummel it with their strong young hands. They discard their finery for the ordeal and retain only their loin skins. Most of the spectators beat a cautious retreat, and the women, especially royalty, are carefully removed.

The sound of the mournful *Incwala* hymns rings out from the older men, who remain performing, apparently unmoved by fear or curiosity. Inside the *inhlambelo* the king strikes the bull with a wand of *masweti* timber and 'though it may have been one of the most docile animals when it entered the *inhlambelo* it comes out as vicious and wild as a buffalo' (*mzululeke*). The boys are after it. Madly the animal rushes towards a gateway. One year it broke right through the palisade and streaked across the veld. The few intrepid onlookers grow wildly excited. One of the 'pure' youths is abreast of it. He grabs its tail. He is pulled along the ground and lets go his hold. Another lad takes his chance. He hangs on to the tail till the rest catch up. The shout goes forth: 'They have overcome it.'

To throw the bull with naked hands is a trial of strength and a test of purity. Every boy is eager for fame. Before the event the boys boast to each other of what they will do, and afterwards the first to grab the beast is highly praised for his skill and bravery. Swazi are convinced that if someone 'impure' has managed to gather the sacred *lusekwane*, without his guilt being detected, his sin will be exposed by the *umdvutshulwa*. There is doubt, however, as to whether the punishment will be meted out directly or vicariously. Some informants insist that no matter how hard an innocent boy be thrown or even trampled upon, he will suffer no real hurt, while if the sinner be only touched the injury will be severe. Others insist that the beast selects a scapegoat and when, in 1936, a youth had his leg broken, it was not against him that most criticism was levelled. Youngsters themselves tend to regard vicarious punishment as the rule, and when I suggested to a very immature boy that there was no possibility of his being hurt, he replied lugubriously that the bull doesn't look for the sinner, but the sin. If someone is hurt, the sinner should be discovered and punished, though the damage has already been done: his wand is in the *inhlambelo*, his hand is on the beast that is needed to doctor the king.

The word *umdvutshulwa* is derived from *kudvuɓula*—to thump or pummel. During the years I witnessed the ceremony, the youngsters, vigorously singing the lullaby, pummelled the beast with their hands the moment it was thrown, and those who could jumped on it, till it was barely alive when they dragged it to the *inhlambelo*. I was told 'the hands of all the boys should come to the *umdvutshulwa* like the waters of all the world go into the medicine for the king'. Sobhuza insists that the animal should never have been jumped on, and since I left, he has ordered the boys not to pummel or stamp on it, but merely to throw it and pull it as fast as possible into the *inhlambelo*. The time from the emergence of the beast until its final capture was between thirty and fifty minutes in the years 1934–6; with the change in procedure it takes only a few minutes.

As a result of pressure put on the nation by the government, every effort has been made to compress the 'killing of the bull' into the shortest possible time. The government acted because of representations made to it by the S.P.C.A., who were urging the complete abolition of the ritual on the grounds of cruelty. At a meeting I attended in 1935, where the matter was heatedly discussed, the councillors proclaimed that the rite could not be abolished: 'it was law from the beginning'; 'the *umdvutshulwa* is tied to many things—the *lusekwane*, the water, and all that is done in the *inhlambelo*. Without it there could be no *Incwala*.' A coloured man with whom I discussed the position later asked bitterly: 'Is it better to kill a bull for religious reasons than to destroy a nation with colour prejudice?'

The *umdvutshulwa* is killed by the *ɓelwandle* in the *inhlambelo* and special portions are taken to doctor the king. One of the priests cuts a deep incision in the right side where the ribs end, someone puts in his hand and breaks the windpipe, and as the animal bellows its last the men give its spirit the royal whistle. The *ɓelwandle* cut off snippets of the different inner organs, liver, entrails, silverside steak; they cut a bit of the ear, the tongue, lower lip and other parts that 'have power' and they remove the gall bladder very carefully. That night the dismembered

P

animal is kept in the shrine hut of the nation; part of it is used to 'put strength into the king'.

The next rite of this, the third day, seems to be connected with the potency of the king. The 'pure' are summoned to drive into the cattle byre a black ox. This ox is known as the *incwambo*, and on it the king sits and is washed with sacred waters. The *incwambo* holds a unique place in the royal herd, it must not be beaten, maltreated or used for any mundane task. When it loses its vigour a young substitute is found, but the old one is never killed. *Incwambo*, according to some informants, is a physiological term applied to a muscle near the testicles. The *incwambo* animal is forced to the ground, the king sits on it naked, and the right-hand *insila* washes his right and the left-hand *insila* his left side. The water is powerful with foamy medicines that bestow personality and include *umtfuso*, from *kutfusa* (to stir or awaken) a prescription given to bulls to make them strong and quick to climb the cows, and to men to stir virility. The *incwambo* is so powerful that all those who touch it must wash their whole bodies, and when the *incwambo* dies it is ritually burnt by old men and people should not go near the smoke lest by inhaling it they go mad. The king, as he sits on the *incwambo*, is made 'the bull of the people'. Amongst the medicines that he is given to eat is a small hard lump near the liver, known as the *impundvu*. This may never be eaten by young men, for it is believed that it would make them lose their way, go astray, and be disrespectful; it is the food of the old men no longer able to fight. When the king comes to this piece, he calls the attention of the *Belwandle*, who start with simulated anger and surprise: 'Hau—you are eating the *impundvu*.' And as he bites it, but does not swallow it, the crowd is given the sign to applaud his development. It is believed that he has staved off harm in the coming year.

All this time the regiments have been chanting their songs, and as night falls they are organized into a circle in the same way as at the Little *Incwala*. The *simemo* ritual is again enacted with different medicines. Sometimes rain falls but even if the men get drenched they must not seek cover. They finally go to the river to wash, but the *Belwandle* remain in the *inhlambelo* busily preparing for the morrow, when the drama reaches a dramatic denouement.

7. The Great Day

The fourth day is the great day, the *Incwala*, sometimes spoken of as the day of throwing the gourd. On this day the king appears in all his splendour, and the ambivalent attitude of love and hate felt by his brothers and by his non-related subjects to him and to each other is dramatized.

Before dawn the people begin singing and dancing for the king. Only the sacred *Incwala* songs and no *imiguɓo* may be chanted on this day. Two tunes are heard at once—the lullaby song of the boys as they drive the *incwambo* into the *inhlambelo* and the chant of hate from the men and women. As the sun rises the king is bathed by his *tinsila* and when they have done, the scene of action moves from the cattle byre to the harem The regiments go out of the lower gate and the women through the upper and form arcs in the space between the harem and the queen mother's enclosure leaving a small pathway for the king.

The king walks from his sanctuary to the hut where he solemnized his first recognized marriage, his marriage with the Matseбula queen. He is naked but for a glowing white penis cap of ivory—*lupondvo lwendlovu*—and as he passes the people whom he rules, the women weep and the song of hate rings out with penetrating melancholy. Later, when I asked the women why they had wept, the queen mother said: 'It is pain to see him a king. My child goes alone through the people', and the queens said: 'We pity him. There is no other man who could walk naked in front of everybody', and an old man added: 'The work of a king is indeed heavy.' On either side of him are his priests, one of whom carries a pot of sacred medicine. They go with him into the hut and the councillors order silence. The lullaby sung by the youths who remained on the cattle byre to take out the *incwambo* is heard dimly in the distance. The king takes a mouthful of the medicine (unstrained beer mixed with *umtfuso*), and as he is about to spit it out the councillor gives the signal, 'Eh eh! he stabs it' and the crowd responds. He spits the medicine through two small holes, one in the front (east) over the doorway and the other at the back (west). Into this hut were placed special ropes connected with national well-being and as the king spits his strength goes 'right through' and awakes his people. In this rite the king reveals his potency. Sobhuza recalls how on his marriage to Matseбula a similar rite was performed. Some old councillors tell him that on that occasion he should have cohabited with her and the cry, 'Eh! he stabs it' would have marked their union.

By now he is sufficiently strong to bite (*luma*) the most powerful of the new season's crops, and after that his people can perform their own 'first fruits' ritual. He returns to his sanctuary and the women and warriors encircle it as he spits for the last time to the east and west with a medicine made of the water of the sea, green foods and portions of the *umdvutshulwa*.

The regiments leave the byre, and after a while the king goes to the harem and all the immature children living at the capital are summoned to the *inhlambelo* to eat the meat of the *umdvutshulwa* and receive special purifying medicines to bite. Despite their love of meat, the children go unwillingly, for they find the flesh of the *umdvutshulwa* rather revolting —it is bruised and tasteless, the blood is clotted, the essence has gone. The bones must not be cracked open, and, with the remainder of the meat, they are carefully carried to the ritual hut of the queen mother's enclosure. When the children have finished eating, they go to the river to wash.

The different representative status groups in the nation *luma* during the morning of the great day. In this context, *luma* (literally 'bite') is a type of sacrament. There is a separate potsherd for the king's wives, for his brothers' wives, for his sisters and brothers, for his children, for his councillors and for his priests. His mother and her co-wives have a separate ritual the following day. The regiments do not *luma*; the king, their leader, *lumas* for them, but the men often perform private ritual before eating the green foods. The king's children *luma* in the *inhlambelo*, the others in the veld, at the back of the capital. An *indvuna* is in charge of each pot to see that only those entitled to the sacred mixture partake, and to show the people how to use it. The mixtures are slightly different, though the basic ingredients in each are the same—a little gourd and long strips of sugar cane black with charred medicine and boiled with various wild greens. Within each group the members *luma* in order of seniority, for example among the queens Matseбula 'bites' first, then Motsa and so on down to the king's recognized sweethearts. Each nibbles off a little bit of gourd, spits it out, takes another bite and swallows it, repeats the process with the sweet reed, takes a small piece of each and taps her joints saying aloud 'strengthen joint', finally washes her hands and goes away. They fear that otherwise their joints would be brittle as the new grass, that their stomachs would not 'be right' and that they would fall sick and quickly die. To-day there are many cases of non-performance, especially among converts to Christianity.

Towards midday the command is given for the people to dress in full *Incwala* clothing and go to the cattle byre. Each male age class has a distinctive crown of animal skin below the small tight cap of ostrich feathers. The queen mother wears a cloak of leopard skin, thus standing out from among her co-wives in their cloaks of hide. The young queens on this day must discard their cloth shawls and wear only native clothing and they look extraordinarily dignified in their leather skirts and aprons, their hair specially prepared, and black feathers, tied over their ears, falling softly on their cheeks. A special man is appointed to put the red feathers into the hair of the little princes and princesses, whose clothes are carefully chosen, alike for each sex. Everyone who comes to the *Incwala* wears his best clothes; it is an occasion for the utmost display.

It has become customary for the Resident Commissioner or his representative to come to the afternoon of the great day and look around. Sobhuza and his bodyguard, all in full *Incwala* clothes, lead the members of the European government past the men as they stand and sing in the cattle byre, and then the Europeans sit and watch from the tent specially sent down and erected by native police in the morning. Quite a few other Europeans also come to look on, and near them hover a number of native men in European clothes. The presence of the Europeans in no way interferes with the ceremony, and they leave before the climax. They see and hear only three of the very impressive *Incwala* dance-songs, which continue as the sun moves from its height towards its resting place.

There is feverish activity in the *inhlambelo*. Strange medicines are brought in; others are taken out. At one stage the constant bodyguard of the queen mother leaves her side, removes his elaborate clothing, and, dressed only in his loin skin, moves unostentatiously towards the king and leads him to the *inhlambelo*. After a short period the king returns to his regiment, and a little later the companion, carrying a small bundle of medicine, goes inconspicuously towards the Mdzimba hills. He is holding in his hand the quick-growing evergreen parasite, the *ihlatsi*, first cord of medicine to protect every child of the king. The *ihlatsi* is typical of so many of the ingredients—green, quick-growing.

Late in the afternoon the *Incwala* enters a new phase. The male members of the royal clan surround the king, the rest of the army surges behind and the song changes abruptly:

'We shall leave them with their country,
Whose travellers are like distant thunder,
Do you hear, Dlambula, do you hear?'

and the women sing

'Do you hear?
Let us go, let us go.'

The words and the tune are wild and sad like the sea 'when the sea is angry and the birds of the sea are tossed on the waves'. The royal women move backwards and forwards in small, desperate groups uttering their cry. Many weep. The men's feet stamp the ground vigorously and slowly, the black plumes wave and flutter, the princes come closer, driving the king in their midst. Nearer and nearer they bring him to his sanctuary. The crowd grows frenzied, the singing louder, the bodies sway and press against the sides of the enclosure, and the king is forced within. The priests follow; the princes draw back a little; an old man in full *Incwala* finery jigulates in the doorway, spurring on the dancers, keeping them from seeing what is happening to their king.

What does it mean? I received two possible interpretations, or, rather, two speculations: first, 'The Malangeni (royal group) want to migrate once again. They want their king to come with them, they want to leave the people whom they distrust in the country where they stayed a little while.' The second suggestion was: 'The Malangeni show their hatred of the king. They denounce him and force him from their midst.'

The next act seems to support the second version. The song changes once again. The princes lunge with their sticks against the small doorway and beat their shields in agitation, draw back slowly and beseechingly, try to lure him out, beg him with praises: 'Come from your sanctuary. The sun is leaving you, You the High One. Dlambula' and the song continues:

'Come, come, king of kings,
Come, father, come,
Come king, oh come here king.'

There emerges a figure weird as the monster of legends. He is *Silo*, a nameless creature. On his head is a cap of black plumes that cover his face and blow about his shoulders, and underneath the feathers is glimpsed a head-band of a lion's skin. His body is covered in bright green grass and evergreen shoots that trail on the ground. In his left hand he holds a shield smeared with fat of the sacred herd, the *mfukwane*. His right hand is empty and as he moves it gleams with lines of dark medicine. The fatty tissue (*umhlehlo*) of the *umdvutshulwa* is tied cross-wise on his chest and the blown up gall bladder lies on the costume. Round his loins is a belt of silver monkey skin.

Each item of the costume has meaning and ritual association. The green grass is the *umuzi*, razor-edged, strong, from which are made the mats in the shrine hut that are kept from one reign to another, a symbol of the life and continuity of the nation. The *mfukwane* are the sacred animals of kingship that have the tip of their tails cut off to brand them for work of kingship. They are rarely killed and those who eat of their meat cautiously lean forward so that no drop of fat may touch the body and cause madness, 'their milk is red and they have human feelings'. The king, his mother and the great ritual wife, Matse6ula, smear themselves with the fat. They alone are powerful enough to withstand it and are made more powerful by using it. The silver monkey has the power of life—'no one has ever seen it die'. It is used as a sling for an heir apparent to the throne; it is 'his health'.

In this powerful costume the king appears reluctant to return to the nation. He executes a crazy, elusive dance with knees flexed and swaying body. The movements are an intuitive response to the rhythm and situation, a dance that no ordinary man knows and that the king was never taught. The old teachers who trained him in all his duties explained: 'We do not know it; we are not kings; it will come to you at the time.' Suddenly he crouches low and disappears into his hole, and the *tinsila* follow close behind picking up any bits that drop off the sacred costume, lest they be used by enemies to ruin the nation. The princes spring forward crying: 'Come out, king of kings.' They draw back, pause, sway forward. At last he responds. At his approach they retire, enticing him to follow, but after a few steps he turns back and they close behind him again. Everyone is urged to dance. The *tindvuna* bring down their batons and shout: 'Beat your shields.' The people dance with vigour; here more than at any other stage they keep their king alive and healthy by their own movements. The mime goes on with increasing tension, each appearance of the king making a sudden startling and unforgettable impact. His eyes shine through the feathers as he tosses his head, his face is dark with black medicine, dripping down his legs and arms are black streaks—he is terrifying, and as the knife-edged grass cuts into his skin he tosses his body furiously in pain and rage.

During this scene the men who took part in the capture of the *umdvutshulwa* come in with special large black shields (*tihlangu*), which are like the ancient war shields and not the ordinary shields (*emahawu*) used every day for dancing and display. The *tihlangu* are kept all the year round in a special shelter in the barracks at the capital, and are cut from the hides of cattle slaughtered by the rulers. If anyone by accident during the year touches the black shields, he immediately goes to wash, for among them are shields touched, as we shall see, by the powerful doctored calabash. The men with the *tihlangu* move to the front row of dancers and the music changes:

'Thunder deep,
That they hear the thundrous beat,
dji, eh, eh.'

The men in the front row pommel the large shields with clenched fists and the king dances towards them. In his right hand he holds a long black wand. At his approach the warriors retreat, he retires and returns. After two or three appearances during this song, he appears with nothing in his right hand, and the men see that the end is near. Aliens and royalty are told to leave the amphitheatre, and the king comes out with a vivid green gourd in his hand. It is *luselwa lwembo*—the wild gourd from 'Embo', the direction from which the Dlamini first migrated. Two gourds are fetched each year; the king 'plays' with one, and the other is kept till the following year and burnt. The gourd that looks so green is therefore not the gourd plucked that year, but the previous year. The king retreats into his lair, tantalizing the men. They place their shields horizontally, waiting for the fruit that must not be allowed to fall to the ground. Finally, he lurches purposefully forward and throws the gourd lightly on to one of the *tihlangu*. There is a wild stamping of feet and frantic hissing and thumping. Some informants insist that in olden days, had the recipient of the gourd gone to war he would have been the first killed, since he was selected to hold the powerful vessel symbolizing the past. It seems to me that he is a national scapegoat, a sacrifice for the future.

The dancers disperse; the men with the black shields go to the river, and only the king remains in the *inhlambelo* with his priests. They remove his elaborate costume and take it to the shrine hut, where lie the remains of the *umdvutshulwa*. They leave the paint on his body and face and lead him to the hut of the Matseбula queen to spend the night.

8. *Seclusion*

After he has thrown the gourd, the king remains *cungiwe* (painted in blackness) and *emnyameni* (in darkness); he is unapproachable, dangerous to himself and to others. He must cohabit that night with his first ritual wife, or, if she is ill, with the second; if both are indisposed, with any other queen of the Matseбula clan. It is a bad thing if he spends the night alone, but, apart from these women, there is no one strong enough to stand such intimate contact.

The entire population is also temporarily in a state of taboo and seclusion. Ordinary activities and behaviour are suspended; sexual intercourse is prohibited, no one may sleep late the following morning, and when they get up they are not allowed to touch each other, to wash the body, to sit on mats, to poke anything into the ground, or even to scratch their hair—an act most essential for many a person's comfort. The children are scolded if they play and make merry. The sound of songs that has stirred Loбamba for nearly a month is abruptly stilled; it is the day of *бacisa* (cause to hide). The king remains secluded with men of his inner circle, who see that he breaks none of the taboos. All day he sits naked on a lion skin in the ritual hut of the harem or in the *inhlambelo*. Only the ritual queens may see or speak to him, while the other wives may not even pass the entrance of the hut where he slept and a special doorway is broken for them in the reed fence.

Spies appointed by the *бelwandle* see that the people respect the taboos and impose a fine graded according to the seriousness of the offence: for scratching, folding the arms, etc., a string of beads or any trifle is sufficient, but for washing or having sexual relations the punishment is a beast.

On this day the identification of the people with the king is very

marked. The spies do not say, 'You are sleeping late' or 'You are scratching', but 'You cause the king to sleep', 'You scratch him (the king)', etc.
It is worse for a prince than for a commoner to break a taboo, 'for their
blood is one with the king's' and, secondly, the princes 'should teach the
people the law'.

It is rather a shock to a Westerner to find that most of the men try to
'steal', and break the taboos quite happily unless they are found out. This
coincides with a great deal of Swazi ethics that appears at first incomprehensible: morality is not so much a question of character and individual
conscience as of overt behaviour and group conscience. The sense of
personal moral guilt is not well developed, but once a Swazi is discovered
committing a wrong against the group he is deeply penitent and ashamed.
As long as a king does not know that a prince is having sex relations on
the forbidden day, the prince is not affected, but if it is made public he
brings danger to himself; moreover, he is considered 'to have soiled the
nation and he must atone'.

The queen mother and her co-wives are given treatment the day after
the king and his close relatives. A ritual specialist of the Mkonza clan
slaughters a black ox and takes special portions. He makes medicine for
her to *luma* and gives a separate pot to her co-wives. Then in a secluded
corner of her enclosure he paints her with a black mixture, he marks her
face so that it resembles a half-moon, in contrast to that of her son, who
is painted on both sides like the full moon, and he stripes her right foot
and hand. For the rest of the day she sits quietly (*kufukama*) in her
enclosure and sees few people till, on the following day, she washes her
paint off with doctored water and comes again into 'lightness' and
normality.

Although so many activities are restricted, there are no prohibitions on
food on the day of *Bacisa*, and cattle are killed by the queen mother to
feed the people. Most of the meat will be eaten on the morrow, but a
little is always roasted as soon as the beast is dead. Though food may
abound, there is so little freedom that the people are glad when the day
draws to a close.

9. *The Fire*

The sixth day is the day of final purification, when the objects no
longer required are burnt and the king and his mother—hence the nation
—are left strengthened to face the coming year.

A huge pyre is built in the cattle byre. The regiments collect branches
and the old councillors carefully select those without thorns—'so that the
king will not be scratched'. The veterans, stripped but for a loin skin,
fetch the articles to be burnt—the costume worn by the king on the great
day, the perishable remains of the *umdvutshulwa*, the hide of last year's
umdvutshulwa, last year's gourd, utensils that are no longer usable, fines
collected from the people by the *Bemanti*, and, finally, blankets and clothing discarded by the king during the year. 'The filth of the king and all
the people lies here on the fire.' The hide of the new *umdvutshulwa* and
the new gourd are kept carefully stored till the following year.

The king must be finally cleansed (*kupotfula*—to turn around, to
normalize), the end of all doctoring. The cattle are driven into the byre,

a black cow is killed and the gall bladder carefully removed and taken into the *inhlambelo*. The king goes to the pyre and takes fire sticks, one male, one female, and by friction starts a spark; after which a councillor takes over and soon the wood is crackling. Then, accompanied by special attendants holding a finely-plaited dish with medicated waters in which is the gall of the newly killed cow, the king wanders naked round the pyre amongst the herd, and washes off his paint. The water drops on the ground and 'helps the rain'. Moreover, the *Belwandle* throw on the fire leaves believed to 'have connection with rain'. The king retires to dress in his more simple *Incwala* clothing.

About noon the warriors and the women enter the cattle byre dressed as on the first day. They take their places and sing, but the *Incwala* songs are closed for a whole year and only the *imiguɓo* may be chanted. The nation, with the king in its midst, stands and sings as the sun moves slowly to its height and then gradually descends.

As the people dance they 'know' that rain must fall to quench the flames. The older men, to whom Christianity is vague, speak of the fire as a purification and as an offering (*umnikelo*) to the ancestors, who must acknowledge it with rain. Twice in the lives of my older informants no rain came, and the nation feared misfortune. No matter how heavy the storm, the people do not seek shelter, till, drenched to the bone, they finally round off the performance with the national chant.

The last day of the *Incwala* ends with feasting and revelry. Huge platters of meat and bowls of beer come from the queen mother's enclosure and the harem to the people ranged as usual in order of birth and locality. There is a general well-being, the rain falls, the crops can safely be eaten, the king and the nation are strong; in the evening the king chooses the wife he desires, young bloods are free 'to hunt the birds', and in the huts and in the veld there is gaiety and love-making.

A last service remains to be performed for the rulers—the weeding of the fields. Early the next morning the warriors collect in the cattle byre, sing ordinary march songs, and leave for the queen mother's biggest maize garden. It usually takes a couple of days to weed, then the regiments slowly drift back to their districts. The permanent royal battalion moves over to the king's gardens and, having cleared them, usually works in the gardens of the queens. Throughout the country the local contingents serve their local chiefs, demonstrating in the order of their service the hierarchy of their society. And everywhere, before the people eat of their food, the conservative headmen collect the members of their homesteads and ritually partake of the crops of the new season; those chiefs who were sufficiently important not to attend the king's *Incwala* have a more elaborate rite than the commoners about them.

10. *The Ceremony during the King's Minority*

The *Incwala* is so intimately bound up with the king that it reflects each stage of his development. During the minority of a king the *Incwala* is slowly being developed, and as he grows to maturity the ritual increases in potency. Swazi speak of the pre-*Incwala* ceremonies as 'things that support the *Incwala*', and these reflect the stages of growth of kingship.

I obtained descriptions of this early ritual from Ntshwebe, the old man who nursed Sobhuza when a child ; from the queen mother, Sobhuza, Ngolotsheni Motsa (the left hand *insila*) and governors of royal villages. The average Swazi was of little help, saying: 'This is a thing of kingship; we do not enter.' 'There is no dog that touches things of the kingship.'

In Chapter IV I briefly outlined the growth of a capital and showed how it paralleled the development of the heir apparent to full maturity. During the time that the *Umntfwana* (child king) and *NaBomntfwana* (his mother) are in the *umstangala* (the mourning village) the whole country is 'in blackness'. There is a minor ritual to ensure the eating of new foods in safety and the strengthening of the new rulers and the country. At the time when, during a monarchy, the big *Incwala* would take place, the *Bemanti* come to the young king and give him medicines. A tiny beast—'measured against the child'—is killed to doctor him. *Luma* medicines are also prepared for the princes, led by the prince regent. The 'mother of the child' and the queen regent are treated by the Mkonza doctors. There is no assemblage of all the men of the nation, no festive regalia, no sacred songs. During this period the nation is not strong internally and should not fight against external enemies.

When the future ruler moves to the embryonic capital of the new reign there is a more elaborate ceremony known as the *Simemo*. Like the *Incwala*, it is divided into two parts. It opens with a simple celebration of the dying year, but only the *simemo* and the *imiguβo* songs are sung and the water is fetched from the rivers and not from the sea. In the interim period there is tribal work and preparation for the big *Simemo* and the regiments of the nation come to the embryo capital. The big *Simemo* opens with the child king in the sacred enclosure at moonrise—there is no gathering of the *lusekwane* nor of the *emacembe*. The warriors wear partial *Incwala* clothing—the skin head-ring and the little soft black feather cap are not allowed. The following afternoon the *umdvutshulwa* is killed. This animal is 'measured against' the king himself, so if the heir is very young it is a small animal, and if he is already nearly full grown the animal is large. It can only be caught by the 'pure' but it is not sufficiently strong to be a trial of strength. It is killed and used to treat the child. Later he sits on the *incwambo*, which is also chosen with regard to his size. There is no throwing of the powerful gourd. On the third day the boy and his mother are painted, but the boy is painted like a half-moon and his mother like a crescent. He does not sit on a lion skin, but on an *inkatsa* (grass ring) made from pieces of thatch taken stealthily from the huts of enemies and subjects. His mother, who is being 'made big' to assume her future position, is treated with a cow, and the old queen mother with a pitch black goat. On the fourth day the pyre is burnt and is extinguished by the rain. In the *Simemo* period the country is more united than during the years of mourning, but it is still not wise for regents to send out an army against a strong enemy. The year the child reaches social maturity, he is circumcised and wedded to his ritual wives. At this stage the *Incwala* is almost, but not quite, complete. The king is said to 'steal the *Incwala*': when he dresses in his strange costume he wears a head-band which looks like the lion's skin, but is not. A few significant ingredients are omitted from the medicines.

It is not till the following year that the *Incwala* is 'danced' with full pomp.

From this brief account of the pre-*Incwala*, or *Simemo*, it is clear to what an extent the development of the nation through the person of the king is symbolized in the *Incwala*. Immediately after the announcement of a king's death, the country is in chaos; formerly wizards were smelt out, princes rose against princes. During the *Simemo* period the people are still anxious and distressed, wondering what will happen to their country. The young heir is kept secluded, the people cannot come freely into his section of the village. Then the king is appointed, the *Incwala* is danced, and the monarchy is secure. Once the *Incwala* is danced, it must be continued till the death of the king, or it is believed that the nation will end. Even in war, if the king and his people are in hiding, they have to try to execute every act.

Interpretation of the Incwala

We are now in a position to summarize the meaning of the *Incwala* in terms of its effects on social stratification. The *Incwala* has been considered by Cook as pre-eminently a 'First Fruits Ceremony'; Marwick goes further when he says he is of the opinion that 'it is in effect a pageant in which the early life of the Swazi is re-enacted in dramatised form' (p. 191). Schoeman comes to the conclusion that 'die seremonie van die eerste vrugte is eigenlik . . . 'n groot versoeningsgees' (p. 21). From the evidence, it appears to me that the *Incwala* is first and foremost a ceremony which, as Swazi say, aims at 'strengthening kingship', at 'showing kingship', 'to make stand the nation'. It is not the specific economic, ritual, or political powers of the king that are emphasized, but the sum total of kingship. The sacrament of the first fruits is an essential rite in a complex series of rites. Nothing could show this more clearly than the way the *Incwala* develops with the king, identifies him with the well-being of the nation, ceases with his death, and blossoms with his successor. The fruits of the fields ripen each year, and each year the people protect themselves against danger but—not by the full *Incwala* ceremony.

The *Incwala* is also one of the economic weapons of kingship, since no one should eat of the new foods before the king nor plant spring foods once the ceremony is over. The man who produces an early crop has a curb placed on his supposedly ambitious industry.

But the *Incwala* controls the consumption of only a limited number of foods, and those not the staple crops. And in cases of dire need the men eat of the mealies before the king. Moreover, in the early years a special species of millet and not maize is said to have been the staple crop, and millet ripens long after the *Incwala*. For this and other green foods (e.g. *siβaca*) which mature later in the year, and for certain insects (e.g. the caterpillar, *manyamane*) the people have distinct, but relatively insignificant, *luma* rituals. The plants used at the *Incwala* have primarily a ritual virtue and many of them are inedible. The essence of the plant medicines are: greenness, toughness, freshness, quick growth. Ngolotsheni Motsa told me that 'the crops used at the *Incwala* are those privileged to combine with it'. When one asks why the *Incwala* should coincide with the *luma* of the sweet reed and cucurbitaceous plants, and not, for example, with the *luma* of the caterpillars, Swazi reply tolerantly: 'Do not forget the *Incwala* goes with the sun.' The time of the *Incwala* as a ceremony of kingship and of new strength is regulated by the natural phenomena, moon and sun, which link mystically with stages of human destinies, and not by the agricultural routine, which the people themselves largely control.

At the *Incwala* there are feasts, but there is not always regular food. People never say, 'We are going to the *Incwala* to eat.' On most days the masses receive nothing at all from the rulers, and if they have no friends they say they almost starve. The men who fetch the sacred branches realize that hunger is part of their work, while to eat is part of their reward. At the same time, when food is given, it appears in quantities no commoner could provide, and the dependence of the people on the riches of the rulers is made manifest. In 1934 eighteen beasts, in 1935 and in 1936 sixteen beasts, were killed, and each year over two bags of mealies and two of corn were used in the making of beer by the rulers. At present, when the Swazi can say, 'money is our best friend', and food is purchasable from the nearby shop, there is not the same correlation between hunger and dependence on the royal hospitality.

As kingship alters, and has altered, additions and adaptations are, and have been, made to the ritual. I have not attempted to suggest here its evolution, nor have I tried to show which elements were borrowed, and when, from neighbouring Bantu tribes, and how changes in organization —such as the development of independent chieftains, the formation of regiments on a local and not kinship basis—may have reacted on the construction of the *Incwala*. Swazi themselves think that the efficacy of the ritual lies in exact repetition, or, if change is essential, that it is better to add than to discard. When kingship was an expanding concept, this was an effective approach, but now that the powers of the king are limited and checked, it is impracticable. Open attack against the *Incwala* was launched by a few Churches, which excommunicated members who attended, and the ritual was incapable of coping with those converts who obeyed Church law. Sobhuza is attempting to induce the converted among his subjects to participate in the *Incwala*, and will give them, if necessary, another 'uniform', so that the *Incwala* can once again extend as a unifying factor through all sections of the country.

The *Incwala* unites the people under the king, and at present there is a fairly general appreciation of its nationalizing value. 'We see we are all Swazi; we are joined against outside foes.' I have heard an onlooker rebuked: 'This is a thing of your people. Why abandon us for Europeans?' The people must be united in friendship and co-operation; bloodshed at the *Incwala* is a terrible thing. Yet, because the *Incwala* is a mass celebration, and, moreover, since it is connected with food and well-being, the people are known to be highly excitable and ready to fight. So the men must not carry spears, and trusted councillors exercise discipline. In a fight in 1938 that started between warriors on their way to the *lusekwane*, Sobhuza himself intervened. Energy is canalized in the song, dance, and service. Sobhuza, with sociological insight, explained: 'The warriors dance and sing at the *Incwala* and so they do not fight, although they are many and from all parts of the country and are jealous and proud. When they dance they feel they are one and they can praise each other.'

It is not surprising to find that the *Incwala*, which made for internal solidarity, was often the precursor of an announcement of war against external enemies. After the *Incwala* the men returned to their chiefs to show their loyalty, and then they came back to the capital and were actually fortified for attack. The *Incwala* has certain similarities with the old war ritual, and the men's clothing is identical with battle dress except for the plain sticks instead of spears and knobkerries. The *Incwala* united the nation internally in its hierarchical structure; the war medicine made the nation invulnerable to a specific external enemy.

The *Incwala* dramatizes actual rank developed historically: it is 'a play of kingship'. In the ceremony the people see which clans and people are important. Sociologically, it serves as a graph of traditional status on which, mapped by ritual, are the rôles of the king, his mother, the princes, councillors, priests, chiefs, queens, princesses, commoners, old and young. Just as in the dance, clothing, service, feasting, *luma*, the laws of rank are expressed in action, so in discussing the ceremony they are consciously articulated. The major adjustment, the balance of power between the king, his mother, the princes, and commoners, is a central theme. A study of groups and individuals who do not participate in the *Incwala* completes the graph of rank in Swazi society, and reflects the situation of European dominance over an increasingly stratified society.

CHAPTER XIV

CONCLUSION

THE approach to the data presented in this book has been influenced primarily by the necessity, stressed again and again by Malinowski, of studying societies in action.[1]

The culture of each society is a whole greater than the sum of isolated traits. A trait, whether it be an item of material culture or of less tangible social structure, assumes its meaning through association in the total context; hence a change in any particular trait or complex of traits— hereditary chieftainship, the cattle complex, belief in witchcraft, an age-grade military organization—has repercussions in greater or lesser degree throughout the society.

Not only is every society a whole, but it has dominant orientations, and interests,[2] which give to it a specific configuration, or pattern.[3] Whether each pattern is unique or not cannot as yet be stated, but the plurality and relativity of cultural types has been amply indicated by the works of the American 'configurational' or 'typological'[4] school. Thus Benedict describes the Zuni as a people who value sobriety and inoffensiveness above all other virtues and whose 'interest is centred upon their rich and complex ceremonial life' (p. 59); in contrast are the jealous, aggressive, suspicious Dobu, who exalt in their institutions 'extreme forms of animosity and malignancy' (pp. 130–73); different again is the culture pattern of the wealthy Indians of the north-west coast of America, whose behaviour is dominated at every point—inheritance, marriage, death, economic exchange, religion—'by the need to demonstrate the greatness of the individual and the inferiority of his rivals' (pp. 214–15). The laboratory of the social scientist is shown to consist of a variety of cultural types, each possessed of a specific and consistent individuality.

From the description of the conservative Swazi, there emerges a picture of a society in which pedigree is used to evaluate members on a social scale, and determines duties, privileges, and attitudes. Individual variability does not of itself create differences in classes;[5] birth overrides

---

[1] Cf. Bronislaw Malinowski, *Argonauts of the Western Pacific*, London, 1922; *Crime and Custom in Savage Society*, London, 1926; *The Sexual Life of Savages*, London, 1929; *Coral Gardens*, London, 1935. This does not mean that I accept the Functionalist approach *in toto*.

[2] Cf. R. Linton, *Study of Man*, London, 1936. Chaps. XXIV–XXVI.

[3] This stimulating and provocative concept was first developed for anthropology by Ruth Benedict. See Ruth Benedict, *Patterns of Culture*, London, 1935; also Margaret Mead, *Sex and Temperament*, London, 1935; Gregory Bateson, *Naven*, Cambridge, 1936.

[4] A term coined by S. F. Nadel. For an excellent criticism of the main exponents, see his article, 'The Typological Approach to Culture', *Character and Personality*, Vol. V, pp. 267–84.

[5] Cf. G. Landtman, *The Origins of the Inequality of the Social Classes*, Kegan Paul, 1938, p. 36. 'The earliest form of inequality . . . is the variation of social status depending on different personal endowments. Such individual dissimilarities naturally do not form any social classes, and it is only in conjunction with certain economic and industrial factors that they co-operate in building up classes.'

this as well as other issues. Specialization is limited because of the simple peasant economy, and such specialization as exists is largely influenced by hereditary rights. Only the aptitude and skill of medicine men and diviners have been recognized in the formation of an occupational unit with special rating, and the highest practitioners claim their powers from their ancestors. Leading members of the aristocracy exercise administrative and ritual functions which preclude them from other less-honoured occupations (including doctoring and divining), and people not of the royal lineage who are given high posts in the government tend to be identified with the aristocrats by a fiction of kinship. Nor is wealth a primary interest, since the limits of wealth are regulated roughly by the position held in the hierarchy of birth. Begging bestows honour on the donor, and brings no shame to the recipient.

Other principles of social grouping, such as age and sex, revolve round the central theme of noble birth; thus we saw the prerogatives conferred on princes, who were permitted to enter regiments beyond their biological age, and we noted that aristocratic women wielded authority over male commoners in a society which in other respects inculcated the inferiority of females.

The Swazi culture offers certain strong contrasts with our own and with other cultures. Thus while individualism and ambition are curbed, people who claim to be possessed by spirits and who would be regarded by us as neurotics are regarded as blessed by the ancestors and singled out for special dignities. Again, generosity—*noblesse oblige*—follows partly from the perishable nature of Swazi possessions and the absence of luxury goods, and is effectively embodied in the political structure with its kinship nucleus. Scientific experimentation is practically unknown, and ritual flourishes in its stead. Rivalry for power is expressed through the medium of witchcraft within a social framework established by birth. Thus, witchcraft operates primarily along lines indicated by the stereotyped kinship alinements and antagonisms, especially between co-wives and between classificatory brothers.

To interpret a society in terms of orientations involves selection, as well as abstraction, of data; here I feel that the American writers tend to oversimplify, to short-cut, the complexity of a culture, in order to reduce it to a 'consistent pattern'. Emphasis is placed on 'unconscious canons',[1] 'potential purposes and motivations',[2] and fundamental trends whereby 'culture' (highly personified) 'integrates' into autonomous, *gestalt*-like wholes.[3] To these wholes, the American writers attach terms descriptive of the individual psyche—prudish, passionate, arrogant, unco-ordinated, casual—which qualities are then related back to a limited (in some cases, extremely limited) number of activities and features of the social structure.

[1] Ruth Benedict: 'Consistent patterns "arise" in accordance with unconscious canons of choice that develop within the culture, op. cit., p. 48.

[2] Ibid., p. 237.

[3] Ibid., especially pp. 45–56. Also Margaret Mead, *Sex and Temperament*, p. 14: '. . . each culture creates distinctively the social fabric in which the human spirit can wrap itself safely and intelligibly, sorting, reweaving, and discarding threads in the historical tradition that it shares with many neighbouring peoples. . . .'

The integration of the culture is interpreted through these psychological qualities; they involve particular types of education, sex-expression, religious cult or kinship affiliation. Using this technique, analysis of society is transferred from the working of institutions to 'motives', 'ambitions', and 'drives'. So, for example, Margaret Mead describes the gentle, unacquisitive Arapesh, brought up in a happy, co-operative society, where leadership is unwillingly assumed and warfare is practically unknown. In highly emotive language she contrasts the Arapesh with the aggressive, suspicious, malfunctioning Mundugomor, living in hate-ridden kinship groups and indulging in raiding, head-hunting, and cannibalism. So violent are the contrasts, so simple each pattern, that the reader looks for (and finds) contradictions in the evidence, and is led to wonder if the orientation described for the culture does not lie partly in a bias of the investigator. And what measure, one asks, is used to gauge the emotions so colourfully painted? What, for instance, is meant by 'the warm and maternal temperament of both men and women' of the Arapesh (p. 40), especially when a few pages earlier (pp. 32–3) we were told that these kindly people, preferring boys to girls, sometimes resort to infanticide of girl babies. Not only are emotive terms relative to each culture: the man whom the Arapesh consider kind may appear to us brutal: but they may also reflect the disposition of the investigator—a bellicose twentieth-century male may label cowardly and effeminate a group that to his docile female companion appears courteous and charming.

To interpret the Swazi culture type, I analysed its characteristic social units (the polygynous patriarchal family; the hierarchy of clans and lineages; the dual monarchy; the age grades; the groups of specialists), and discussed their focal behaviour and associated beliefs. The consistency of the pattern then appeared as the result of the interaction of concrete processes in a historical setting; there was no need to resort for explanation to the 'selectiveness of a culture', or to any vague 'purpose' or 'goal' or 'drive'; the psychological qualities were the products of, and in turn influenced, the structure and activities.

Neither the structural nor the psychological consistency must be over-stressed; society is not a mosaic in which each stone is set with conscious care. The units of society are difficult to disentangle one from the other, and reflect a diversity of social currents and a multiplicity of aspects. The polygynous family of the aristocrats recognizes inequalities among wives, sons and daughters, based on seniority and sex and expressed in rights over property and religious responsibilities. On the death of the polygynist the principle of seniority is overridden by that of the parentage of the wives, the heir being chosen by the pedigree of his mother, though she may be a newcomer in the harem and he a babe in arms.

Nor are the psychological qualities always harmoniously combined. The varied situations arouse a wide range of human emotions, and expression fluctuates accordingly from courtesy to arrogance, humility to pride, gentleness to aggression. The major institutions of society place more emphasis on some qualities than on others, but never on one category exclusively. The Swazi mother's tender affection towards her own babe does not eliminate hatred and jealousy of the children of a rival for

her husband's love; the restraint imposed on ambition by the age-grade
system is accompanied by self-display among contemporaries. These
different emotions appear in different situations; they need not be complementary, nor need they consciously conflict with each other.

A valid interpretation of social facts must be inclusive and logically
consistent. From the material presented in this book, an attempt might
be made to show that the Swazi are orientated towards warfare and
aggression; emphasis could be laid on the training of males, on regimental
exploits and rewards, the privileges of warriors, the religious bias in
favour of the paternal (warrior) line. But some facts—the rank of royal
women, the privileges of young princes beyond the military sphere—
would conflict with such an interpretation, and other facts—the influence
of kinship ties and the rating of clans and lineages—would find no place
in it. Nor would the simple psychological emphasis be valid; young men
are expected to be hot-headed and eager to fight, but the older, married
men are more respected for caution in war and skill in maintaining peace.
Killing, even in battle, is an achievement fraught with danger and pollution which requires to be neutralized by elaborate treatment, so that the
desire to kill does not continue.

Furthermore, no society is ever static. Its culture alters from within,
albeit slowly, through the drives of outstanding personalities, the impetus
of new discoveries, and the cumulative nature of tradition itself. Culture
also alters from without, through contact with other groups, and the
greatest stimulus is provided by long-term association with a society
possessed of a more highly developed technology. The process of cultural
growth involves contradictions, juxtapositions, alternatives, and the
existence of majorities and minorities.

Each stage, though rooted in the past, is distinctive. Social development is not mechanical, and is difficult to predict because of the innumerable factors which are involved in each case. Bearers of a new culture
may be interested in conquest, or trade or conversion; they may be few or
many; predominantly male or female; they may speak an entirely foreign
language and have 'strange customs and beliefs'. Their reception may in
one case be friendly, in another hostile, and different items may be
absorbed by or forced upon the existing culture. This historical process,
which must inevitably change the pattern, receives scant attention in the
writings of the configurationalists; yet every study of society, being made
at a particular period of time, should provide us with illustrations of
survivals, and conflicts between different outlooks. We find in the conservative Swazi milieu the decline of the clans in the interest of national
expansion; the decay of the old ritual and the birth of new; shortage of
land, leading to new systems of tenure and overlordship. Under the
influence of the European, we see the rights of a hereditary aristocracy
challenged by the claims of the 'school educated' and of *nouveaux riches*;
the superiority of men weakened by new rights granted by European laws
to women; worshippers before the ancestral shrines cursed by the priests
of other gods.

Transition is both a morphological and a psychological process. In the
last two hundred years, Swazi society underwent two major changes:
firstly, the structure based on the equality of clans gave place to a nation

Q

under a hereditary monarchy, and, secondly, contact with Western civilization introduced a system based on colour discrimination and orientated towards the accumulation of wealth. Taking into account the complex nature of cultural growth, it seems a dangerous oversimplification to state that societies only borrow what is in accord with their 'emotional and intellectual mainsprings".[1]

The pattern of a society is inculcated into each generation by a process of conscious and unconscious educational activities, and gives rise to ideal personality types. These naturally vary with the culture; the Swazi prince, princess, chief, specialist, commoner, have characteristics different from those prescribed for the lady gentleman, diplomat, professional man, or layman of twentieth-century Western European society. The ideal types outlast the actual status holders, and provide standards of social judgement. To the people concerned, their standards alone are usually 'right' and 'good' and 'just'; the average European does not praise a 'leader' who does not make decisions; the average Swazi condemns a chief who 'pushes himself forward'. The ethnocentric bias of cultures is illuminated by a realization of the arbitrariness of 'ideals'.

People have some difficulty in verbalizing the qualities which the social stereotypes imply, but they know the behaviour expected in specific situations. It is not surprising that the Swazi, with their orientation to rank, have formulated most clearly the ideal of the aristocratic ruler, and other types are adapted, and complementary, to his. It is by reference to the moulding situations that we are able to describe the characteristic patterns of the conservative Swazi.

No individual (chief or commoner, man or woman) conforms completely to his, or her, status personality, but the institutions of the society are flexible enough to admit of some deviation in behaviour and belief. Those who diverge too widely from the standards of their society are deprived (temporarily or permanently) of status privileges. The mean and aggressive chief loses his followers, or even his life; the youth who abandons the sex restraint imposed on his age mates is debarred from sharing the national honours they enjoy; the over-ambitious commoner is condemned as a sorcerer. It is necessary to point out that cultural deviants[2] are as much the products of their society as their more fortunate, better adapted fellow men, and the possibilities of maladjustment are inherent in the social structure.

The interest of a simple society may be similar to that of one very much more complex—for instance, both may venerate pedigree, and in one society it may be maintained by a military system, while in the other it may be enshrined in inalienable rights over the land. On the other hand, despite the apparent similarity of certain traits, the configuration may be entirely different. An aristocracy of birth may be associated in one society with wealth and warfare, and in another with the arts of peace.

The Swazi, as described in this book, can be compared with other societies both morphologically, and from the angle of orientation. Such

---

[1] R. Benedict, op. cit., p. 46.

[2] 'The individual who is at variance with the values of his society', Margaret Mead, op. cit., p. 291. 'Those whose characteristic reactions are denied validity in their society', Ruth Benedict, op. cit., p. 258.

comparison has not yet been attempted for Africa, over which vast continent are scattered hundreds of tribes, each with its distinctive structure and interests. Even the near neighbours of the Swazi show marked differences: the conservative Zulu have a single male ruler, and formerly were organized into an aggressive military nation; the Thonga of Portuguese East Africa are without a powerful central organization, and possess highly developed arts; the Venda have a complicated political hierarchy, and ritualize extensively all individual and national occasions; the Lovedu recognize a female ruler who takes unto herself 'wives', and whose power rests largely on mythological claims.

Configurational differences must be sought in the operation of historical factors in a particular geographical milieu, inhabited by, and interpreted by, individual men and women, who are born into a culture with a specific, yet flexible, structure. Thus, the regimental system and the predatory character of many of the South African tribes developed only with the rise of Shaka, the Zulu despot, himself the product of a period of unrest. The Swazi were only one of the nations which developed at that time. Black and white had already come into conflict with each other in the south and east, and peaceful expansion northwards was checked by the existence of other clans and tribes. The semi-nomadic economy was restricted. Those people who settled in Swaziland were fortunate in finding a fertile land, where grain and cattle throve, whereas some of their early fellow migrants from the distant north had been forced to adapt themselves to a harsh, tsetse-ridden environment. On the basis of the existing kinship structure, equipped with limited tools and protected by their simple ancestral faith, the Dlamini chiefs gradually established themselves as the ruling aristocracy.

A study of society from the angle of its major orientation also has practical implications. Now that primitive societies are no longer isolated, but are directly or indirectly under the control of highly industrialized civilizations, the aims and methods of future development are being carefully considered. In the light of the relativity of cultural interests, the rulers of 'backward peoples' must revaluate their selection of traits, and plan in measures less weighted by their own stereotyped predilections. Full consideration must then be given to the major structural units and activities, the social determinants of attitudes and personality types.

ROYAL GENEALOGY FOR LAST EIGHT GENERATIONS

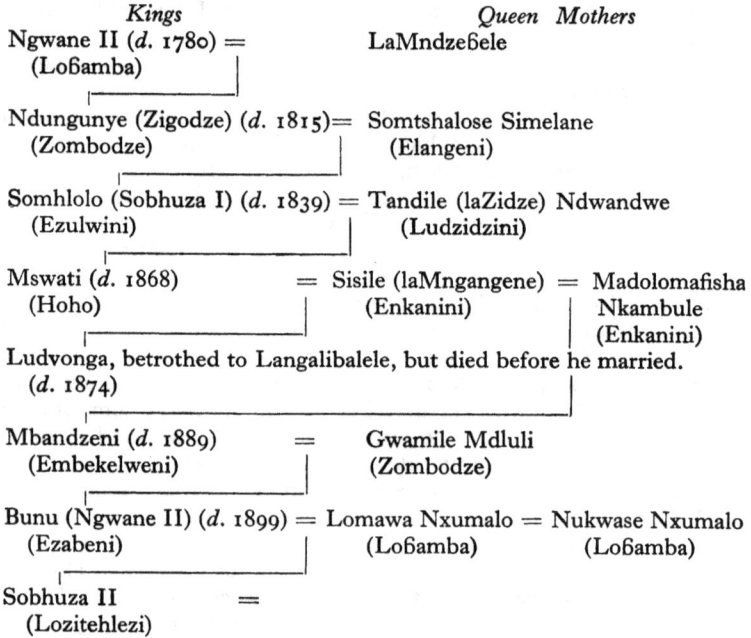

Kings	*Queen Mothers*

Ngwane II (*d.* 1780) =   LaMndzeɓele
  (Loɓamba)

Ndungunye (Zigodze) (*d.* 1815)= Somtshalose Simelane
  (Zombodze)   (Elangeni)

Somhlolo (Sobhuza I) (*d.* 1839) = Tandile (laZidze) Ndwandwe
  (Ezulwini)   (Ludzidzini)

Mswati (*d.* 1868)   = Sisile (laMngangene) = Madolomafisha
  (Hoho)   (Enkanini)   Nkambule
                                                  (Enkanini)

Ludvonga, betrothed to Langalibalele, but died before he married.
  (*d.* 1874)

Mbandzeni (*d.* 1889)   =   Gwamile Mdluli
  (Embekelweni)   (Zombodze)

Bunu (Ngwane II) (*d.* 1899) = Lomawa Nxumalo = Nukwase Nxumalo
  (Ezabeni)   (Loɓamba)   (Loɓamba)

Sobhuza II   =
  (Lozitehlezi)

The royal genealogy goes back some thirty generations, but there is agreement on the order of the last eight rulers only. The name after each ruler is the name of the royal village at which he or she lived. The queen mother's village is always the capital.

APPENDIX II

SWAZI CLANS

Nkosi Dlamini
Nkosi Ginindza
Nkosi Mamba
Nkosi Dvu
Nkosi Magutfulela
Nkosi Magongo
Mhlanga
Madvosela
Mavuso
Fakudze

Hlophe
Mndzeɓele }

Matseɓula
Mkabele }

Lulale

Motsa
Thwala }

Lukhele
Mdluli
Nkonyane } [1]

Shiɓa
Mwanazi }

Ngcampalala
Shongwe
Matse
Kunene
Gamedze }

Tsabetse
Ndzimandze
Ntshalintshali
Ɓembe
Manana
Sukati
Zwane
Malokothwako

EMAKHANDZAMBILI—THOSE FOUND AHEAD

Gama
Magagule
Maziya
Maseko
Kubonye }

Mnisi
Maphosa
Shaɓalala
Gweɓu
Shaɓangu }

LABAFIK'EMUVA—LATE-COMERS, INCORPORATED INTO THE NATION

Sotho Elements

Nkambule
Nkomolo
Hlengethwa
Mathunjwa
Luɓetsi

Nguni elements

Manyatsi

Mkatshwa
Nxumalo }

Mtsetfwa
Nzima
Dladla
Hlatswhakho
Mapholole
Dvuɓa
Nsiɓandse
Mngometfulu
Maɓasa
Mbamali
Masuko
Tsela

[1] Brackets indicate that intermarriage is prohibited, i.e. the clan has split into sub-clans.

Zikalala

Ɓiyela

Msimango

Mayisela

Biɓeko

Mgidzini

Sifundza

Vilakati

Tonga Elements

Sigwane

Thomo

Nyoni

Masilela

Nkala

Mabila

Mathunjw

Vuɓu

APPENDIX III

DIAGRAM OF THE CAPITAL, LOBAMBA, (1935)

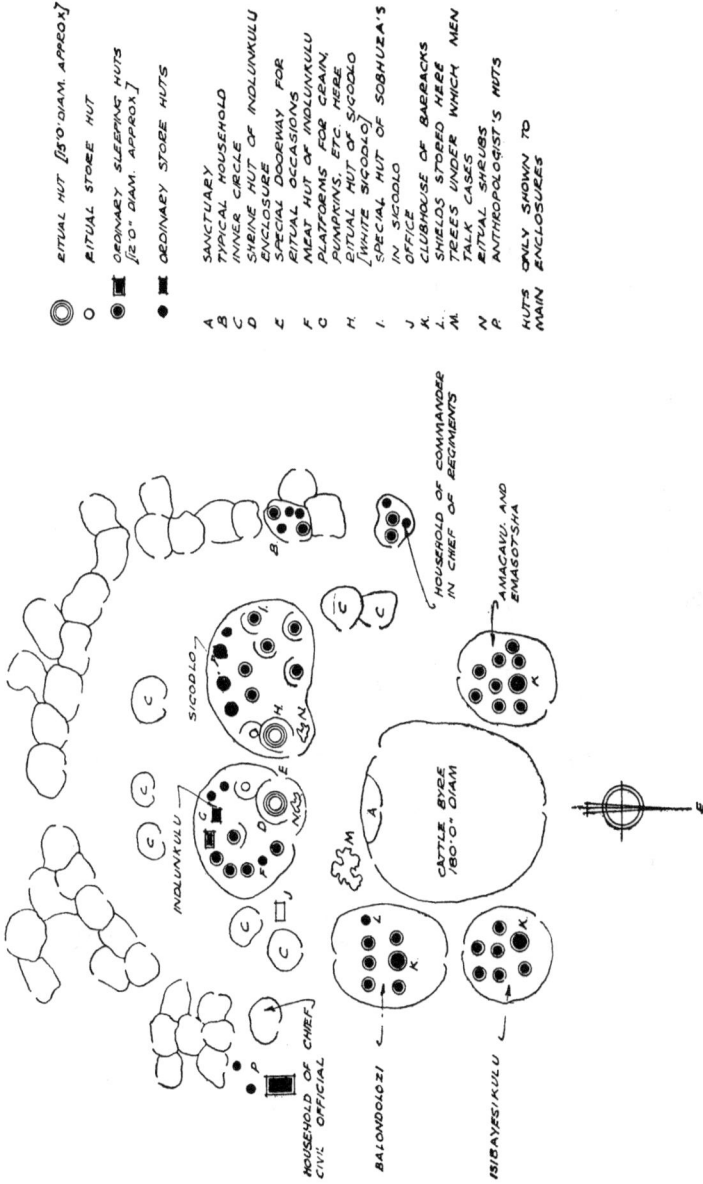

◎ RITUAL HUT [15'0 DIAM. APPROX]

○ RITUAL STORE HUT

◉ ORDINARY SLEEPING HUTS [12'0" DIAM. APPROX]

◆ ORDINARY STORE HUTS

A SANCTUARY
B TYPICAL HOUSEHOLD
C INNER CIRCLE
D SHRINE HUT OF INDLUNKULU ENCLOSURE
E SPECIAL DOORWAY FOR RITUAL OCCASIONS
F MEAT HUT OF INDLUNKULU
G PLATFORMS FOR GRAIN, PUMPKINS, ETC. HERE
H RITUAL HUT OF SICODLO [WHITE SICODLO]
I SPECIAL HUT OF SOBHUZA'S IN SICODLO
J OFFICE
K CLUBHOUSE OF BARRACKS
L SHIELDS STORED HERE
M TREES UNDER WHICH MEN TALK CASES
N RITUAL SHRUBS
P ANTHROPOLOGIST'S HUTS

HUTS ONLY SHOWN TO MAIN ENCLOSURES

HOUSEHOLD OF COMMANDER IN CHIEF OF REGIMENTS

AMACAVU AND EMASOTSHA

CATTLE BYRE 180'0" DIAM

SICODLO

INDLUNKULU

HOUSEHOLD OF CHIEF CIVIL OFFICIAL

BALONDOLOZI

ISIBAYESIKULU

APPENDIX IV
EMBRYO CAPITAL, SHOWING LUSASA

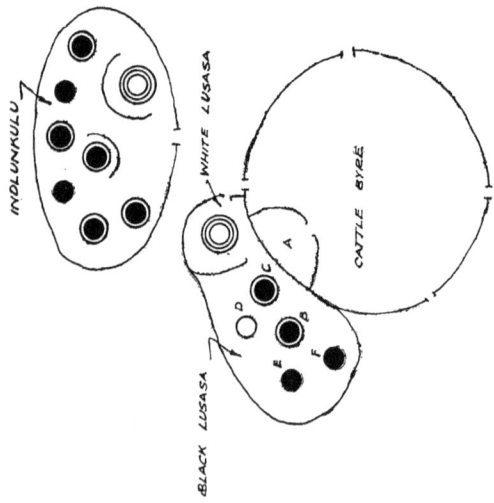

INDLUNKULU

WHITE LUSASA

BLACK LUSASA

CATTLE BYRE

SLEEPING HUT
STORE HUT
RITUAL HUT

A. SANCTUARY
B. KING'S BED ROOM
C. HUT FOR MEN
D. RITUAL STORE HUT
E. KITCHEN USED BY OLD WOMEN
F. MEAT HUT

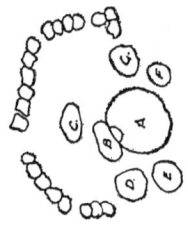

A. CATTLE BYRE
B. LUSASA
C. INDLUNKULU
D. ABALONDOLOZI
E. KWABAYESIKULU
F. EMSIZINI
G. AMAGAVU

APPENDIX V

A MYTH OF KINGSHIP

THERE was a king who had many queens and many children. The name of one of the sons was Madlisa, and of another Madlebe. Madlebe's mother was a junior queen with her hut on the veld, where the other wives threw away their rubbish. Now, Madlebe was not like other children: he was born with a magic bracelet on his hand and when he cried he cried tears of blood and his bracelet wept '*tsi tsi*'.

The king wanted to point out his heir, and summoned together his people. They came bringing cattle and goats as homage. The queens sat separate, and the mother of Madlebe sat with her little son humbly at a distance.

The king said: 'He whose spittle travels further than where I stand shall be the Little Chief.' He hit the boys with a hippo whip. Madlisa's spittle fell on his chest. He hit Madlebe. His spittle went far away. Then the heavens roared and Madlebe wept blood and his bracelet cried, '*tsi tsi*'. The people wondered.

His father gave him a clay pot, a gourd and a wooden spoon. He told him the pot must never be broken. The pot and the gourd were for sour milk. They were kept high on a shelf in the hut where the children could not reach them.

One day Madlisa said, 'I'm hungry, let us eat that food of yours.' Madlebe answered, 'I can't reach there.' On the morrow Madlisa again said, 'My brother, let us eat. We are hungry. Our mothers are hoeing.' Madlebe agreed. He reached for the pot and it fell.

Madlisa ran to the king and reported this. The king mourned, and was angry. Warriors took Madlebe to the forest to kill him, but when they were going to touch him the thunder rolled and lightning struck the earth. They were afraid. 'Hide in another country. We do not know how to kill you.' Madlebe went away. His mother carried mourning robes for her child.

Years passed. The king died. The moon drew near for throwing off the mourning. Madlebe came to his home and stood in his mother's yard. A beautiful girl came to him and he made love to her. She wept and wept blood. Madlebe exclaimed: 'Hau! Do you also weep blood?' The girl told her mother: 'There is a man who says I weep blood even as he does.' The mother came from her hut and saw Madlebe. And the warriors looked at him and recognized him and feared. But the council rejoiced exceedingly. They appointed Madlebe king.

APPENDIX VI

FAILURE OF MALE ISSUE TO A MAIN WIFE

THE CASE OF PRINCESS SENCABAPHI

LIVING at the queen mother's village is the Princess Sencaɓaphi, daughter of the late king Bunu and widow of Dinane, Chief of the Ndwandwe. When Sencaɓaphi was still a schoolgirl, her father's full sister Tonga Tonga was sent in marriage to Dinane. The marriage was executed with full pomp and the Ndwandwe contributed 100 cattle for her loɓola. She accompanied them to her home, paying her first visit there since marriage. Soon after her arrival she fell ill and died. Her people 'were broken'. They did not know what to do. They feared that the Ndwandwe thought they had killed her, and to return the loɓola would be an outrage. It was essential to find a suitable substitute. The Dlamini elders met and agreed that Sencaɓaphi, the greatest princess of her generation, should be sent. She had recently returned from Lovedale, in the Cape, where she was being educated with Sobhuza.

Between the young king Sobhuza and Sencaɓaphi was a deep attachment, and when she was asked if she would 'waken the house of Tonga Tonga', she agreed 'to help kingship'. So she doffed her 'Christian clothing', piled her hair into the bun of a married woman, and left for the husband whom she did not know to fill the place in his homestead of the wife who had died three years before. A lover of her own choice, whom, because of her coming marriage, she realized she would have to give up, followed her and tried to shoot Dinane. The case came before the European court, European lawyers were employed. Sobhuza himself was cross-questioned on whether or not he had 'forced' the marriage. Sencaɓaphi supported the arranged marriage as the marriage of aristocrats.

She bore Dinane two children. Both were daughters. When the baby was a few weeks old Dinane died. He left behind many widows and children. Who was to be the heir?

The Ndwandwe family council was unanimous on Sencaɓaphi's superior pedigree. She had not only taken the place of the great Tonga Tonga, but her own marriage was an elaborate document of her status. The Ndwandwe gave for her an additional sixty head of cattle—but this time the bride remained at the husband's home.

The problem was to find a 'son' to 'put in the stomach' of Sencaɓaphi, as main heir. With the Princess Tonga Tonga had come as junior wife a less important sister, Bono, but Bono was also childless. With Sencaɓaphi had come a handmaiden who bore Dinane a son, and Sencaɓaphi was prepared to adopt this boy as her own. However, the majority of the Ndwandwe council wished to appoint a son by another wife. This woman, Siboshiwe, was daughter to one of Bunu's lesser queens by the levirate. Siboshiwe's marriage ritual was insignificant compared to Sencaɓaphi's, but it included a beast (the *umgano*), signifying that she was an independent wife and not an attached sub-wife (*inhlanti*).

Sencaɓaphi refused to accept Siboshiwe's son. She feared that on maturity he might try to remove her and raise his own mother to her position. 'Two great people cannot sit in a seat for one', said Sencaɓaphi.

The position was further complicated by the character of the guardian and regent, a brother of the deceased Dinane. One of his duties was to cohabit with the main widow, but it appears that he was impotent, Actually, had she borne a son, the position would have been even more complicated, since a son by the levirate is usually only made the main heir if there is no physiological son of the deceased. Moreover, the brother was considered violent, to the verge of madness, and was disliked and feared by his brother's widows and children.

When I left Swaziland, the position was that the huts of the Ndwandwe chief were empty, his family scattered, and his property squandered. Some of the widows moved to other men, and some returned to their own families, where they were in the unhappy position of married women living at their girlhood homes. Though Sencaɓaphi commanded overt respect, she was aware of the gibes of enemies, who condemned her for abandoning her responsibilities to her dead husband. The latest news was that Siboshiwe's son was definitely appointed, and, since Sencaɓaphi refused to accept him, Siboshiwe would really be in control, while Sencaɓaphi and her daughters remained at the national capital.

REBUILDING OF THE SHRINE HUT

A DESCRIPTION of the rebuilding of the *kaBayethe* or shrine hut of Loɓamba in August 1935 will give an idea of the complexity of a national enterprise, and the interaction of work and ritual.

Building must always be completed before the spring rains, and the essential materials—saplings, ropes, and different varieties of grass—can only be obtained in their proper season. Grass may only be cut when it is dry, and the middle of autumn is the usual time. The period for building the *kaBayethe* was strictly dependent on the Swazi belief that if rain struck the building before it was complete, there would be devastating storms and national disasters.

The queen mother-in-council sent runners to different principalities to tell the chiefs that material was required. Though expert builders are able to estimate roughly how much is needed for a hut, no specific amount was demanded from any area. The queen mother anticipated that more than was necessary for the ritual hut would be brought, and the surplus could then be used for other buildings. If too little arrived, she explained that she would organize the people from the capital to bring in tribute. There is a growing scarcity of good grass and saplings in native areas, and very often they must be bought from European farmers, but no purchases were necessary for the *kaBayethe*.

Age classes from eighteen different principalities arrived with tribute. On some days as many as three local contingents, each with thirty to sixty men and/or women, came from distances ranging from a couple of miles to over thirty miles away. They contributed: seventeen bundles of saplings, twelve huge coils of plaited ropes, over 100 bundles of *iqunga* grass, and twenty-two bundles of *umuzi* grass.

The arrival of each contingent was an exciting occasion for the people at the capital. Throwing down their gifts before the Great Hut, the men and women, in festive clothing, sang and danced in front of the queen mother and her court. The old men collected the bundles and stacked them neatly against the cattle byre, and then the leading *indvuna* thanked the workers. Sometimes the queen mother provided them with beer, sometimes with meat, and sometimes with no food at all. When she killed a beast, a portion went to the inhabitants of the capital, and there was general rejoicing. Eight oxen were killed in the seven weeks during which the supplies were brought to the capital. If the workers came from very far, they spent the night at the capital or nearby villages, and left with pomp and glory the following day.

The queen mother and the main civil *indvuna* organized the work. It was necessary to demolish the old hut with elaɓorate care and ritual before reconstruction could begin. Before dawn the sacred objects were removed from behind the screen and taken to the sacred store hut. Workers were carefully selected, not for their skill, but for their ritual purity. The tasks of climbing to the top of the hut, taking off the horns of the sacrificial animals, removing the ornamental doctored pinnacle and unrolling the surface mats, were allotted to old women past the menopause. Other women stood at the bottom and unravelled the binding ropes and cleared away the rubbish. Dlamini women and wives of the king were not allowed to participate. The Dlamini were 'too close to the dead with whom the hut is associated', and the young queens were 'too hot' (sexually impure) to touch the hut of the powerful in-laws. The *Indlovukati* did not do any of the actual work; she supervised from her courtyard, where she dealt in between whiles with cases and visitors. While the women worked, they sang popular ditties of the day and carried on a jolly conversation.

Though there was no solemnity observable among the workers, the building was associated with supernatural powers. One night a terrible gale blew, uprooting fences, tossing thatching from the binding ropes, tearing down doors, and shrieking through the empty spaces. The next morning a terrified people discussed the reason for the havoc. Some said it was because the rain wanted to fall and the *Indlovukati* stopped it, but the wind was sent instead. Others blamed a few women who after work went to the river to wash, instead of washing in the enclosure of the hut.

When the women had stripped the hut of all but a sacred mat of *umuzi* grass stretched cross-wise over the framework, the delicate task of rebuilding began. This required special skill, and two male experts, trained in the royal barracks, had been summoned by the *Indlovukati*. Together they discussed how best to construct a new framework without entirely removing the old, for 'That would endanger the nation'. 'Not for one day should the capital be without a ritual hut.' Finally, the builders arranged to erect the two halves separately. They set to work, aided occasionally by trusted elders of the capital, and after thirteen days the framework was ready to be joined. The joining was marked with special ritual—all the *Emathonga* (aliens) were ordered outside and the workers sang a sacred song associated with the king's puberty ceremony, his marriage with his ritual wife, and the marriage of leading princesses. The *Emathonga* included clans prohibited from witnessing the most important rituals at the great annual ceremony of kingship (see Chapter XIII). The day ended with singing and feasting, and on the following morning thatching began.

The age class of married women at Loɓamba, the *Emadonda*, were summoned to thatch. Roughly thirty women appeared at the royal enclosure early the next morning, and an old woman fixed the first mat across the top. The first mat in all living huts is known as the *umcengo*; the same word is used for the head ornament worn by women to whom respect is due from in-laws at marriage ceremonies and other occasions. The *umcengo* of the hut is usually explained as a sign of respect to the headman. When the *umcengo* of the kaɓayethe was fixed, other mats were rolled down and straightened over the framework. It was finally covered with three layers—first the *tihlansi*, resembling crudely-made sleeping mats which in this case were of *umuzi* grass; then came the *emashigi* of loosely-tied grass stalks wound round from the base with the loose ends of grass downwards; and, finally, the *emakhenya*—mats of uncombed grass—with the ends of the grass upwards.

The grass mats were firmly sewn down with grass rope threaded through a wooden needle nearly one foot in length. Only old women were allowed inside the hut to draw the needle from their side and push it back again. On top of the hut an old woman placed again the *incongwane* (ornamental pinnacle) with its base of *impumputse* (long, uncombed grass). The sewing of the mats took three days, and then the final binding took place.

Binding is done with strong cords of plaited rope and is usually the work of women, but on this occasion expert male builders were again employed. Among the binding ropes was the *lutfungu* (sacred cord) used from one generation to another, and symbolizing national continuity.

The entire building took thirty days, and when everything was ready, doctors were summoned to treat the supporting poles, made of special *umlenzangulube* wood, and the ornamental pinnacle. The old materials were burnt, but not as firewood. Though wood was difficult to obtain, no one thought of using the material of the sanctuary for mundane purposes, and everything was burnt in the veld behind the village. The skulls of oxen slaughtered to feast the workers were put over the doorway, and the hut was ready for use.

Cattle were sent to the royal graves to inform the dead, and ask their blessing. It was time for the rains, and agricultural work. That year the *Indlovukati* performed an interesting agricultural ritual—an irregular event, but one which she and her advisers considered necessary because the crops had been so poor. And because the rains still did not come the queen mother and her son, together with their trusted assistants, spent nearly three weeks working the rain ritual in the new shrine hut built by the joint effort of many subjects.

BIBLIOGRAPHY

In preparing the present volume, the author has derived particular assistance from the following works:

BENEDICT, RUTH. *Patterns of Culture*. Routledge, 1935.

BOAS, F. *The Mind of Primitive Man*. New York, 1911.

DURKHEIM, E. *Division of Labor in Society*. New York, 1933.

EVANS-PRITCHARD, E. E. *Witchcraft among the Azande*. Oxford, 1937.

FIRTH, R. *Primitive Economics of the New Zealand Maori*. London, 1929.

FORTES, M., and EVANS-PRITCHARD, E. E. (Editors). *African Political Systems*. Oxford, 1940.

GLUCKMAN, MAX. 'The Kingdom of the Zulu of South-east Africa' in *African Political Systems*.
'Mortuary Customs and the Belief in Survival after Death among the South Eastern Bantu', *Bantu Studies*, Vol. XI, No. 2, 1937.

GOLDENWEISER. *History and Psychology and Culture*. London, 1933.

HERSKOVITS, M. J. *The Economic Life of Primitive Peoples*. London, 1940.

HOERNLÉ, A. W. 'The Importance of the Sib in the Marriage Ceremonies of the South Eastern Bantu', *S.A.J.S.*, 1928.

JUNOD, H. A. *The Life of a South African Tribe*. Macmillan, 1927.

LANDTMAN, G. *The Origin of the Inequality of the Social Classes*. Kegan Paul, 1938.

LINTON, R. *The Study of Man*, London, 1936.

LOWIE, R. H. *Primitive Society*. New York, 1920.
The Origin of the State. New York, 1927.

MACIVER, R. M. *Society, Its Structure and Changes*. Toronto, 1931.

MALINOWSKI, B. *Argonauts of the Western Pacific.* London, 1922.
Coral Islands and their Magic. 2 vols. London, 1935.

MEAD, MARGARET. *Sex and Temperament*. New York, 1935.

RADCLIFFE-BROWN, A. R. *The Andaman Islanders*. Cambridge, 1922.

RADIN, P. *Primitive Man as Philosopher*. New York, 1927.
Method and Theory of Ethnology. New York, 1933.

RIVERS, W. H. R. *The History of Melanesian Society*. 2 vols. Cambridge, 1914.

RICHARDS, A. I. *Land, Labour and Diet in Northern Rhodesia*. Oxford, 1940.

SUMNER, W. G. *Folkways*. Boston, 1907.

SOROKIN, P. *Contemporary Sociological Theories*. 1928.

SCHAPERA, I. *Handbook of Tswana Law and Custom*. Oxford, 1936.

THOMAS, W. I., and ZNANIESKI, F. *The Polish Peasant in Europe and America*. New York, 1927.

VEBLEN, T. B. *The Theory of the Leisure Class*. New York, 1927.

WISSLER, C., *Man and Culture*. New York, 1923.

Select Bibliography of Swazi Material

BEEMER, HILDA. 'The Development of the Military Organization in Swaziland', *Africa*, Vol. X, No. 1, 1937.

'The Diet of the Swazi in the Protectorate', *Bantu Studies*, Vol. XIII 1939.

Introductory article on the Swazi. *The Bantu Tribes of South Africa*, Vol. III, Section IV. Cambridge, 1941.

BRYANT, A. T. *Olden Times in Zululand and Natal*. Longmans, London, 1929.

COERTZE, P. J. 'Volkekundige Studies in Swazieland', *Tydskrif vir Wetenkap en Kuns*, 1930–1.

COOK, P. A. W. 'The First-fruits Ceremony', *Bantu Studies*, Vol. I, 1930.

ENGELBRECHT, J. A. 'Swazi Customs relating to Marriage', *Ann. Univ. Stellenbosch*, 8, Sect. B, No. 3, 1930.

Financial and Economic Situation of Swaziland. Cmd. 4,114, H.M.S.O., 1932.

MARWICK, A. G. *The Swazi.* Cambridge, 1940.

SCHOEMAN, P. J. 'Die Swazis se jaarliks seremonie van die eerste vrugte'. *Ann. Univ. Stellenbosch*, 15, Sect. B, No. 3, 1937.

INDEX

ADMINISTRATION, 60 ff., 156–7. *See also* Political structure.

Adultery, 54, 67, 103–4, 158, 172, 189

Age, 117–19

Age classes, 15, 62, 240
itilomo, 119–20
men's, 119 ff.
siceme, 120
system of, 117 ff.
units in, 120
women's, 129–32, 241

Agriculture, 35, 36, 37–8, 137, 139, 145. *See also* Crops; Land.

Ancestors (*emadloti*), spirits of and cult of, 42, 87, 106, 108, 162, 163–4, 171, 186 ff., 227
Incwala and, 199, 221
life of, 186–7, 196
priests and, 191, 192
Umkhulumcandi, 191

Animals, 127, 128, 150, 169, 184, 194
husbandry, 50–3
kingship and, 218
licabi, 192
See also Cattle.

Anthropology, 1 ff., 8, 226 ff.
Africans and, 1, 3–4

Arapesh, 228

Aristocracy, 111, 115, 129, 133, 153, 227

Aristocrats (rulers), 56, 70–1, 77, 93–4, 117, 119, 126, 137, 139, 141, 144, 152, 154, 181. *See also* Chiefs; Councils; Dlamini; Kings; Lineage; Princes; Queens.

Army, 15. *See also* Regiments.

BANTU, SOUTH-EASTERN, 39
Southern, 83 *n*. 1.

bayethe (royal salute), 42, 64, 78, 193

Beer, 36, 42, 55, 70, 121, 144, 145, 146, 147, 148, 154, 157, 186, 191, 193, 194, 195, 240
Incwala and, 199, 200, 202, 206, 208, 209, 221, 224

belwandle. *See* Incwala: priests.

bemanti. *See* Incwala: priests.

Birth, 74–5

Blood, ties of, 13, 58, 78 ff.
Swazi beliefs about, 105 ff.
See also Kinship; Relationship.

Boer War, the, 29

Boers, the, 20, 21, 22, 25–6, 27

bomage (classificatory mothers). *See* Relationship: classificatory mothers.

Boys, 117, 152

'Bull', the *Incwala*, 211–14

Bunu, 26, 29, 99, 102
capital and establishment of, 41
trial of, 28–9

Burial ritual, 180 ff. *See also* Death.

CALABASHES (*inkosatana*), 199, 200, 202

Capitals (*umpakatsi*), 39, 40, 41, 72–4, 235, 236

Cattle, 28, 36, 55, 68, 103, 107, 123, 131, 140, 148, 150–2, 155–6, 169, 171
byre (*sibaya*), 38, 47
Incwala and, 203–4, 220–1
marriage (*lobola*), 54, 59, 80, 81, 93, 96, 97–8, 99, 100, 101, 104, 151, 152–3, 238
mfukwane, 151
ritual and, 59, 87, 151, 193
royal graves and, 193 ff.
royal herds, 42, 55, 72, 73, 85, 98, 151, 155, 202
sisa relationship and, 155–6
See also 'Bull'; *Incwala*: cattle.

Ceremonies. *See* Ritual.

Character, 103–4, 108, 158, 188.
See also Personality.

Chiefship and chiefs, 15, 39, 40, 45, 57, 58, 63–4, 65, 67, 68 ff., 78 *n*. 1, 101, 112, 115, 139, 169, 170, 230
cattle and, 151–2
death and, 86 *n*. 1, 185, 186
diviners and, 170–1
doctoring of, 170
Incwala and, 198, 200, 221
land and, 45, 46, 47, 149, 150
main wife of, 97–8
personality, 70–1
ritual specialists and, 170–1
subjects and, 48, 49, 68–71, 127, 141, 144, 147–8, 189

Chieftainship, 69–70

Children, 37, 90, 92, 99, 108–9, 113, 151, 153, 154, 179, 181
birth of, 74–5
death and, 180, 184
Incwala and, 215
royal, 74 ff.
See also Education.

Clans, 11, 13, 18, 32–3, 60, 83, 105, 107, 110 ff., 114 ff., 233–4
chiefs' medicines, 172
death and, 86 *n*. 1
hierarchy, 110 ff.
king, the, and, 83

Clans, marriage and, 105
  name, 110, 113, 114
  ritual of blood transference and,
    78
  royal clan, 111 ff.
  sub-division and fission of, 110–11
Clanship, 32, 110 ff. *See also* Clans.
Classificatory relatives. *See under*
  Relationship.
Communal enterprises, 144–8
Conception, 108
Concessions, 24–6, 30
Conquest, 32
  Swazi and, 11 ff.
Councillors, 67, 201, 202, 212. *See
  also Tindvuna.*
Councils, 62–4, 88
  kinship, 64–5, 89–91
  Libandla, 62, 63–4, 65, 131
  Liqoqo, 62, 63, 64
Crafts, 142–3, 161. *See also* Work:
  specialization.
Crops, 107, 137, 221, 223. *See also*
  Agriculture.
Culture-contact, 1 ff., 7–8, 9, 19 ff.,
  229–30
Cultures, 11, 226, 227 ff.
Curses, 159
Customs, 9, 17, 18, 150
  clan, 113

Dancing and dancers, 122, 131,
    132, 147, 154, 168, 195
  Incwala, 203, 204, 205, 206, 207,
    208, 209, 211, 217, 221, 223
Death, 86, 89, 107, 177 ff., 185
  explanations of, 177, 180, 197
  in warfare, 125
  king, the, and. *See under* King.
  main wife, of, 99–100
  mdzambane ritual and, 185–6
  old people and, 177, 180
  social meaning of, 182 ff.
  social status and, 180, 182
  widows and, 183–4, 188–9
Dinane, 238
Dingane, 14, 125
Dingiswayo, 13
Divination and diviners, 87, 108,
    162, 163–6, 167–8, 169, 170,
    171, 186, 188, 189, 192
  payment of, 169
  switch of (*lishoba*), 167
  ukuphotula ceremony of, 164
Dlamini, 11 ff., 15, 17–18, 57, 62, 76,
    84, 86, 94, 107–8, 109, 111, 113,
    153, 165, 170, 231
  rain-making and, 172
  'true Dlamini', 12
Dreams, 187
Dreamers, 158
Dzambile, Princess, 12

Education and training, 109,
    117–18, 127–8, 130
Elangeni, 14, 55
emabutfo, 117, 119, 120, 122, 126
  women's, 130
  See also Regiments.
Emadloti. See Ancestors.
Emanzawe, 125–6
Ematinta, 76
Embekelweni, 21
Enemies, 174
  'smelling out' of, 170, 175
Eshiselweni, 12, 79, 113
Europeans, Swaziland and, 4, 32.
  See also Concessions; Culture-
  contact; Great Britain.
Exogamy, 95, 113

Famine, 36
Fines, 29, 63, 64, 67, 69, 118, 128,
    131, 152, 200, 202, 219, 220
Food, 36, 45, 50–3, 132, 139, 141,
    155, 156, 220, 223, 224
  warriors and, 126, 127

Generosity, 154–5
Gifts, 154, 156, 164, 169
Gininza, Mahutfulo, 143
Girls, 118, 129, 130, 151, 152
  puberty ceremonies of, 130–2
Goats, 77, 86, 87, 94, 155, 159, 169,
    178, 192
Gourds, the two, 219
Grandparents, 95, 96
Great Britain, Swaziland and, 24 ff.,
    28 ff.
Grey, George, 30–1
Guardianship, 101–3
Gwamile Mdluli, 26, 29, 31, 41, 55,
    102, 103
Gwebu, 45, 112, 125, 233

Harems. *See under* Wives.
Havelock, Sir Arthur, 27
Headmen, 38, 39, 45, 150, 182 ff.
  death of, 179, 182 ff.
  homestead of, 48
  land and, 149
  main heir of, 39–40
  'mother' of, 38–9, 40
  widows of, 183
  wives of, 84
  See also Umnumzana.
Head-rings, 77–8, 80, 128
Heirs and succession, 56, 88 ff., 93,
    94, 99 ff., 103, 118, 119, 184
  laws of, 101–4
  main, 39, 47, 181, 182, 183
  tests for, 94
Herbalists, 162, 166–7, 169
Heredity, 105, 108, 109. *See also*
  Inheritance.
History of Swazi, 11 ff.

Homestead, 36 ff., 149
head of, 64
huts, 36, 74, 138
lilawu, 38, 39, 40, 41, 44, 121
moving of, 47–9, 145
royal, 40 ff.
sacred store hut, 42, 199, 202
shrine hut (*kabayethe*), 42, 202, 214, 240–2
sigodlo, 43, 74
three structures in, 38 ff.
Huts. *See under* Homestead.

IDIOTS, 109, 158
Imigubo, 204, 205, 211, 221, 222
Impahla (goods), 148, 149
Incest, 190
Incusakati, 129, 130
Incwala, the (annual ceremony), 9, 35, 42, 62, 82, 83, 86, 112, 113, 128, 172, 197 ff.
Big, 208 ff.
bull of, 211–14
cattle and, 203–4, 214, 220–1, 222
chiefs and, 198, 200, 221
costumes, 203, 207–8, 212, 216, 217–18, 220, 221, 222
Dancing. *See under* Dancing.
Fire, the, 220–1
Great Day, the, 215 ff.
interim period, 206–8
interpretation of, 223–5
king, the, and. *See under* King.
Little, 201, 202 ff.
luma and, 215–16, 220, 222, 223
medicines, 198 *n.*, 200, 201, 202, 212, 215, 216, 220, 222, 223
medicines of king and. *See under* King: *Incwala* medicines.
Ox and. *See under* Ox.
preparations for, 199–201
priests of, 198, 199, 200, 212, 213, 215
queen mother and. *See under* Queen mother.
Silo, the king as, 217–19
sun and moon and, 201–2
tihlangu (shields), 218–19
tinsila and, 198, 199, 214
work and, 206, 221
See also Inhlambelo.
Incwambo, 214, 222
Indlovukati. See Queen mother.
Indlunkulu (great hut), 38, 39, 42, 73
Indvuna (councillor), 58, 60–1, 65–6, 130, 131, 203, 240
lenkulu (great councillor), 43, 60, 61, 63, 64
yemabutfo, 43, 119
See also Tindvuna.
Ingwenyama, 1, 54, 55, 56. *See also* Kings.

Inheritance, 88 ff., 152, 157
king and, 88
See also Heirs; Heredity.
Inhlambelo (sacred enclosure), 42, 199, 202, 204, 205, 211, 212, 214, 215, 216
Inkosana. See under Political structure: little chief.
Inkosatana. See Calabashes; Princesses.
Inkosi, 55, 80. *See also* Kings.
Insila. See Tinsila.
Inyanga, 77, 79, 161 ff., 172. *See also* Herbalists; Sorcery and sorcerers.
Isangoma. See Divination and diviners.
Isisiwe, 155

Kabayethe (national shrine hut), 42, 202, 214, 240–2
King, 15, 17, 54 ff., 57, 72 ff., 105, 151, 154, 157, 237
age classes and, 119
birth and childhood of, 74 ff.
blood, transference of, 78 ff.
cattle and, 55, 151, 155–6
death and, 73, 77, 81–2, 85–7, 102, 178, 180, 181, 185–6, 201, 205
divination and, 165
embalming of, 86
enemies of, 207
female relatives of, 58–60
First Circumcised of, 92
functions and prerogatives of, 54–5
genealogy of, 232
government and, 64
health of, 85–6
homestead of, 40 ff.
Incwala and, 197 ff., 212 ff., 223–5
Incwala, dancing of, 209, 218–19
Incwala medicines and, 204, 214, 215, 218, 222
land tenure and, 44 ff., 149
legends of, 94
main wife, 85, 94
marriage and, 111
marriage cattle and, 152–3
medicines, ritual, and, 42, 70, 75, 77, 79, 80, 81 ff., 85
minority of, and the *Incwala*, 197, 221–3
mother of, 17, 40, 43, 45, 54, 85, 99, 222. *See also* Queen mother.
political structure and functions of, 54 ff., 114
puberty ritual and, 77
rain-making and, 171
regency of, 101–2
relatives and lineage of, 56 ff.

King, ritual and, 44, 55, 72 ff., **77** ff.,
  169
  royal graves and, 193, 195
  simeno and, 205
  sister of, 59
  succession of, 54
  tinsila and. *See Tinsila.*
  title of, 54
  unmarried girls and, 112
  Umcwasho and, 132
  Umntfwana, 73, 74, 76 n., 78
  warfare and, 123
  wives and harem of, 7, 17, 41, 43,
    60, 74, 81, 82 ff., 84–5, 99–100,
    153, 203, 205
  wives, ritual queens, 78, 80, 81,
    82 ff., 94, 215, 218, 219, 222.
    See also Queens.
Kingship, 15, 44, 54, 57, 73, 78,
  141, 170
  cattle and, 80–1, 151
  myth about, 237
  See also Cattle: royal herds; Kings.
Kinship and kinsmen, 32, 37, 60,
  105 ff., 118, 144, 182
  council, 88, 89–90, 97
  death and, 181, 182, 191. *See
    also* Death.
  groups, 40
  land and, 47
  locality and, 114–16
  marriage and, 95–6
  'mothers', 105
  ties of, 47, 48.
  See also Relationship.
Kukhonta, 67–8
Kuper, Hilda, Swaziland and, 1 ff.

LABOUR. *See* Work.
Land, 30 ff., 35, 44 ff., 115, 149–50
  division and organization of, 44 ff.
  European and Native ownership,
    31–2
  inheritance of, 47
  grants, 25, 30
  partition of (1907), 30, 32
  seasonal rhythm and, 35–6
  tenure, 44 ff.
Liɓovu (red ochre), 108
Lidloti. See Ancestors.
Lihlambo (ritual hunt), 87
Lihlumbi, 159
Lilima. See under Work: parties.
Lineage, 56, 89, 111 ff., 114–15
  ruling, 8, 56. *See also* Heirs;
    Kinship; Relationship.
Lingangadu, 73
Lisokancanti, 92
Loans, 156
Loɓamba, 1, 12, 41, 42, 43, 67, 72,
  74, 126, 127, 208, 235

Loɓola. See Cattle: marriage cattle.
Lomawa, 31
Lozitehlezi, 55
Lubelo, 16
Ludvonga, 100, 101
Lugunga, 159
Lusekwane, 208–11, 213, 224
Lusendvo, 114–15

MAɓONYA, 40
Maɓuzo, 201
Magagule, 172
Magicians, 86, 158, 161 n. *See also*
  Ritual: specialists in.
Mahlalela, Chief Sidloko, 169, 177
Makontolo, 189
Malangane. See Princes.
Malunge, 29, 55, 102
Mandanda Mtsetfwa, 60–1
Mapoko, 14, 20
Marriage, 92 ff., 105
  arranged, 93–5, 238
  cattle. *See under* Cattle.
  cross-cousin, 96
  Dlamini and, 12
  intermarriage, 12, 17
  'marrying-up', 113
  preferential, 95–6
  regiments and. *See under* Regi-
    ments.
  two types of, 92 ff.
  See also King: wives of; Queens;
    Wives.
Mats of shrine-hut, 241–2
Matseɓula, 80, 81, 82, 84, 85, 92,
  114, 215, 218, 219, 233
Maziya, 172, 233
Mbaɓa Siɓandze, 61
Mbandzeni, 8, 9, 12, 20, 21, 22, 24,
  45, 100, 101, 112, 123–4
  Europeans and, 21 ff., 112
Mbozongo, 40, 59
Mdluli, 79, 81
Meat, 45, 145, 147, 155, 191, 240
  Incwala, 206, 208, 220, 221
Medicine men, 75, 77
Medicines, 62, 84, 101, 154 n., 162,
  164, 165, 166, 167, 168, 169,
  170, 190, 192, 200, 201
  death and, 183, 184, 185
  Incwala and, 198 n., 200, 201, 202,
    212, 215, 216, 220, 222, 223
  king, the, and. *See under* King.
  queens and, 81
  rain medicines, 171, 172
  ritual, 76, 77
  war and, 125
  witchcraft, 173
Memezi, Chief, 90–1
Men, 38, 134, 160
  work of. *See under* Work.

Menstruation, taboos and, 107
Mgwedjeza, 198
Mkonza, 220
Mlokotwa, 40
Mngometfulu, 16–17
Mnisi, 110–11, 172, 233
Mnisi, Prince, 144–5, 152
Monogamy, 37
Moon, the, 201–2, 208
    infants and, 76
Morality, 220
Motsa, 79, 80, 84, 92, 110, 111, 114
Mourning, 178–9, 180 ff.
    national, 73, 87, 180
Mpande, 19
Mshudulwane Zwane, 60
Mswati, 15, 16, 17, 19, 20, 45, 125
    wives of, 17
Mtsetfwa, 13, 233
Myth, 177, 237
Mzululeki, 189

NATION, THE, SWAZI AND, 115–16,
    117, 123
    cattle of, 151
Navel cord, 75 and n., 113
Ndungunye, 12
Ndwandwe, 13, 40, 102, 123, 172
Ndzaßankulu, 47, 56
Neighbourliness, 48
Ngolotsheni Motsa, 40, 58, 78, 79,
    82, 151, 161, 223
Nguni, 13, 18, 95 n., 113, 114, 233
    Embo, 11, 13
Ngwabadla Duba, 198
Ngwane I, 9
Ngwane II, 12
Nkambule, 81
Nkosi, 111, 233
Ntshingile, 40
Nukwase, 99–100

Ox, 86, 178, 192
    Incwala and, 199, 204, 212, 214,
        220
    incwambo, 214, 222

PARTITION PROCLAMATION, 30
Personality, 49, 70, 71, 158 ff.
    treatment for, 160
    See also Character.
Political structure, 32–3, 54 ff.,
    88 ff., 114, 115–16, 169 ff., 180
    Little Chief (inkosana), 88, 92
    See also Clanship.
Polygyny, 37, 84–5, 88, 112, 152,
    153, 228. See also King: wives
    and harem of; Wives.
Population, 32, 46
Possession, 163–6, 227

Praise names, 110, 172
    songs, xi–xii, 12, 47, 144, 151,
        193, 203
Priests, 161, 192, 198
    family, 191, 192
    Incwala priests. See under Incwala.
Princes, 46, 56–7, 75, 112, 119, 127,
    137, 141, 178, 197, 198
    Incwala, the, and, 197
Princesses, 59, 93–4, 98, 151, 203
    marriage of, 93–4
    puberty ceremony of, 130–2
Principalities, 46, 57, 58, 65, 149
Psychic attributes, 159
Puberty, ritual for, 77, 130–2

QUEEN MOTHER (Indlovukati), 31, 41,
    42, 55–6, 64, 70, 72 ff., 89–90,
    98, 102, 112, 129, 141, 155
    co-wives of, 59
    death and, 102, 178, 186
    functions of, 55
    genealogy of, 232
    Incwala and, 199, 203, 206, 208,
        215, 216, 218, 220, 221, 222
    rain-making and, 171, 172
    relatives of, 59
    shrine hut and, 240
    title of, 54
    See also King: mother of; Queen
    regent.
Queen regent, 26, 27, 72 ff., 75, 197.
    See also Queen mother.
Queens, 40, 43, 44, 57, 60, 74, 81,
    84–5, 87, 99, 137, 143, 153
    harem (sigodlo). See under King:
    wives and harem of.
    Incwala and, 215, 216, 217
    Matseßula. See Matseßula.
    ritual and senior, 81
    sisulamsiti. See under Wives.

RAIN, 221, 240, 241
    making and the rites of, 42, 110,
        171–2, 221, 242
Rank, 5, 6–7, 113, 141, 156, 175, 225
    death and, 177 ff.
    See also Aristocracy.
Regency, 101–3
    Incwala and, 197
Regiments, 35, 43–4, 55, ᴏᴉ, 77,
    78, 117, 120–1, 195. See also
    emaßutfo.
    Incwala and, 198, 203 ff., 222
    king's marriages and, 80
    marriage and, 121, 128, 209. See
    also Warfare.
Relationship: classificatory mothers,
    59, 99, 105, 184
    classificatory system, 90, 98, 101,
    105, 118
    See also Blood; Heirs; Kinship.

Religion, 177, 190 ff., 199. *See also* Ancestors; Death; Ritual.
Reserves, 30 ff.
Ritual and rites, 12, 38, 42, 44, 50–3, 54, 59, 77, 107, 154, 155, 157, 160, 161 ff., 169 ff., 191 ff.
  agricultural, 30, 242
  blood and, 108
  cattle and. *See under* Cattle.
  childhood and, 74 ff.
  death and, 86–7, 178 ff., 185 ff.
  head-rings and, 77–8
  Incwala. See Incwala.
  main wives and, 85
  marriage, 93, 97, 108
  national. *See Incwala.*
  puberty, girls', 130–2
  shrine hut and, 241
  social structure and, 176–7
  specialists in, 142, 161 ff., 169 ff.
  transference of the king's blood, 78 ff.
  war and, 125
  See also Ancestors; Rain-making; Royal groves.
Robinson, Sir Hercules, 22
Royal groves and graves (*embilini*), 12, 193–4
  annual ritual at, 193 ff.

Sacred Tree, the, 208–11
Sacrifice, 151, 188, 189, 192, 193, 194, 195
Sacrilege, 61
Sandlana Zwane, 61
Seasons, the, 35, 50–3
Sencaβaphi, Princess, 100, 126, 148, 238–9
Sexual intercourse, 84, 108, 128, 131, 219
Shaka, 13, 14, 15, 125, 231
Shepstone, Sir Theophilus, 19, 22–3
Shepstone, Junior, Theophilus, 23, 27
Shiβa, 79, 233
Shwapa Mdluli, 82
Siboshiwe, 238
  son of, 238–9
Sickness, ancestors and, 182, 188, 189, 190, 192
  diviners and, 163–4
Sifuba Twala, 144
Sifunza, 114
Silwane, 40
Simelane, 13, 40, 59, 113
Simemo, 204–5, 206, 207, 214
  king's minority and, 222
Singing and songs, 38, 80, 87, 122, 129, 130, 132, 147, 164, 168, 186, 194, 195, 203, 241
  Incwala, 203, 204 ff.
Sitozi, 159

Slavery, 68
Smith, work of the, 142–3
Snakes, 187
Snuff, 199, 200
Sobhuza I, 12–13, 14, 19, 125
Sobhuza II, 1, 29, 31, 41, 43, 45, 56, 57, 58, 59 n., 60, 62, 63, 69, 70, 73, 82, 85 n., 102, 117, 121 n., 141, 143, 152, 170, 238
  capital and villages of, 41
  daughters of, 206 n.
  Incwala, the, and, 197, 199–200, 208, 213, 215, 224
  land and, 31–2
  mother of, 13, 41, 112
  praises of, xi–xii
  puberty ritual of, 77
Social structure, 137 ff., 161, 175, 225
  sorcery and witchcraft and, 175–6
Sociology, 226 ff.
Solowako, Chief, 189
Sorcery and sorcerers, 87, 103, 107, 108, 159, 160, 170, 172 ff., 190, 197
  death and, 177, 185
Sotho, 15, 18, 20, 83, 95 n., 233
Space, Swazi conception of, 36
Succession. *See* Heirs and succession.
Sun, the, 201–2
Swazi, 3, 12
  'true Swazi', 13–14, 18, 33
Swaziland, 21, 34–5
  topography of, 34

Taboos, 38, 39, 42, 75, 77, 81, 86, 107, 109, 113, 125, 141, 142, 143, 164, 194, 195, 198, 202–3, 219–20
Taxation, 7, 28, 31
Technology, 137–8
Tembe, 12, 19
Theft, 154, 190
Thwala, 81
Tikhondzi, 17
Timbers, 142
Time, Swazi and, 8–9, 36
Tindvuna (councillors), 46, 55, 60, 61, 65–6, 193. *See also* Indvuna.
Tinsila (*insila*), 58, 78, 79–80, 82, 83, 86, 214
  death and, 81–2
  Incwala and, 198, 199, 214
  junior, 81
  marriage of, 80–1
  senior, 81–2
Tinyanga, 62, 77, 169, 170, 175. *See also* Divination and diviners; *Inyanga*.
Tonga, 234
Transvaal, Swaziland and, 29
Twins, 180

Ukuqoma, 17
Umbango, 88
Umbondvo ordeal, 168
Umbutfo, 122–3, 126, 127
Umcwasho, 130–3
Umdvutshulwa, 212–14, 215, 220, 222
Umfana, 2
Umntfwana. *See under* Kings.
Umnumzana (headman), 36, 38, 64
Umnyakaza Gweɓu, 2
Umshengu, 58
Umtsakatsi, 172–3, 174, 175
Umuti. See Homestead.

VASSALAGE, 67–8
Vilakati, Josiaha, and the Vilakati, 113, 233
Villages, royal, 14, 15, 40 ff., 55, 56, 66, 72 ff., 86, 122, 198
    age-classes and, 122, 127
    plan of, 42–4
    national shrine hut, 42

WARFARE, 33, 123–6, 225
    intertribal, 119–20, 123
    ritual and, 125
Warriors, 208, 209, 221. *See also emaɓutfo*; Regiments.
Wars, Swazi and, 20
Wealth, 137 ff., 227
    distribution of, 148–9
Weapons, 124, 203
Widows, 35, 37, 81, 82, 84, 90, 178, 183, 185, 188–9
Witch doctors, 9–10
Witchcraft and witches, 48, 82, 101, 103, 159, 160, 168, 170, 172 ff., 192, 227
    transmission to children and others of, 173
Wives, 39, 56, 88–9, 91 ff., 103–4, 139, 148, 152–3, 180
    adultery and, 103–4
    'break the stomach' ritual and, 104
    children and, 100

children 'put in the stomach' of, 92, 94, 100, 101, 238
    death of, 179, 180
    first wife, 91, 92–3
    harems, 17, 92 ff., 117
    inhlanti (subordinate co-wife), 39, 94, 100
    main wife, 88, 91, 92 ff., 97–8, 99–100, 101, 103, 104
    main wife, failure of male issue to, 238–9
    senior, 39
    sisulamsiti, 80, 84, 91, 92
    See also King: wives; Marriage; Women.
Wizards, 26, 125, 154, 180
Women, 38, 104, 135–6, 160, 165
    Incwala and, 203, 208, 212
    kinship council and, 90–1
    kugana (lover relationship), 96–7
    land and, 149
    mourning and, 181
    royal women, 198, 212. *See* Queen mother; Queens.
    specialists in ritual, 165–6
    work of, 35, 45, 117, 130, 140, 142, 165, 241–2
Work, 50–3, 61, 126, 137 ff.
    children and, 140
    division of, 139–41
    Incwala, the, and, 206, 221
    men and, 35, 139–40, 142
    parties, 144–8
    rank and, 141
    specialization and crafts, 142–4, 161
    tribute labour, 85, 122–3, 144, 148
    warriors and, 126–7
    women and, 35, 45, 117, 130, 140, 142, 165, 241–2

ZANDE, 106
Zidze, 13
    daughter of, 14
Zulu, 15 *n.* 2, 46 *n.*, 59, 82 *n.*, 83 *n.*, 83–4, 88, 124–5, 231

Reprinted by lithography in Great Britain
by Jarrold & Sons Limited, Norwich

For Product Safety Concerns and Information please contact our EU
representative GPSR@taylorandfrancis.com
Taylor & Francis Verlag GmbH, Kaufingerstraße 24, 80331 München, Germany